# Jane Austen

## New Perspectives

# Jane Austen: New Perspectives

Women & Literature, Volume 3
(New Series)
Edited by Janet Todd

Previously published as a quarterly, the new series of *Women & Literature* will appear in this annual format. Each volume will focus on a specific theme in literary or artistic criticism. Standing orders for the series are invited.

# JANE AUSTEN
## NEW PERSPECTIVES

Women & Literature
New Series     Volume 3
Edited by Janet Todd

**HM**

HOLMES & MEIER PUBLISHERS, INC.

NEW YORK · LONDON

WOMEN & LITERATURE,
the journal devoted to women writers and
the portrayal of women in literature,
is published annually

All editorial correspondence should be addressed to:
Janet Todd
Department of English
Rutgers University
New Brunswick, N.J. 08903

Articles should be submitted in duplicate and accompanied by a
stamped, self-addressed envelope. They should be 15–30 pages long
and conform to the MLA style sheet.

Correspondence relating to subscriptions and advertising only should
be addressed to:
Holmes & Meier Publishers, Inc.
30 Irving Place
New York, N.Y. 10003

*Text design by*
Stephanie Barton

*Library of Congress Cataloging in Publication Data*
Main entry under title:

Jane Austen: new perspectives.

(Women & literature; new ser., ISSN 0147-1759; v. 3)
1. Austen, Jane, 1775–1817—Criticism and interpretation
—Addresses, essays, lectures.   I. Todd, Janet M.,
1942–    .  II. Series
PR4037.J32   1983        823'.7        83-254
ISBN 0-8419-0863-X
ISBN 0-8419-0864-8 (pbk.)

# CONTENTS

# INTRODUCTION

There is a wonderful passage in Fanny Burney's diary when the company at Mrs. Thrale's house at Streatham assembles to contemplate the "tearful eyes" of Miss Sophy Streatfield. "I would ensure her power of crying herself into any of your hearts she pleased," announces Mrs. Thrale. "I made her cry to Miss Burney, to show how beautiful she looked in tears." When the audience is ready, Miss Streatfield cries, although smiling all the while. " 'There now,' said Mrs. Thrale, 'she looks for all the world as if nothing had happened; for, you know, nothing *has* happened.' "

This is very much Jane Austen's opinion of physical emotional displays and their contemplation, that indeed nothing has happened, but it is an opinion running counter to sentimental thought, which found such displays both aesthetically satisfying and morally improving. In *The Theory of Moral Sentiments*, Adam Smith derives morality from feeling, itself often resulting from a contemplation of feeling in another. The one contemplating changes places with the one suffering and feels a similar emotion. So strong is this kind of sympathy through specular contemplation that emotion is raised even if the original cause is unknown. The philosophical emphasis on spontaneous emotion through looking at emotion is connected with the use of tableaux of domestic affection and distress, a common element in the sentimental work of, for example, Henry Mackenzie and Helen Maria Williams.

To Jane Austen, such emotional looking seemed as absurd as it did to Mrs. Thrale when she thought of Sophy Streatfield crying her way into anyone's heart; a refusal to provide sentimental tableaux to educate the emotions marks Austen's novels, especially the early ones, written when sentimental literature was still dominant. In *Northanger Abbey*, where one might expect the tableau of family separation, one hears that Mrs. Morland parted from her daughter "with a degree of moderation and

1

composure, which seemed rather consistent with the common feelings of common life." Tableaux when they come are in fact fraudulent, created for display, and as emotionless as Sophy Streatfield's tears. So Isabella forces the unsentimental Morlands into false configurations of friendship or lengthy farewells that are inappropriate and unnecessary.

Looking at people in a Jane Austen novel rarely brings illumination. Those who are regarded have often set themselves up for it, like Isabella with her "two odious young men" and, more culpably, with Captain Tilney on the public bench. Those who gaze usually misinterpret, like the General staring at Catherine as heiress or Mrs. Jennings of *Sense and Sensibility* when she watches what she thinks is a proposal scene of Colonel Brandon and Elinor. And yet Jane Austen is certainly not against looking, and *Northanger Abbey* can in a way be interpreted as a pedagogy of sight. But the gaze is an intellectual not an emotional one and is best educated on things and oneself before being turned on other people. In this attitude, Jane Austen is closer to William Gilpin than to Adam Smith; in *Essays on Picturesque Beauty; on Picturesque Travel; and on Sketching Landscape,* the look is intellectual and moral, occasionally epiphanic indeed, but mostly calmly pleasurable. Although there is much irony in Catherine's specular education on Beechen Cliff, she does make progress in the appreciation of the picturesque. In addition, under Eleanor Tilney's tutelage, she learns to love a hyacinth. "By accident or argument?" asks Henry Tilney of this interesting achievement, and it is clearly the latter. Spontaneous looking with the stupid Mrs. Allen has produced only indifference.

Jane Austen's emphasis on learning to look is heartening to her critics, often accused by readers of an inappropriate ingenuity in interpretation. But, if the novels give license to careful, particular readings, they also warn against the quick judgment and inappropriate analysis. The warning is echoed by several of the essays in this volume about Jane Austen looking and about looking at Jane Austen.

Joel Weinsheimer, for example, in *"Emma* and Its Critics: The Value of Tact,"* emphasizes tact in interpretation. He notes that criticism of Austen has been a conservative enterprise, tending to avoid new contexts. He believes that criticism ought to adjudicate between the historical approach, which stresses differences between Jane Austen's world and the present, and the modern approach, which emphasizes similarity. The question of course is which context to choose for interpretation— philosophical, psychological, critical—or whether to combine all or to use none. Weinsheimer takes Barbara Hardy to exemplify the criticism that aims at neutrality in the English commonsensical tradition, but he finds her work slightly patronizing to Jane Austen and her readers and notes that Lacanian terminology might have helped the interpretation. The opposite problem is exemplified in Bernard Paris, who uses Karen Horney, not accepting the reciprocity of text and context, but imposing Horney's ideas on Austen in such a way that Horney is never in jeopardy. This Weinsheimer finds a failure in tact. Susan Morgan illuminates Austen's epistemology not through the usual Samuel Johnson but through her contemporary, Shelley, whom she never read. Why not, asks Weinsheimer, if one is writing on epistemology, use Kant instead? He then tries on Austen a passage from the first *Critique* concerning the conjunction of conception and perception and the lack of rules for judgment. He ends by asserting that new critical contexts are not a priori inappropriate and their use can only be determined by tact. He warns that "inflexible diffidence" is as dangerous as "inflexible openness."

David Monaghan in "The Complexity of Jane Austen's Novels" again takes up the matter of critical disagreement, even about the most basic aspects of Jane Austen's art. Some critics, he declares, see her as timeless, either escapist or universal in her pictures; others require a late eighteenth-century context, which may however be conservative or subversive. Monaghan finds the disagreement a result of the critical habit of seeing parts, not the whole of novels and of failing to observe the relationships between the main courtship plots and the subplots. The subplots, he argues, are not reaffirmations or alternatives, but in dialectical relationship to the main plots, yielding a synthesis which is the total novel. The main plots primarily dramatize conservative ideology, but they also have the structure of a fairy tale, with separation, testing, and reintegration. The subplots, however, transcend ideology and complicate archetype, although they do not thereby make the main plot into a conformist front, since main plot and subplot remain of equal importance; in their union, Monaghan asserts, a dramatization of conservative ideology becomes a rich world vision, wrought out of imperfect elements.

In "Jane Austen and the Conflict of Interpretations," Alistair Duckworth presents himself squarely as a historical critic, but he argues that historical criticism must question itself. For this enterprise, he uses Jane Austen as an exemplary focus. Summarizing many conflicting perspectives, he questions how we are to respond to disagreement, noting, however, that recent criticism appreciates openness of the classic to a variety of productive interpretations. But he takes his stand on the preeminence of historical criticism over other modes; the problem then, as for Weinsheimer, is the choice of context. This is resolved when one accepts that Jane Austen has no single one, since there is much "textual sedimentation" in her texts; she speaks with many voices. In this situation, historical criticism can either investigate the intertextuality, as Edward

Copeland and Jocelyn Harris do in their articles, or separate out her individual voice, probing and correcting anachronistic and suspicious criticism.

The historian David Spring makes clear in his "Interpreters of Jane Austen's Social World" the difficulty of the historical enterprise advocated by Duckworth, when he argues that many historical literary critics, including Duckworth, are mistaken in their interpretation of Jane Austen's fictive world. He assesses some recent critics, beginning with those who, like Lionel Trilling, see Austen as having no comprehensive view of society and so portraying an idyll. But Spring points out that her England of the local rural elite is as real as another person's and that her social vocabulary, avoiding the modern language of class, well fits this society. The bulk of Austen interpreters see her world as real, but differ about how to characterize it. Some term it bourgeois because so concerned with money. Marvin Mudrick is an example, but he also questions the word, ultimately finding the society not simply bourgeois but a hybrid. Spring agrees with this finding and names three groups: the landed aristocracy and gentry, differing mostly in size of income and style of life; and a group often called bourgeois by critics but which Spring terms the pseudo-gentry of professional and rentier families. These were not landowners in a large way, but they resembled the gentry; they aimed at their habits and status by acquiring the right attributes and making the correct marriages. Austen's father illustrates the type: he was the son of a country surgeon and so of low status, but he moved up through education, entry into the church, and an improving marriage. His sons became admirals, a churchman, and a great landowner. Finally, David Spring notes that, despite the desire of critics, the aristocracy in Austen's time was not dying out, improving parks, or engaging in class struggle, but in fact growing businesslike and booming. He ends with a plea for more awareness between historians and literary critics.

Two very different biographical approaches come from Joan Austen-Leigh and Margaret Kirkham. In "The Austen Leighs and Jane Austen, or, 'I have always maintained the importance of Aunts,'" Joan Austen-Leigh writes on her own family connection with Jane Austen, the "most important Aunt." She notes that, with a few exceptions, all the primary biographical works were written by descendants of James Austen, the Austen-Leighs, who became the guardians of Jane Austen's memory. In this family can be found the models for several of Jane Austen's characters; for example, Mary Lloyd Austen, second wife of James, had a grandmother known as the cruel Mrs. Craven who may have inspired Lady Susan, and a father who seems seminal to Mr. Watson. After her death, Jane Austen suffered years of obscurity, for her irony and wit seemed unappealing to the Victorians; later her reputation revived to a point where James Edward Austen Leigh felt obliged to write the *Memoir,* so providing valuable information on her life. Ultimately, however, as Joan Austen-Leigh concludes, Jane Austen can maintain her own importance. Margaret Kirkham is less happy about the family's possession of the Austen memory, and she begins her essay, "The Austen Portraits and the Received Biography," with a glance at Cassandra's unpretty sketch of her sister Jane, noting how little it resembles her brother Henry's sweet picture of domestic virtue and the improved and standard portrait which gives charm and femininity to its subject. Kirkham notes too that J. E. Austen Leigh's Victorian *Memoir* was written not to give a clear picture of the novelist but to provide a respectable version that would not embarrass the family. The charming portraits in painting and writing became standard, Kirkham notes, and Jane Austen escaped her vigorous Enlightenment and feminist contexts. Among her early critics, only Richard Whately shows that he understood something of this context and of her intellectual point of view, so revealing that, in 1821, Austen's stance as a moralist was still intelligible. Later critics were misled by their ignorance of the feminist controversy and by the received image of Austen.

Finally in this series of critical assessments comes my own piece on Virginia Woolf's reaction to Jane Austen. The earlier novelist often appears a kind of talisman in her successor's criticism, standing for reality, comedy, and perfection against the flawed moderns. In most ways she seems to fulfill Virginia Woolf's requirements of the good artist: she does not preach or intrude her personal life into her texts and she is aware of her craft. And yet, strangely enough, Jane Austen is frequently denigrated in Woolf's pages, and her great qualities of perfection, reticence, and artistry are found irritating. She is belittled in domestic images and her ironic works are denuded of irony and rewritten in the Woolfian prose of sensibility. Clearly Jane Austen annoys Virginia Woolf, and one can only speculate on the causes. Perhaps, unlike other women Virginia Woolf chooses to describe, Austen fails to fit in with her views of female writers as suffering and sensitive. Partly, too, Austen may rebuke her as woman, in her class, her childlessness, her marital state, and her sisterly love, all of which worried Woolf in her own life. In addition, Jane Austen intrudes into Woolf's own fiction through critics' comments and through Woolf's fear of both repetition and failure.

Zelda Boyd, Mark Hennelly, Martha Satz, and Jane Nardin scrutinize not interpretations of Jane Austen but the novels themselves, the way characters learn to look and interpret. In "The Language of Supposing," Boyd finds one lesson for the characters of *Sense and Sensibility* in the opposition between actual and hypothetical or between existing states of affairs on the one hand and wishes, desires, and suppositions expressed by modals on the other. Modals are the language of all reasoning, and hypothesis is inescapable; politeness requires reticence and the indirection of modals, which also bind human society and create necessary fictions. But these fictions are dangerous, Boyd argues, and the novel may teach that one should not rely too heavily on imaginative realms; hypothetical constructs must touch base with the actual.

Mark Hennelly studies the looking of characters through a similar opposition of appearance and reality, but arrives at a slightly different conclusion from Boyd. In *Pride and Prejudice,* the ocular drama is between proud and prejudicial first impressions and forgiving hindsight. Eyes and sight are used in character presentation, plotting, theme, and technique. In this, Austen is holding to British empiricism, which emphasizes the primacy of perception; Elizabeth and Darcy must learn to accept the visible fact, instead of fabricating fantasies. Yet Jane Austen is close to Romantic ideas of insight as well, and characters must also penetrate the phenomenological mirage into inner truth; external and internal, vision and insight are necessary. Jane Austen manipulates point of view so that there is a revolving dialectic between the eye and the I, and the controlling viewpoint remains flexible.

In "An Epistemological Understanding of *Pride and Prejudice,*" Martha Satz again takes the opposition between perception and interpretation, or subjectivity and objectivity, but she focuses on a progress to understanding distinct from those described by Hennelly and Boyd. She argues that, in the main first part of the book, comments and discussions about knowledge and the erratic and variable interpretations on which they rest supply the central subject. *Pride and Prejudice* illustrates the overwhelming problem of acquiring knowledge, the frustrating fallibility and insufficiency of evidence, and the relativism of all interpretations. Evidence and judgment depend on the perceiver, and alternative explanations are always possible. With this view, Austen is, for Satz, close to modern structuralism, which stresses the creative and arbitrary nature of perception. At the same time, Jane Austen puts forward a different and definite view, which dominates the last part of the book after Lydia's elopement, that moral virtues are the equivalent of knowledge and that reason should be controlling. *Pride and Prejudice* is thus cleft between pride in reason to find truth and humility at the recognition of the prejudice of mental process. The ironic distance between narrator and character, clear even with Elizabeth in the first part of the book, closes in the last part. Where Hennelly found the viewpoint of the novel flexible to the end, then, Satz sees it becoming rigid; Elizabeth, chastened and cured of ironic detachment and arrogance about knowledge, is the pattern for the chastening of narrator and reader.

In "Children and Their Families in Jane Austen's Novels," Jane Nardin finds the road to proper perspective through judgment of the formative family. In her works, Jane Austen avoids the tableaux of domestic piety of the sentimental novel, which signify the heroine's absolute virtue, and instead depicts a range of misalliances that mark and mar the children born of them. For correct vision, some discipline either from family circumstances or from later affliction is necessary, Nardin argues. The characters who are not parental favorites, like Fanny Price and Elinor Dashwood, possess the hidden advantages of control and criticism and are less liable to stray than the favored Emma and Elizabeth.

Several articles put forward interpretations using the various critical methods already theoretically discussed. First are the two pieces that examine silence in the novels, finding, contrary to Monaghan's point of combining sub and main plots, much rich material in a probing of parts. Angela Leighton in "Sense and Silences" looks at *Sense and Sensibility*, investigating what the text refuses to say openly and finding Jane Austen's greatness in the way she lets the reader hear the silence. In the subplot, Marianne's progress from self-indulgent emotionalism to humiliation and despair is told in Austen's discreet, ironic, and deceptive style; her feelings are treated first with irony, then, as she really suffers, with understatement, then with neglect. Marianne *almost* screams and then is reduced to illness, to "inarticulate sounds." Marianne's silence is of nonconformity and emotional powerlessness, and Margaret Leighton finds in her a hidden story related to the stagy and seemingly distanced tale of the two Elizas; the figure of the fallen woman haunts her from the moment she "falls" at Willoughby's feet. At the end Marianne is saved and can talk again, but, now socialized, she has nothing to say; her story has been a choice of silences.

Marylea Meyersohn, in "What Fanny Knew," again looks at silence, but as approved and firmly written into the main plot. She scrutinizes Fanny Price, the heroine who will not express herself, and notes that talking in *Mansfield Park* becomes equated with play and, through the Crawfords, with sexuality. Fanny, the virgin, is silent through most of the novel, although her speeches lengthen as her social status rises. Meyersohn terms Fanny a center of nonenergy and control through passivity and suggests that the novel as a whole reveals the dangers to society of self-expression. In "Jane Austen's Dangerous Charm," Nina Auerbach takes up from Meyersohn the ever-intriguing question of the unpleasing Fanny Price and examines why Jane Austen avoids pleasing. She notes that Fanny as a character appeals little to readers but captivates critics as an emblem. Ranging over Romantic literature from *Beowulf* through Shakespeare's *Hamlet* to Byron to find analogues for Fanny's jealous hunger, Auerbach constructs a reading in which the heroine becomes the Romantic villain, spoiler of ceremonies and fellowship, monstrous and marginal, unloved and validated by no family. She is the spectator, linked disturbingly with the solitary reader, and here looking, so much the subject of these essays, becomes powerful. Fanny's assertive negative resists acting and realistic fiction; she is judged a relentlessly uncomfortable figure in the Austen domestic romance.

Margaret Kirkham accepts the unpleasantness that both Meyersohn and Auerbach find in Fanny but argues that it is part of Austen's purpose. For Kirkham, *Mansfield Park* can best be interpreted through its ideological context, since Jane Austen was not as separated from rational feminists like Mary Wollstonecraft as many critics have supposed. In her weakness and in the sexually arousing religiosity she seems to some characters to possess, Fanny Price is close to conduct-book heroines and to Sophie of Rousseau, whom both Jane Austen and Mary Wollstonecraft deplored. But, unlike conduct-book heroines, Fanny Price is also intractable and rational, and, in this side of her presentation, Jane Austen comes close to the Mary Wollstonecraft of *A Vindication of the Rights of Woman* and the novel *The Wrongs of Woman*. As allusions in the text suggest, Jane Austen laughs at certain aspects of Fanny Price, for example her conduct-book acquiescence in injustice, and treats her with irony. But the Austen irony is also turned on the reader who may approve these aspects. *Mansfield Park* is, Kirkham asserts, a great comic novel, "regulated by the sane laughter of an impish, rational feminist."

Avrom Fleishman tries not myth or historical analogy on the novels but psychoanalysis. In "Two Faces of Emma," he translates the book into modern scientific language, offering a diagnosis of the heroine as a case history in projective neurosis, repressed homosexuality, and phobic delusions. But, although he terms her an incurable neurotic who sows confusion wherever she goes, Fleishman also excuses her on the grounds of her banal environment and lively mind. In the end he finds Emma's own word "imaginist" a far more appropriate one than the diagnostic terms of science.

Two articles interpret Jane Austen through intertextuality, which is also to some extent Margaret Kirkham's method with Mary Wollstonecraft. Both articles use Jane Austen's favorite novel, *Grandison*, but Jocelyn Harris's adds a more unusual perspective through Chaucer's Wife of Bath. In "The Burden of *Grandison*," Edward Copeland looks at the family harmony and unity in *Grandison* and notes their wreckage in the novels of Jane Austen's female contemporaries of the 1790s. He considers this a reflection of the shift in society's concept of family owing to economic forces. The Richardsonian plot remains in these late novels, but real activity falls to interlopers and to financial ogres. London becomes the place less of sophisticated vice and frivolity, as in Richardson, than of mean-spiritedness and the evils of a ruthless economy. Finding Austen's family less negative than Jane Nardin does, Copeland argues that it is not in retreat as in the novelists of the 1790s, although he admits that it is represented less on the grand public scale of Richardson than in small private groupings.

In "Anne Elliot, the Wife of Bath, and Other Friends," Jocelyn Harris looks at *Persuasion* as a search for the true Grandison; in it the false Grandison, Mr. Elliot, is rejected for the true, Captain Wentworth, and the unmasking, unsatisfactory in both Austen and Richardson, is similarly contrived. Harris also finds echoes of the Wife of Bath's prologue and tale in Anne Elliot's famous statement that the pen has been in male hands and in the discussions of control in marriage—the Wife's struggles with Jankyn may be behind Louisa's jump and near death to prove her willfulness. The story of the Loathly Lady, who changes from ugliness to beauty, resembles Anne Elliot's progress from decay to bloom through love, while Chaucer's ideas of gentillesse as good deeds rather than rank, wealth, and finery find echo in the contrast between Sir Walter and Mr. Elliot on the one side and Captain Wentworth and Admiral Croft on the other.

Katrin Burlin takes the sister art of painting, rather than other writings, to illuminate Austen. In " 'Pictures of Perfection' at Pemberley," she investigates how the novelist uses painting to expose the illusion that life is like art and to laugh at perfection. In *Pride and Prejudice*, art is represented by the miniature and the full-size portrait and by the exploitation of *ut pictura poesis* to structure the imaginary art gallery of Pemberley. Elizabeth moves from the art of nature through the miniatures of Darcy and Wickham and the picture gallery, with its full-size smiling portrait of Darcy, to the "conversation piece" of real women talking in embarrassment and hostility. In the first three, Darcy expands; the portrait is felt to be giving the truth, for Elizabeth learns of another's more perfect point of view. But the conversation piece is a necessary corrective to the artistic idealizations of both the portrait and the natural prospects. Ultimately, Pemberley becomes an art gallery, not of perfection, but of characters in need or in search of perfection.

As Alistair Duckworth notes, Jane Austen is a classic, remaining open to many approaches and perspectives. Unlike the audience before the tears of Sophy Streatfield, the reader feels, after experiencing her reticences and irony, her silences and generalizations, that something has happened. It is of course the novels that teach this something, guiding the reader in the art of intellectual looking and interpreting, but the criticism may be an aid. And here I hope it is "tactful" to use Austen's admired Samuel Johnson on editors to illuminate the purpose of the critics.

In his *Preface to Shakespeare*, Johnson was wryly pessimistic about the critical and conjectural enterprise. No tears can validate a response, as in sentimental theory, and sympathy must always be scrutinized, not indulged. Error is ever possible, Johnson noted, and, if the critic succeeds, "he produces perhaps but one reading of many probable." No perspective is final in Johnsonian criticism, for "human judgment . . . never becomes infallible." In evaluation, as several of the critics in this volume argue and many of the interpretations imply, there is "no system, no principal and axiomatical truth." Yet, Johnson valued criticism, especially that which worked by comparison and examination, that learned to look, like Catherine Morland at the hyacinth, not by accident but by care and argument; "in the productions of genius nothing can be stiled excellent till it has been compared with other works of the same kind," he declared. He saw appreciation and criticism not as the sure pronouncements of a few scholars, but as a communal and lengthy effort of many. The value of a work only slowly reveals itself, and the process requires "a long succession of endeavours."

# The Austen Leighs and Jane Austen

## or "I have always maintained the importance of Aunts"

"I have always maintained the importance of Aunts."[1] So wrote Jane Austen in 1815 to her niece, Caroline. Caroline was ten years old and had just herself become an aunt on the birth of a child to her half-sister, Anna Lefroy.

For us, in the Austen family, to maintain the importance of our most important Aunt has been the pleasure of successive generations. In fact one might almost say that Jane Austen has been to us what the baronetage was to Sir Walter Elliot: "occupation for an idle hour, and consolation in a distressed one."[2]

As a small child I was taught that because I was related to Jane Austen, I was special. My infant mind was unable to grasp who Jane Austen was, but the sense of being unique remained, and, as it happens, it is to our branch of the family, the Austen-Leighs, that the maintenance of Jane's importance has chiefly fallen.

The reason is not hard to discover. Of Jane's brothers' decendants, Edward Knight's children became landed gentry, officers, and clergy; Francis Austen's sons and grandsons, naval officers and clergy; Charles's descendants fell on evil times. Although his son, Charles John, was a naval officer, his grandson Charles John was a telegraphist, and *his* son Charles John drove a bread van and his brother, Francis William, was a grocer's assistant.[3]

It was the Austen-Leighs, descendants of her eldest brother, James, who became scholars and writers, heads of colleges and schools. Apart from the "Biographical Notice" by Henry in 1817, and two books, Lord Brabourne's *Letters of Jane Austen* (London: Richard Bentley & Son, 1884) and *Jane Austen's Sailor Brothers* (London: The Bodley Head, 1906) by her great-nephew J. H. Hubback and his daughter, Edith, all

11

the primary biographical works have been written by James's decendants. The first was the *Memoir of Jane Austen* (London: Richard Bentley, 1870) by his son (my great-grandfather) James Edward Austen (Leigh, 1837), the only biography by one who actually knew her.

R. W. Chapman, when speaking of understanding the family ramifications, said:

> The task is not easy; for the Austens and their relations by marriage were numerous and prolific; and their historian, labouring to be lucid, is embarrassed by their tendency to marry twice, and to change and amplify their surnames.[4]

In addition to James Edward's taking the name of Leigh, Mrs. Austen's brother, James Leigh, added the name of Perrot, and Jane's brother Edward changed his name to Knight.

In this essay, to clarify further, the name Edward always refers to my great-grandfather, James Edward Austen Leigh. He was over seventy when he began writing his *Memoir*, in which task he was greatly helped by his younger sister, Caroline Mary Craven Austen. She had a retentive memory and a deep interest in family conections. She was aided, also, by her mother's diaries. For many years her mother (James's second wife, Mary Lloyd) kept pocket books or diaries, small red leather notebooks. But, as Caroline says, "She scarcely ever added any remark to the fact which she wrote down."[5] Mary was perhaps a very reserved person; still, it does seem strange that, after nursing Jane in her final illness at Winchester for several weeks, she wrote down no more in her notebook, on July 18, 1817, than the bald fact that on this day Jane had died.

Possibly it is for this reason that Caroline determined when she was in her sixties to record her own reminiscences. It is fortunate for us that she did so.

> The entries in my Mother's well-kept pocket books are the authorities on which I write of these events and give their dates . . . she was the first who gave me any histories of the past, to which when quite a child I delighted to listen, it comes most naturally to me now, to begin my recollections with her family. (*Reminiscences*)

Mary Lloyd was a granddaughter of the Honorable Charles Craven, Governor of South Carolina in the reign of Queen Anne. It is said that Jane used Mrs. Craven, known as the cruel Mrs. Craven, as her model for Lady Susan. Caroline writes that Mrs. Craven was a "most courteous and fascinating woman in society, but of a stern tyrannical temper." She mistreated her five daughters, depriving them even of food.

Not surprisingly, the daughters ran away from home, marrying whatever husbands they could get. One of them settled for a horse dealer.

Mary Lloyd's mother took the Reverend Nowys Lloyd. They lived at Enborne Parsonage and had three daughters, Eliza, Martha, and Mary, the two last-named marrying, as second wives, two of Jane's brothers. Caroline writes of her grandfather:

> Mr. Lloyd became a sad nervous invalid, keeping much in his own room, and some days equal to nothing. His malady had no name then, but I have heard it was thought afterwards that it might have been suppressed gout. When better, he liked to amuse himself by playing at cards, and then his daughters were summoned to play with him. At first it was some childish game which they knew, for he was too nervous to teach them anything; but he was glad when he found their Mother had taught them whist, and afterwards they always played it. They played for money—some small stake—*he* always paying, whichever side might lose. Sometimes he would like backgammon, and then two were left at liberty. Such constant card-playing was very irksome to these young girls, though to a degree it soothed his nervous sufferings.

Thus do we gain insight into the style of living and the people with whom Jane was acquainted, if not personally at least by reputation. And is it to be believed that Mary, who had told all this to her own daughter, did not tell it also to Jane, some years earlier when they were both in their teens, the tiresome father dead, and the two Lloyd girls and the two Austen girls intimate friends together before the Lloyds left the neighborhood to live at Ibthorp?

Then there is the time when Jane, about to pay a visit to the Lloyds, writes to Martha:

> You distress me cruelly by your request about Books; I cannot think of any to bring with me, nor have I any idea of our wanting them. I come to you to be talked to, not to read or hear reading. (*Letters*, p. 89)

In fact the evidence seems overwhelming that the Reverend Nowys Lloyd was seminal to Mr. Watson:

> Mr. Watson had not been well enough to join the party at dinner, but was prevailed on to come down & drink tea with them.—"I wish we may be able to have a game of cards tonight," said Eliz. to Mrs. R. after seeing her father comfortably seated in his arm chair.—"Not on my account my dear, I beg. You know I am no card player. I think a snug chat infinitely better. I always say cards are very well sometimes, to break a formal circle, but one never wants them among friends." "I was thinking of its being something to amuse my father," answered Eliz. "—if it was not disagreable to you. He says his head won't bear Whist—but perhaps if we make a round game he may be tempted to sit down with us."—"By all means my dear Creature. I am quite at your

> service. Only do not oblige me to chuse the game, that's all. *Speculation* is the only round game at Croydon now, but I can play anything.—When there is only one or two of you at home, you must be quite at a loss to amuse him—why do not you get him to play at Cribbage?" (*The Watsons*, p. 354)

Those readers who choose to find Mr. Woodhouse a selfish and self-centered old man might wish to discover that he, too, is a descendant of the Reverend Nowys Lloyd. Others, who, like myself, delight in him as a lovable and loving person (though heaven forbid one should be his guest unless Emma were present)—indeed, Jane herself tells us that he was "everywhere beloved for the friendliness of his heart and his amiable temper"—would staunchly deny any relationship between him and the querulous Mr. Watson.

Caroline has some amusing remarks to make on the subject of education:

> Everybody knows that a hundred years ago, there was not much trouble taken with the education of young ladies. A Governess was unknown in Parsonage houses and not very commonly found in the Squire's mansion.

One is reminded, inevitably, of Mrs. Morland, "whose time was so much occupied with lying-in and teaching the little ones" (*Northanger Abbey*, p. 15).

Caroline continues:

> The daughters of Enborne Parsonage got about the average allowance of education, as bestowed in their time. Certainly fully as much as their Mother had ever received, though she was born in a higher position than they were. No language beyond their own was thought of and they learned *that* by ear, and although they spoke and wrote it with as few mistakes as did the younger and better taught generation who afterwards grew up around them; I doubt if they could have assorted their words by any rules of grammar. . . . As to accomplishments, if music had been desired, I suppose it would not have been very easy to find an instructor. For singing none was thought needful. If girls had good voices, they would sing like birds, by nature, so what would be the use of teaching them? and if they had not voices, clearly it would be of no use at all. A young nightingale or lark, if you let it alone, would be sure to find its own song, but with all your teaching, you would never get a note worth hearing from a sparrow or a cock. . . .

This information is echoed in Lady Catherine's catechism of Elizabeth Bennet:

> "Do you play and sing, Miss Bennet?"
> "A little."

"Oh! then—some time or other we shall be happy to hear you. . . .
Do your sisters play and sing?"

"One of them does. . . ."

"Your mother should have taken you to town every spring for the
benefit of masters."

"My mother would have had no objection, but my father hates
London."

"Has your governess left you?"

"We never had any governess."

"No governess! How was that possible? Five daughters brought up
at home without a governess!—I never heard of such a thing. . . .
Without a governess you must have been neglected."

"Compared with some families, I believe we were; but such of us as
wished to learn, never wanted the means. . . . Those who chose to be
idle certainly might." (*Pride and Prejudice*, p. 164)

Jane and Cassandra, of course, never wanted the means, though they
were only briefly at school. The education of boys was another matter,
and continued to be so on into the twentieth century, as even Virginia
Woolf was later to lament.

Jane's brothers were prepared at home by their father for entrance to
the university or the naval academy; there is the famous story of Mr.
Austen objecting to his third son's proposed visit to the Knights, because
his Latin would suffer. The next generation of Austens, being more
prosperous, were sent away to school. All Edward Knight's boys and
James's son, Edward, were at Winchester. Even Caroline was sent away
to school.

One of Edward's school reports still exists, a report that would gladden
any parent's heart. It is from the headmaster to his father, and is dated
December 1814; Edward had just turned sixteen.

Dear Sir:
    To the very favourable reports which I have had the pleasure of
making to you from time to time on the conduct of your excellent son,
I can add nothing.

Your faithful and obedient servant,
H. D. Gabell[6]

Jane, too, had a good opinion of Edward. She wrote to a friend in
1817:

We have just had a few days visit from Edward. He grows still, and still
improves in appearance, at least in the estimation of his aunts, who love
him better and better as they see the sweet temper and warm affections
of the boy confirmed in the young man. (*Letters*, p. 475)

Six months later, Jane died. Edward Austen was the youngest person
to attend her funeral. Years afterwards he wrote:

I was young when we lost her; but the impressions made on the young are deep. And though in the course of fifty years I have forgotten much, I have not forgotten that Aunt Jane was the delight of all her nephews and nieces. We did not think of her as being clever, still less as being famous; but we valued her as one always kind, sympathising, and amusing.[7]

Caroline, his younger sister, remembered:

*She* was the one to whom we always looked for help—She would furnish us with what we wanted from her wardrobe, and *she* would often be the entertaining visitor in our make believe house—She amused us in various ways—*once* I remember in giving a conversation as between myself and my two cousins, supposed to be grown up, the day after a Ball.[8]

As we know, at Jane's express wish, her authorship was a closely guarded secret. The title pages of her novels merely stated "By a Lady." She was thirty-five years old in 1810, when *Sense and Sensibility* was published. She wrote that she could no more forget it than could a mother forget her "sucking child." Three years later *Pride and Prejudice* appeared. "My own darling child," she called it. She received the book from London and wrote to her sister, Cassandra, who was staying with their brother Edward Knight at Godmersham:

Miss Benn dined with us on the very day of the books coming & in the evening we set fairly at it, and read half the first vol. to her, prefacing that, having intelligence from Henry that such a work would soon appear, we had desired him to send it whenever it came out, and I believe it passed with her unsuspected. She was amused, poor soul! . . . she really does seem to admire Elizabeth. I must confess that I think her as delightful a creature as ever appeared in print. . . . (*Letters*, p. 297)

A few days later, she wrote again:

My dear Cassandra
Your letter was truly welcome, and I am much obliged to you for your praise: it came at a right time, for I had had some fits of disgust. Our second evening's reading to Miss Benn had not pleased me so well, but I believe something must be attributed to my mother's too rapid way of getting on: and though she perfectly understands the characters herself, she cannot speak as they ought. (*Letters*, p. 299)

It is an interesting comment on the manners of the age, and the respect that a younger person was obliged to accord to an older, that it should be *Mrs. Austen*, not Jane, the author, who should have the privilege of reading the book aloud for the first time. Moreover, such was Jane's modesty and reticence that she did not wish even a close friend like Miss Benn to be told who wrote it, or to share in her joy on its being published.

We can imagine what an exercise in self-discipline it must have been for her brother James and his wife, Mary, who lived only a few miles off at Steventon, to refrain from confiding in their son, Edward, who had read and delighted much in the novels without having any idea of their author's identity.

Then Henry, the weakest character in the family, hearing *Pride and Prejudice* praised by a titled acquaintance, could not forbear from boasting that the author was his sister. Jane wrote to Frank, then away at sea, that in future, "I shall rather try to make all the money than all the Mystery I can of it."

That is what she said, but it is not what she did. She never capitalized, never allowed her name to appear on any of her works in her lifetime. It did mean, however, that, now the secret was out, the younger generation and friends like Miss Benn could be told. On hearing the news at school, Edward promptly addressed a verse to his aunt, of which I shall give a part:

TO MISS J. AUSTEN

No words can express, my dear aunt, my surprise
Or make you conceive how I opened my eyes,
Like a pig Butcher Pile has just struck with his knife,
When I heard for the very first time in my life
That I have the honour to have a relation
Whose works were dispersed through the whole of the nation.

Oh dear, just to think (and the thought drives me mad)
That though Mr. Collins so grateful for all
Will Lady de Bourgh his dear patroness call.
'Tis to your ingenuity really he owed
His living, his wife, and his humble abode.'

From that day forward Edward and his two sisters, Anna and Caroline, began also to write novels and to besiege Aunt Jane for her opinion. No remnants of these youthful effusions remain, alas. Perhaps if Jane had lived longer, they might have continued writing. As it is, we know that Anna destroyed her manuscript, could not bear to carry on after her beloved aunt was dead. But we can be grateful that these attempts produced from Jane a hint as to her own methods. In 1816 she wrote to Edward the famous description of her work:

By the bye, my dear Edward, I am quite concerned for the loss your Mother mentions in her Letter; two chapters and a half to be missing is monstrous! It is well that I have not been at Seventon lately, & there-fore cannot be suspected of purloining them; two strong twigs and a half towards a nest of my own, would have been something. I do not think however that any theft of that sort would be really very useful to me. What should I do with your strong, manly, spirited Sketches, full of Variety and Glow? How could I possibly join them on to the little bit (two inches wide) of Ivory on which I work with so fine a Brush, as produces little effect after much Labour? (*Letters*, p. 468)

At the time she wrote the above letter, four of her novels had been published, *Emma* had been reviewed (anonymously) by Sir Walter Scott, and *Sense and Sensibility* had been translated into French. Yet the recognition she achieved in her lifetime was not striking. How could it be? As Edward points out in the *Memoir:*

Few readers knew even her name, and none knew more than her name. I doubt whether it would be possible to mention any other author of note, whose personal obscurity was so complete. (*Memoir*, p. 143)

Edward tells us that she mingled not at all with the literary world, although she lived within comparatively easy distance of London, and was often staying there with Henry. He cites Fanny Burney, who from an early age was petted by Dr. Johnson; Maria Edgeworth, who corresponded with Sir Walter Scott; and Charlotte Brontë, who left the gloomy isolation of her Yorkshire parsonage to attend a reception given by her publisher.

No parties were given by John Murray for Jane. She called him a rogue, but a civil one. He did offer, however, to lend her new books, providing the pages had already been cut, and she, in return, promised that any she might borrow, he could "depend on their being in careful hands."

It is hardly surprising, with so little notice taken of her when she was alive, that Jane's death should pass unremarked by the public. She was mourned by her relations as a valued member of the family only, not as a great author too early lost to literature.

On her grave in Winchester Cathedral, among the Christian virtues customarily extolled, there is only an oblique reference to "the extraordinary endowments of her mind."

Half a century was to pass before Edward used the profits from his *Memoir* to erect a tablet in the wall of the cathedral stating that "she was known to many by her writings." Later still, a stained-glass window was subscribed by admirers in England and America.

For many years after her death no new edition of the novels was published. The only one extant through most of the nineteenth century had small, hard-to-read type. it was printed in 1837, then not again for thirty years, though an American edition did appear in 1833 in Philadelphia.

It seemed only too probable that Jane Austen and her works would sink into complete oblivion. It would appear to be uphill work for the family to maintain the importance of their aunt. There was so little importance to maintain.

Jane Austen did not appeal to the generality of Victorians, to which fact her books' not being reprinted bears testimony. Fashion had abandoned the "horrid" novels of her youth, though, to be sure, some of Walter Scott's medieval romances and the Brontës' melodramatic stories come perilously close. Favorite reading of the Victorians was often about magnanimous Anglicans: witness Trollope or Charlotte M. Yonge. But who reads Charlote M. Yonge now? Or Walter Scott? Dickens, of course, was wildly popular. But he painted extravagantly on a large canvas, very different from Jane's little bit of ivory. When the final installment of the *Pickwick Papers* came out, 40,000 copies were printed. Yet twenty years earlier, in 1816, John Murray had published only 2,000 of *Emma*. Jane Austen's cool, detached realism bears little resemblance to the florid prose admired by the Victorians, who could hardly be expected, therefore, to appreciate a passage such as this:

> The real circumstances of this pathetic piece of family history were, that the Musgroves had had the ill fortune of a very troublesome, hopeless son had the good fortune to lose him before he reached his twentieth year; that he had been sent to sea, because he was stupid and unmanageable on shore; that he had been very little cared for at any time by his family, though quite as much as he deserved; seldom heard of, and scarcely at all regretted, when the intelligence of his death abroad had worked its way to Uppercross, two years before.
>
> He had, in fact, though his sisters were now doing all they could for him, by calling him "poor Richard," been nothing better than a thick-headed, unfeeling, unprofitable Dick Musgrove. (*Persuasion*, p. 50)

Yet, however shocking many Victorians found these sentiments, a hard core of admirers persisted. Public demand for information goaded Edward Austen-Leigh into writing the *Memoir*. If he had not made the attempt at the age of seventy-two to recall and revive a life by half a century obscured, if he had not by his example inspired his son and grandson, his sister and daughter to still further research and exertions, it is likely that the surviving letters—those that Cassandra did not destroy—would be our sole source of knowledge.

Also, if Edward had been rector of the remote and tiny parish of Steventon in Hampshire, as his father and grandfather had been before him, instead of Vicar of Bray, a populous town a few miles from Eton and Windsor, it is doubtful if he would have been made aware of the indispensability of publishing a biography of his aunt.

His involvement in academic, scholarly, and civic matters must be ascribed not only to his own considerable ability and charm, but also to his coming into an inheritance from another aunt, which made him a person of consequence. As Jane says, "the rich are always respectable," and "money will come, you may be sure, because they cannot do without it" (*Letters*, p. 231). The money came from Mrs. Jane Leigh Perrot, always "my aunt" in Jane Austen's letters. She had been Jane Cholmeley, niece of Sir Montagu Cholmeley, before she had married Mrs. Austen's brother, James. She was a most extraordinary and redoubtable woman, of whom Jane wrote to Cassandra after they had received a letter from her:

> In spite of all my Mother's long & intimate knowledge of the Writer, she was not up to the expectation of a letter such as this; the discontentedness of it shocked & surprised her—but I see nothing in it out of Nature—tho' a sad nature. (*Letters*, p. 232)

Mrs. Austen's brother, James Leigh, had inherited through his greatgrandfather an estate, money, then the name of Perrot and a crest—a parrot holding a leaf in its claw. The Leigh Perrots were an exceedingly devoted, though childless, couple. After they had been married forty-two years, he found himself obliged to spend a few days from home on business. He wrote to his wife daily. One of his letters concludes: "If I was able to say How much I love you and how much I long to be with you, perhaps you would not believe me. You must, therefore, not have one more Word, my dearest Jenny, from yrs. sincerely James Leigh Perrot" (*Austen Papers*, p. 241).

So her husband doted on her, though the Austens did not. She hardly endears herself to Janeites by her opinion of *Emma*, expressed to Edward in 1828, eleven years after Jane Austen had died:

> I have been reading Emma a second time. But I still cannot like it so well as poor Jane's other novels. Excepting Mr. Knightley and Jane Fairfax, I do not think any one of the characters *good*. Frank Churchill is quite insufferable. I believe *I* should not have married him, had I been Jane. Emma is a vain meddling woman. I am sick of Miss Bates. (*Austen Papers*, p.280)

In 1799 Mrs. Leigh Perrot was accused of stealing a card of white lace from a shop in Bath. The details do not concern us here; those interested will find an excellent account of the trial in Sir Frank MacKinnon's book *Grand Larceny: Being the Trial of Jane Leigh Perrot* (London: Oxford

University Press, 1937). Suffice it to say that she had bought a card of black lace and paid for it with so large a note that she could easily have purchased the white lace also. But, it being found in her parcel, such was the law in those days that she was sent to Ilchester jail to languish until she could be tried, her devoted husband insisting upon going with her, though he was so badly afflicted with gout that he was "unable to move but with two sticks."

There were cells, of course, for the felons, but those who could afford to pay were lodged in the house of the jailer, one Edward Scadding. Mrs. Austen offered her two daughters as companions to their aunt, but the offer was refused. It is amusing to speculate, had it been accepted, whether Jane would have written a Dickensian type of novel set in a prison.

Mrs. Leigh Perrot was allowed to have visitors. One friend, Mrs. Goodford, knew the jailer and had at one time done him some service. Mrs. Leigh Perrot wrote to her cousin Montagu Cholmeley that after such a visit Mrs. Goodford had taken Scadding aside

> . . . and told him that, as She should be coming two or three times a week and should probably bring other friends with her, it would be absolutely necessary that we should have a room to ourselves—this the Man seemed to take as a reproof and said he had on my first coming told me that the Dining Room I was to consider as my own whenever I chose to be alone—and so it was till Fires began; but this Room joins to a Room where the Children all lie, and not Bedlam itself can be half so noisy, besides which, as not one particule of Smoke goes up the Chimney, except you leave the door or window open, I leave you to Judge of the Comfort I can enjoy in such a room. (*Austen Papers*, p.193)

It is thought possible that Jane took her descriptions in *Mansfield Park* of the Portsmouth scenes at the Prices' from her aunt's account of her incarceration in Ilchester jail. This is what Mrs. Leigh Perrot has to say about eating with the Scaddings, meanwhile extolling the uncomplaining fortitude of her husband:

> My dearest Perrot with his sweet composure, adds to my philosophy; to be sure he bids fair to have his patience tried in every way he can. Cleanliness has ever been his greatest delight and yet he sees the greasy toast laid by the dirty children on his knees, and feels the small Beer trickle down his sleeves on its way across the table unmoved. Mrs. Scaddings knife, well licked to clean it of fried onions helps me now & then—you may believe how the mess I am helped to is disposed of— here are 2 dogs and 3 cats always full as hungry as myself. (*Austen Papers*, p. 195)

Now here are the Portsmouth scenes, which were much admired in Jane's own family, especially by her brothers. Fanny compares her father's house with the well-ordered home she has left:

> Here everybody was noisy, every voice was loud. Whatever was wanted was halloo'd for, and the servants halloo'd out their excuses from the kitchen. The doors were in constant banging, the stairs were never at rest, nothing was done without a clatter, nobody sat still, and nobody could command attention when they spoke. (*Mansfield Park*, p. 392)

This is what Fanny thought of meals at the Prices':

> She was so little equal to Rebecca's puddings, and Rebecca's hashes, brought to table as they all were, with such accompaniments of half-cleaned plates, and not half-cleaned knives and forks, that she was very often constrained to defer her heartiest meal till she could send her brothers in the evening for biscuits and buns. (*Mansfield Park*, p. 413)

The penalty for shoplifting in 1799 was death or transportation to Australia. In anticipation of the latter, James Leigh Perrot had already made arrangements to sell up Scarlets, his property in Berkshire. The case created quite a furor at the time. A drawing was circulated of the Perrot crest, a parrot holding in its claw a card of lace. When the case finally came to court some 2,000 persons attended, and the trial lasted seven hours.

In those days counsel was not permitted directly to question the accused, nor could Mrs. Leigh Perrot or her husband testify in her defense. Eventually, however, she was invited to speak, but she was so overcome, and her voice was so low, that her counsel had to repeat her words to the court.

> "Placed in a situation the most eligible that any woman could desire, with supplies so ample I was left rich after every wish was gratified. Blessed in the affections of the most generous man as a husband, what could induce me to commit such a crime?" (*Grand Larceny*, p. 104)

Many of those present wept. It is reported that her husband broke down in sobs and covered his face with his handkerchief. The jury took less than a quarter of an hour to find her not guilty, after she had spent seven months in jail!

It has always been assumed that Mrs. Leigh Perrot was a victim of blackmail. The shop was in financial difficulties and her husband was rich. Indeed there are letters extant which seem to prove this. Alas, we shall never know the truth, nor can we know what was Jane's opinion. No letters of hers exist from June 1799 to October 1800, a period which includes her aunt's imprisonment and trial.

An interesting postscript, however, may be found in a note written inside a first edition of *Northanger Abbey* and *Persuasion* at the Victoria and Albert Museum. The writer, named Dyce, had been at Exeter College, Oxford, with James Edward Austen and wrote of him:

> He is now (1844) the Rev. James Edward Austen Leigh, having added Leigh to his name since he succeeded to the property of his aunt, Mrs. Leigh Perrot the lady last mentioned Miss Austen's sister [*sic*] had an invincible propensity to stealing & was tried at Bath for stealing lace, the printed account of her trial is extant. The family were dreadfully shocked at the disgrace which she brought upon them.[10]

Once Mrs. Leigh Perrot was released, the greatly relieved couple resumed their life together for another seventeen years. Then, in the words of *Sense and Sensibility*, "the old gentleman died; his will was read, and like almost every other will, gave as much disappointment as pleasure" (p. 4).

James Leigh Perrot, like Mr. Dashwood, distressed his family by leaving his money to his wife for her lifetime, and his two houses, one Scarlets, the other at Bath, at her disposal absolutely. All the nieces and nephews had had expectations, even Mrs. Austen, his sister. In fact the will was a disaster as far as the family was concerned. There was a distinct danger that Mrs. Leigh Perrot would leave Scarlets to one of her Cholmeley relations. Over the next nineteen years she threatened at different times to make various of her nephews her heir. At one period Francis was the favorite. He, in compliment to his aunt, prudently christened his eleventh child Cholmeley. After a few months the child, as children were wont to do in those days, died.

Edward, meantime, had rather disqualified himself as a potential heir by taking orders. Mrs. Leigh Perrot, like Mary Crawford, could not abide clergymen. Later, however, he reinstated himself in her good graces by making a match with a most eligible young lady, Miss Emma Smith, sister of Sir Charles Smith, baronet, of Suttons, Tring Park, and Portland Place, London. When, nine months after their marriage, a son was born to Edward and Emma, they judiciously named him Cholmeley.

Mrs. Leigh Perrot finally succumbed at the age of ninety-one. Edward became master of her beloved Scarlets, moving there with his wife and five children. As a condition of the inheritance he took, by Royal Licence, the name and arms of Leigh. A testimony to that obligation still exists at Scarlets in a stained-glass window over the main staircase, incorporating the Austen and the Leigh crests together with the date, 1836.

Scarlets proved a happy home to the Austen-Leighs. There five more children were born, making a sterling Victorian family of ten. As Jane says, "A family of ten children will be always called a fine family where there are heads and arms and legs enough for the number" (*Northanger Abbey*, p. 13). This particular fine family was exceptionally gifted, literate, and clever, and included in its members at least two future biographers of Jane Austen.

This is perhaps the more remarkable when one considers that Edward, although still a parish clergyman, educated all of his seven sons at home. Each boy in turn began Latin the day after his seventh birthday and Greek exactly two years later. They worked with their father for half an hour before breakfast, and one and a half to two hours afterwards, with another lesson to be prepared for the evening. All he required was that his children give him their undivided attention during the time he taught them. His four older sons went on to Harrow, Winchester, and Cheltenham. When it came time for the three youngest to go to school, it was suggested that they might try for scholarships to Eton. Their father, while preparing them for the examination, had no idea of their being successful. His daugther, Mary Austen-Leigh, the family historian, recalls:

> It happened that for some years past a private school in the neighborhood, where boys were made to work excessively hard, had obtained a monopoly of the top places in the list of entrances. This was not much approved of at Eton, and when the custom was broken through by an unknown amateur teacher, and by boys brought up at home, who without any cramming took, two of them the first place, and the third the second place among all their respective competitors, there was secret satisfaction amongst the Eton staff. (*James Edward Austen Leigh*, p. 217)

These three boys, Augustus, Edward, and William, became respectively: Augustus, Provost of King's College, Cambridge; Edward, Head of the Lower School, Eton; William, Fellow of King's and co-author of the definitive *Life and Letters of Jane Austen*.

Mary goes on to mention her father's profound admiration for Sir Walter Scott: "an author whose writings gave him extreme pleasure" and that "Lockhart's 'Life of Scott' was constantly in our father's hand" (*J.E.A.L.*, p. 162). One cannot escape the heretical notion that Edward thought more highly of Scott's works than of those of his own aunt. He refers to Jane Austen's juvenilia as being "in a humbler way" than Scott's early efforts (*Memoir*, p. 62).

Mary continues:

> Still better, if possible, was his reading of the Austen novels, and here he probably had some remembrance and inherited knowledge of the way in which their author had herself read them aloud, to guide him.

The result was that to his children their characters appeared to be perfectly real people, amongst whom we grew up, knowing them in part from our earliest years, and learning as we became older to understand and appreciate them better and better. . . . Jane Austen's books appeared to us then, and for a long time afterwards, to be a family and almost a private possession. Our father looked upon it as an accepted fact that to enjoy them required a mind of a peculiar order, and that it was not to be expected she could ever become a great favourite with the general public. (*J.E.A.L.*, p. 163)

It seems to me rather touching, this large family of Austen-Leighs, devoted to the novels, and so seldom meeting in that Victorian period anyone who shared their taste, or who cared about the importance of this aunt.

In the last years of their lives, William Austen-Leigh, the youngest of the Eton boys, and his sister, Mary, set up house at Roehampton, calling the place Hartfield and constituting themselves guardians of the reputation of their great-aunt. They had a curious opportunity to exercise this privilege in an affair which I stumbled on quite by accident. I was leafing through the bibliography at the back of Mary's own copy of the *Life and Letters of Jane Austen,* given her by her brother William, the author, and inherited by me, where I found a printed listing:

*Jane Austen: a Criticism and Appreciation.* By Percy Fitzgerald, M.A., F.S.A. London: Jarrold & Sons, 1913. [The frontispiece is a reproduction of a bust of Jane Austen executed by Mr. Fitzgerald.]

Against this prosaic entry is an indignant notation in Mary's handwriting: "From his own imagination only!"

Then followed several lines of explanation, which led me to the files of *The* (London) *Times,* where I discovered that Percy Fitzgerald, an eccentric author and sculptor, much addicted to donating his works to whomever he could prevail upon to accept them, had given a bust of Jane Austen to the Pump Room at Bath. The occasion had been marked with suitable pomp and ceremony, but William and Mary had not been included.

One can imagine their rage on reading this account in *The Times* next morning at breakfast. They sallied forth, like Lady Catherine, to scold the Mayor and Council, not into harmony and plenty, but into having the bust removed.

I have seen a photograph of it. The bust is labeled "Jane Austin," for a start. The lady depicted is a long-faced, supercilious woman with a vulgar leer.

From his own imagination, indeed! Mary's penciled note relates that Mr. Fitzgerald's bust

> was placed, according to his wish, in the Pumproom, opposite a bust of Dickens, also executed by Mr. Fitzgerald. No intimation of this intended proceeding had been made to the Austen-Leigh family nor was any member of it invited to the ceremony of unveiling the bust. When in a few months time the bust was seen by W.A.L. & his sister M.A.A.L. and was found to bear no resemblance to Jane Austen they requested the Mayor to have it removed. After some delay this was done and a bust of Garrick now takes its place.

Unhappy Mr. Fitzgerald. Some years elapsed before the bust of Garrick came to rest among the potted palms of the Pump Room. It had been previously offered to the City of London and declined. It is also ironical that if Percy Fitzgerald did not know what Jane looked like, neither did Mary Austen-Leigh. The frontispiece of her book, *Personal Aspects of Jane Austen*, written in 1920 when she was eight-two years of age, includes a portrait of Jane Austen by Zoffany. For many years this was believed to be authentic. It is now entirely discredited by art historians.

William Austen-Leigh had inherited Jane's writing desk (a small mahogany box, now in my possession) from his Aunt Caroline, who had had it from her aunt, Cassandra. Edward describes in his *Memoir* how Jane wrote

> upon small sheets of paper which could easily be put away or covered with a piece of blotting paper. . . . In that well-occupied female party there must have been many previous hours of silence during which the pen was busy at the little mahogany writing-desk, while Fanny Price, or Emma Woodhouse, or Anne Elliot was growing into beauty and interest.

In 1922, Caroline Ticknor, an American author, went one day to tea at Hartfield to see this desk. She wrote about it afterwards in a book called *Glimpses of Authors* (Boston: Houghton, Mifflin Co., 1922). The show put on for her benefit at Hartfield seems to have been curiously theatrical. Caroline Ticknor describes her introduction to "Mr. Austen-Leigh" and her invitation to tea at Hartfield, which she speaks of as a "charming country house" "skirted by beautifully trimmed lawns" and "backed by the prettiest of English gardens." The hostess, Mary, was not available when the guest arrived, so she sat waiting by long windows and presently Mary approached along a garden path, "a basket of cut flowers upon her arm, dressed in flowing gray silk, and bringing with her a delicate impression of what her great-aunt might have been." The author goes on to say that as they sat at tea and "listened to some delightful reminiscences, the decorative background of trees and flowers seemed like some cleverly painted stage scenery, and the interior a dainty bit of Cranford. 'Will you bring Aunt Jane's desk?' the hostess said to her brother . . . and when the cups were emptied, he entered with the precious desk which he placed on a table and opened reverently."

Jane has had to weather many winds of change. But in her quiet way she has survived, survived the "horrid" novels of the Regency, survived the sentimentality of the Victorians, the archness of the 1920s, and the devastation of two World Wars. Now, in the 1980s, there is perhaps a juster appreciation.

But it doesn't really matter, because whatever the Austen-Leighs might say or do or write, howsoever fashions may vary, whatever the Percy Fitzgeralds might choose to perpetrate, is in the final analysis inconsequential. Jane Austen can very comfortably maintain her own importance, and I venture to suggest that so long as books are read, her novels will continue to involve, charm, entertain, provoke, and comfort those who love her.

*Joan Austen-Leigh*

# NOTES

1. R. W. Chapman, ed., *Jane Austen's Letters to her Sister Cassandra and Others*, 2nd edition (London: Oxford University Press, 1952) (subsequent references to the *Letters* are to this edition and are in the text), p. 428.
2. R. W. Chapman, ed., *The Novels of Jane Austen*, 5 vols., 3rd edition (London: Oxford University Press, 1932–34), *Persuasion*, p. 3.
3. The source of this information is *Jane Austen's Kindred* by Joan Corder, unpublished, in possession of the College of Arms, London.
4. R. W. Chapman, *Jane Austen, Facts and Problems* (Oxford: Clarendon Press, 1949), p. 2.
5. These diaries and reminiscences, now in the possession of my cousin Lawrence Impey (whose grandfather was Cholmeley Austen-Leigh), have been published in part under the title, *My Aunt Jane Austen, a Memoir* by Caroline Austen, printed for the Jane Austen Society in 1952. It is to Mr. Impey that I owe thanks for permission to quote from unpublished portions.

6. R. A. Austen-Leigh, ed., *Austen Papers* (privately printed by Spottiswoode, Ballantyne & Co., 1942), p. 328.
7. J. E. Austen-Leigh, *A Memoir of Jane Austen* (London: Richard Bentley, 1870), p. 3.
8. Austen, *My Aunt Jane Austen.*
9. Mary Austen-Leigh, *James Edward Austen Leigh: A Memoir,* privately printed 1911.
10. For this information I am indebted to Mr. Sidney Ives, Librarian, University of Florida, Gainesville, Florida.

# The Austen Portraits and the Received Biography

$T$wo portraits of Jane Austen are reproduced with this essay. They raise some interesting questions about a good deal more than the author's appearance. The first, usually known as "Cassandra's sketch," is the only authentic portrait in existence. It depicts a young woman in a plain muslin dress, sitting bolt upright on what appears to be a simple, country-made ladderback chair, such as might have been found in a country vicarage or prosperous farm at the turn of the eighteenth century. Her arms are crossed in a somewhat uncompromising fashion; the neckline of her gown is unadorned by frills or ruching; the cap is very plain, and the slightly absurd, unruly curls stick out beneath a black, or dark-brown, headband. What is unmistakable is the penetration of the dark, staring eyes and the unsmiling, unpretty mouth. Perhaps there is the faintest suggestion that a sardonic smile might be about to break and to bring this face into animation, but you can see that it would not transform this young woman into anything remotely resembling a contemporary portrait of female softness and modesty. As a portrait of the author of Mr. Collins, Aunt Norris, Mrs. Elton, and Sir Walter Elliot it is convincing; as a portrait of the beloved sister who, according to Henry Austen, "always sought, in the faults of others, something to excuse, to forgive or forget" and who, "in the bosom of her family . . . was . . . thankful for praise, open to remark, and submissive to criticism,"[1] it simply will not do.

The second portrait, which is much more familiar and continues to be reproduced as the standard portrait of Austen on the dust jackets of most modern critical books about her, "improves" the subject as to charm and femininity. The whole face is softened, the mouth is prettier, the harsh lines from nose to mouth have been faded out, the eyes no longer stare so boldly. The arms are composed more decorously and disappear into the mists of a white muslin skirt, which appears to stick out like a crinoline. The cap and neckline have acquired some pretty frills and ribbon, the curls have lost their absurdity. The sash and headband are now a delicate, virginal pale blue, and the eye-color has been lightened. Finally, the figure is seated on a quite anachronistic Victorian chair. This Jane Austen might, just, have been the modest, devoted aunt of the nineteenth-century family biographies, but ought we to take her seriously? If we attend to how she was created, we must surely ask some critical and skeptical questions about our received portrait of Jane Austen, both as she appears in the Victorian adaptation of Cassandra's sketch, and in the received, largely Victorian, biography.

The Victorian portrait of Jane Austen was created by "Mr. Andrews of Maidenhead," who was commissioned by J. E. Austen Leigh to "improve" Cassandra's sketch, so that an engraving might be made to form the frontispiece of the 1870 *Memoir*. At this time, Jane Austen had been dead for fifty-three years, Cassandra for twenty-five. All her brothers were dead, and the two nieces who had known her well, Anna Lefroy and Fanny Knight, were now Victorian grandmothers, well into their seventies. Fanny Knight, by then Lady Knatchbull, expressed at about this time some reservations about her distinguished aunt, which bear upon the way she is represented in the *Memoir*. Writing to her daughter, she says:

> Yes my love it is very true that Aunt Jane from various circumstances was not so *refined* as she ought to have been for her *talent*, and if she had lived fifty years later she would have been in many respects more suitable to *our* more refined tastes.[2]

This letter tells us a good deal about the attitudes of the now aged nephew and nieces who in 1870 authorized, reluctantly, a highly selective account of Jane Austen's life which, together with the selection of letters which "family sources" have chosen to make public, remains the basis of our received biography. J. E. Austen Leigh's decision to write the *Memoir* caused acute anxiety in the surviving nieces, as R. W. Chapman makes plain.[3] An important motive in publishing it at all was to insure that what was made public would not cause embarrassment to the Austens alive in the late nineteenth century, and by then remote in sympathy and understanding from the world in which an uncompromising young woman, with black, staring eyes and an absence of Victorian refinement, had written novels that were so "clever" as to be slightly disturbing. J. E. Austen Leigh's intention in preparing the *Memoir* was not to give the

*The "Cassandra Sketch" of Jane Austen*
*copyright National Portrait Gallery, London*

public a full, clear portrait of the author in the context of her time, but to provide an acceptable, unembarrassing portrait of such an aunt as need make no respectable Victorian blush for her. It was not, considering the temper of Austen's pen, an easy task, but he did it well. "St. Aunt Jane of Steventon-cum-Chawton Canonicorum" was, with Mr. Andrews of Maidenhead's "picture," established as the accepted author of *Pride and Prejudice, Mansfield Park,* and *Emma*—works which, had they been seen

as written by an outspoken, irreverent young woman, who grew up and
began to write in the decade when Mary Wollstonecraft made such a stir,
might not have escaped embarrassing censure.

The biography of no other major author rests so exclusively on "family
sources" as does Jane Austen's. Henry Austen's brief "Biographical
Notice"—"Hagiographical Notice" might be a better title—starts, in
1817, the process of neutralizing what Austen has to say in her novels by
presenting us with an author who "recoiled from everything gross" and
"never uttered a hasty, a silly, or a severe expression." His hagiographical
portrait is enlarged and given authority by the 1870 *Memoir*, written by
Jane Austen's nephew, to whom she was not particularly close, and who
had but recently left school when she died. James Edward Austen Leigh
was over seventy, and a respectable Victorian clergyman, by the time he
collected his materials, commissioned Mr. Andrews, and published the
*Memoir*. It would be unthinkable to suppose that his Jane Austen had
read Mary Wollstonecraft with sympathy, was aware of the feminist
controversy of the late years of the eighteenth century, or was conscious
of the extent to which the "Sense/Sensibility" question in literature,
especially fiction, bore on Enlightenment feminism. But then his and Mr.
Andrews' Austen could not have written *Pride and Prejudice* either.

The received "life" of Jane Austen, together with general ignorance
about the development of feminist ideas from the beginning of the eighteenth century, has obscured her importance as a feminist moralist of the
age of Enlightenment. The family biographers created, as far as they
could, a portrait of a conventional, domesticated spinster, who happened, in between more important occupations, like playing spillikins
with her brothers' children, to write some very amusing, but quite innocuous novels. It is probable that by the time W. and R. A. Austen-
Leigh wrote *Jane Austen: Her Life and Letters* in 1913 they were
genuinely unaware of the controversial aspect of Austen's work, and did
not at all understand how carefully "family sources" had censored what
was to be made public, in order to insure that no controversy arose. J. E.
Austen Leigh probably had no more than an inkling of what Henry
Austen and Cassandra clearly understood and guarded against in their
selection of what it was proper for the public to know. Henry's "Biographical Notice" and Cassandra's suppression of the bulk of her sister's
correspondence were, I believe, designed to eliminate from the public
record anything that might connect the novelist with the "feminist controversy" of the late eighteenth and early nineteenth centuries, a period
covering Austen's formative years and unsuccessful attempts at publication. It will be remembered that, following Mary Wollstonecraft's death
and the publication of Godwin's *Memoirs of the Author of a Vindication*

*Mr. Andrews's Portrait of Jane Austen*
*courtesy of J. Butler-Kearney*

*of the Rights of Woman,* in 1798, a virulent attack on women writers who did not make a point of displaying a proper feminine submissiveness was made. The Reverend Richard Polwhele made it clear that *authorship* in itself was suspect in females, that it was wrong to treat the work of women on its merits, like the work of men, and that "the sparkle of confident intelligence" in a woman novelist was a breach of modesty.[4] It was at precisely the period when this view was being advanced by such "moralists" as Polwhele that Jane Austen, with the help of her admirably

unprejudiced clerical father, first attempted publication. She was not successful in this venture, either in late 1797 or in 1803, *First Impressions*
being rejected by Thomas Cadell, and *Susan* being purchased and adver-
tised, but "unaccountably" suppressed by Richard Crosby—the London
publishers to whom they were submitted. Had she achieved publication
at this time, when the heat was still on "Unsex'd Females," she would
have been unlikely to escape all remark. Nor should the possibility be
ruled out that Messrs. Cadell and Crosby realized that the works rejected
or suppressed might be found objectionable.

As it happened, by the time she did, at her own expense, achieve
publication, in 1811, the feminist controversy was dying away. By the
time *Susan*, retitled *Northanger Abbey*, appeared posthumously, in 1818,
it was virtually over, the battle having been largely lost by the feminists.
The rational feminism of the age of Enlightenment was to remain dor-
mant until Harriet Taylor and J. S. Mill rediscovered it in the mid-
nineteenth century. By 1818, Scott had become the major novelist of the
age, and by the time the women novelists of the midcentury began writing, the anti-Romanticism of Mary Wollstonecraft and Jane Austen was
no longer fully intelligible. Charlotte Brontë and George Eliot were no
longer in touch with the tradition of rational feminism of the eighteenth
century, which had led Wollstonecraft to denigrate Madame de Staël
(whom they admired) as a betrayer of the women's cause.[5] The feminist
controversy of an earlier time was now obscure. They were not attracted
by the portrait of the author appended to the posthumous edition of
*Northanger Abbey* and *Persuasion*, but saw no reason to question it.
Henry Austen's portrait of his sister, stressing her complete contentment
with the uneventful life of a country spinster and her abhorrence of the
public role of author, helped to convince them, and almost everyone else,
that she was too unremarkable a person to have had anything arresting or
controversial to say. And this was exactly what Henry Austen had intended, for he was old enough to remember the nature of turn-of-the-
century feminist controversy, and close enough to the author who "was
not so *refined* as she ought to have been for her *talent*," to feel that her
reputation (and that of her surviving family) needed guarding by the
closest editing of her life and opinions.

Among the nineteenth-century critics of Austen, only the liberal-
minded Richard Whately, writing in 1821, shows that he understood
something of the novelist's point of view as a moralist, and connected it
with Enlightenment feminism, to which he is clearly sympathetic. He
places the Austen novels in a philosophical context and shows that he
understands the author's religion to have been that of an enlightened,
Christian feminist. He praises her for not dealing in male "fiends" and

female "angels," for creating a heroine (Fanny Price) who was "not satisfied with religious belief and practice in herself, and careless about them in her husband." In this, he says:

> She presents a useful example to a good many modern females, whose apparent regard for religion in themselves, and indifference about it in their partners for life, make one sometimes inclined to think that they hold the opposite extreme to the Turk's opinion, and believe men to have no souls.[6]

Whately shows that he understands the importance of Sir Thomas Bertram's wrong beliefs about the moral responsibilities of women, sees that *Mansfield Park* asserts the equal moral accountability of both sexes and attacks the hypocrisy of the "double standard" of sexual conduct. His allusion to "the Turk's opinion" shows he was acquainted with feminist use of pejorative reference to "Turkey" as symbolizing Islamic exclusion of women from the moral status which rational Christianity ought to allow them. He praises Austen for showing women as much the same in their mixture of good and bad traits of character as men, and contrasts her in this with Richardson and Marivaux—thus showing that he understands the opposition of feminist opinion to the idealistic representation of women, in sentimental fiction, as peculiarly "virtuous" and peculiarly "frail" creatures.

Whately's perceptiveness about Austen is of great interest, partly because it shows that in 1821 her stance as moralist was still intelligible to a young critic (he was twenty-four) versed in the arguments associated with the earlier feminist controversy, and because it is the only instance of such clear understanding in nineteenth- and early twentieth-century critical writing. Whately was able to see that Austen's religion, upon which her brother laid such stress, was compatible with the views of an enlightened feminist, and he saw that what she had to teach about morals was taught not through preaching, but through demystifying the female character and showing it to be as various, as prone to fault, and as capable of principled conduct as the male. Rightly identifying her subject as the moral nature and capacity of man and woman, Whately places her as a moral teacher to those capable of learning anything "from productions of this kind," and here he foreshadows such twentieth-century critics as F. R. Leavis, Laurence Lerner, and Lionel Trilling, who have cast her in this role. The difference is that he, close to Austen in age (he was twelve years younger), knows what she can teach us *about* and, no doubt familiar with the hagiographical tendency in female biography, and the reasons for it, is not deceived by the pietism of the "Biographical Notice."

Unfortunately, many twentieth-century critics, including some who

have admired the Austen novels greatly, have been deceived, being unaware of the suspicion attached to "confident intelligence" in a woman
author in the early nineteenth century. A pseudo-problem about the
"slightness" of Jane Austen's subject matter and "the authority of the
manner," to quote Ian Watt,[7] has arisen. The "authority" is seen as a
matter of artistic technique, and excessive respect for it is sometimes
thought to indicate the separation of aesthetic from moral value, requir-
ing the treatment of the Austen novels as "autonomous verbal structures," without inquiring whether anything of importance about life is
revealed through them. This is a pseudo-problem because it ignores the
significance of the assumption of authority in an author who makes a
point of declaring her sex, even though she published anonymously.
Watt, writing in 1963, says:

> In the case of Jane Austen it is still difficult to reconcile the apparently
> trivial nature of her subject matter with the absolute command of expe-
> rience implied by the way it is presented.[8]

Marilyn Butler, going several steps further, advances the view that Austen's innovations in narrative technique were not merely unconnected
with her subject matter and political point of view, but that they turned
out to be so inimical to her purposes as a conservative moralist that she
was obliged to backtrack on them, thus destroying the formal coherence
of *Mansfield Park*.[9]

    If it were true that Jane Austen's moral concern was similar to that of
the "social critics" and "social-problem novelists" of the nineteenth century, it would also be true that there is a genuine problem about matter
and manner, but it was not. Her subject is "The Man and Woman Question," not the "Rich and Poor Question," and the authority she acquired
in fictional technique is itself an aspect of her criticism of patriarchal
prejudice. The "message" (if such an expression can be allowed in connection with an author who took such pains to embody meanings in
fictional structures rather than in preaching) is in the commanding manner as much as in the delineation of character and conduct which it
controls. By her refusal to disguise "the sparkle of confident intelligence"
with "the crimsoning blush of modesty," Austen implies, as Polwhele
would certainly have said—had he read *First Impressions* in 1798, or
*Susan* in 1803—active interest in the feminist "War of Ideas." Critics like
Arnold Kettle have recognized the importance of Austen's "highly critical concern over the fate of women in her society,"[10] but without seeing
that it is a politicized literary concern, the assumption by women of
serious and confident authorship being in itself a means of criticizing not

only the institutions of contemporary society but the assumptions of patriarchal moralists, poets, novelists, and critics. Lionel Trilling says:

> The extraordinary thing about Emma is that she has a moral life as a man has a moral life. And she doesn't have it as a special instance, as an example of a new kind of woman, which is the way George Eliot's Dorothea Brooke has her moral life, but quite as a matter of course, *as a given quality of her nature* [italics added].[11]

This is perceptive, but it is not seen as an aspect of Austen's philosophical feminism, connected with her development of a narrative style which can accommodate both the authoritative command of lady-novelist-as-moralist and the representation of "mixed" female characters, whose mistakes, humiliations, and moral growth may be truthfully depicted as representative of human nature in general rather than a female subspecies of it.

Such critics have, perhaps, been more misled by ignorance of "the feminist controversy" than by the received "life" and the censored letters, in which all reference to anything controversial has been almost completely hidden. Female critics have been even more strongly affected than men by what they believed about the woman. Charlotte Brontë in her brief but hostile comments betrays a lack of sympathy not merely with the Austen novels but with the received image of the novelist. Virginia Woolf, who admired the novels very much, was so misled by the "life" as to suppose that Jane Austen was largely unaware of contemporary literary opinion and dinner-party gossip about current trends. And it never occurred to her to ask if Austen had borrowed Wollstonecraft from a circulating library in Bath, or even bought a copy of Godwin's *Memoirs*. Of course, we can't be sure that she did, but we can be sure that failure to mention it in the "Biographical Notice" or the unburnt letters is no proof that she did not. Margaret Drabble's treatment of Austen in *The Waterfall* reveals an attitude not unlike Charlotte Brontë's, and the new feminist criticism of the last decade has, in general, accepted with too little skepticism something like Mr. Andrews' Austen as the author of *Pride and Prejudice*.

It is a long time since Q. D. Leavis put an end to the notion of Jane Austen as "a practically uneducated genius," but it is as true now as it was in 1942, when she wrote it, that

> . . . the conventional account of Miss Austen as prim, demure, sedate, prudish and so on, the typical Victorian maiden lady, survives.[12]

Surely it is time to give Andrews' Austen decent burial, and to reconstruct what we can of the *author* glimpsed in Cassandra's "unfinished"—

and unrefined—sketch. For never was the "sparkle of confident intelligence" so plainly shown in a *lady* novelist, and there is every reason to think that Austen was well aware of the feminist implications of such an open and unashamed display of it.

*Margaret Kirkham*
*Bristol Polytechnic*

# NOTES

1. Henry Austen, "Biographical Notice of the Author," prefixed to the first (posthumous) edition of *Northanger Abbey* and *Persuasion,* 1818; reprinted in R. W. Chapman, ed., *The Novels of Jane Austen* (London: Oxford University Press, 1931–34).
2. Quoted in Jane Aiken Hodge, *The Double Life of Jane Austen* (London: Hodder & Stoughton, 1972), p. 93.
3. R. W. Chapman, *Jane Austen, Facts and Problems* (Oxford: The Clarendon Press, 1949), pp. 140–45.
4. The Reverend R. Polwhele, *The Unsex'd Females,* 1798.
5. Mary Wollstonecraft, *Vindication of the Rights of Woman,* Chapter 5, Section IV.
6. Item 16 in B. C. Southam, ed., *Jane Austen: The Critical Heritage* (London: Routledge & Kegan Paul, 1968), p. 100.
7. Ian Watt, Introduction to *Jane Austen. A Collection of Critical Essays* (Englewood Cliffs, N.J.: Prentice-Hall, 1963), p. 12.
8. Ibid., p. 4.
9. Marilyn Butler, *Jane Austen and the War of Ideas* (Oxford: The Clarendon Press, 1975).
10. Arnold Kettle, "Jane Austen: *Emma*" in David Lodge, ed., *Emma* (Nashville: Aurora Publications [Casebook Series], 1970), p. 102.
11. Lionel Trilling, "*Emma* and the Legend of Jane Austen," originally the introduction to the Riverside edition of *Emma;* also included in the *Casebook,* p. 154.
12. Q. D. Leavis, "A Critical History of Jane Austen's Writings," *Scrutiny,* 1, 1944.

# Jane Austen and the
# Conflict of Interpretations

To discuss Jane Austen in the context of her literary predecessors is, at some point, to raise questions about historical criticism, its relation to other forms of criticism practiced today, and its claims to be, if not the only, then the best access to objective literary meanings.[1] As the recipient of diverse and contradictory interpretations, Jane Austen is, in fact, an exemplary focus for such questions. Consider some recent studies. In 1975, Marilyn Butler confidently proposed that Jane Austen was a thoroughly orthodox author, of a distinctively anti-Jacobin kind, whose fiction gave "flesh to the conservative case as no one else had done except Burke."[2] Her argument has not received universal assent. In fact, critics since 1975 have often disagreed, though with no unanimous voice. Julia Prewitt Brown considers Austen as revolutionary an author "in her own way" as Mary Wollstonecraft, and argues that her morals have "anthropological" rather than social or historical roots.[3] Susan Morgan views Austen, not in the context of her eighteenth-century predecessors, but in the context of her contemporaries, the romantic poets, and she argues that her central concerns are neither social nor ethical but "epistemological."[4] Bernard Paris applies Karen Horney to Jane Austen and discovers neurotic character traits behind the rhetorical and thematic unities of her fiction.[5] And Sandra Gilbert and Susan Gubar stress the early works, which, because they lack the "organic camouflage" of the mature novels, offer a more direct measure of the depth of Austen's alienation from the patriarchal society in which she was compelled to live.[6]

It is a curious situation, this conflict of interpretations, the more curious for the lack of reflection it has elicited from readers of Austen criticism. We seem willing, on the one hand, to entertain the most

contradictory of proposals—Jane Austen was at home in her culture; she
seethed with repressed anger—or, on the other, to adopt positions of
dogmatic repudiation—Jane Austen *was* at home in her culture; her regulated hatred has been *vastly* exaggerated—but not to seek to understand
the existence of the contradictory interpretations in themselves. Why do
contradictory interpretations exist? And how are we to evaluate dis-
agreements among interpreters?

Following one line of skeptical thinking, we might argue as follows:
literary meanings cannot be definitively recovered as a function of the
historical moment, nor can they be definitively analyzed as a formal
property of the text; instead, literary meanings are everywhere and always a function of the institutional model (the intellectual "pre-
understanding") brought to bear on a work.[7] The merit of such an
argument is obvious; at a stroke, it explains the current plurality of
readings of Austen. By bringing anthropological, romantic, post-
Freudian, and feminist expectations to Austen's novels, critics have been
able to come up with anthropological, romantic, post-Freudian, and
feminist readings. And, beyond its value as explanation, the skeptical
argument has the merit of according with recent criticisms or
redefinitions of the "classic": far from valuing a work for its ability to
enshrine universal truths in pleasing and complex form, critics from various standpoints have valued works for their ideological reticence—or
"hesitation," or "undecidability"—and for their consequent openness to
an indefinite variety of productive interpretations.[8]

Whatever the merits of this line of argument, historical critics are likely
to have problems with it and, even if they grant that any interpretative
"understanding" implies and depends upon some form of "pre-
understanding," they are likely to claim superior truth for the frame of
pre-understanding they bring to Austen's texts. That is, even as they
concede the possible *significance* of "anachronistic" criticism, they are
likely to claim priority for the *meaning* that is disciplined by a recognition of intellectual and generic contexts and by an attempt to recover the
author's intentions, conceived of in other than superficial ways.[9]

How compelling is a historical case of this kind? Several considerations
give us pause. E. D. Hirsch's celebrated distinction between meaning and
significance, which so conveniently cuts the Gordian knot of critical
disagreement for some critics, is not exactly homologous with his other
distinctions between "historicist" and "anachronistic" interpretation. As
a "dimension of hermeneutics," historicism, like "anachronism" (or the
imposition of later and alien frames of expectation upon historical texts),
is vulnerable to theoretical objections. Which is not to say that it is
*equally* vulnerable. Hirsch is obviously more sympathetic to a historicist

like Schleiermacher than he is to an anachronist like Heidegger. Even so, when in *Aims of Interpretation* he argues on behalf of the recovery of authorial intention in a historical context he does so on ethical, not theoretical grounds.[10]

In the second place, when one turns to the historical contexts which, critics have claimed, illuminate Jane Austen's intentions, one discovers a rather broad range of proposals, and the question arises as to which context allows the best access to Austen's intended meanings. For Brian Southam (reading *Sanditon*) the best context is a Regency England featuring "improvers" like Repton and Count Rumford and novelists like Thomas Love Peacock and Thomas Skinner Surr.[11] For Marilyn Butler it is the war of ideas between Jacobin and anti-Jacobin writers of the 1790s. For C. S. Lewis we breathe the air of the *Rambler* and the *Idler* in Austen's novels.[12] For Gilbert Ryle the best context is the ethics of Shaftesbury, for Philip Drew the theology of Bishop Butler.[13] For Douglas Bush, the context extends to an even wider and more distant past: nothing less than the Christian humanism of Spenser and Milton, as well as of Johnson and Burke.[14] And to all these intellectual contexts one must add the studies that have more narrowly focused on Austen's literary predecessors, novelists in the Richardson–Burney tradition, Richardson himself.[15] Clearly, there is a wide variety of contextual possibilities of pre-understanding, permitting a variety of interpretative emphases.

A literary historian might well counter that the existence of a variety of contexts is not damaging to the historical case, since various interpretations may be complementary and cumulative as regards meaning. There is considerable merit to this time-honored assumption of literary historiography. The studies mentioned and, until recently, historical scholarship generally, tend to concur in the discovery of a moral and conservative author, who is as respectful of such inherited values as sense and prudence, properly defined, as she is accepting of such social facts as the rule of primogeniture. Even so, there are frictions among various historical approaches, as I shall note presently, and the problem of multiple *historical* contexts for interpretation remains a real one. There is an undoubted interest in an approach to Austen's novels via Richardson's fiction, and an equally undoubted interest in an approach via the fiction of the anti-Jacobins. But it may be doubted whether these approaches, and the interpretative results they obtain, may simply be added to one another in a process conducing to the goal of interpretative truth and completion.

An even greater problem for the goal of consensus regarding Jane Austen's meaning (here considered in terms of the disposition she displays toward her inherited culture and its values) is the persistence in

Austen studies of an "alternative" critical tradition. Recent Austen criticism has often continued the "subversive" strain of Reginald Farrer, D. W. Harding, and Marvin Mudrick. In a related sense (Paul Ricoeur's), such criticism is a criticism of "suspicion."[16] Seldom explicitly Marxist, Nietzschean, or Freudian in its argument (Bernard Paris's carefully argued post-Freudian approach is the exception rather than the rule), such criticism nevertheless adopts, in however filtered a form, the iconoclastic procedures of Ricoeur's three great critics of suspicion. Thus, it is suspicious in that it distrusts the formal unities of her texts (her "verbal icons"), preferring to discover her real intentions behind the countercathectic or ideological screens of her moral rhetoric. Nor can such criticism always be labeled anachronistic. In the 1970s, indeed, a school of feminist criticism has returned to Austen's historical world to tell a very different story from the official one, a story in which Austen's novels presage an egalitarian sexual ideology and in which her characters penetrate to the secrets of patriarchal rule.[17]

Such arguments, some literary historians may feel, are misguided, but they can hardly be dismissed out of hand. The sheer persistence of "subversive" criticism suggests to reasonable people that there is a textual basis for "suspicious" views, and, by referring to recent theories of "textuality," we may perhaps understand both why suspicious criticism exists and will continue to exist *and* why historical criticism should take it into account.

Jane Austen's novels have no single contextual origin; they show traces and residues of many earlier texts. One can track her everywhere in Richardson's snow, but if Addison, Johnson, Cowper, and Burke had their own from her, there are (one might say, echoing Dryden) few serious thoughts that are new in her. Her novels—their plots, themes, characters, values—are "overdetermined," the result of her more or less conscious collaboration with an indefinite number of earlier texts. And the consequence of this textual sedimentation is inevitably a certain indeterminacy of meaning. There is "a surplus of signification" in her texts, permitting the reception of various "healing" messages.[18] Thus it is that she can speak therapeutically to Romantic scholars and to feminists, though for most historical critics she is neither Romantic nor feminist. The former simply do not hear the conservative signals in the text; they are too busy hearing other signals. Nor, as already suggested, is this simply a matter of their foisting an unhistorical framework on Austen's novels. Even in historical terms, the novels offer an "overflow of possibilities," so that any reading, considered as a Gestalt selectively constructed from textual evidence, will exist in the presence of other potential emphases, even in the presence of "alien associations."[19] What might seem a dangerous individualism in the context of a villain like Lord James Marauder (in Lucas's *The Infernal Quixote*) may be read as an admirable individualism if the context chosen is that of a Grandisonian "patrician hero," whose insufferably complacent virtue needs and receives its comeuppance.

Like all authors who enter the textual labyrinth, then, Jane Austen speaks with many voices, and her messages are more "equivocal" than the Chicago critics would have us believe.[20] But where do we go from this recognition? If her novels fail to achieve "univocal" certainties, do they leave us with radically ambiguous or undecidable possibilities of meaning? Does the "intertextual" character of her fiction imply the death of Jane Austen, considered as the voice of a coherent social and moral vision? And the birth of a fortuitous textuality, in which Austen can be "Miltonic" or a precursor of Simone de Beauvoir, depending on where one enters her discourse and how one writes her story?

A growing number of critics, I suspect, would answer yes to these questions, and welcome the availability of Jane Austen's texts to *écriture* and deconstruction. Within current protocols two responses are to be expected from historical critics. Each is a valid response, but neither comes close to resolving the question of the conflict of interpretations. First, it may be pointed out that while intertextuality may be a new term it is hardly a recent discovery, nor is it a concept that has always caused anxiety in the past. Jane Austen may not have her meaning alone, but she remains a domestic version of T. S. Eliot's authentic poet, writing with a good deal of eighteenth-century literature in her bones. In a more Augustan sense, she invades authors like a monarch, and what might be theft in others is victory in her. This is especially true, as Jocelyn Harris has most recently shown, of her relations with Richardson.[21] When we consider, for example, the Pemberley scenes in the first chapter of the third volume of *Pride and Prejudice* we may observe that Jane Austen's talent is not burdened by the past but liberated into "originality." The housekeeper's praise of the master, the view of the tastefully improved grounds from the windows of the house, and the tour of the picture gallery where the hero at a younger age is on display, are all coded sequences "lifted" from *Sir Charles Grandison*. Yet the visit to Pemberley radically changes Elizabeth's view of its owner, rather than simply confirming an admiration already arrived at, as in the instance of Harriet at Grandison Hall. And Mrs. Reynolds' remarks about Darcy's good nature provide new information on the hero's character, rather than simply adding more evidence that he is a paragon. What had been inert in Richardson becomes dynamic in Austen, and what had been a somewhat redundant illustration of character becomes, in rhetorical terms, a brilliant pivot of plot and themes.

A second response, equally confident that Jane Austen's voice can be separated from its various textual inheritances, may seek to establish a legitimate author by correcting what it takes to be the excesses or errors of anachronistic or suspicious criticism. Recent years have, in fact, produced proposals which, taken out of context, are enough to induce apoplexy in a Janeite (in context they often have an unimpeachable logic). There have always been, of course, critical voices claiming that despite Jane Austen's intentions, or in keeping with her real but suppressed feelings, Fanny Price is an insufferable prig and Marianne Dashwood is the real heroine of *Sense and Sensibility*. Others have argued that, far from being humiliated, Emma Woodhouse is not even morally educated in any convincing way. Recent critics have often buttressed such proposals.[22]

Others have made even more polemical arguments. It has been argued, for example, that Henry Tilney is a misogynist and Mrs. Norris a surrogate of her author; that Elizabeth Bennet is a critic of entailed estates, and that Anne Elliot is a critic of a patriarchal society. Such arguments, often made with verve and conviction, deserve to be aired and evaluated, but it has been a feature of much recent criticism not to engage dialectically with opposing views. Often the opportunities are there but not seized. There is, for example, an interest in common between two studies that in most respects are diametrically opposed. I refer to Marilyn Butler's *Jane Austen and the War of Ideas* (pp. 237–42) and Sandra M. Gilbert and Susan Gubar's *The Madwoman in the Attic* (pp. 160–66). Each study notes in Austen's fiction a thematic opposition between speech (or noise) and silence, or between bustle and stillness (or lethargy). But their evaluations of Austen's dialectic differ widely, as a brief summary may indicate. For Butler, Fanny Price's "silences are the appropriate social demeanour of the Christian heroine" (p. 240), and, despite a certain rhetorical failure in characterization, Austen says what she wants to say, which is that traditional religious orthodoxy (associated with order, silence, Mansfield Park, and Edmund Bertram) is to be preferred to a modern worldly subjectivity (associated with noise, bustle, Portsmouth, and the Crawfords). For Gilbert and Gubar, by contrast, Fanny "resembles Snow White not only in her passivity but in her invalid deathliness, her immobility, her pale purity" (p. 165). For the novel to be authentic, they suggest, her silence needs to be integrated with Mary Crawford's outspokenness; in this way Austen's self-division—her commitment to wit and the imagination, on the one hand, and her guilty sense that wit and the imagination are unfeminine on the other hand—could be accommodated in a dialectic of emerging self-consciousness; but integration does not of course occur, and as Fanny is destined to follow the example of the "corpse-like" Lady Bertram at the end of the novel, and her potential "sister," Mary, is expelled from the park, Jane Austen's usual accommodation fails, the cost of repressing wit is exposed, and the fictional split implies a split in the author's personality. This split is symptomatic of a society that requires women to be silent rather than noisy, to learn "the intricate gestures of subordination" (p. 163) rather than retain the freedom enjoyed in adolescence.

Even thus crudely summarized, these studies may be seen to represent a clear opposition between historical criticism and a criticism that is at once anachronistic and suspicious. Both studies achieve strong "understandings" that derive from "pre-understandings" of a very different kind. Can they be reconciled? Is one right and the other wrong? Does Butler's approach interpret Jane Austen's "meaning" and that of Gilbert and Gubar her contemporary "significance"? Or, taken together, do these studies support the skeptical argument that literary meanings are the consequence of the conceptual models applied to textual evidence?

I don't think we have begun to answer such questions.[23] My own sense of Jane Austen, shaped in an atmosphere respectful of historical and formalistic methodologies, is close to that of Marilyn Butler, and, in reading *Jane Austen and the War of Ideas*, I am persuaded that historical scholarship may play a corrective role vis-à-vis certain anachronistic readings; throughout this excellent study there is a rich fund of evidence for such corrections. By setting Austen's values and attitudes against those of the sentimental tradition and the fiction of the Jacobin writers, and by showing how close her responses often are to the anti-Jacobin novelists at the turn of the nineteenth century, Butler provides by far the best measure we have of her author's conservatism. Promiscuous comparisons with *The Vindication of the Rights of Woman* carry little force in the light of her findings. Yet whether, in the instance of the present contrast, her argument is decisively more persuasive and compelling may be doubted. Her stress on the "partisan" stance of *Mansfield Park* seems excessive, and in her insistence on partisanship in other novels she disallows not only anachronistic readings but historical readings that view Austen's conservatism in more flexible and liberal terms than she is willing to allow.[24] Moreover, in her conclusion she comes close to identifying Austen's orthodox position at the cost of conceding its lack of significance, its irrelevance, to modern readers. "Her morality is preconceived and inflexible," she writes, "of a type that may be antipathetic to the modern layman" (pp. 298, 296). Surely this is a high price to pay for the recovery of "meaning" and its separation from "significance."

One could, of course, argue that even in historical terms Austen's conservatism may be read more flexibly and, on the important question of the individual in relation to authority, as granting a much greater degree of spontaneity and freedom than Butler allows. I have argued previously that the theme of laughter is central to the meaning of *Pride and Prejudice*.[25] In the light of the recent work of Keith Thomas, that theme seems to take on even greater relevance.[26] Thomas argues that the association of open laughter with ill-breeding was an attempt by the Augustan aristocracy to establish a supremacy based on a cultural hegemony of manner and deportment as much as on the realities of political and economic power. And having stressed the social, even political, importance of manners—the area, we may say, of Austen's supreme expertise—he goes on to describe how the upper classes distinguished themselves from the rest by their gravity, decorum, and deportment, but also by their ceasing to use folk sayings and proverbs. Though he is not concerned with Jane Austen, and his period is earlier, Thomas's argument bears interestingly on the behavior of both Darcy (all gravity, decorum, and deportment) and Elizabeth, who does, when she wishes, use folk sayings and proverbs as weapons of a kind. When Elizabeth keeps her breath to cool her porridge, or disingenuously mistakes the fuss over Lady Catherine's arrival at Hunsford to be caused by pigs loose in the garden, she in effect challenges the hegemony that Darcy represents and seeks to maintain. But Jane Austen's criticism of the aristocracy in *Pride and Prejudice* is nicely balanced against her exposure of vulgarity in the speech and behavior of Elizabeth's aunt at Meryton and of her sister Lydia; so that her position, far from being that of a leveler, supports certain rural values of the gentry, who feel pressures from above and below.[27]

The social significance of laughter, both as a conservative and as a radical force, increased in post-Reformation England.[28] By the eighteenth century, in the wake of Shaftesbury's *Essay on the Freedom of Wit and Humour* (1709), the battle over laughter engaged Addison, Fielding, Warburton, Akenside, Lord Chesterfield, Allen Ramsay, and many others. In 1791, Vicesimus Knox published an essay entitled "On the Ill Effects of Ridicule When Employed as a Test of Truth in Private and Common Life." The whole debate, relevant to much of Austen's fiction, has a special relevance to *Pride and Prejudice*, and not only to the scene at Netherfield, where Miss Bingley and Elizabeth disagree over the question of whether Darcy is to be laughed at or not. Laughter divides the characters along the lines of the thematic dialectic of noise and silence already referred to; as it is deployed in the novel, laughter dramatically enacts a "position" on the relation of the individual to authority. This position is conservative, but attractively so; it is reached not dogmatically but irenically. It is a position that can be measured against the arguments of a dozen sources from Addison's *Spectator* (e.g., Nos. 494 and 598) to Gisbourne's *Duties of the Female Sex.* As an epigraph for the novel, one might choose a sentence of Lord Kames: "Let us bring ridicule under proper culture if we can, without endeavouring to pull it up by the root."[29] Or one might choose another from *Spectator,* No. 494: "It is not the business of virtue to extirpate the Affections of the Mind, but to regulate them."

To argue thus, however, is not only to attempt to "fine-tune" one historical emphasis with another, it is to claim a special privilege for a certain mode of thematic analysis. When I'm feeling especially protective of Jane Austen, it seems to me that such analysis is the way to truth. To recognize the rich historical texture composing a central theme in her novel is not, it then seems to me, to practice literary archaeology; it is rather to recover the aesthetic strategy of an author considered as a single and trustworthy source of meaning. The motif of laughter is so dramatically integrated into characterization, so well choreographed with other motifs in the dance of her dialogues, that the wonder is not that conflicts are suppressed in her novels, but that they are so well "exposed" and resolved.

But what if, under the guise of protecting Jane Austen, I am really protecting a method of reading, sanctioned by an institution, whose vested interest lies in the control and organization of critical discourse? What if, by positing an author as the origin of a coherent vision, I am blinding myself to what is surplus, or fortuitous, or uncontrolled in her texts? What if, seeking to separate truth from falsity in commentary, I am bringing scientist expectations to textual material, which will verify far more and falsify far fewer hypotheses than one might think? Such questions, obviously derived from Michel Foucault,[30] are doubtless pitched too high; one finds it difficult to conceive of Austen critics (already so dispersed and fragmented) as engaged in a conspiracy to suppress the free dissemination of textual meanings. Yet there may be enough truth in the questions to give us pause. In another place, Foucault writes of "the author [as] the principle of thrift in the proliferation of meaning."[31] And it may be the case that, faced by texts whose stability and determinacy seem more and more uncertain, critics have projected on Jane Austen the responsibility for an economy of meanings which their own procedures have initiated and predetermined. If this is so, then it may also be time to question the will-to-truth that characterizes both historical and anachronistic criticism.

Between (or perhaps beyond) the alternatives of a legitimist search for the recovery of meaning and a skeptical acceptance of the view that all interpretations are more or less concealed political interventions, future Austen studies may wish to concern themselves, not with further "readings" of Jane Austen's novels (six chapters of explication preceded by a brief introduction providing a hypothesis), but with the question of what "reading Jane Austen" signifies and entails. They are likely to discover that no easy distinction is to be made between "reading" Jane Austen (being receptive, objective, attentive to rhetorical signals and to informing historical contexts) and "writing" Jane Austen (being productive, subjective, suspicious of rhetoric, anachronistic); that both "reading" and "writing" may be equally intent on the discovery of "truth" and on the appropriation of Austen's name for particular purposes. One need not doubt or deplore that historical criticism will retain its right to correct lazy and ignorant readings (nor doubt that such readings will appear); but one may hope that historical criticism will refrain from staking too proprietary a claim. Future research into her various historical contexts will surely open new perspectives on the fiction, as, I have argued, Keith Thomas's sociology of laughter illuminates a central theme of the novels; but the stress should remain on "open"; and the tendency of historical criticism, especially when it works in alliance with modes of rhetorical and thematic analysis, to close Austen's meanings, to seek to provide a complete and true definition of her vision, should be viewed with reservations. The danger of legitimist criticism, rather like Darcy's threat in *Pride and Prejudice,* is silence; when research is complete and analysis is exhausted, then the truth is known, and no more need be said. Against such authority, assuming passive and obedient reading procedures, there is always likely to be rebellion, taking the form of the delightful laughter of Elizabeth Bennet, or the more raucous, less appealing noise of her sister Lydia.

*Alistair M. Duckworth*
*University of Florida*

# NOTES

1. This paper is a slightly revised version of a talk given at the meeting of the American Society for Eighteenth-Century Studies in Washington, April 10, 1981.
2. Marilyn Butler, *Jane Austen and the War of Ideas* (Oxford: Clarendon Press, 1975). The quoted phrase is from p. 228, where the context is the description of Sotherton, with its "curious blend of stylization and naturalism."
3. Julia Prewitt Brown, *Jane Austen's Novels: Social Change and Literary Form* (Cambridge, Mass., and London: Harvard University Press, 1979). For a more extended consideration, see my review in *Criticism*, 21 (1979): 374–76.
4. Susan Morgan, *In the Meantime: Character and Perception in Jane Austen's Fiction* (Chicago and London: University of Chicago Press, 1980). For a more extended consideration, see my review in *Modern Philology*, 79 (1981): 96–101.
5. Bernard Paris, *Character and Conflict in Jane Austen's Novels: A Psychological Approach* (Detroit: Wayne State University Press, 1978). Contending that Jane Austen is at once conservative, satirical, and detached, Paris argues that the relationship among these stances is to be understood in terms of her conflicts.
6. Sandra M. Gilbert and Susan Gubar, *The Madwoman in the Attic: The Woman Writer and the Nineteenth-Century Literary Imagination* (New Haven and London: Yale University Press, 1979). Quoted phrase is from p. 153. It should be added that not all recent works on Austen are in implicit or explicit disagreement with Marilyn Butler. Two works taking a historical approach and discovering a conservative author are: Warren Roberts, *Jane Austen and the French Revolution* (London: Macmillan, 1979), and David Monaghan, *Jane Austen: Structure and Social Vision* (Totowa, N.J.: Barnes & Noble Books, 1980); while Lord David Cecil's biography, *A Portrait of Jane Austen* (1978; reprinted New York: Hill and Wang, 1980) sees its subject as comfortably rooted in eighteenth-century cultural and moral assumptions.
7. Compare the argument of Stanley Fish, *Is There a Text in This Class? The Authority of Interpretive Communities* (Cambridge, Mass.: Harvard University Press, 1980).
8. See, for example, Frank Kermode, *The Classic* (New York: Viking, 1975); Roland Barthes, *S/Z*, trans. Richard Miller (New York: Farrar, Straus & Giroux, 1974); and Jacques Derrida, *Of Grammatology*, trans. Gayatri C. Spivak (Baltimore and London: Johns Hopkins, 1974).
9. Compare the argument of E. D. Hirsch, Jr., in *The Aims of Interpretation* (Chicago and London: University of Chicago Press, 1976), especially chapters 1 and 5.
10. See chapter 5, "Three Dimensions of Hermeneutics." It should be added that Hirsch's goal is the enlargement of an area of theoretical agreement among critics—an agreement as to principles that are independent of any particular

set of values. Whether interpretation can ever be free of value preferences is precisely the point in question.

11. Brian Southam, "*Sanditon:* The Seventh Novel," in Juliet McMaster, ed., *Jane Austen's Achievement* (London: Macmillan, 1976), pp. 1–26.

12. C. S. Lewis, "A Note on Jane Austen," *Essays in Criticism*, 4 (1954): 359–71. See also Peter L. DeRose, *Jane Austen and Samuel Johnson* (Boston: University Press of America, 1980).

13. Gilbert Ryle, "Jane Austen and the Moralists," in B. C. Southam, ed., *Critical Essays on Jane Austen* (London: Routledge & Kegan Paul, 1968), pp. 106–22; Philip Drew, "Jane Austen and Bishop Butler," *Nineteenth-Century Fiction*, 35 (1980): 127–49.

14. Douglas Bush, *Jane Austen* (New York: Macmillan, 1975).

15. See, for example, Mary Lascelles, *Jane Austen and Her Art* (London: Oxford University Press, 1939); Henrietta Ten Harmsel, *Jane Austen: A Study in Fictional Conventions* (The Hague: Mouton, 1964); Kenneth L. Moler, *Jane Austen's Art of Allusion* (Lincoln: University of Nebraska Press, 1968); Jocelyn Harris, " 'As if they had been living friends': *Sir Charles Grandison* and *Mansfield Park,*" *Bulletin of Research in the Humanities*, 83 (1980): 360–405.

16. For Paul Ricoeur's distinction between a "hermeneutics of recovery" and a "hermeneutics of suspicion," see his *Freud and Philosophy: An Essay on Interpretation*, trans. Denis Savage (New Haven: Yale University Press, 1970).

17. The culmination (thus far) of this school is provided by *The Madwoman in the Attic* (see note 6), especially "Part II. Inside the House of Fiction: Jane Austen's Tenants of Possibility." But the position forcefully argued here has been prepared by such other scholars as Nina Auerbach, "Austen and Alcott on Matriarchy," *Novel*, 10 (1976): 6–26, and Lloyd W. Brown, "The Business of Marrying and Mothering," in Juliet McMaster, ed., *Jane Austen's Achievement* (London: Macmillan, 1976), pp. 27–43. Leo Bersani's *A Future for Astyanax* (Boston: Little, Brown, 1976) seems also to have been a general influence. A comprehensive list of feminist criticism of, or bearing on, Austen would include works by Patricia Meyer Spacks, Elaine Showalter, and Janet Todd.

18. For this structuralist concept, which is also important to the thought of Roland Barthes and Jacques Derrida, see Claude Lévi-Strauss, "Introduction à l'oeuvre de Marcel Mauss," in Marcel Mauss, *Sociologie et Anthropologie* (Paris: Presses Universitaires de France, 1950).

19. See Wolfgang Iser, *The Act of Reading: A Theory of Aesthetic Response* (Baltimore and London: Johns Hopkins, 1978), especially Part 3, "The Processing of the Literary Text." Opposing the notion of a "structured prefigurement" in texts, Iser explains how readers typically synthesize meanings by constructing Gestalt groupings that result from a process of anticipation and fulfillment in relation to textual signals. Such Gestalten, however, are not only selective, they are, to a greater or lesser extent, subjective configurations; however dependent on textual authority, therefore, they contain "traces of illusion."

20. Wayne Booth, "Control of Distance in Jane Austen's *Emma*," in *The Rhetoric of Fiction* (Chicago: University of Chicago Press, 1961); Stuart M. Tave, *Some Words of Jane Austen* (Chicago: University of Chicago Press, 1973). Both of these fine studies exemplify the Chicago insistence that texts are wholes, in which the separate parts contribute to an overall coherent meaning, and that authors (an aesthetic, not biographical term) speak with single, trustworthy voices.

21. See article cited in note 15.

22. Bernard Paris *(Character and Conflict)* argues that the education of Emma Woodhouse may be viewed, in Horneyan terms, as Jane Austen's glorification of self-effacement as a defensive strategy. Susan Morgan *(In the Meantime)* denies that *Emma* is "a book about mature understanding replacing immature fancy. . . . It is about the powers of the individual mind . . . and about how these powers can find their proper objects in the world outside the mind" (pp. 38–39).

23. Similar questions are raised in David Monaghan's introduction to *Jane Austen in a Social Context,* ed. David Monaghan (Totowa, New Jersey: Barnes & Noble, 1981).

24. Marilyn Butler's insistence on Austen's orthodox and anti-individualistic stance in *Pride and Prejudice* leads her not only to dispute the cogent interpretations of Samuel Kliger and Lionel Trilling, but to question also the arguments of Kenneth Moler (in *Jane Austen's Art of Allusion*) regarding Austen's deflation of her "patrician hero," Darcy. The point here is one of emphasis. *Pride and Prejudice* as a conservative work is not endangered by Moler's reading. If the hero's social attitudes are criticized, so too is the heroine's individualism. By minimizing the criticism of the "patrician hero," by considering it as a nonessential vestige of an original burlesque intention (vis-à-vis the heroes of Burney as well as Sir Charles Grandison), Butler overstresses Austen's orthodoxy at the possible cost of making her author's position "antipathetic" to modern readers. It is the mutuality of the concessions made by Elizabeth and Darcy that makes the novel such a satisfying work. Elizabeth's individualism is corrected, but it is not eradicated; it remains as an essential, though nonthreatening, element of Austen's social vision. It may be added that in *The Watsons* Austen portrays another "patrician hero" in Lord Osborne. Like Darcy, he is to be rebuked and educated by the heroine.

25. Alistair M. Duckworth, *The Improvement of the Estate* (Baltimore and London: Johns Hopkins University Press, 1971), pp. 132–40.

26. Keith Thomas, "The Place of Laughter in Tudor and Stuart England," *Times Literary Supplement,* January 21, 1977.

27. Compare David Monaghan's argument in *Jane Austen: Structure and Social Vision.*

28. See William Darby Templeman, "Warburton and Brown Continue the Battle over Ridicule," *Huntington Library Quarterly,* 17 (1953–54): 17–36; and Stuart M. Tave, *The Amiable Humorist* (Chicago: University of Chicago Press, 1960).

29. Lord Kames, *Elements of Criticism* (Edinburgh, 1762), II: 57.
30. The questions and language of this paragraph come from Michel Foucault, "The Discourse on Language," Appendix to *The Archaeology of Knowledge*, trans. A. M. Sheridan Smith (New York: Harper & Row, 1976), pp. 215–37. The translation of the Appendix is by Rupert Sawyer.
31. Michel Foucault, "What Is an Author?" in *Textual Strategies*, ed. Josué V. Harari (Ithaca: Cornell University Press, 1979), p. 159.

# Interpreters of Jane Austen's Social World
## Literary Critics and Historians

### I

Jane Austen observed in *Emma*: "Seldom, very seldom, does complete truth belong to any human disclosure; seldom can it happen that something is not a little disguised or a little mistaken."[1] This chastened mood, I think, is appropriate to an examination of the variety of conflicting interpretations of the social world of Jane Austen's novels which is the purpose of this essay.

I come to this task as a social and economic historian and not as a literary critic. My chief interest is the history of English landed society from the eighteenth to the twentieth centuries. Like many other devotees of Jane Austen, I first read her simply for the pleasure of it, which I still do. Then, as a university teacher, I found that I was expected, among my graver duties—for reasons never very clear to me then or afterwards—to attend doctoral examinations of candidates in English literature, some of whom were Austen specialists. This was the beginning of my perplexities. Students of English literature, I found, were little interested in English history—so little interested that my favorite question became: Do you know who George Macaulay Trevelyan was? Unhappily this indifference revealed itself in their discourses on Jane Austen. Some of them, when in need of historical background, invented a sort of bogus history. Some of them on occasion went so far as to invent—the better to further their argument, I would guess—some part of the text of the novels. Or so it seemed to me.

I was thus led to look into Jane Austen scholarship. My initial reaction, I am afraid, was both uncharitable and unwarranted. I began to dwell

shrilly on the frailties of literary critics, going so far as to suggest that if
literary critics got their history straight they would be better literary
critics. Much of this I regret as unseemly and to some extent unfair. My
own understanding of eighteenth-century English society—and thus of
Jane Austen's world—has come distressingly slowly, and it is clear to me
now that part of the literary critics' troubles probably began with the
historians. Moreover, as I became more familiar with the work of literary
critics, I found that, far from being wrongheaded, some had already seen
something that I came to see for myself, and that others showed me
something that I had not yet seen or might never have seen. It follows
that I have remained unrepentantly a believer in the utility of students of
literature and students of history talking to one another more often than
they do.


# II

The method of this essay will be to group and assess opinions about
Jane Austen's society under various heads. I will begin with those students, relatively few but of high distinction, who find that in having no
comprehensive view of society she in fact portrays no real society. One
such student thus argues that she portrays an idyll. Another argues that
her society, although in a sense real, is hardly more than an extended
family.

The first is best represented by Lionel Trilling in a remarkable essay on
*Emma.* He wrote there that "any serious historian will make it
sufficiently clear that the real England was not the England of her novels,
except as it gave her license to imagine the England which we call hers.
This England, especially as it is represented in *Emma,* is an idyll. All too
often it is confused with the actual England, and the error of the
identification ought always to be remarked."[2]

Like some other notable judgments by Trilling, this one has puzzled
both literary critic and historian. One critic has asked whether it is not
the result of something lacking in the modern (and American) mind,
which has "difficulty in taking for granted the reality of Jane Austen's
social units"[3] and which finds social reality in the fleeting, ever-changing
quality of present-day life. It is not, of course, especially rewarding to
speculate why Trilling delivered himself of this judgment. Plainly enough
it has failed to convince—and, I would think, for good reasons.

One is that a "serious historian" would be hard put to make much of
"*the* real England."[4] He is more likely to think of several real Englands
coexisting. Admittedly Jane Austen's was not the England of the Durham
coal miners, or of plain-living aesthetes like the Wordsworths, or of

London shopkeepers like Francis Place, or of London bohemians like the Prince Regent—to name but a few of the real Englands. Instead, her England was that of the local rural elite. She called it "neighborhood"—one of the prime words in her social vocabulary. She meant by it not the tenant farmers, the rural laborers, the country-house servants, or the village tradesmen. They did not belong to the world of neighborhood. Rather she meant by neighborhood their social superiors, who lived in large houses and whose dining, dancing, and marrying provided the substance of her stories.[5]

A second reason for skepticism is Jane Austen's social vocabulary—one that fits her world of the rural elite. This vocabulary, however, is something different from the modern (largely nineteenth-century) language of class. Perhaps only on one occasion—in *Persuasion*—does she make use of the language of class, and even there it strikes the modern eye as a bit stilted and odd.[6] Otherwise the reader finds no "working class," "middle class," or "upper class"—or any of the variations on these that the nineteenth century produced. This is perhaps understandable, given that the language of class had as a major (if implicit) assumption that society was becoming relatively fluid. Jane Austen, however, had no great liking for social fluidity. Hence that interesting remark in *Emma* about Frank Churchill: "His indifference to a confusion of rank bordered too much on inelegance of mind."[7]

What, then, is her social language? "Neighborhood" has already been noted as comprising the rural elite. Expressions like "the very great," or "resident landholder," or "profession" designate groups within that elite—all of them covered by the word "gentleman." For those parts of society in varying degree inferior to her elite she uses a variety of expressions such as "the second rate and third rate," or "half gentlemen," or, for the very lowest, "the poor." Or she may specify these inferiors as "yeomen," "laborers," "tenant farmers," or "in trade"—all of them, as she would say, "in a low line." The word "line"—like such words as "sphere," "circle," or "rank"—does some of the work that the language of class would do later to indicate large divisions within society. All this would suggest that Jane Austen was not bereft of a notion of social reality, although it may be unlike our own.[8]

These reasons for skepticism also apply to the second sort of interpreter, best represented by Richard Simpson, the Victorian critic,[9] and by Oliver MacDonagh, a contemporary historian.[10] If I understand the latter correctly, he is in substantial agreement with Simpson, who wrote over a century ago that "there is nothing in her novels to prove that she had any conception of society itself, but only the coterie of three or four families mixing together . . . of organised society she manifests no idea." Simpson later qualified this statement. "Perhaps the assertion that she had no powers of portraying or understanding society as such should be modified in favor of one special class. . . . She thoroughly understood the naval officer whom she could study at home in her brothers."

That Jane Austen's novels deal with little more than an extended family has a bit of plausibility: we are all familiar with her advice to her novel-writing niece: "Three or four families in a Country Village is the very best thing to work on."[11] But her families exemplify a variety of social types, all of which go to make up a larger society, the nature of which she is clearly aware of. They do not exist in a social vacuum. Even Simpson admits that she was a close student of a least one social type—although his assertion that only sailors were the successful object of her studies would seem to be farfetched.

After all, her domestic opportunities for the study of social types were not confined to sailors. If two brothers were sailors, two were parsons; so was her father, as well as numerous friends and relations. Another brother was a large-acred Kentish and Hampshire landowner, and both in Steventon and Chawton the gentry families were well known to her. Nor is it really clear that she understood sailors better than she understood parsons or landowners or soldiers (her favorite brother, Henry, was once a soldier as well as a failed banker before he rushed precipitately into the church). Indeed, a case might be made that her sailors are in some ways the least convincing of the social types in her novels. How does she put it at the very end of *Persuasion*? "That profession which is, if possible, more distinguished in its domestic virtues than in its national importance."[12] But in all likelihood she had heard of Horatio Nelson and his domestic infelicities. Something bordering on sentimentality prevents her sailors from sharing those human frailties that she saw so clearly in the rest of the human race. Even their prize money—Captain Wentworth's £25,000—assumed heroic proportions.

### III

It would be fair to say that the bulk of Jane Austen interpreters have had no trouble in agreeing that the world of her novels is real, a part of the real England. But they have had trouble in agreeing on what to call it, on how to characterize it. In the course of more than a century and a half, Jane Austen interpretation has boxed the compass of social respectability. It began by describing her as the annalist of the "middle classes," of "ordinary and middle life." Later she was said to be the aristocracy's annalist, or more commonly the gentry's. Most recently interpretation seems to have turned back to its beginnings and plumped for a bourgeois Jane Austen.[13]

High on the list of reasons for calling Jane Austen's society bourgeois, it would seem, is the ubiquity of money in her novels. Things and persons seem all to have their price. Even naval officers go to sea in a great war to make money. This pervasive monetarization of the novels was in itself perhaps enough to catch the eye of literary critics. But there were also historians, looking to other evidence than the novel, who reinforced this conclusion. So influential an historian as R. H. Tawney, in his famous essay on the gentry, characterized sixteenth- and seventeenth-century landowners as bourgeois because they were more intent on making money than their predecessors. For later centuries, something like this was also said by Marxist historians like the equally influential E. P. Thompson.[14] Not surprisingly, the bourgeois label found wide acceptance.

But some critics have had their doubts. Graham Hough, for example, observed in 1970 that the bourgeoisie was "too blunt an instrument to have much explanatory value."[15] And almost two decades earlier, in one of those revealing footnotes where professors choose to argue with themselves, Marvin Mudrick said almost as much. His admission is especially interesting, for in the text of the same book he came down heavily on the bourgeois nature of Jane Austen's novels. He wrote there, for example, of "the particularities of bourgeois courtship," meaning by this its monetary aspects. He also described Captain Wentworth in *Persuasion* as "possessed of all the new bourgeois virtues—confidence, aggressiveness, daring, an eye for money and the main chance." On the other hand, in his interesting footnote he observed that expressions like "middle class" and "bourgeois" did less than justice to a society which in his opinion was a hybrid society—one that combined "dying feudal tradition and progressively self-assertive bourgeois vigor."[16]

Mudrick's dilemma is well worth pondering. It touches on a number of confusions that have marked Austen interpretation—and, for that matter, the writing of eighteenth-century English history. It would be worthwhile to identify these confusions. Three suggest themselves. The first has to do with what Mudrick calls the hybrid nature of Jane Austen's society, of the world of neighborhood. What were its several elements? The second has to do with the group that Mudrick calls bourgeois. Who precisely made up this group, and in what ways was it related to the others? The third has to do with the group that Mudrick sums up as possessed of "a dying feudal tradition." Who were they, and were they dying, let alone feudal—at any rate, any more so than the group called bourgeois?

The world of neighborhood, the world of the rural elite, was indeed hybrid, hence the disagreement on what to call it. Strictly speaking, it contained three groups, two of which—the landed aristocracy and gentry—were less distinctive one from the other than both were from the third group. What brought them close together was the ownership of landed estates. They made their money in the same way—mainly by letting land to tenant farmers, as Mr. Knightley did to Robert Martin in *Emma,* although some also let land to housebuilders and mining entrepreneurs.[17] A few even embarked on such enterprises themselves, as Mr. Parker seems to have done in *Sanditon.* Where the aristocracy and gentry chiefly differed was in what—to use one of her favorite phrases—Jane Austen called "style of living," that is, in their status, in how they spent their money.

Aristocratic landowners, having more money, had more to spend. A few had a great deal more to spend, as much as £100,000 of gross income annually. To appreciate what a very great deal this was, remember that in the first decade of the nineteenth century a skilled worker with a family to support would have been fortunate to enjoy an annual income of £100, an unskilled worker of £40.[18] Even the lowest annual income of an aristocratic landowner was something like £5,000 to £10,000, Mrs. Bennet's measurement of the lordly life. Aristocratic incomes, therefore, made for splendid status: great houses, great estates (perhaps several), great parks, a house in London, a seat or seats in the House of Commons for sons and relations, a hereditary seat in the House of Lords for titled fathers, perhaps a position at Court. Like the gentry, the aristocracy had local roots, but they also enjoyed a more metropolitan existence. They were less likely to marry locally: they traveled more, as Elizabeth Bennet once suggested to Darcy, up to London, and among "a range of great families."[19]

The gentry had less money to spend—although relative to the income of a working man, even modest gentry incomes were still impressive, probably on a level with the income of a large town merchant and exceeding the incomes of most professional men. A modest gentry income was something like £1,000 to £2,000 a year. It was Mr. Bennet's income in *Pride and Prejudice,* Colonel Brandon's in *Sense and Sensibility.* Delaford, the latter's estate, was (according to Mrs. Jenkins) "a nice place . . . exactly what I call a nice old-fashioned place, full of comforts and conveniences." At £4,000 a year income, Henry Crawford's estate in Norfolk was judged "a pretty estate." At £12,000 a year, the peak of gentry income, Mr. Rushworth's Sotherton was a great gentry estate: with its lordly income, as Mary Crawford put it, "a man might represent the county with such an estate." At the other end, at somewhat below £1,000 a year, at the income of John Willoughby's estate in *Sense and Sensibility,* the gentry landowner approached that uncomfortable region, so aptly summed up by Jane Austen as "comparative poverty," where status demands outran income, where the affliction of frustrated expectations became acute.[20] To the unpleasant but aristocratic Lady Catherine de Bourgh, even Mr. Bennet's Longbourn with its £2,000 a year was scarcely adequate: deficient in park, servants, and whatever else was needed to impose on the imaginations of social inferiors. But these modest gentry estates, covering England in their thousands, managed to supply their owners with comfort and status sufficient to make them the natural leaders of their local communities. Assisted principally by the resident Anglican clergy, they ran their parishes and counties, acting as overseers of the poor, and as magistrates. They were more at home in the local county town than in London's West End.

Of the two, gentry and aristocracy, Jane Austen preferred the former. Not that she was uncritical of the gentry. She had her gallery of gentry fools like Sir John Middleton and Sir Walter Elliot. But socially she stood closer to the gentry than to the aristocracy, especially to the smaller-incomed gentry. Morally she approved of their more settled habits, of their less ostentatious patterns of consumption, of their limited capacity—compared with that of the Court aristocracy led by the Prince Regent—to perpetrate a national scandal. Her novels are thus not much populated with aristocratic figures. Moreover, when they appear, they are almost invariably silly, both men and women. If I am not mistaken, the single aristocrat in her novels whom she looks upon kindly is the young nobleman in *Northanger Abbey*, suitably obscure, who marries Miss Tilney. Emma Watson, we are told, if her story had been completed, would have rejected Lord Osborne's offer of marriage in favor of a parson, the much humbler Mr. Howard. Perhaps there is an appropriateness here, a reflection of Jane Austen's social background. Like Emma Watson, she was not a landowner's daughter, although it is still being said by some interpreters that she was a daughter of the gentry. Instead, like Emma Watson, she was a parson's daughter, and although she was not likely to marry below a parson's position in society, she was also not likely to marry much above it.

Strictly speaking, then, Jane Austen belonged to neither of the first two groups in that hybrid world of the rural elite—neither to the aristocracy nor to the gentry—but to a third group, so far unnamed. This group comprised the nonlanded: the professional and rentier families, first and foremost the Anglican clergy; second, other professions like the law—preferably barristers rather than solicitors—and the fighting services; and last, the rentiers recently or long retired from business. I have described them as nonlanded, by which I mean that if they owned land, and doubtless many of them owned some, they owned comparatively little, perhaps 100 acres and less. Sometimes they merely rented a house and its adjoin-

ing land, as did the Bingleys in *Pride and Prejudice;* and often, notably in
the case of the Anglican parson, they held land (and sometimes farmed it)
for life.[21] By and large, they were neither lords of manors nor collectors
of rent from tenant farmers. But they lived in big houses, held or owned
enough land to assure privacy, that most cherished of social delights, like
the Woodhouses in *Emma,* who owned a corner of Mr. Knightley's
Donwell Abbey estate. Some did with less land, less privacy, less floor
space of an impressive sort. These were lower in the scale of the nonlanded, a sort of village patriciate, like the Coles in *Emma* or the Edward-
ses in *The Watsons,* and inferior to them, touching the very bottom of the
rural elite, within a hair's breadth of falling out of it, the humble and
garrulous Miss Bates, the impecunious spinster daughter of a defunct
parson, living with her mother and two servants behind a village shop.

This third group, the nonlanded, is the one most likely to be described
by Jane Austen interpreters as bourgeois—although some (as we have
seen) have also described the entire world of neighborhood as bourgeois.
The word, however, ill suits both the smaller as well as the larger social
unit. For bourgeois evokes an urban—or at least an actively trading—
milieu. It also evokes a degree of social hostility—of class antagonism, to
use the Marxist phrase—that was also inappropriate to the several groups
within the world of neighborhood. There were tensions within that
world, but these were something different from the deeply divided outlook of class antagonism. In sum, a word that breeds such misunderstanding might well be scrapped—at least in this particular context.
Compared with sociologists and anthropologists, historians are timid
inventors of language, a practice admittedly not always advantageous.
But here, I suggest, it would be useful to find a new word.

As it happens, this has already been done. Some years ago, the Leices-
ter historian Alan Everitt invented the word pseudo-gentry as a helpful
substitute for the word bourgeois, having in mind the latter's misleading
overtones. He used it first for seventeenth-century English society, later
for a time more appropriate to Jane Austen's society.[22] There is some sign
that it is being taken up, although as yet there is no great rush to do so. It
strikes me, however, as a profitable addition to the social historian's
language, as well as to the language of the historian of culture.

The pseudo-gentry were "pseudo" because they were not landowners
in the same sense as the gentry and aristocracy were. They cannot be said
to have owned landed estates. But they were gentry of a sort, primarily
because they sought strenuously to be taken for gentry. They devoted
their lives to acquiring the trappings of gentry status for themselves and
especially their children: the schooling, the accent, the manners (from
style of conversation to dressing for dinner), the sports, the religion, the

habit of command, the large house in its own grounds, servants, carriages and horses, appropriate husbands and wives, and, last but not least, an appropriate income, which Jane Austen called "independence," that most desirable of all social states. In short they had a sharp eye for the social escalators, were skilled in getting on them, and (what was more important) no less skilled in staying on them. They were adept at acquiring what the economist Fred Hirsch has aptly called "positional goods"— those scarce services, jobs, and goods which announce social success.[23] In this they helped to inaugurate a "positional competition" inevitably more widespread than that indulged in by landowners, which has set the style for all modern societies, once those societies achieve a certain level of wealth and enterprise sufficient to feed the voracious appetite for positional goods.

Of this positional competition, central to the lifestyle of the world of neighborhood, no one knew more than Jane Austen. Her novels are full of it. She saw its range and idiosyncrasies and absurdities as someone might who among other things combined the gifts of an estate agent, family lawyer, and auctioneer. Who else among novelists, male as well as female, knew how to calculate the value of a next presentation? Or was familiar with that technical refinement in the practice of strict family settlement which allowed father and son jointly to break a family entail, the better to allow for habits of expenditure? She knew the male as well as the female side of fashionable consumption. On the male side, there were rich young men like Henry Crawford, skilled in turning an ordinary house into something more than a gentleman's seat, into a "place . . . as to make its owner to be set down as the great landholder of the parish."[24] On the female side, there were well-to-do young women like Emma Woodhouse who measured precisely how status was affected by setting up one's carriage or keeping dining company—or less sensibly, as in Mrs. Elton's case, by burning wax candles in the schoolroom.

Marriage, of course, had an important place in positional competition. As anthropologists have told us, marriage makes society and tends to confirm its arrangements. Jane Austen's was a rich, differentiated society, and marriage, being largely endogamous, tended to keep it that way. This is not to say that marriage among the pseudo-gentry and their superiors was exclusively a matter of status. That "trade of coming out," to use Jane Austen's bitter phrase, managed as it was reputed to be by marriage-making mothers, furnished increasing room in the eighteenth century for marriages of affection. But status accommodation was never lost sight of. Emma Woodhouse, maker of marriages although not a mother, out of genuine scorn resolutely blocked Robert Martin's marrying Harriet Smith—a mere tenant farmer marrying a lady like herself, a daughter of the pseudo-gentry. Later her scruples were removed when she removed Harriet herself from the ranks of the pseudo-gentry.

In the business of positional competition, none among the pseudo-gentry equaled the strivings of the Anglican clergy, particularly its upper reaches, that is, the rectors and vicars who held prosperous livings. They derived their income mainly from tithes, thus being ultimately dependent, as landowners were for their rents, on the fortunes of agriculture.[25] Of clerical incomes, as might be supposed, Jane Austen had a precise and extensive knowledge. She knew the terrible depths to which an impoverished curate might fall—"a country curate without bread to eat." Colonel Brandon's living at Delaford was only £200 a year—a sum judged in all quarters as too small to permit Edward Ferrars' marrying; even £350 was found inadequate to supply "the comforts of life." Only when clerical incomes began to approach the lower levels of gentry income—somewhere above £500 a year—did they begin to give some assurance of gentlemanly status. Henry Crawford summed up Edmund Bertram's Thornton Lacey income of £700 a year as "a fine thing for a younger brother." Dr. Grant's £1,000 was plainly more than enough to guarantee that "unpretending comfort of a well-connected Parsonage" which Jane Austen found so agreeable a prospect.[26]

This was the scale of clerical income which permitted the Anglican clergy to come closer to realizing the ideal of the English country gentleman than any other pseudo-gentry type. The rise of the clergy was an eighteenth-century rise, partly a product of the agricultural revolution, of the beneficial effect of enclosure on the receipt of tithe.[27] Not surprisingly, many of the clergy became enthusiastic farmers of their glebeland; some of them became agronomists, acting as enclosure commissioners and writing county agricultural reports. Some of them hunted; one of them wrote a treatise on fox-hunting. A good many of them became justices of the peace, in some counties virtually taking over the business of local government; and some of them became local political bosses. In their religious capacity, they were among other things the chief agents of social legitimacy and whatever measure of social control was attainable. In short, enjoying a superior education to that of most Englishmen, they were well fitted to becoming a kind of rural managerial class for the landed gentry, forebears of a sort of the modern service class.

The rise of George Austen and his family paralleled the general rise of the clergy. The orphaned son of a country surgeon—and country surgeons came low in Jane Austen's social scale—he managed in the seventy years after his birth in 1730 to make a secure position for his large family in the world of the pseudo-gentry. Luck, family connections, the eighteenth-century patronage network, a superior marriage—all joined together to do the trick. His prosperous, kindly solicitor uncle, Francis Austen, started him off, steering him away from the apprentice-oriented but less gentlemanly callings. He went to Tonbridge School, which had its special road to Oxford and a St. Johns fellowship. From there the rest of the road into the church was easy: his uncle's help again, and a distant cousin's (Thomas Knight of Godmersham in Kent), made him a pluralist, the holder of two clerical livings, at Steventon and Deane in north Hampshire. He also married Cassandra Leigh, of the Leighs of Adlestrop, a family whose genealogy reached social heights unattained by the Austens. Six sons and two daughters came of this marriage. Five of the six sons did well; one was an incurable invalid. Luck would have it that one son was adopted by the childless Knights, to become in time the master of a great gentry estate of the order of Mr. Rushworth's in *Mansfield Park*. Two other sons followed their father into the church. The remaining two, like Horatio Nelson, also a parson's son, entered the Navy, eventually to become admirals. The daughters fared less well, remaining spinsters and dependents, both luck and family doing less for them than for their brothers, although doing much for the world in supplying the raw material for some of the greatest novels in the English language.

The story of the Austens is but a single episode in the general rise of the pseudo-gentry. The historian Alan Everitt found the origins of the psuedo-gentry in the late seventeenth century; they were then an urban phenomenon. Sometime during the eighteenth century, presumably, they also became a rural phenomenon, settling on the outskirts of towns and villages. Many came from London, like the Coles and Westons in *Emma*, or from some other thriving center. Their numbers by the first half of the nineteenth century were impressive. Look into an early *Kelly's Post Office Directory* for any English county, and there you will find the pseudo-gentry in their hundreds and thousands, arranged alphabetically under the proud title of "Court," as opposed to the humdrum and inferior title of "Trade." Historians have long dwelt on the rise of the bourgeoisie and the rise of the gentry. They might now profitably turn their attention to the rise of the pseudo-gentry, which was well under way during the years Jane Austen composed her novels. In a sense, her novels celebrated that rise.

## V

We are left with the last of Mudrick's perplexities—what to make of that group in Jane Austen's world of neighborhood to which he attaches a "dying feudal tradition." This group, as we have seen, was in fact two— the aristocracy and the gentry, the titled and untitled owners of large and small landed estates. It has seemed to many interpreters of Jane Austen's novels—Mudrick among them—along with many historians, that landowners were in some important sense effete, reactionary, something of a precapitalist remnant. This influential opinion needs scrutiny.

In fact, as historians are only now coming to agree, eighteenth-century English society was not, like the French, an *ancien régime* society.[28] Eighteenth-century English landowners were thus neither effete nor reactionary; instead, they were strong and progressive. They were, first and foremost, a political class, predominant in the localities and at Westminster, in effect England's governing class. They were to remain in this position of strength, in spite of an occasional faltering, throughout the nineteenth century. As a political class, unlike contemporary European landed elites, they were libertarian rather than repressive: the state they governed was not a police state. Finally, they were a businesslike, capitalist class. This last, perhaps, is central to the removal of misunderstandings among Jane Austen interpreters. Although English landowners were not commercial or industrial capitalists, they were agrarian capitalists. In their own sphere, they were economic modernizers, in no important sense hostile to other spheres of economic modernity; on the contrary, by reason of the importance of agriculture in the national economy, they helped mightily in generating England's pioneering achievement, the industrial revolution, and managed as well to derive profit from it.

Their businesslike agriculture was—as landowners would have said—an improving agriculture: improving cultivation, improving rents, and at the same time undertaking a massive transformation of the English landscape in the shape of the enclosure movement. This was what was chiefly meant by estate improvements in Jane Austen's day—not landscape gardening, as seems to have been suggested in a recent and interesting study of her novels.[29] Landscape gardening was a minor department—if it was a department at all—of estate business, and indicated nothing of major significance in landowners' attitudes to their estates. If I understand it correctly, this study suggests that opposing certain forms of landscape gardening was opposing estate improvements and thereby protecting the landed estate from its despoilers. This is, of course, to obscure the modernizing, capitalist thrust of English landownership in the eighteenth century by which estates were increased and strengthened rather than despoiled.

By promoting the enclosure movement—or the first agricultural revolution, as it has come to be called—English landowners after long effort put an end to a traditional and communal agriculture and a backward, truly reactionary peasantry, thereby promoting the forces of economic individualism in the rural community. In their way landowners were not unlike merchants and manufacturers. They sought for productivity, and in the form of increased rents for an increase in their profits. They were not, however, as singleminded as a merchant or manufacturer in the pursuit of profit, inasmuch as they wanted other things as much or more, notably the exercise of political power. They were likely to conclude, therefore, that a landowner who racked his tenants showed little political wisdom. Still, theirs was a capitalist money culture. Well before Jane Austen's lifetime, they had ingeniously turned a variety of landed resources into money. Not only wheat and turnips but also coal and town-building sites had been converted into cash crops. In the eighteenth century their money incomes grew markedly, as did their borrowing.

Oblivious to landowners' political power and progressive economics, some interpreters of Jane Austen have seen weakness and crisis and change in landed fortunes, where they should instead have seen strength and stability and continuity. Major turning points have been found in what in fact was the same old story. Take, for example, the case of Mr. Parker in *Sanditon*. Mr. Parker is a local landowner who turns town developer, as we would call him in the twentieth century, the promoter of a new bathing resort on the Channel coast. Brian Southam, among English critics the most worthy to succeed R. W. Chapman, has seen in Mr. Parker a new social phenomenon—as he puts it, "the member of the landed gentry who capitalizes his property and goes into business."[30] But in fact Mr. Parker was not a new figure in landed society. Ever since the early seventeenth century a large part of the chief towns and cities of England had been built by landowners, who let their land to builders on very long leases. With the growth in popularity of sea-bathing in the eighteenth century, bathing resorts like Sanditon came to be built in this way all round the coast of England from Blackpool and Southport to Eastbourne and Hastings.

Or take that silly old goose, Sir Walter Elliot, in *Persuasion*, whom some Austen students have made into a doom-laden figure, a portent of the imminent downfall of landed society. Sir Walter vacates his estate at Kellynch Hall, renting it to Admiral Croft. This has been taken to mean that "the fundamental order of Sir Walter's world is changing fast."[31] But letting country houses to someone who paid a good rent and going to live elsewhere more cheaply—as in Bath or on the Continent—was an ancient expedient for debt-ridden landowners. Sir Walter, advised by a reliable agent, was doing what prudence and custom dictated. Ordinarily foolish, he was now being eminently sensible. In a year or two, perhaps longer, he would be able to scale down his debt and return to Kellynch, once more to adorn its numerous mirrors. In the history of English landed society, this had been a favorite device of embarrassed landowners, as

they went through the cycle of feasting and starvation, of overspending
and enforced abstinence.

This facility for uncovering landed crises has gone to remarkable
lengths. One scholar in search of an explanation for Jane Austen's ear-
nestness in *Mansfield Park* has sketched out a general economic crisis in
gentry fortunes, rooted both in the lowering of agricultural prices at the
end of the Napoleonic Wars, and in the decline of the West Indian
plantation system.[32] The truth of the matter, however, is that the years
1811–1813, when *Mansfield Park* was being composed, saw mostly an
economic boom, not a serious economic downturn; wheat prices in these
years reached their highest point in English history. As for the West
Indian plantation system, even if it were in a state of decline (which is
now being questioned), there is only a modest connection between plantation ownership and English landed society. Sir Thomas Bertram in
*Mansfield Park* was, as the owner of an Antigua plantation, almost as
unusual as the Sir Thomas who chose to go halfway round the world in
the middle of a great war to oversee the management of his distant property. This was very unlikely behavior for a great landowner, who would
normally leave such matters to an inferior agent.[33]

A landed crisis would not be complete without a class struggle of some
sort. Austen students who found the bourgeoisie entrenched in Jane
Austen's world have sometimes spoken of a victory of the rising middle
class over the landowners, or with more particularity have sometimes
singled out the professions as the victors. Malcolm Bradbury has observed that *Persuasion* testifies to "Jane Austen's desire to explore two
salient forces in her society, two classes in interaction, in a way that she
has never chosen to do before."[34] These were landed gentry and professional naval officers. Foolish Sir Walter yields up his house to Admiral
Croft, and eventually his daughter to Captain Wentworth, whose addresses he had once contemptuously dismissed. As one student has
bluntly put it, "*Persuasion* is set in the historical context of the rising
importance of the Royal Navy and the declining importance of the titled
gentry."[35] Presumably this may be attributed to what Marvin Mudrick
called Wentworth's "new bourgeois virtues—confidence, aggressiveness,
daring, an eye for money and the main chance."

Recently, in an otherwise useful book, this theme of landed decay and
crisis has been taken to extremes.[36] The author's interpretation rests
chiefly on a reading of *Mansfield Park*. Two quotations will suffice. The
first goes as follows:

> At the close of the 18th century, the gentry were beginning to experi-
> ence the financial decline that would gather force through the century.
> The increase in population, particularly an urban population,

threatened the traditions of the relatively small gentry. In *Mansfield Park* we witness the gentry's resistance to urban values. The historical suggestiveness of the social picture of *Mansfield Park* seems to me to be tolerably profound for a supposedly ahistorical novelist. All of these changes in the economic and social life of the nation are registered in the personal lives of the characters. From its economic to its spiritual condition, the world of *Mansfield Park* is a world in transition and decline.

The second quotation reads thus:

> The rise to favor of the Price children, Susan and William, is seen as one of the true hopes for the future at the close of the novel. Susan and William seem to represent the new breed, strong, fearless, able to endure. They possess a secular integrity, which is perhaps another term for solid bourgeois values.

Plainly we have come back to the Mudrick perplexities put forward a quarter of a century ago—but, alas, without his interesting and candid footnote.

It needs therefore to be said again that the world of the rural elite was neither going bankrupt in the early nineteenth century nor disintegrating spiritually and socially. No group within it was casting out the others. There were no simple winners or losers. Moreover, those virtues ascribed exclusively to the bourgeoisie, or, as I have called them, the pseudo-gentry (if I may list them again)—confidence, aggressiveness, daring, an eye for money and the main chance—were far from being unknown to landowners. They simply practiced them elsewhere—not in small wooden ships (although some were to be found there) but at the hustings, in quelling riots, in the hunting field, and in the management of their estates. Nor is it odd that landowners' behavior was so like sailors' behavior. After all, landowners and sailors were often kin, brothers, sons, and uncles; or, if not kin, then they were schoolfellows or neighbors.

It might be said, of course, that Jane Austen thought otherwise: that she read the nature of her society differently from the way we might; in short, that she saw a crisis threatening her society. Indeed, at least one student of her novels has suggested that in her last years she went so far as to switch her allegiance from a corrupt and expiring landed society to the brave new world of the Royal Navy and the fashionable watering place.[37] This has been denied by other students—and I should think that their judgment is more plausible.[38] Jane Austen's loyalty to the world of neighborhood remained steadfast. *Sanditon* was not intended to declare a new allegiance, but rather to express her longstanding uneasiness at the sight of restless, anonymous, shapeless communities like Bath and London. This always disturbed her, and it may be that what she saw became more disturbing in her later years. On the other hand, I should draw the line at making her into a crank like William Cobbett, who was sure that landed society was being eaten alive by *nouveaux riches*—as if the history of landed society was not also the history of new men entering it and becoming part of it. Admittedly Jane Austen was always critical, always a moralist. She was not the daughter of the clerical pseudo-gentry for nothing. But even so, I hesitate to assert that she was intent on diagnosing and averting what she took to be the imminent ruin of landed society— or, for that matter, that it was her major preoccupation. Her major preoccupation, it seems to me, was the fate of women in that society. That, however, is a large and quite different subject, best considered elsewhere.

## VI

Let me conclude with these reflections. On the matter of Jane Austen's world of neighborhood, it is important to keep in mind how peculiarly English a world this was. It is unlikely that European landed elites had so close a relation with a part of the so-called bourgeois world as the English landed elite had with its pseudo-gentry, or that the pseudo-gentry in European societies was so formidable a phenomenon as the English. Both Matthew Arnold and Alexis de Tocqueville suggested that this was the case.[39] This would mean that social historians must walk more warily than they have done—as must students of society generally, whether they be literary critics indulging in social discourse or social scientists indulging in historical speculation.

Historians have been fond of viewing social change dramatically—and in the English case this has helped mislead interpreters of Jane Austen's world. For that world did not function dramatically. Its component groups, landowners and pseudo-gentry, were not in collision. The former provided the pseudo-gentry with what sociologists call a reference group—that is, a model for their lifestyle as well as with jobs of all sorts. In turn the pseudo-gentry provided the landowners with ideas and specialized capacities and services. If the several groups had a common name, it was that of gentleman. They shared a common view of England's society and economy and a common aspiration to dominate them. In this sense they formed a sort of partnership in a highly prosperous firm—one which political scientists call the ruling class, or highbrow journalists the Establishment. The firm remained in business well into the twentieth century. It is said in some quarters to be still intact. In the course of time, the nature of its business changed, as did the relations among the partners. The pseudo-gentry, junior partners in Jane Austen's day, were by

1914 at least equal partners, on the way to becoming senior partners. In all this there was a quiet, undramatic continuity as well as change, in which the partners rubbed off on each other in a kind of two-way traffic, a sort of social symbiosis.

On the matter of interpretation I should like to end with the plea that among the interpreters of Jane Austen's novels, notably among historians and literary critics, there might well be more awareness than now exists of what the others are doing. At present, in both literary and historical studies, there is a markedly rising interest in society, in the changing nature of the family, in male and female consciousness. This is a difficult kind of history to investigate. Take, for example, the history of women. What women did and what they thought has generally been left to men to record: "the pen," as Anne Elliot declared in *Persuasion*, "has been in their hands,"[40] with the result that women's story has been poorly told, if it has been told at all, and that the evidence is scarce and not easy to interpret. Given these difficulties, it would be a happier state of affairs if historians and literary critics did more in the way of looking over each other's fences. By doing so they might speed each other's work; and they might make themselves more intelligible and interesting to a wider reading public. Such goals, in all likelihood, would have seemed very sensible to Jane Austen.

*David Spring*
*Johns Hopkins University*

# NOTES

1. *Emma*, p. 431. All references to Jane Austen's novels are keyed to R. W. Chapman, ed., *The Novels of Jane Austen* (London: Oxford University Press, 1931–34).
2. Lionel Trilling, *Beyond Culture* (Harmondsworth: Penguin, 1965), p. 61.
3. J. Bayley, "The Irresponsibility of Jane Austen," in B. C. Southam, ed., *Jane Austen: The Critical Heritage* (London: Routledge & Kegan Paul, 1968), p. 9.
4. See also C. Kent, "'Real Solemn History' and Social History," in D. Monaghan, ed., *Jane Austen in a Social Context* (Totowa, N.J.: Barnes &

Noble, 1981). This essay has many merits, especially its historical view of literary criticism.

5. Something of the same point was made by R. Williams, *The English Novel: From Dickens to Lawrence* (New York: Oxford University Press, 1970), p. 24.

6. *Persuasion*, p. 74.

7. *Emma*, p. 198.

8. On how different it was from our own, see Bayley, "The Irresponsibility of Jane Austen"; and Williams, *The English Novel*.

9. R. Simpson, in B. C. Southam, ed., *Jane Austen: The Critical Heritage*.

10. O. MacDonagh, "Highbury and Chawton: Social Convergence in *Emma*," *Historical Studies*, April, 1978.

11. R. W. Chapman, ed., *Jane Austen's Letters* (London: Oxford University Press, 1959), p. 401.

12. *Persuasion*, p. 252.

13. The early critic was Sir Walter Scott, in B. C. Southam, ed., *Jane Austen: The Critical Heritage*, p. 100. For a modern critic who assigned her to the aristocracy, see D. Daiches, "Jane Austen, Karl Marx and the Aristocratic Dance," *The American Scholar*, Summer, 1948; for one (among many) who assigned her to the gentry, see D. Monaghan, *Jane Austen: Structure and Social Vision* (New York: Harper & Row, 1980).

14. R. H. Tawney, "The Rise of the Gentry, 1558–1640," *Economic History Review*, XI, No. 1, 1941; E. P. Thompson, "The Peculiarities of the English," *The Socialist Register* (London: Merlin Press, 1965).

15. G. Hough, "Narrative and Dialogue in Jane Austen," *Critical Quarterly*, Autumn, 1970.

16. M. Mudrick, *Jane Austen: Irony as Defense and Discovery* (Princeton: Princeton University Press, 1952), p. 15, footnote 26. The quotation about Captain Wentworth is on p. 235.

17. There is a very large literature on this subject. See especially G. E. Mingay, *English Landed Society in the Eighteenth Century* (London: Routledge & Kegan Paul, 1963); F. M. L. Thompson, *English Landed Society in the Nineteenth Century* (London: Routledge & Kegan Paul, 1963); D. Spring, *The English Landed Estate in the Nineteenth Century: Its Administration* (Baltimore: Johns Hopkins University Press, 1963).

18. See H. Perkin, *The Origins of Modern English Society 1780–1880* (London: Routledge & Kegan Paul, 1969), pp. 20–21, for a table of the several categories of income.

19. *Pride and Prejudice*, p. 178; *Emma*, p. 221.

20. *Sense and Sensibility*, p. 196; *Mansfield Park*, pp. 118, 161; *Sense and Sensibility*, p. 321.

21. For a good account of the eighteenth-century Anglican clergy, see G. F. A. Best, *Temporal Pillars: Queen Anne's Bounty, the Ecclesiastical Commissioners and the Church of England* (London: Cambridge University Press, 1964).

22. See A. Everitt, "Social Mobility in Early Modern England," *Past and Present,* April 1966; and A. Everitt, "Kentish Family Portrait: An Aspect of the Rise of the Pseudo-Gentry," in C. W. Chalklin and M. A. Havinden, eds., *Rural Change and Urban Growth 1500–1800: Essays in English Regional History in Honour of W. G. Hoskins* (London: Longman, 1979).

23. F. Hirsch, *Social Limits to Growth* (Cambridge, Mass.: Harvard University Press, 1974). See also C. Kent, " 'Real Solemn History' and Social History," who makes something of the same point.

24. *Mansfield Park,* pp. 243–4.

25. On tithes generally, see E. J. Evans, *The Contentious Tithe: The Tithe Problem and English Agriculture, 1750–1850* (London: Routledge & Kegan Paul, 1976).

26. For the several quotations from the novels, see *Persuasion,* p. 19; *Sense and Sensibility,* pp. 302–303, 319; *Mansfield Park,* p. 226.

27. See W. R. Ward, "The Tithe Question in the Early Nineteenth Century," *The Journal of Ecclesiastical History,* April 1965.

28. See Perkin, *The Origins of Modern English Society.*

29. A. M. Duckworth, *The Improvement of the Estate: A Study of Jane Austen's Novels* (Baltimore: Johns Hopkins University Press, 1971).

30. B. C. Southam, *Jane Austen's Literary Manuscripts* (Oxford: The Clarendon Press, 1964), p. 114.

31. D. Mansell, *The Novels of Jane Austen: An Interpretation* (London: Macmillan, 1973), p. 188. B. C. Southam makes the point even more strongly in his *"Sanditon,* the Seventh Novel," in J. McMaster, ed., *Jane Austen's Achievement* (London: Macmillan, 1976), p. 7: "The landowner [Sir Walter Elliot in *Persuasion*] is bankrupt. A new social order, born of the war, has come into being, and he is forced to receive an Admiral into his family home and a mere Captain into the family itself."

     Mr. Southam in this same essay refers to my differing with him on these matters in a conference discussion some years ago (p. 25). Our differences, I am afraid, still persist—although perhaps not in the way he has described them. If, by a "new social order" emerging during the Napoleonic Wars, he means the rise of industrial towns with their factory proletariat, I should of course agree. But that was not the question at issue, as I understood it. The question at issue was whether *landed society*—so important to Jane Austen's world—had undergone radical change in these years, of the sort suggested by the juxtaposing of the 1790 landowner (General Tilney) with the 1815 landowner (Mr. Parker), the first presumably an example of the *old,* the second of the *new.* Instead of a radical change in landed society I see a heightening of what had been going on for a long time before 1790.

32. A. Fleishman, *A Reading of Mansfield Park: An Essay in Critical Synthesis* (Baltimore: Johns Hopkins University Press, 1967).

33. See M. Craton, *Searching for the Invisible Man: Slaves and Plantation Life in Jamaica* (Cambridge, Mass.: Harvard University Press, 1978). This study of Jamaica planters gives some examples of planters resident in England visiting

their plantations—but the planters were not owners of large English estates, as Sir Thomas Bertram was.

34. M. Bradbury, "*Persuasion* Again," *Essays in Criticism*, October 1968.
35. J. Wiesenfarth, "History and Myth in Jane Austen's *Persuasion*," in *The Literary Criterion*, Winter 1974.
36. J. P. Brown, *Jane Austen's Novels: Social Change and Literary Form* (Cambridge, Mass.: Harvard University Press, 1979), pp. 85–86, 97.
37. Mansell, *Jane Austen*, p. 189.
38. Notably M. Butler, *Jane Austen and the War of Ideas* (Oxford: The Clarendon Press, 1975), p. 286.
39. For Matthew Arnold, see *The Works of Matthew Arnold* (London: Macmillan, 1904), 15 vols., X: 143, 157–58. For Tocqueville, see D. Spring, "An Outsider's View: Alexis de Tocqueville on Aristocratic Society and Politics," *Albion*, Summer 1980.
40. *Persuasion*, p. 234.

# Children and Their Families in Jane Austen's Novels

Because her focus is on solid, middle-class people and her mode is one of domestic realism, Jane Austen never permitted herself to have recourse to a device for providing excitement that was greatly favored by sentimental and gothic novelists of her era: the unprotected orphan. Austen always develops her central subject, maturation, within the context of an enveloping, protective family life, though the families involved are often more complicated units than the modern nuclear family of two parents and their children. In Austen's novels the tensions and conflicts with which the central characters must deal come from within their own families and not from the absence of family protection.

In each of her novels Austen faces the same basic problems of construction: the heroine's family background must be made known to the reader; at least a few members of the family must be present as characters in the novel; the family must be credible as the heroine's point of origin, yet must fail to guide and protect her completely, so that her coming to maturity will not lack interest. Her family background must help to explain her good traits, as well as her serious flaws and her early errors. In order to accomplish these things, Austen employed several postulates concerning family interactions and the development of children. It is noteworthy that this set of ideas changed very little in the course of Austen's writing career: the family pressures which explain characters in the three late novels are not much different from those which Austen used in the three novels she drafted before 1800. This, for a writer who was always trying to solve new artistic problems, to extend her range of theme and characterization within the consciously limited subject matter she had appropriated as her own, is surprising and may be evidence of the depth of her early convictions on the subject of families.

73

Often Austen's heroines find themselves in trouble because, through a complex set of hereditary and environmental influences, they grow up closely resembling one or both of their seriously flawed parents. Such a heroine's main task is to develop a critical perspective concerning the family which has formed her, and most frequently the guide who helps her develop this perspective is her future husband, the product of a different family.

Catherine Morland, the heroine of *Northanger Abbey,* is a character whose initial approach to life, a reflection of her parents' attitudes, gets her into some mild trouble. To stress the difference between *Northanger Abbey* and the gothic and sentimental novels whose conventions she is mocking, Austen gives her heroine a particularly ordinary, sensible, functioning family. The Morlands expect life to proceed for everyone in the same orderly, prosaic fashion in which their own lives have passed. And like her kindly, humorless, honest parents, Catherine is straightforward and conscientious, no more ready to look for falsity and pretense in others than to practice them herself. The thought that wit might illuminate truth has never entered her mind.

Away from home, Catherine encounters a series of people who cannot be judged adequately on the basis of her parents' assumptions about life. Isabella and John Thorpe and General Tilney are deceitful, and Catherine must learn to look critically at their pretensions. In this process of developing her critical abilities, Catherine's guide is Henry Tilney, a witty young man whose pedagogical method is the humorous exaggeration, rather than the plain statement favored by Catherine's parents. Originally, Catherine's reaction to Henry's teasing is at least partially disapproving: she feared "that he indulged himself a little too much with the foibles of others" (*Northanger Abbey,* p. 29).[1] But as she puzzles over his cryptic witticisms, Catherine's own wit sharpens. The girl whose response to her mother's straightforward, rote methods of teaching was "not remarkable" (*Northanger Abbey,* p. 14) starts to flower, and Henry's humor becomes increasingly admirable to her: "His manner might sometimes surprise, but his meaning must always be just" (*Northanger Abbey,* p. 114). Beginning as the product of her family, Catherine matures by refining, if not rejecting, many of their basic, tacit assumptions about human nature, good manners, and ordinary life.

Catherine Morland is the only heroine of a completed Austen novel possessing a pair of well-matched parents who are both alive at the time of the story, and the reason for this is undoubtedly Austen's desire to place Catherine in an initial situation which differs as dramatically as possible from the orphaned, unprotected condition of the sentimental or gothic heroine. With her other heroines, this particular contrast is not needed, and so they all begin in less favored family situations. If their parents were a fairly well-matched couple, like the Dashwoods in *Sense and Sensibility,* one parent is dead. If both parents are alive, as are the Bennets in *Pride and Prejudice* or the Prices and Bertrams in *Mansfield Park,* their marriage is seriously flawed. In *Persuasion,* Anne Elliot is not only the product of an unsatisfactory marriage, but also suffering from the death of her more intelligent, admirable parent.[2] Thus the question of parental influence upon the heroine is more complex in the other novels than in *Northanger Abbey,* where the very straightforwardness of family influence is a source of humorous contrast to the inexplicable perfection of many gothic or sentimental heroines.[3]

In *Pride and Prejudice,* Austen first experimented with a heroine who is the product of a misalliance. Elizabeth Bennet's character has been influenced, more deeply than she realizes, by her father, the parent she naturally resembles. Elizabeth's quick intellect and sparkling wit come to her from her father, and she is his favorite daughter precisely for this reason. Elizabeth's mother—perhaps through jealousy or perhaps because she cannot dominate her clever daughter any more than she can dominate her elusive husband—finds Elizabeth "the least dear to her of all her children" (*Pride and Prejudice,* p. 103). Mrs. Bennet prefers the daughters who most resembler *her:* the beautiful Jane and the thoughtless, high-spirited Lydia. In spite of the tension between them, Elizabeth does resemble her mother in one important trait. Each woman tends to judge people unfairly, on the basis of the way they affect her own ego or interests, though Mrs. Bennet's crude misjudgments are mere parodies of Elizabeth's clever perversities.

And it is this element of clever perversity in her judgments that Elizabeth derives from her well-loved father. Mr. Bennet reacted to his disappointment in marriage by withdrawing from active participation in family life and allowed himself to be "contented with laughing" at the follies of his wife and younger daughters, without attempting to correct their misbehavior (*Pride and Prejudice,* p. 213). Mr. Bennet is amusing and, because he has paid so heavily for his mistake in marriage, worthy of sympathy, but his familial irresponsibility is deeply wrong.

Further, there is strong evidence that Austen wants her readers to accuse Mr. Bennet of social irresponsibility in his role as a landowner. Until many years after the birth of their fifth daughter, the Bennets still hoped to have a son who "was to join [with his father] in cutting off the entail as soon as he should be of age," so that suitable provision could be made for his mother and sisters, through the sale of portions of the estate (*Pride and Prejudice,* p. 308). It was not unusual for aristocratic families of immense estate to exempt, for this purpose, a small percentage of their land from the strict settlement arrangements which ruled that the estate should descend intact to the eldest son.[4] But if a family of gentry, like the Bennets, whose estate was only a moderate £2,000 a year, cut off the entail altogether and provided for a large number of daughters from land sales, this would probably mean its demise as a landed family. Breaking up an estate was highly repugnant to the gentry of the period because it meant the loss of the family's local social and political influence. And so the strict settlement of the entire estate was almost invariably renewed from generation to generation.[5] In planning to cut off the entail and dismantle his estate for the benefit of his dauthers, Mr. Bennet may at first seem to be an egalitarian taking a stand in favor of fairness. But since he has chosen this course simply to avoid economizing on family expenses as an alternative means of providing for his daughters, Mr. Bennet is in fact irresponsibly proposing to destroy a landed estate—that basic prop of the English constitution—for his own convenience.[6] His plan for portioning his daughters is of a piece with his general approach to his parental duties: to avoid personal trouble at whatever cost.

Elizabeth is indeed her father's daughter. Though she claims that "I never ridicule what is wise and good," like Mr. Bennet she has acquired the ominous habit of laughing off things which should be taken seriously (*Pride and Prejudice*, p. 57). When her friend Wickham attempts to contract a reprehensible mercenary marriage, Elizabeth is ready with an exculpatory witticism: "handsome young men must have something to live on, as well as the plain" (*Pride and Prejudice*, p. 150). Her father often encourages Elizabeth to joke even when she is rightly disinclined to feel amused. "Your sister is crossed in love," Mr. Bennet quips when he and Elizabeth discuss the failure of Jane's romance, "I congratulate her. Next to being married, a girl likes to be crossed in love a little now and then" (*Pride and Prejudice*, p. 137). Elizabeth, deeply sympathetic with Jane and well aware that no remark could be less applicable to Jane's quietly heroic suffering, nonetheless answers lightly. To please her father, she will participate in his ridicule of the wise and good Jane, though she does try to turn the joke away from Jane and toward herself: "We must not all expect Jane's good fortune" (*Pride and Prejudice*, p. 138). As incidents like Lydia's elopement with Wickham make Elizabeth increasingly aware that her father's irresponsibility is a serious matter, she finds herself less able to laugh along with him. She can "only force one most reluctant smile" when he teases her about her romance with Darcy, with no sense that the subject might be a sensitive one (*Pride and Prejudice*, p. 320). Catherine Morland must learn the value of wit, which her parents overlook, but Elizabeth needs to improve upon her father's understanding of humor's legitimate limits.

Some of the social attitudes which Elizabeth must qualify can also be traced to her father's influence. Though Elizabeth and Jane have often tried to explain "the nature of an entail" to their uncomprehending mother (*Pride and Prejudice*, p. 62), Elizabeth does not understand it thoroughly enough to see that she might well censure her father for his intention to break up his estate. Perhaps because she has absorbed her father's attitudes, she does not fully understand the great responsibility of the landed proprietor, the serious consequences which his most personal decisions may have, until she visits Pemberley and sees a well-run great estate in action. Only after receiving this object lesson in the way an estate which has been kept intact and conscientiously cared for can become a beneficent social force, does Elizabeth understand, and partially excuse, both Darcy's self-importance and his unwillingness to marry into a family which shows so little regard for the proprieties as her own. Elizabeth comes to realize that her readiness to censure the person who weighs *any* social consideration when he forms a personal relationship is, in part, a selfishly defensive reaction to her own mixed social background—paralleling her father's irresponsible and selfish approach to such social questions as the entail of estates. Of course, this is not to say that Elizabeth's egalitarian views concerning personal relations are all wrong, or that Darcy's family pride is completely justified, but only that both need to qualify—through each other's teaching—attitudes absorbed too unthinkingly from their own families.

In Austen's novels the kind of love that leads to marriage is usually the only influence potent enough to loosen the strong tie that binds many parents to their children. Austen varies this pattern in *Sense and Sensibility*, where the guide who helps Marianne Dashwood reevaluate some of the attitudes she has absorbed from her mother's teaching is not her lover but her sister, Elinor. This must happen because, unlike any of Austen's other heroines, Marianne falls deeply and lastingly in love with the wrong man, and her growth to maturity must therefore involve a rejection of her lover, as well as of the ideas which led her to choose him in the first place. Marianne loves Willoughby for his liveliness, spontaneity, spirit, and self-reliant readiness to act on impulse. It is easy to ascribe Marianne's valuing of these qualities entirely to her reading of sentimental fiction and to overlook her mother's influence on the process. But "the resemblance between [Marianne and her mother] was strikingly great" (*Sense and Sensibility*, p. 6) precisely because Mrs. Dashwood consistently encouraged Marianne's natural sensibility and impetuosity. Mrs. Dashwood feels it is wrong to count the cost or exercise prudent restraint where even a minor principle or emotion is concerned. Only because Marianne has a mother who completely accepts all the basic assumptions of the cult of sensibility, does she feel emboldened to endorse them so wholeheartedly and to love so violently the man who seems to share them too. Marianne's difficulties are caused by faulty parental influence and not by adolescent rebellion.

Ironically, it is Willoughby's willingness to follow an emotional impulse without calculating its consequences that leads him to jilt Marianne. Though he loves her, Willoughby panics at the prospect of poverty as Marianne's husband, and when his rich cousin disinherits him, he obeys his lowest, most selfish impulse and hastily proposes to a rich and available woman. From this betrayal by her chosen lover, Marianne learns that impulses can be evil as well as good and that the considerations which might lead a person to discipline his impulses need not be meanly prudential ones, but may in fact be moral or altruistic in their nature. The lover whom she has chosen in accordance with tastes she and her mother share has brought Marianne to this plight—and therefore he cannot, except negatively, be the guide who extricates her from it. Only her sister, Elinor, who has inherited the self-control and prudence that characterize her father's side of the family, as well as her fair share of her mother's strong feelings, can explain to Marianne the real relationship between emotion and moral conduct. The Dashwood family is sufficiently complex so that the cause and cure of Marianne's ills can both come from within it.

At first glance it would seem that no child ever less resembled a parent than the clever, domineering Emma Woodhouse resembles her slow-thinking, valetudinarian father. A second look, however, reveals a family likeness between them—more subtly concealed than the parent/child links in the early novels, but present nonetheless. Using his poor health and his neurotic fears to gain the sympathy of family and friends, the gentle Mr. Woodhouse has unconsciously established a tyrannical control over his environment that Emma, with her more active methods of domination, never even approaches. He is so pathetic that no one can bear to cross him. And like his daughter he is always trying to promote the welfare of those he dominates. His hungry guests are forced to practice "unwilling self-denial" when he sends their suppers back to the kitchen, but his only motive is concern for their health (*Emma*, p. 213). When Emma forces Harriet Smith to deny herself the pleasure of becoming Robert Martin's wife, at least a part of her motive is a similar altruistic concern.

A tendency to deluded imagination is another trait Mr. Woodhouse shares with Emma. Because of his invalidism and because he lives the isolated life of a man who simply draws an income from his funds and does not have a profession or an estate to give him active employment,[7]

Mr. Woodhouse lacks practical experience on which to base his judgments, which therefore have become most peculiar. He is the victim of subjectivity and idle fancies, and so, in similar ways, is Emma—for she is as effectively isolated from experience by her role as his nurse, and by her fastidiousness and snobbery, as he is by his complete withdrawal from all sorts of activity.

The resemblances between Emma and her father are clear; their genesis is more problematic. Perhaps their tendency to domineer is partly the result of the high status and unvarying deference they share—but not entirely, for Knightley's high rank has not had this effect upon his character. Or perhaps her father's great admiration for Emma's intelligence, and the subtle flattery implicit in being much cleverer than one's parent, have helped to convince Emma that her judgment is nearly infallible. In this late novel, the mechanisms of parent/child influence are not as simply spelled out as they were in such early novels as *Northanger Abbey* and *Sense and Sensibility,* but the existence of the influence and its primarily destructive nature are obvious. Like the earlier heroines, Emma must change, and she finds a guide to this process in Mr. Knightley, an involved, busy landowner whose many interactions with all sorts of people have given him both the evidence upon which to base sound judgments and a respect for the rights and autonomy of his social inferiors. As we have seen, Emma, when asked for advice, pressures Harriet Smith into refusing Robert Martin's attractive offer of marriage. But Knightley, in a parallel scene where Robert asks him for counsel, ascertains that Robert can afford to marry and is really in love, and then simply tells him to follow his own inclination.

The influence of one or both living parents, then, goes a long way toward accounting for the problems of several Austen heroines. But in some cases the more adequate and influential of the heroine's two parents has died, leaving her to struggle with the bad guidance provided by her remaining parent. Elinor Dashwood apparently gets her sound common sense from her dead father, while Anne Elliot inherits her intelligence and has learned her moral values from her late mother. Emma Woodhouse, as we have seen, suffers from the influence of her living parent, but the absent-parent syndrome also plays a part in her problem. Though she does indeed resemble her father, Emma also "inherits her mother's talents and must have been under subjection to her," had she lived (*Emma,* p. 37). Henry and Eleanor Tilney are totally unlike their father. They resemble only their dead mother, whose absence they continue to mourn. The dead parent is invariably the more intelligent, sensible parent; his or her virtues explain the virtues of the child, while his or her absence often explains the fact that the child has gone somewhat astray.

Anne Elliot is the most pathetic victim of this particular family mishap. One feels sure that Anne's engagement to the impecunious Captain Wentworth would not have ended so disastrously had her mother, a woman "whose judgement and conduct . . . never required indulgence" after she made the youthful mistake of marrying Anne's father, lived to be her adviser (*Persuasion*, p. 4). Instead, poor Anne—a conscientious girl with a strong sense that youth ought to respect the wisdom of age—is left to the guidance of an imbecile father, who values only good looks and good birth in a prospective suitor, and a too-worldly surrogate mother, Lady Russell. Her well-motivated acceptance of their bad advice leads to tragedy. Here again it is not childhood rebellion but poor parental judgment that causes the heroine's basic difficulty. Bereft of her lover, Anne is left in a family that does not understand or value the virtues she inherited and learned from her mother. Much of the emotional interest of *Persuasion* derives from Anne's heroism in dealing with this situation, and thus Lady Elliot's death is the pivot upon which the novel turns.

Elinor Dashwood's problem is similar to Anne's. Though Mrs. Dashwood loves Elinor well, she definitely prefers Marianne and tends to see Elinor's prudence as closely akin to mean suspicion. Without her father as an ally, Elinor initially lacks the power to influence either her mother or Marianne. She must stand by and watch Marianne's rejection of self-control and propriety in favor of unrestrained emotion bring her to the brink of death. As in *Persuasion*, so also in *Sense and Sensibility* the heroine's stoic grace in bearing suffering inflicted by her family, theoretically her nearest and dearest, defines a moral ideal.

Emma suffers in a different way from the absence of her more intelligent parent. In her mother "she lost the only person able to cope with her" (*Emma*, p. 37). She was left in the care of an excessively affectionate father, who, though he is able to get his own way in such matters as diet and drafts, is incapable of providing much guidance. The moral lessons which Mr. Woodhouse is not bright enough to articulate are provided by Emma's governess, Miss Taylor—but Miss Taylor is prevented by her sweet and accommodating temperament, and by her inferior social position, from backing up those lessons with criticism or effective discipline. Mr. Knightley tries to fill the gap, but his role as friend of the family does not give him a socially recognized position from which to influence Emma's conduct, and the restraint he is able to impose is too little and too late. He later realizes that Emma responded to his admonitions by asking herself, "What right has he to lecture me?" (*Emma*, p. 462). It is natural that Emma should grow up vain and domineering, and she does. Both her mother's genes and her mother's absence have had dramatic effects in making Emma what she is.

As we have seen, the death of Mrs. Woodhouse harms Emma more because it deprives her of discipline than because it deprives her of guidance. And Austen repeatedly stresses the importance of discipline in forming character. If some effective, consistent way of disciplining childish impulses is present in a family situation, the children are likely to turn out well, even if the parents are gravely deficient. But in the absence of adequate discipline, even a child of naturally good intelligence and disposition is likely to run into problems. Austen believes that people—or, rather, some people—can learn to control their selfish, harmful impulses and correct their character flaws, but from her Christian viewpoint no one is naturally so good that his impulses can invariably be trusted. If discipline is not provided in childhood, it can be learned later on only through the lessons of affliction.

Although *Mansfield Park*, to which we will turn shortly, is the novel in which Austen gives the most extended, serious consideration to the importance of childhood discipline, characters in her other novels also suffer from its absence. Emma Woodhouse and Marianne Dashwood, as we have seen, are such characters. Fitzwilliam Darcy's parents, "though good themselves," spoiled their heir and only son, encouraging him to "be selfish and overbearing, to care for none beyond [his] own family circle" (*Pride and Prejudice*, p. 369). The combination of self-importance, snobbery, and shyness which this upbringing managed to produce in the naturally able and decent Darcy is the serious flaw he must overcome in order to be a suitable match for Elizabeth. And Elizabeth, too, is a sufferer from lack of discipline. Her mother saw her young daughters as merchandise to be effectively displayed and promoted, not as human material to be molded, and she had no sense of her daughters' faults. "They are all of them very clever," is a remark which typifies her tendency to overrate them (*Pride and Prejudice*, p. 29). Mr. Bennet was more clearsighted, but this hardly mattered, since he refused to become actively involved. "Those who chose to be idle, certainly might," says Elizabeth when asked about her sisters' education (*Pride and Prejudice*, p. 165). Elizabeth has not been as idle as her younger sisters, but her upbringing has forced her neither to apply herself nor to acknowledge her own faults, and thus has encouraged her belief that if she follows her own impulses, she cannot well go wrong. She takes pride in the fact that she has progressed in music only as far as impulse has moved her, that she "would not take the trouble of practising" (*Pride and Prejudice*, p. 175). She despises application for the sake of reward and doesn't think she needs to study situations diligently in order to judge them justly. Thus, in a different way from Darcy but to an almost equal degree, Elizabeth is a victim of spoiling.

Many Austen characters are victims of their parents' unwillingness to criticize them. In *Northanger Abbey*, Mrs. Thorpe's remark that her children are "all of them more beloved and respected in their different situations than any other . . . beings ever were" helps the reader to identify the approach to child-rearing which has produced the odious young Thorpes (*Northanger Abbey*, p. 32). The unvarying admiration of her father, whom she closely resembles, is one cause of the insufferable smugness that characterizes Anne Elliot's sister, Elizabeth. And so the Austen characters who are not parental favorites almost invariably turn out to be possessors of a hidden advantage: criticism and control. Even if the criticism is most unfair, as Mrs. Dashwood's attacks on Elinor, Mrs. Norris's on Fanny Price, or Sir Walter Elliot's on Anne generally are, it helps to remind the child that she is not perfect and that she must learn to accommodate herself to a harsh and sometimes unreasonable world.

In *Mansfield Park* the problems of discipline are studied in three separate family situations. In the Bertram family a strange combination of insufficient and excessive discipline has warped the children's development. The unbending attitude of their harsh, reserved father has driven the Bertram children to seek out their Aunt Norris as a substitute parent, for she is a sycophant of the worst sort and encourages them in the belief that they are perfection itself. Thus the Bertram children escape parental discipline by evading it. "Maria was indeed the pride and delight of them all—perfectly faultless—an angel," Mrs. Norris tells the family of a prospective suitor (*Mansfield Park*, p. 39). Like Mrs. Bennet, Mrs. Norris is a parental promoter, not a parental critic, and she also resembles Mrs. Bennet in playing favorites even among children whom she will not criticize, by apportioning the excess of her praise unfairly.

Henry and Mary Crawford were raised by a married uncle and aunt who did not get along and who used their orphan charges as weapons in their marital disputes, Admiral Crawford choosing to adore and idolize Henry, his wife making Mary her special pet. Thus both children managed to receive the damaging upbringing accorded a family favorite. In the Price family, likewise, favoritism was rampant. The lazy and coarse Mr. Price preferred his sons, the foolish and inefficient Mrs. Price her sons and youngest daughter—both parents having a special soft spot for their eldest son, William. However, the older daughters, Fanny and Susan, received little love and constant carping criticism, treatment very similar to what Fanny experienced later when she went to Mansfield Park as a poor relation.

The results of all this are mostly what one would expect on the basis of Austen's other novels, but there are a few significant surprises. Tom, Maria, and Julia Bertram, and Henry and Mary Crawford, do indeed turn out vain, selfish, and more ready to rationalize their bad impulses than to attempt to govern them. Julia's willfulness, predictably, is a bit less destructive than that of the more favored Maria. In this group of characters, lack of discipline has the expected effect, while excessive discipline, though it causes suffering and creates some problems for Fanny and Susan Price, does indeed make them into hard-working, extremely conscientious women. The timidity and self-doubt which characterize Fanny, and which are a response to continual censure, seem a reasonable price to pay for the strong conscience that even the unfair discipline she received has nurtured in her.

The surprise comes in Edmund Bertram and the other Price children, all of whom turn out remarkably well in spite of poor guidance, favoritism, and spoiling. The reason for this is that professional discipline supplies the place of parental discipline in forming their characters. Unlike the other Bertram children and the Crawfords—all people of independent fortune—Edmund must train and discipline himself to fit the role of clergyman, by which he is to live. William Price, endangered by favoritism, is easily saved by naval discipline. And the need to make their way in the world similarly disciplines the other young Prices.[8]

In *Mansfield Park,* as in Austen's other novels, the discipline that helps create the moral adult need not necessarily be administered in early childhood. Frequently, as we have seen, it is not—for its absence is useful in helping to create the problems with which the novel deals. But if adequate discipline is lacking in childhood, it must be supplied later, and this happens only when the character learns "the lessons of affliction" (*Mansfield Park,* p. 459). Only after immaturity, selfishness, and excessive self-confidence have produced error, trouble, and real suffering, can the adult begin to teach himself or herself the habits of criticism and self-control which should have been inculcated in childhood. The humiliation of learning how mistaken she has been in her belief that she can read the hearts of all her friends, the fear that she has lost Knightley—these are the afflictions that discipline Emma, and they are remarkably similar to the troubles that help to change Elizabeth Bennet. Marianne Dashwood and Tom Bertram are both chastened by serious illnesses, which their thoughtless behavior has helped bring on. Tom, remarks the narrator of *Mansfield Park,* "was the better forever for his illness. He had suffered and he had learnt to think, two advantages that he had never known before" (*Mansfield Park,* p. 462).

When Mr. Knightley tells Emma that "nothing very bad" will happen to little Anna Weston as a result of the thorough parental indulgence she is certain to receive—"she will be disagreeable in infancy and correct herself as she grows older"—he is exaggerating the ease with which this process generally occurs (*Emma*, p. 461). And indeed we might expect a man who has fallen in love with Emma, that quintessential spoiled child, to minimize the consequences of spoiling in this way. Nonetheless, though Knightley speaks from his overflowing joy and with less than his usual persuasiveness, he is here, as on most other occasions, essentially correct.

Austen sometimes finds that the exigencies of her plot and themes, or the need to explain the genesis of a complex personality, demand that she give characters adoptive or surrogate parents whose influence modifies the influence of their natural families. In *Mansfield Park*, Fanny's dual-family upbringing helps both to explain her personality and to develop the novel's themes. As we have already seen, Fanny's neurotic insecurity and strong sense of duty were produced by her nurture in not one, but two homes which denied her emotional security. Her underprivileged origin accounts for her intense desire to please the Bertrams, while her education in their home gives her the literary and moral sophistication without which she could not be the heroine of an Austen novel. But Austen needs the contrast between the uncivilized milieu of Fanny's natural family in Portsmouth and the civilized, decorous, yet too worldly milieu of her adoptive family at Mansfield in order to develop her social themes, no less than she needs it in order to account for Fanny's character.

In *Emma* there are two characters, Frank Churchill and Jane Fairfax, who have been raised by adoptive families. But the complicated family backgrounds of these two characters are necessitated by considerations of psychological coherence and by the demands of plot, with thematic concerns playing a much smaller role than in *Mansfield Park*. Frank's mixed psychological nature is suggested by his mixed parentage and upbringing. Like his father, he is affectionate, well-meaning, and so optimistic that his judgment can hardly be trusted. But, as Mr. Knightley points out, Frank differs from his father in one important way: Mr. Weston's "sanguine temper" is governed by his "upright and honorable" principles, whereas Frank's optimism leads him to hope that he will get away with serious wrongdoing (*Emma*, p. 445). Thus, when Frank violates the novel's ideal of openness and secretly engages himself to Jane, trusting hopefully to "any thing, every thing—to time, chance, circumstance, slow effects, sudden bursts, perseverance and weariness, health and sickness," his action has no real parallel in his father's conduct (*Emma*, p. 437).

The dishonesty and moral elasticity which Frank displays here are partly explained by the influence of his adoptive parents, the Churchills. The Churchills are proud and snobbish and, though she is not herself well-born, Mrs. Churchill nonetheless despises other upstarts. She is jealous of Frank's father and encourages Frank to slight him. Further, she is a hypochondriac who demands constant sympathy and attendance. This immoral and deluded woman is able to impose her vision of reality upon the family in which Frank was raised, and he knows that his chance of affluence depends on her affection for him. Her example of selfishness and self-deception, combined with the necessity that he satisfy her unjust demands, undermines Frank's natural decency, and he begins to lie and distort—both to others and to himself.

Jane Fairfax's character, on the other hand, has suffered no such harm from the influence of her adoptive family, the Campbells. Like Jane's natural family, the Campbells are fine people, and, though the element of insecurity in her relationship with them has certainly had some share in producing Jane's habitual caution and restraint, it is hard to see that having to reconcile the conflicting demands of two families has affected her character in any other way. Jane's dual-family situation is necessitated more by the demands of plot than by those of psychological explanation. She must be poor, or else the Churchills would simply accept her as a bride for Frank and there need be no secret engagement. She must have a home in Highbury, so that she can be there during the relevant portions of the story. Yet she must spend long periods away from Highbury, both to provide a pretext for Emma's unjust suspicions of her conduct and to give her an opportunity to fall in love with Frank offstage. Frank, too, must for reasons of plot have homes both in and away from Highbury. Thus, for both characters, the dual-family arrangement serves the demands of *Emma*'s intricate plot as simpler family backgrounds could not do.

Sometimes Austen uses a hypothesis of surrogate parenthood in order to add a last touch of delicate verisimilitude to a subtle psychological and moral dilemma. Readers of *Persuasion* might ask themselves why Anne's surrogate mother, Lady Russell, is needed in the story. The answer, I think, is that Anne's mother, as we noted above, must be a truly good woman, or Anne's own virtues would seem unexplained and anomalous. But such a woman would not have opposed Anne's engagement with Wentworth, and, therefore, had she lived there would have been no novel. On the other hand, Anne's father is so foolish and wrongheaded that it is impossible to believe that he could singlehandedly have convinced his intelligent daughter to break with her lover. So a third character is needed: a surrogate mother at once decent, sensible, and beloved enough to influence Anne, yet worldly enough to wish, from prudential motives, to separate two young lovers. Anne's dilemma is so complex, her character so nicely defined, that the influence of three "parents" is really necessary to explain the basic conflict of the novel. In *Persuasion*, as in the other novels which build adoptive or surrogate parents into their characters' backgrounds, Austen has in mind a structure of theme, plot, and character so intricate that its demands simply cannot be satisfied by the provision of a single family for each character.

The violent type of father, as described by Fielding, Richardson, Smollett, and Sheridan, had disappeared from English literature by the early nineteenth century, as Samuel Butler accurately noted in *The Way of All Flesh,* but although "the parents in Miss Austen's novels are less like savage wild beasts than those of her predecessors . . . she evidently looks upon them with suspicion."⁹ And so she does. Many of these parents and surrogate parents are no more grown-up or wise than their youthful charges; they tend to die when they are most needed and they abdicate responsibility through laziness, stupidity, or fondness. Children get into trouble by imitating them, far, far more frequently than by rebelling against them. Parental inadequacies set the scene for the maturation drama in all Austen's novels—and they do this in ways that change very little between the early and the late novels. But after a few painful collisions with reality, Austen's intelligent heroines and heroes learn to evaluate themselves and their families critically and to become the true adults that their parents rarely were.

*Jane Nardin*
*University of Wisconsin–Milwaukee*

# NOTES

1. All quotations from the novels incorporated in the text are taken from R. W. Chapman, ed., *The Novels of Jane Austen,* 3rd ed., 5 vols. (London: Oxford University Press, 1966).
2. And this is exactly the state of affairs in the Tilney family as well.
3. Austen also stresses the Morland family's comic homogeneity in her treatment of Catherine's older brother, James. In the other novels, siblings often bear little or no resemblance to one another—the Bennet girls exemplify this tendency—but James is very like his sister in his innocence, gullibility, and sweetness.
4. F. M. L. Thompson, *English Landed Society in the Nineteenth Century* (London: Routledge & Kegan Paul, 1963), pp. 66–68.

5. Ibid., p. 68.
6. In "The Business of Marrying and Mothering," Lloyd W. Brown says that "in the light of Austen's personal concern about the single woman's choices, we may very well discover a complex reaction on our part to Mrs. Bennet's obsession with the entailment of the Longbourn estate." Had cutting off the entail been the Bennets' only way of securing their unmarried daughters' prosperity, we could indeed sympathize with Mrs. Bennet's obsession—but this is not the case. Had the Bennets saved only one quarter of their income for the twenty-four or so years of their marriage, Mr. Bennet would have had a satisfactory £16,000 to leave his heirs by the time the novel opens. His decision to trust the future of his daughters to so chancy a course as trying to end the entail is like Lydia's decision to spend her lunch money on a bonnet: a thoughtless disregard of the future, based on the hope that someone else will foot the bill. Lloyd W. Brown, "The Business of Marrying and Mothering," in *Jane Austen's Achievement*, ed. Juliet McMaster (London: Macmillan, 1976), p. 34.
7. Hartfield is only a country house with pleasure ground attached, forming a sort of notch in the estate of the local squire, Mr. Knightley.
8. Several critics have discussed a related factor which helps to determine the way these characters turn out: the sort of formal education they have received. See, for example, D. D. Devlin, *Jane Austen and Education* (London: Macmillan, 1975) or Marilyn Butler, *Jane Austen and the War of Ideas* (Oxford: The Clarendon Press, 1975).
9. Samuel Butler, *The Way of All Flesh* (New York: The Modern Library, 1950), p. 30.

# The Complexity of
# Jane Austen's Novels

Jane Austen does not strike the reader as a particularly complicated or opaque novelist. Nevertheless, there is a remarkable lack of critical agreement about some of the most basic aspects of her art. One school of thought holds, for example, that Jane Austen's novels have few roots in the larger political or social issues of their day and thus exist in a kind of timeless vacuum. On the contrary, another argues, her fictional worlds can be understood properly only when they are recognized as finely detailed microcosms of late eighteenth-century English society. Even within these critical camps there are further factions. For some critics Jane Austen's timelessness manifests itself as a wish-fulfillment escape from reality;[1] for others as a Shakespearean ability to capture the universal aspects of human character and behavior.[2] Critics who favor the social approach are similarly split between those who see her microcosms as supportive of the status quo[3] and those who consider her to be ultimately subversive.[4]

An understanding of Jane Austen's novels, I would argue, will be achieved, not by choosing between these various critical stances, but by adopting a more complex stance that reconciles their apparent contradictions. The critics disagree, by and large, not because they interpret the whole of Jane Austen's novels differently, but because they have taken parts of the novels and made them serve for the whole. The effect has been, at best, to simplify the novels and, at worst, to warp them. This tendency to take the part for the whole, I am going to suggest, results mainly from a failure to understand the nature of Jane Austen's main plots and the kind of relationship that exists between the main plot (that is, the courtship of hero and heroine) and the subplot (other courtships) in all her novels.

For Jane Austen the subplot is not simply a way of reaffirming the points made by the main plot. Neither does she use it to present an alternative view of things to the one proposed in the main plot. Rather, there is a dialectical relationship between subplot and main plot which yields the synthesis we can call the total novel. To take either in isolation is inevitably to miss the point. For example, Jane Austen's view of marriage in *Pride and Prejudice* is not contained within Darcy and Elizabeth's relationship any more than it is in that of the Bennet parents. On the contrary, it emerges out of the tensions that exist between all the marriages in the novel. An interpretation that ignores Mr. and Mrs. Gardiner or Jane and Bingley, or considers Charlotte Lucas's union with Mr. Collins to be of more significance than Lydia's with Wickham will inevitably reveal at best only a part of the truth. The same is true for the ethical debate contained in the title of *Sense and Sensibility*. Jane Austen's definition of "sense" is based as much on Lucy Steele and the John Dashwoods as on Elinor and Colonel Brandon, and only by taking into account Mrs. Jennings along with Marianne and Willoughby can the reader begin to grasp her notion of "sensibility."

A proper sense of Jane Austen's complexity must derive, then, from an examination of some of the more important lines of tension that run between her main and subplots. Before proceeding to do this, however, we must focus on some problems of interpretation that have obscured the nature of her main plots. Up until about twenty years ago, it was almost a truism among critics that Jane Austen was a poorly educated and socially unaware spinster who, while remaining entirely unconscious of the process by which she did it, nevertheless managed to write delightfully escapist or universally profound novels.[5] A large part of the achievement of recent criticism has been to demonstrate the inadequacy of this assumption. First of all, it was pointed out that her novels do indeed reveal a knowledge of the great issues of her day. The Napoleonic wars are clearly there in references to the militia in *Pride and Prejudice* and to the Navy in *Persuasion*.[6] Similarly, the great social revolution lies behind the characterization of the vulgar upstart Mrs. Elton and the declining gentleman Sir Walter Elliot. Having shown that Jane Austen is on occasion overtly social, critics then engaged in the more significant task of demonstrating how even the tiniest details of her novels are loaded with microcosmic significance. Thus, instead of being a pleasant escape from the realities of life in England at the beginning of the nineteenth century, Highbury becomes England itself as it struggles to hang onto and to revitalize established values while dealing with new social realities.

The social critics have made an invaluable contribution to our understanding of Jane Austen. However, by insisting that they have discovered

the correct way to read her works, they are simply replacing one orthodoxy with another and are bringing us no closer to a full understanding of them. For in actual fact, Jane Austen's main plots are capacious
enough to accommodate socially specific and timeless readings. The relationships between hero and heroine in all the novels are certainly deeply
embedded in social reality. Indeed, at a fundamental level they are nothing less than dramatizations of conservative ideology, as an examination
of *Pride and Prejudice* will reveal. In this novel Jane Austen takes pains to
establish the precise social positions of hero and heroine; Darcy is fixed
firmly within the aristocracy, while Elizabeth occupies an uneasy position on the borderline between lesser gentry and trade. Furthermore,
Jane Austen attributes a great deal of the antagonism that exists between
Darcy and Elizabeth to these differences in rank. Elizabeth's view of
Darcy is obscured by the middle-class prejudice that all aristocrats are
snobs, and he is blinded by the aristocratic conviction that to be middle-
class is to be automatically vulgar. Darcy and Elizabeth must transcend
these social stereotypes and come to appreciate that, in spite of their
different functions, each class is motivated by the same basic ideals of
duty and concern for others, before they can reconcile their personal
differences. Consequently, Elizabeth's visit to Pemberley, which
epitomizes all the aristocratic virtues, and Darcy's meeting with those
gentlemanly tradespeople the Gardiners are the two most crucial incidents in their relationship. Because these are its origins, their marriage
becomes an emblem of the conservative ideal of a society made up, not of
classes in conflict, but of a series of ranks, separated in role and economic
status, but united in a concern for the common good. As Edmund Burke
puts it, "The constituent parts of a state are obliged to hold their public
faith with each other, and with all those who derive any serious interest
under their engagements, as much as the whole state is bound to keep its
faith with separate communities."[7]

*Mansfield Park* and *Emma* also dramatize basic aspects of conservative
ideology. According to conservative philosophy, the state is not an arbitrary creation of man that can be dismantled and rebuilt in accordance
with whatever abstract principles might prevail at any given time. Rather
it is a living organism, from which faulty parts can be pruned away,
leaving room for fresh shoots to grow, but whose essential shape is not to
be altered. Burke often uses organic metaphors in talking of the state; on
one occasion he calls it "a plant," on another, "the British oak."[8] However, a building metaphor is employed in one of his most succinct descriptions of the total process of "conservation and correction": "At both
these periods [the Restoration and the Glorious Revolution] the nation
had lost the bond of union in their ancient edifice; they did not, however,

dissolve the whole fabric. On the contrary, in both cases they regenerated the deficient part of the old constitution through the parts that were not impaired. They kept these old parts exactly as they were, that the part recovered might be suited to them."[9]

The stories of Fanny Price's and Emma Woodhouse's childhood, maturation, and marriage can be accommodated within the terms of the organic metaphor. They are new shoots on the plants of Mansfield and Highbury society, and as they take shape in relationship to the main body of the social organism, so they reveal the need for some adjustments and pruning within that main body. As a result, the societies with which we are presented on their wedding days are much more vigorous and healthy than those with which the novels open. Yet, and this is the important point, they are not essentially changed. Mansfield Park has done no more than commit itself anew to values that were in danger of atrophying away and being replaced by the urban, materialistic code of the Crawfords, and Highbury, once threatened by social and moral ossification, has guaranteed its future vitality by simply transferring leadership from the moribund Mr. Woodhouse to Emma and Mr. Knightley.

Jane Austen's main plots are, then, deeply embedded in their time. Recognition of this, however, should not be allowed to exclude other possibilities, for, at an equally fundamental level, they can also be read in terms of the structure of myth or fairy tale. According to Joseph Campbell, the myth and the fairy tale, which he describes as a "domestic myth," are essentially narrative versions of the initiation ritual.[10] As such, they reiterate the tripartite structure of ritual—separation, testing, and reintegration—and carry the same statement of faith in the ability of the individual to engage himself successfully in rites of passage,[11] thus achieving personal maturity and a healthy relationship with his social group. Of Jane Austen's heroines only Catherine Morland in *Northanger Abbey* is completely separated from her family during the testing period she endures at Bath and Northanger. Nevertheless, all effectively experience periods of separation as they make their first excursions to the ballroom and the dinner party where they are tested, through the medium of polite intercourse, in their knowledge of the ways of adult society. Having been proved worthy, they achieve reintegration into society through marriage. The mythic aspect of Jane Austen's plots is nowhere more evident than in the fact that the marriage is always with the group's most worthy male and in the promises of complete felicity for hero and heroine with which her novels end. Of Henry Tilney and Catherine Morland, Jane Austen says, "To begin perfect happiness at the respective ages of twenty-six and eighteen, is to do pretty well" (p. 252),[12] and of Emma and Mr. Knightley, "The predictions of the small band of true friends who witnessed the ceremony, were fully answered in the perfect happiness of the union" (p. 484).

In seeing one level of Jane Austen's main plots, critics seem typically, then, to have had their view of the other blocked. This is because there is a remarkable lack of strain between them. How this could be the case when the author is engaged simultaneously in what Northrop Frye sees as the two extremes of the possibilities of literary expression[13] can be explained by keeping in mind that, for all her close observation of the minutiae of daily life, Jane Austen's relationship to the society around her, as revealed by her main plots, is finally ideological. Ideology is the means by which a ruling class explains and justifies the social reality it has created. As such it glosses over inconsistencies and is intolerant of ambiguity, thus achieving an illusory resolution of real conflicts. As Clifford Geertz states, "Ideology bridges the emotional gap between things as they are and as one would have them be."[14] In other words, it is a form of wish-fulfillment, and as such operates at approximately the same distance from reality as myth. There is, thus, correspondence rather than conflict between the two levels at which Jane Austen's main plots operate, and it is not surprising that when the outline of one is laid over the other it tends to obscure it.

Recognition of the ideological and archetypal aspects of Jane Austen's main plots is an essential step toward understanding the complexity of her novels. But it is not, in itself, enough, for it leaves us with a slightly oversimplified picture of an essentially conformist, optimistic, and escapist Jane Austen. Subplot must also be taken into account in order for us to see that wish-fulfillment, whether social or universal, is only a part of Jane Austen's vision of the world.

We might begin by returning to *Pride and Prejudice*, in order to consider the social implications of its subplot. What one notices almost immediately is that once Wickham, Lydia, Mr. Collins, Charlotte Lucas, and so on are admitted into Darcy and Elizabeth's world things assume a much darker aspect. The marriage of hero and heroine is emblematic of the ability of human beings to achieve personal maturity and act out of a concern for the greater good of society. The universality of this conclusion is challenged, however, by Charlotte Lucas and Mr. Collins, who marry out of an empty concern for social status; by Wickham and Lydia, who are united by lust and kept together by Darcy's willingness to satisfy Wickham's greed; and even by Jane and Bingley, whose union, delightful and affectionate as it may be, carries with it no implications that either personal maturity or a large, social vision has been achieved.

The sense conveyed, by a consideration of marriages, that people can be less than intelligent, rational, benevolent, and socially aware, is confirmed by the behavior of a number of the novel's other minor characters. Mrs. Bennet is silly and solipsistic; Mr. Bennet hides from responsibility behind a screen of ironic humor; Caroline Bingley is a self-seeking snob; and Lady Catherine is selfish and a bully.

Different as major and minor characters may be—and of all the minor characters only the Gardiners can be considered anything near the intellectual and moral equals of Darcy and Elizabeth—nevertheless, they do ultimately belong to the same fictional world. It is not good enough, therefore, to pay serious attention only to the main plot and to dismiss the subplot as a somewhat sour counterpoint to an essentially affirmative vision. Nor can the main plot be taken as mere conformist window-dressing designed to mask the truly subversive vision expressed by the subplot. Main plot and subplot are of equal importance to Jane Austen, and it is in her union of the two that she fleshes out her dramatization of conservative ideology into a rich world vision.

The subplot in *Pride and Prejudice* functions not to contradict the main plot's affirmative vision of society but to reveal that this vision is wrought out of very imperfect elements. What is crucial to Jane Austen is not that everyone achieve the same degree of maturity as her hero and heroine, but that Darcy and Elizabeth maneuver themselves into a position of leadership. If they can manage this, they will be able to encourage virtue, keep the silly, the selfish, and the vicious in check, and thus insure that society operates in an ordered and harmonious way. Final judgments about Jane Austen's view of society in *Pride and Prejudice* must be based, then, not on Darcy and Elizabeth or on the minor characters but on the relationship into which they enter at the novel's conclusion. When one approaches *Pride and Prejudice* in this way, it emerges as one of Jane Austen's most affirmative and generous novels. There is a place for almost everyone in the configuration that forms around Pemberley. Nearest to the center are those who can most actively contribute to the good of society. Thus, the Gardiners are "on the most intimate terms" (p. 388) with Darcy and Elizabeth; Georgiana and Kitty live at Pemberley, where they mature under Elizabeth's tutelage; and Jane and Bingley live only thirty miles away. But even those who remain unreformed can be accommodated. Mr. Bennet nourishes his one genuine emotional attachment by visiting his beloved daughter Elizabeth, "especially when he was least expected" (p. 385). Lady Catherine learns no more than that she cannot bully Darcy and Elizabeth, and Lydia nothing at all. Nevertheless, each is occasionally received at Pemberley. In fact, only Wickham is completely excluded from Darcy and Elizabeth's circle, and even he receives help in his career from Darcy.

A similar relationship between main plot and subplot can be found in

*Mansfield Park* and *Emma*, and these novels end with the minor characters grouped appropriately around Edmund and Fanny, and Mr.
Knightley and Emma. *Emma* is like *Pride and Prejudice* in its faith that
society has a place for almost everyone. Marriage takes the disruptive
Frank Churchill away from Highbury, but union with Jane Fairfax
guarantees him reentry at any time. And while Mrs. Elton is not invited
to Mr. Knightley and Emma's wedding, she retains a place in the community as wife of the vicar. Everyone else is included in the tight and
intimate "band of true friends" (p. 484) that will encircle Hartfield in
order to pay attention to the old patriarch, Mr. Woodhouse, and, more
important, to benefit from the moral and spiritual leadership of Emma
and Mr. Knightley.

Subplot and main plot in *Mansfield Park* come much closer to repre-
senting alternative worlds than in any other of Jane Austen's novels apart
from *Persuasion*. However, even though some severe pruning is involved
in the process, the novel does manage to achieve a synthesis of its diverse
elements, and is thus able to affirm the ability of society to experience
change and growth without altering its essential shape. The Crawfords,
Mrs. Norris, and Maria Rushworth all pose too great a threat to
Mansfield's hard-won tranquillity to be included within Edmund and
Fanny's circle. This circle nevertheless remains the novel's single point of
focus. Mrs. Norris and Maria are quite literally exiles from the only social
group that might have given their lives meaning, while the Crawfords
have inculcated enough of Mansfield standards to see a future from which
Edmund and Fanny are absent only in terms of lack. Everyone else is
granted a place somewhere in Edmund and Fanny's group. Sir Thomas,
Tom, and Julia have all learnt enough from their mistakes to welcome this
new and firmer leadership; Susan is imported from Portsmouth; and
Lady Bertram, as a moral nonentity, can continue to be tolerated.

In arguing that these novels move from ideology to world view I am
not trying to suggest that Jane Austen cuts her ties with Burkean conservatism. In fact, Burke is extremely conscious that society is made up of
imperfect elements, and bases his argument for the primacy of the state
on the limitations of the isolated individual: "We are afraid to put men to
live and trade each on his own private stock of reason; because we suspect
that this stock in each man is small, and that the individuals would do
better to avail themselves of the general bank and capital of nations, and
of ages."[15] Nevertheless, because he is writing apologetics for the status
quo, Burke tends to substitute his beautiful metaphor of the organic state
for the struggle actually involved in establishing a functioning society.
Putting Lady Catherine in her place or ridding Mansfield Park of the
Crawfords is a much more difficult and messy business than can be

captured by the almost deterministic image of society cutting away deformed growth as it continually tends toward its ideal shape. As a result, Jane Austen conveys the sense that her optimism is based on an acute awareness of how things really are, while Burke always remains within the ideal world of how things ought to be. In this difference lies the distinction between world view and ideology.

Just as Jane Austen uses her subplot to transcend ideology, so she uses it to complicate archetype. The view of human nature offered by the subplots, like that of society, seems at first sight to contradict the affirmative vision of the main plot. Far from achieving personal maturity and ideal marriages, Jane Austen's minor characters serve as emblems of how fallible, petty, lustful, greedy, and foolish human beings can be. However, much as characters like Mr. Collins, Mrs. Bennet, Lydia, and Wickham might seem to offer a grotesque alternative to the intelligent, rational, responsible, and mature world of Darcy and Elizabeth, they must finally be considered as part of the same total vision. What Jane Austen appears to be trying to do with her antithetical portraits of human nature and experience is to capture the tensions of real living. To ignore the imperfections of human nature is certainly to be escapist, but equally, to fail to acknowledge the will to transcend these limitations is to deprive human experience of much of its dignity. We do not live in a world of objective fact, any more than we do in one of wish-fulfillment. Rather, we oscillate between the two. Moments of vision of complete harmony and felicity, such as those with which Jane Austen ends her novels, are transitory but nonetheless true. To recognize that Mrs. Elton will at times annoy Emma, or that life at Hartfield with Mr. Woodhouse will not always be easy for Emma and Mr. Knightley, is not to invalidate Jane Austen's claims "for the perfect happiness of the union." The two realities exist simultaneously at different levels: life in process is full of imperfections, but the individual moment can be perfect. The union of hero and heroine is always for Jane Austen one of those points at which all tensions, imperfections, difficulties are resolved for an instant, and life matches up to myth.

Main plot and subplot, however, do not exist simply to illustrate the different levels at which we live. Jane Austen draws them into a much tighter synthesis than this by claiming that the ability to achieve the ideal state is directly dependent on a willingness to be involved in the imperfections of daily life. Elizabeth Bennet's pursuit of maturity is not carried out in isolation from her mother, Mr. Collins, or Lady Catherine. On the contrary, she comes into contact with these people far more than with Darcy, and her final transcendence owes as much to the education she receives from them as it does to self-analysis or to Darcy's influence. The

Crawfords, Maria and Julia Bertram, and the Price family are similarly an essential part of Fanny's education, and Emma would not be the person she finally is were it not for her involvement with Mrs. Elton, Frank Churchill, and Miss Bates. The view of experience revealed in these novels is thus similar to that expressed by Stein in *Lord Jim*, since for Jane Austen too, in order "to follow the dream," we must "in the destructive element immerse."[16]

What I have tried to do in this paper is no more than to sketch in the outlines of a complete reading of Jane Austen's novels. However, I hope I have done enough to suggest that, while it may be valid to put her into roles as varied as conservative ideologist, critic of the status quo, idealistic fantasist, and jaundiced observer of human foibles, to reduce her to any of them is to miss the complexity of her achievement. Jane Austen assumes each of these roles, and her total vision of society in particular and humanity in general comes out of her synthesis of them.

*David Monaghan*
*Mount Saint Vincent University*

# NOTES

1. See, for example, H. W. Garrod, "Jane Austen: A Depreciation," *Essays by Divers Hands: The Transactions of the Royal Society of Literature*, 8 (1928):22–41.
2. This school of criticism takes its inspiration from Richard Simpson's unsigned review of J. E. Austen-Leigh's *Memoir of Jane Austen*, published in *North British Review*, 52 (April, 1870): 129–52, and reprinted in B. C. Southam, ed., *Jane Austen: The Critical Heritage* (London: Routledge and Kegan Paul, 1968), pp. 241–65.
3. Recent interpretations of Jane Austen as conservative include Marilyn Butler, *Jane Austen and the War of Ideas* (Oxford: The Clarendon Press, 1975); Alistair Duckworth, *The Improvement of the Estate: A Study of Jane Austen's Novels* (Baltimore: Johns Hopkins University Press, 1971); David Monaghan, *Jane Austen: Structure and Social Vision* (London: Macmillan, 1980).
4. This approach was established by D. W. Harding, "Regulated Hatred: An Aspect of the Work of Jane Austen," *Scrutiny*, 8 (1940): 346–62. For some

recent examples, see several of the essays in David Monaghan, ed., *Jane Austen in a Social Context* (London: Macmillan, 1981), particularly Nina Auerbach, "Jane Austen and Romantic Imprisonment," pp. 9–27, and Leroy W. Smith, "*Mansfield Park:* The Revolt of the 'Feminine Woman,'" pp. 143–58.

5. Those most responsible for this view of Jane Austen are J. E. Austen-Leigh whose *Memoir of Jane Austen*, 1870 (Oxford: Clarendon Press, 1926) presents her as "Aunt Jane" (p. 6), a woman more notable for her sense of family obligations than for her artistic abilities, and Henry James, who described her as a writer of "light felicity" whose "fortune with posterity has been in part the extraordinary grace of her facility, in fact of her unconsciousness." See "The Lesson of Balzac," in Leon Edel, ed., *The House of Fiction* (London: Hart-Davis, 1957), pp. 62–3.

6. For a discussion of the inadequacy of the view that Jane Austen's art is defined by its limitations, and for examples of her awareness of the great events of her day, see Donald Green, "The Myth of Limitation," in Joel Weinsheimer, ed., *Jane Austen Today* (Athens: The University of Georgia Press, 1975), pp. 142–75.

7. Edmund Burke, *Reflections on the Revolution in France*, in *The Works of Edmund Burke* (New York: Harper, 1860), I:464.

8. Ibid., 469, 493.

9. Ibid., 464.

10. Joseph Campbell, *The Hero with a Thousand Faces* (New York: Pantheon Books, 1949).

11. See Arnold van Gennep, *The Rites of Passage*, trans. Monika B. Vizedom and Gabrielle L. Caffee (Chicago: University of Chicago Press, 1960), p. 3.

12. All references to Jane Austen's novels are included in the text and are taken from R. W. Chapman, ed., *The Novels of Jane Austen*, 3rd ed. (Oxford: Oxford University Press, 1966); Vol. I, *Sense and Sensibility;* Vol. II, *Pride and Prejudice;* Vol. III, *Mansfield Park;* Vol. IV, *Emma;* Vol. V, *Northanger Abbey* and *Persuasion*.

13. See Northrop Frye, *Anatomy of Criticism* (Princeton: Princeton University Press, 1957).

14. Clifford Geertz, "Ideology as a Cultural System," in his *The Interpretation of Cultures: Selected Essays* (New York: Basic Books, 1973), p. 205.

15. Burke, *Reflections*, I:494.

16. Joseph Conrad, *Lord Jim* (London: Dent, 1935), pp. 156–57.

# The Burden of *Grandison*
## Jane Austen and Her Contemporaries

$R$emembering a novel is not the same as reading it—that's obvious. But the experience of remembering Richardson's three novels and the experience of reading them are so different that the truism takes on some life. In spite of all their diffuseness and length, each one of them comes back in bright, vivid images— *tableaux vivants* of the mind: Pamela and Mrs. Jewkes with the False Nan, for example, or Pamela carving a chicken. In *Clarissa* the unlatched garden gate hovers in the memory with a disembodied intensity caught by no other author I know. Or Clarissa herself returns, not in action, but as the woman observed, alone yet not alone, watched and forever frozen in the frame of tea things, keyholes, and even her own coffin. *Grandison* too comes back in an unperishing image, and one that typifies the solid comforts of its novelistic world just as the anxiety-ridden images of *Pamela* and *Clarissa* do theirs. This is the golden, sun-filled world of the cedar parlor with Harriet Byron in this chair and Charlotte Grandison in that, and Mrs. Shirley over here, and Dr. Bartlett over there. News from the outside world may filter through the walls of Grandison Hall, but none of it can really disturb the serene, kindly, loving world of the cedar parlor. Here is the Golden Age of female domestic felicity, the blissful image of an unsullied, untroubled past, the radiant vision of absolute harmony and security that was to inspire and haunt the followers of Richardson for the next half century.[1]

What Jane Austen and her contemporaries owe most to *Grandison* is paradoxically what they were most unable to take: Sir Charles's unswerving confidence in the family as a symbol of universal order. If you think about it, the wreckage of families in the novels of Jane Austen is unnerving. In the novels of her sister authors it is appalling. These women— Charlotte Smith, Mary Wollstonecraft, Fanny Burney, Maria

98

Edgeworth, among the less obscure ones—describe what was to them a terrifying shift in their society's concept of the family, a profound change that marks the difference between the world of *Grandison,* the world they had lost, and the world in which unhappily they found themselves adrift. The solid world of the anchored, bourgeois family, the Grand Old Middling Way, seemed to them to be on the shoals. Life was just not what it used to be. This is their repeated complaint, as Jane West shows us in an ironic passage of advice to budding novelists: "Let them rub their eyes till they have named all their principal characters, and fixed their residences; for as no one can care about Miss Molly Muggleton of the Minories, or Peter Perkins of Pimlico, so there is some inconvenience in perpetually recurring to the Harlowes, Byrons, Delvilles, and other classical families, as it may produce comparisons, which are truly odious" (*The Refusal,* 1810, II, 17–18).

This changed perception of the family is, I think, the key to the uneasy relationship between Richardson and his literary progeny. Pamela takes comfort in the belief that she can always go back to her "poor father's peaceful cot"; Harriet Byron never worries about her place in the cedar parlor; even Clarissa, whose earthly family does fail her, rejoices in her anticipation of a heavenly father. This is far from the case in the novels of Jane Austen's time. To the heroine of Charlotte Smith's novel *Marchmont* (1796), "the world appeared a desert, in which she stood alone" (I, 69). Fanny Burney's heroine in *The Wanderer* (1814) is, we are told, "a female Robinson Crusoe, as unaided and unprotected, though in the midst of the world, as that imaginary hero in his uninhabited island; and," the author adds, "reduced to sink through inanition, to nonentity, or to be rescued from famine and death by such resources as she could find, independently, in herself" (V, 394–95). No cedar parlors for these heroines. Instead, we find in Mrs. Parson's novel *Lucy* (1794) that the only roof for her orphaned heroine is a castle "tumbling to pieces" where "several of the doors were broken down, and the rooms inhabited by birds of prey" (I, 3–4). As the light from the Grandisonian Golden Age grows more and more dim, our heroine hurtles toward the abyss with her last possession clasped to her breast, a locket containing a picture of her mother—this locket her only remaining proof, if the world were just, that she too has a right to a chair in a cedar parlor of her own.

Before turning to the consequences that such a vision has for the structure, language, and characters of the novel, it seems appropriate to mention here that these women were not imagining things; the harrowing picture that they paint does in fact arise from a society in crisis. In the years between the fall of the Bastille and the Battle of Waterloo the peaceful world of the middle-class British matron was invaded both by philosophical assaults on her station and by an even more unsettling aggressor in the shape of a runaway inflationary economy.[2] Without going into detail, we can simply note that the pressures brought about through the miserable combination of rising prices and fixed incomes, which is what the women were faced with, are enough to cause panic. Although historians of the family can now tell us that the family as a self-sustaining economic unit had long since been a thing of the past and was a myth even in Richardson's time, the novelists of the turn of the century perceived the disparity between myth and economic reality as a hideous reversal of all moral sanctions.[3] Time and again a heroine steps to the edge of the dreaded pit, feels its hot astringent breath waft across her anxious brow, reaches back instinctively for the strong supportive arm of a Grandisonian hero, to find nothing—or as good as nothing: Marianne Dashwood's Willoughby, perhaps, or, not much better, Elinor's weak-kneed Edward Ferrars.

The Richardsonian conventions so freely drawn upon by the authors split apart under the strain. For example, the rambling "No Plot" of *Grandison* wanders where it pleases because there is always in the background the image of the family, a structured society that gives meaning to Richardson's figures. All the palaver about delicacy, duty, manners, and dress fits into a larger picture. As Harriet Byron tells one of her correspondents, families are the "little communities" that "secure the great community, of which they are so many miniatures" (I, Letter VI). Obviously such a structure for anchoring either plot or imagery is not available to a writer who finds her world a moral chaos. The Richardsonian courtship plot, stock-in-trade for the circulating-library novelist, turns hollow, and into the vacuum steps that seductive impostor of form, melodrama. Northrop Frye defines this sort of novelistic melodrama as "comedy without humor," which is exactly what we get from the latter-day Richardsonians, comedy in which marriage bells and a blue lute-string gown do not represent the joyful union of private and public worlds, but are pressed into service in the last volume as tattered emblems of a better day.

Richardson's characteristic practices in style undergo sea-changes in the later fiction as well. In *Pamela, Clarissa,* and *Grandison,* for example, there are coded styles that we recognize immediately: the style of a rake, for instance, or the style of a good person, a good old person, a good young person, an honest servant, and so on with the list. Lovelace and Belford's "Roman Style" is a particularly self-conscious use of a specialized language, demanding an automatic response that goes far beyond any simple parsing of sentences. For Richardson this works because each one of his styles attaches itself to a stable, if casuistical universe. For example, when in *Grandison* Harriet Byron is suspected of harboring a *prepossession,* neither the word nor the condition remains private. Everybody wants to talk it over, to ponder the interesting word. Mrs. Selby introduces it; Mrs. Shirley worries with it; Charlotte Grandison teases with it; Harriet defines and redefines it; and even grave Dr. Bartlett demands a word or two with Harriet about the consequences and moral responsibilities of a *prepossession.* Meanwhile the reader is on tenterhooks: What will Sir Charles say about *prepossessions?* How will he judge poor Harriet? Worse, can a *prepossession,* once contracted, ever be cured? Will it have to be? And what about Clementina?

On the other hand, if one of the unfortunate heroines of the turn of the century should come down with a *prepossession,* she is truly out of luck. She will apply the word to herself as the standard perquisite of a heroine, but in her lonely, hostile world nobody wants to hear about it, nobody wants to ask how, when, why, or any of the usual Richardsonian what if's. Her word and her condition whisper *shibboleth* to the reader: *prepossession,* a ticket to a plot. Bearing her secret in her burdened heart, she has only the recourse of blushes, fine language, good orthography, and a knack for sketching the hero's profile to tell the hero that she is in love. The reader must do the work of all the Grandisonian talkers and questioners, a lonely and profitless job, but one made easy by the utter predictability of the code language assigned to the heroine and her hero, who speaks the same lingo she does—highflown, sentimental, delicate, and spurious. The active Richardsonian styles turn esoteric and arcane in the collusion of library patron and author. Contemporary writers, unable to do much about it, still complained: "We know by the first four pages whether the heroine is to die or be married," observes Mrs. West, wryly adding, "and no other conclusion is admissible, because one of these events always happens to beautiful young women" (*The Refusal,* II, 17–18).

Bringing along their coded styles, almost all the former visitors to the cedar parlor stroll over to the latter-day novels, accompanied occasionally by a recostumed Lovelace, or Anna Howe, or good Mrs. Norton, "educated in the school of affliction." But the reborn Richardsonians are all in miniature, as one of Charlotte Smith's heroines laments: "I know you have a hundred fancies about Colonel Scarsdale," she writes her anxious sister, "and suppose that he is a sort of modern Lovelace; but, believe me, my Fanny, that character does not exist now; there is no modern man of fashion, who would take a hundredth part of the trouble that Richardson makes Lovelace take, to obtain Helen, herself, if she were to return to earth—" (*Desmond,* 1792, II, 25). Nevertheless, Colonel Scarsdale, unpromising as he is, is kept on for the duration for the

same reason as that unpromising Grandisonian, Colonel Brandon, in
Jane Austen's *Sense and Sensibility:* an impotent Lovelace and a broken-
down Sir Charles, still around to take the heroine's hand in one more turn
of the courtship dance, but both, like the heroine herself, somewhat lost
in this unsettling new world.

The problem is still the burden of *Grandison.* Without a coherent
vision of society, the women writers are driven to the unsatisfactory shift
of retiring their Richardsonians to the country and, like Jane Austen
herself, letting such disruptive characters as the Lady Susans, the John
Dashwoods, and the Crawford siblings onto the highroad. Austen is able
to keep these pushy new characters under control through her wit—with
varying degrees of success—but her sister novelists simply let them multi-
ply and people the earth. While the Richardsonian courtship plots wind
their predictable way through the countryside, the real activity in these
novels falls to the interlopers, who, we sense, are far closer to the authors'
own experiences: rude bill collectors, crooked lawyers, unyielding land-
lords, mean shopkeepers, grasping relatives, feckless husbands, default-
ing bankers, greedy doctors, and all the other genuine ogres of a ruthless
economy.

The genteel, Grandisonian heroine of Mrs. Bennett's *Vicissitudes
Abroad* (1806) goes lunatic under the strain: she finds that she does not
have enough money in her purse to pay a rude London coachman, "but it
was impossible to make me understand," she recalls, "either that or the
coarse allusions to 'shabby genteel,' 'scum of the earth' " (I, 102–103).
She is taken by strangers to a charity hospital, where, she remembers, "I
fell into a deep sleep, in which I continued five hours, and awoke perfectly sensible, though weaker than a new born infant. . . . It is impossible to conceive my astonishment, when I beheld the vulgar and pallid
faces that occupied the various beds in a room to which I could see no
end. . . . I found myself literally in a new world, among people as strange
in manner as in face; and too weak to articulate, could only mentally ask
myself, what I had done to deserve being condemned to a residence in
such a place, among such companions" (I, 108). In response to this
horrible new world, the gothic novelist Mrs. Radcliffe attempts to gather
up the shadowy terrors that lie in wait for unprovided, unprotected
women in the symbolic figures of her relentlessly money-minded villains
Montoni, from *Udolpho* (1794), and Schedoni, from *The Italian* (1796),
but her efforts are finally disappointing. The real smell of fresh blood is
found around the minor characters—Mr. Humphrey Hotgoose, the bill
collector, or Mr. Vulture, the lawyer, and a host of other such folk truly
"drawn from the life." Behind the elegant, coldblooded comedy of Mr.
and Mrs. John Dashwood's cheapening of their sister's inheritance in

*Sense and Sensibility,* if we listen, we can hear the stricken ululations of a generation of disinherited women.

If I can be permitted to return to our heroine of the 1790s where we left her at the edge of the abyss, we can imagine that what she saw through the darkness visible was nothing more nor less than London itself—but a different London from the old-fashioned Tom Jonesian center of sophisticated vice and frivolity. This is the London of mean-spirited, aggrandizing people like Mrs. Ferrars and the John Dashwoods, the place where the real connivers of the new economy like Lady Susan or Lucy Steele set up their stands for business. Although Jane Austen's novels are not the most striking examples of the kind of urban distress that dogged the heels of heroines during these years, they are useful here because they are familiar examples and because they do accurately reflect and share in the conventions of the rest of contemporary women's fiction. For example, the old-style Grandisonians of *Lady Susan* (c. 1794), the Vernons and the de Courcys, collapse before the aggressive new consciousness represented by the anti-heroine. The heroines of *Sense and Sensibility* (c. 1797) are saved not by their wits nor by any routing of the new-style villains, but only by the grace of their author, who grants them a couple of kindly eccentrics, who, with old-style Grandisonian generosity of purse, bail them out of trouble—and London. *The Watsons,* begun in 1803 and left unfinished, marks, I think, Jane Austen's recognition that a new settlement had to be found. Austen, having conceived the story along the lines of a fairly commonplace contemporary plot, the genteel-but-poor heroine's move to the city, may have decided that a heroine trained for the cedar parlor would inevitably confront failure in the tatty London suburb of Croydon.

But what was to be done? How was the family to be gotten back together after so distressing a sojourn in the wilderness? How could the conventions of the domestic novel be readjusted to fit the realities of this disturbing new world? Not surprisingly, the solution was found in the now dimmed image of the cedar parlor, the room redecorated and the axis altered, but still recognizable as a descendant of that delightful place. If our memory of *Grandison* enshrines the spacious golden, sunlit comfort of a midcentury great-house parlor, then the equally powerful domestic settings of Jane Austen's novels show both the kinship and the difference in the revised version of the old dispensation.

Although we cannot know the extent of Austen's revisions of *Sense and Sensibility* and *Pride and Prejudice,* novels that took their first births in the 1790s, we can conjecture with some confidence, I think, that Miss Bingley's chilly, hostile drawing room at Netherfield, Lady Catherine's expensive and unfriendly saloon at Rosings, and the splendidly frigid audience chamber of Mrs. John Dashwood and her mother, Mrs. Ferrars, in London, are the leftover architecture of those years of widespread gloom in women's fiction.[4] In *Emma* (1816) and *Persuasion* (1817), Austen abandons them in exchange for the scaled-down interiors of the Hartfield parlor, for example, or the tiny, shipshape quarters of the Harville family at Lyme Regis. But these smaller spaces fill the imagination with a conviction of well-being analogous to that of the Grandisonian cedar parlor. In remembering *Emma,* our mind's eye unfailingly calls up Emma, her father, and Mr. Knightley gathered by the Hartfield hearth; in thinking of *Persuasion,* the Crofts' sitting room at the White Hart inn comes back to us, with a vignette of Anne Elliot before a window in conversation with Captain Harville, Wentworth's desk too close for privacy, and Wentworth's fallen pen, all etched into our memory. This small room in a public inn is truly the home of the heart for Anne, not, as Jane Austen makes pointedly clear, the spacious and elegant double drawing room of her own neglectful family.

*Mansfield Park* (1813) in Austen's work signals the change. Edmund and Fanny's abandonment of the Grandisonian pretensions of Sir Thomas's great house for the more intimate comforts of Thornton Lacey becomes a significant statement of the new tradition. The circle has drawn closer; the family is no longer represented on the grand, public scale that it had been in Richardson's works, but neither is it still in retreat. Highbury, Donwell Abbey, and Thornton Lacey all bring with their occupancy important obligations to the world—on a village scale, perhaps, but nonetheless respected and important. Anne Elliot, too, shares the same new world. From her cozy cabin on her husband's man-of-war, she will do her duty as a British matron, following, it is ironic to note, the tradition of Sir Charles himself out settling the troubles of unruly foreigners. The world comes into focus once again in the woman's novel. Garrets, sponging-houses, prisons, madhouses, gothic towers, the dwelling places of so many innocent heroines during the terrible dark days of the 1790s, are exchanged for an updated version of the cedar parlor, not so grand, but a comfortable enough place to draw up a chair. In the exchange the fine connotations of "gentility" modulate into the firmertoned attributes of "respectability," but one is clearly a descendant of the other.

I wish I could say that language, syntax, and characterization automatically snapped back into shape in the novels of Jane Austen's contemporaries. It didn't happen. But the excesses of the 1790s were left behind as if they were no more than bad dreams. No doubt we see through a glass darkly when we try to measure the state of the contemporary world through the conventions of the ladies' novel, but what is obvious is that the novel once again found a mimetic image that could satisfy the mythic structures of society. In the settling of this image, the burden of *Grandison* held both a curse and a blessing. As curse it tempted more than one heroine and her author into the dark walks of high foolishness and melodrama as they confronted, shocked and outraged, their loss of the old cedar parlor. As blessing, *Grandison* provided the form, focus, and setting for a novelistic accommodation to the new dispensation. Instead of the extended Grandisonian family gathered in the conversation circle of the Richardson novel, we find a smaller grouping of perhaps the wife, the old grandfather, a child or two, and a cat. The heroine, instead of peering out the spacious windows of the old cedar parlor, looks through "casements," as she does in Mrs. Pinchard's *Family Affections* (Taunton: 1816), "entwined [with] many creeping plants, such as jasmine, honeysuckles, etc." And what she would have seen would not have been the monument-strewn, poetic garden of Grandison Hall, but the equally symbolic picturesque scene glimpsed by Mrs. Porter's heroine in *Honor O'Hara* (1826), "a range of romantic hills, backed by the lofty Cheviots; discovering in their recesses, little glens, where wreaths of smoke and cheerful sounds rising above the tufted trees, told of cottages and contented labour" (I, 16–17). Men are welcomed back into the novels: feckless husbands, weak-kneed lovers—Come home! All is forgiven. Conversation keeps up its steady pace, just as it did in the cedar parlor of yore, but now charitable plans, the education of children, village morals, and poultices for the sick occupy the flow of talk.

So far as I can tell, the change cannot be attributed with any certainty to improvements in the consumer economy of Great Britain during these years. Great fluctuations continued throughout the war years and for quite some time afterward. But the field of consumer economics remains in its infancy and may, perhaps, show us in time more than we know now about the period. But that seems to me to be irrelevant to the heart of the *Grandison* legacy. In general terms we all pay lip service to the truism that without Richardson English domestic fiction would not be the same. I would simply like to give the heritage focus in the form of the cedar parlor. Because of it, the novel presents once again a complete world, one only realizable, I would suggest, through the assistance of the backward-looking, golden-tinted, Claude glass vision of that blessed room where, when we look, we always find Harriet Byron in this chair and Charlotte Grandison in that, and Mrs. Shirley over here, and . . .

*Edward Copeland*
*Pomona College*

# NOTES

1. Quotations from *The History of Sir Charles Grandison* are taken from Jocelyn Harris's edition, 3 vols. (London: Oxford University Press, 1972). I am also indebted to Professor Harris for her excellent essay, " 'As if they had been living friends': *Sir Charles Grandison* into *Mansfield Park,*" *Bulletin of Research in the Humanities,* (Autumn 1980): 360–405, which she kindly allowed me to read prior to publication.
2. Any number of sources for confirmation of the sad truth might be suggested: E. M. Carus-Wilson, ed., *Essays in Economic History,* Vol. III (London: Edward Arnold Publishers, Ltd., 1962); E. A. Wrigley, *Population and History* (New York: McGraw-Hill, 1969); Pauline Gregg, *A Social and Economic History of Britain, 1760–1965* (London: George G. Harrap & Co. Ltd., 1965), are three of the more general studies in the long conversation of economic historians about these years. *The Journals and Letters of Fanny Burney (Madame D'Arblay),* ed. Joyce Hemlow, 4 vols. (Oxford: Clarendon Press, 1972), provide firsthand witness to the economic distress.
3. Peter Laslett's provocative study, *The World We Have Lost* (New York: Charles Scribner's Sons, 1965), p. 19, suggests that women were particularly victimized by the economic and social changes of the period.
4. For a discussion of the dates of composition of the early versions of these works, see B. C. Southam, *Jane Austen's Literary Manuscripts* (Oxford: Oxford University Press, 1964), pp.45–62.

# Who's Afraid of Jane Austen?

In her essay on George Eliot, Virginia Woolf wrote of the heroines that "the ancient consciousness of woman, charged with suffering and sensibility, and for so many ages dumb, seems in them to have brimmed and overflowed and uttered a demand for something—they scarcely know what—for something that is perhaps incompatible with the facts of human existence."[1] Suffering and sensibility characterize women for Virginia Woolf, and her reading of their literature is marked by the expectation. In *A Room of One's Own*, her longest description of her female precursors, sensitive women writers are carried relentlessly through suffering to death. Witches evoke the woman poet "who dashed her brains out on the moor or moped and mowed about the highways crazed with the torture that her gift had put her to." When Virginia Woolf fabricates her own female artists, they are similarly doomed. Judith Shakespeare, the "wonderfully gifted sister" of William, passes archetypally through seduction to suicide.[2]

In other essays Virginia Woolf treats individual women extensively, and her choice is often of the odd and unconventional, those thought mad, like the "fantastic and fastidious" Duchess of Newcastle, or bad, like Aphra Behn. Caught in the rush and gush of her prose, the women sob, rage, and suffer, now heroic and vital, now silenced by the needs and sounds of patriarchy. They usually write, but they are not primarily writers and their written work forms a kind of preliterature to the art of woman which Virginia Woolf is presumed now to be creating, a pre-text for her text.

The biographical sketches, written over many years and mostly reprinted in the two *Common Readers,* are partly idiosyncratic, partly typical of the critical and journalistic writing of her period. They are entertaining, readable, impressionistic, sure in judgment, like the portraits of her friend Lytton Strachey, and memorable in metaphor and phrase. Reading several, one is struck by the prose, not the personalities, the phrase that catches, not the woman caught.

Indeed the women seem to merge into each other. Virginia Woolf isolates them from their times, leaving out a history of kings and culture, which she regards as male, and the female subculture of particular women. Her characters exist in their own small tableaux, suddenly and individually illuminated. They are not connected, nor are they consecutive; neither spatial nor temporal relations are allowed them. They live similarly and apart in the Woolfian present tense.

In her sketches Woolf aims to discover a moment, an image, or a stance which exhibits and exposes the life and personality of her character. So Madame de Sévigné is caught in a central relationship: she loved her daughter, comments Virginia Woolf, "as an elderly man loves a young mistress who tortures him" (III, 67). For Harriette Wilson, the discovery is of a moment—when at fifteen she crossed from respectability to freedom and ineradicable impropriety. In Woolf's words, "at once, the instant her foot touched those shifting sands, everything wobbled; her character, her principles, the world itself—all suffered a sea change" (III, 228).[3]

In "The Art of Biography" and "The New Biography" Virginia Woolf wrestles with the problems of the genre, with fact, fiction, and fictionalized fact, and with the presence of the author. In "The Art of Biography" she ties her biographers to fact and sees them opposing the fiction-writers, but in "The New Biography" she admits the distinction is unclear. The light of personality is the biographer's business, and to catch it "facts must be manipulated." Although she stresses their integrity and is uneasy at Harold Nicolson's mixing of fact and fiction in his biographies, she is yet fascinated by the ability of this mixture to transmit personality effectively. "He does not cumber himself with a single fact about them," she writes of his subjects. "He waits till they have said or done something characteristic and then he pounces on it with glee" (IV, 233). And the method has other implications, for, if it can deliver its subject's personality, it can also catch its author's; it is this aspect of the new biography that strikes Virginia Woolf most strongly: "By the end of the book," she says, again of Nicolson, "we realize that the figure which has been most completely and most subtly displayed is that of the author." Fact and fiction mingle to create character and author—both become "at once real and imaginary" (IV, 233).

Virginia Woolf writes evaluatively, as though Harold Nicolson's method were external to her, but in fact it is very close to her own. In her sketches fact is manipulated to expose personality of a particular kind. The women become what Virginia Woolf needs them to be, female heroes or distressed ladies of sensibility, and they write at her dictation. With this method, they do not express themselves so much as they express their author; they become excuses for the reader to watch the musing of Virginia Woolf's mind and see her inspiriting herself with images.

An example is Mary Wollstonecraft. It is difficult to judge exactly what Virginia Woolf knew of her subject, but she had read William Godwin's *Memoirs* of his wife and some of Wollstonecraft's works. Other biographies and papers were available, but she chose to ignore them, and the woman she creates is often freed from fact. Wollstonecraft appears first as hero, forced into the fight through childhood injustice. So Virginia Woolf takes on trust the formative incident of the young girl lying on the landing to guard the mother from the father's wrath, an incident rather close to a famous one in Rousseau, whom Wollstonecraft much admired. One sister in the narrative does duty for another, and, because her subject is for Virginia Woolf essentially alone, it matters not a whit whether it is Eliza or Everina who bites at her wedding ring, or whether she is miserable when being married or afterwards. Mary Wollstonecraft's own misery is supported by Virginia Woolf's exaggeration: so she travels from home to the humiliation of governessing with no stop for her own school, and her father, once a gentleman, becomes simply a farmer, and the red face and dirty hair of his dishonored old age mark his manhood as well. Wollstonecraft becomes the creature of injustice, the fighting feminist who asserts ringingly, "I never yet resolved to do anything of consequence that I did not adhere readily to it," not the wavering woman who lamented that she would remain a fool to the end of her days. Then the hero goes to France and grows all suffering and sensibility, too much so, and the artist Virginia Woolf reduces her two suicide attempts to one. The rather prickly woman who unsettled her lover's vulgar dinner table with her criticisms of his guests becomes a passionate lady in distress, and the problematic relationship with Imlay is caught by one of those memorable images with which Virginia Woolf fixes and simplifies her material and imposes herself all at once: "Tickling minnows, he had hooked a dolphin, and the creature rushed him through the waters till he was dizzy" (III, 193–99).

Mary Wollstonecraft, the complex, self-pitying, insensitive, brave, and thinking woman becomes the Virginia Woolf hero, now fighting, now suffering. It is an inspiring and noble portrait, made possible for Woolf mainly by her own artistic superiority to her subject and her readers' assumed ignorance of the facts.

Mary Wollstonecraft and Madame de Sévigné write, but they are not artists in Virginia Woolf's sense; they are unconcerned with their craft and with form and they need not be judged by standards of art. Indeed, their thrusting and vital personalities, so much praised by Virginia Woolf, are not for the artist and, when she writes of the craft of writing, it is usually to male artists that she looks. Her views on art, which resemble those of her Bloomsbury contemporaries Clive Bell and Roger Fry, are reiterated throughout her criticism. Briefly, she follows Coleridge, Pater, and Henry James in stressing the aesthetic value of art and the closeness of critic and artist—"Indeed, it seems impossible for anyone who is not actually dealing with the problems of art to know the nature of them"— although she does not go as far as Pater in seeing criticism itself as an art.[4] Like Henry James, she regards the work as a living, coherent unit. "A novel," wrote James in *The Art of Fiction*, "is a living thing, all one and continuous, like any other organism, and in proportion as it lives will it be found . . . that in each of the parts there is something of each of the other parts."[5] With such a concept, polemics, preaching, and personality must all be pushed aside. A writer, Virginia Woolf stresses in an essay on Gissing, should not use personal suffering to rivet the reader's sympathy and curiosity; imagination loses its sweep and power and becomes petty and personal when limited to considering a particular case demanding sympathy.[6]

Yet in one respect the writer's situation must (sadly) intrude on the writing. In "The Niece of an Earl" Virginia Woolf writes that "the English novelist in particular suffers from a disability which affects no other artist to the same extent. His work is influenced by his birth. He is fated to know intimately, and so to describe with understanding, only those who are of his own social rank" (I, 221). Class inevitably signs art, then, but other externals should be rigidly controlled.

The women writers Virginia Woolf discusses were chosen for the pain and personality they expressed, for not sticking to what they knew, and for demanding something "perhaps incompatible with the facts of human existence." Women who wrote in the past, then, seem excluded from the group, writers.

Across this antithesis falls Jane Austen, who refuses to be a fighting hero or a distressed heroine, whose small amount of public life is publicly known, and who, ignoring the Woolfian categories, composed *Sense and Sensibility* instead of "Suffering and Sensibility." Jane Austen is the first indubitably great woman writer in English, whether one looks back through F. R. Leavis's great moral tradition or through Virginia Woolf's and Henry James's great aesthetic one. It was inevitable, then, that Virginia Woolf as a woman and an artist should tangle with her great precursor. In *The Anxiety of Influence*, Harold Bloom has described the struggle in literary history as "a battle between strong equals, father and son as mighty opposites, Laius and Oedipus at the crossroads."[7] Ignoring the strident masculinity and simplification of this formula, one can find it relevant to the relationship of Virginia Woolf and Jane Austen. If, to write at all, Woolf had to nullify her eminent Victorian father, Leslie Stephen—"His life would have entirely ended mine," she wrote, speculating what would have happened had he lived—to write as a woman she had to come to terms with the mother of writers, Jane Austen. "Revision—the act of . . . seeing with fresh eyes, of entering an old text from a new critical direction"—Adrienne Rich calls "an act of survival."[8]

Like King Charles's head, Jane Austen is always intruding. She functions in Woolf's essays as a talisman or counter, separated from the scrutiny she suffers elsewhere. For although Virginia Woolf reacts against the Arnoldian touchstone system, modified and adopted by her father in his criticism, she herself is rather apt to hit writers—especially the much despised Edwardian trio of Wells, Galsworthy, and Bennett—with the names of the sacred dead.[9] Of these Jane Austen is usually the only woman, coming with Dickens, Carlyle, and Macaulay to belittle the moderns and provide "that solace, that security, that sense that the human heart does not change. . . ." (II, 263). Elizabeth Bennet will always defeat Arnold Bennett.

Elsewhere Austen represents with Trollope "sober reality" or with Peacock comic genius. When gender is at issue, she is always one of the big four, with George Eliot and Charlotte and Emily Brontë. She even enters sometimes with Stendhal and Chekhov as a creator of real characters or with Turgenev as the pure artist. But usually she is not ranged with foreigners; in her essay "The Russian Point of View," Virginia Woolf distinguishes British from Russian novelists, and her summary of the former could read as a description of Jane Austen. Where Russians worry over souls and great truths, notes Virginia Woolf, the British discourse on class and forms, and incline to satire, looking not at the individual but at society.

On her own, Jane Austen most commonly signifies perfection—a hard, forbidding quality beside the touchstone wit of Meredith, the range of Thackeray, or the "intellectual power" of Tolstoy. Perhaps Woolf comes closest to catching it when she speaks of an Austen successor and mediator for herself, Henry James. "All great writers," she remarks of him, "have . . . an atmosphere in which they seem most at their ease and at their best, a mood of the great general mind which they interpret and indeed almost discover, so that we come to read them rather for that than for any story or character or scene of separate excellence" (I, 270). Jane Austen fulfills all Virginia Woolf's requirements for the great artist. First, she does not preach. In *A Room of One's Own*, commenting on women writers, Woolf exclaims: "What genius in the midst of that purely patriarchal society to hold fast to the thing as they saw it without shrinking. Only Jane Austen did it and Emily Brontë. It is another feather, perhaps the finest, in their caps. . . . Of all the thousand women who wrote novels then, they alone entirely ignored the perpetual admonition of the eternal pedagogue—write this, think that."[10] She reiterated the point in "Women and Fiction": "The genius of Jane Austen and Emily Brontë is never more convincing than in their power to ignore . . . claims and solicitations and to hold on their way unperturbed by scorn or censure. But it needed a very serene or a very powerful mind to resist the temptation to anger" (II, 144).

Secondly, Jane Austen has no personal life in her novels. She does not insist on self. Like the Greeks and Shakespeare, she comes with little baggage. We do not know her as we know Keats in letters or poetry, and our judgment cannot be clouded by our response to the woman. In a review of an anecdotal book on Jane Austen, Virginia Woolf attacks those critics who escape a proper responsibility by delving into biographical irrelevancies: "Only to hear Jane Austen saying nothing in her natural voice when the critics have been debating whether she was a lady, whether she told the truth, whether she could read, whether she had personal experience of hunting a fox is positively upsetting. We remember that Jane Austen wrote novels. It might be worthwhile for their critics to read them."[11]

Virginia Woolf's slightly priggish tone here cannot disguise that she is being disingenuous, for to her it certainly mattered, as to "the critics," what status Jane Austen had. Indeed if there is one judgment that is repeated, it is that Jane Austen is a lady. In a piece on Miss Mitford, Virginia Woolf muses on what a lady is and settles the matter neatly by affirming: "Jane Austen was a lady and . . . Charlotte Brontë was not one" (IV, 105). In the essay "On George Eliot," the novelist is firmly put in her place as "the granddaughter of a carpenter," and Charlotte Brontë is frequently exposed to assure Jane Austen's privilege, her lower-middle-class roots sticking uncouthly through the soil of her genius (I, 198). We do not, Virginia Woolf tells us, read Charlotte Brontë "for a philosophic view of life—hers is that of a country parson's daughter." There is a hierarchy of parsonages, it seems, and breeding will out, certainly in fiction. Jane Austen's Emma knows exactly when she has said enough; Mrs. Casaubon would have talked for an hour and bored her well-bred listener. "One hesitates to call Jane Eyre a lady," writes Virginia Woolf in "The Niece of an Earl," "the Elizabeths and the Emmas of Miss Austen could not possibly be taken for anything else" (I, 221). This class sureness of Jane Austen leads to her third characteristic as an artist, a sureness of tone and subject matter. A lady is never seduced out of her subject: "The writer of perfect judgement and taste, like Jane Austen, does no more than glance across the gulf" into the working classes (I, 220).

Although Austen is no artist-critic like Henry James and Virginia Woolf herself, she is a woman aware of her craft. In "The Anatomy of Fiction," where Virginia Woolf describes ways by which a novelist speaks of art, she finds Jane Austen teaching "how exquisitely one incident relieves another; how definitely, by not saying something, she says it; how surprising, therefore, her expressive phrases when they come. Between the sentences, apart from the story, a little shape of some kind builds itself up" (II, 138).

Of such an artist as Jane Austen, impersonal, nonpolemical, properly classbound, classic, and critically aware, one would expect minute probing, but it is largely missing. Virginia Woolf's most extended description of Jane Austen occurs in "Phases of Fiction," but her art is not really investigated and indeed it seems, like Topsy of *Uncle Tom's Cabin*, to have just "grow'd." Austen is filed here with Dickens among the character-mongers and comedians and praised highly for her sense of organic form, so prized by Virginia Woolf, and her brilliant use of dialogue; she works "by means of perfectly natural question and answer" (II, 75). Other mentions are even vaguer. She is said to have written a female sentence, and to have created a universal, perfect prose, but there is no analysis. Instead there are images; an Austen book is like a shell, a gem, a crystal. Of all great writers, Jane Austen is "the most difficult to catch in the act of greatness." Austen herself exists in the essays without a tradition that would give her meaning and without the novelists of sensibility from Richardson to Fanny Burney who would give her satire point. Indeed, while Virginia Woolf lavishes time on Defoe and Sterne among eighteenth-century writers and on the Duchess of Newcastle and Laetitia Pilkington among women, she is strangely silent on Austen's major predecessors. Fanny Burney, it is true, does appear but mainly in the light, charming piece about her flighty half-sister.

Virginia Woolf is uneasy in the presence of Jane Austen. She renders her lack of ease by modifying those very characteristics which made Austen the great artist, not merely the woman writer. So her impersonality becomes aggravating, her nonpolemical stance passionless, her lady-likeness a limitation, and her artistic perfection negation. And, like any minor woman writer, she is made to submit to the Woolfian personality and sit in silence for her portrait while the author sketches herself.

Impersonal art is reverenced in Shakespeare, but in Jane Austen it seems almost impertinent. "There is Jane Austen," writes Virginia Woolf in her essay "Personalities," "thumbed, scored, annotated, magnified, living almost within the memory of man, and yet as inscrutable in her small way as Shakespeare in his vast one. She flatters and cajoles you with the promise of intimacy and then, at the last moment, there is the same blankness. Are those Jane Austen's eyes or is it a glass, a mirror, a silver spoon held up in the sun? The people whom one admires most as writers, then, have something elusive, enigmatic, impersonal about them. . . . All has been distilled into their books. The life is thin, modest, colourless, like blue skimmed milk at the bottom of the jar. It is the imperfect artists who never manage to say the whole thing in their books who wield the power of personality over us" (II, 275). How can the "small" Jane Austen dare to be so reticent, she seems to ask.

Virginia Woolf's hostility at this control and reticence spills over into belittling images. In the essay "Reviewing," she had asked, "Who would not spout the family teapot in order to talk with Keats for an hour about poetry, or with Jane Austen about the art of fiction?" (II, 213). But in "Personalities" she writes almost with a sneer, "Here is Jane Austen, a great writer as we all agree, but, for my own part, I would rather not find myself alone in the room with her. A sense of meaning withheld, a smile at something unseen, an atmosphere of perfect control and courtesy mixed with something finely satirical, which, were it not directed against things in general rather than against individuals, would be almost malicious, would, so I feel, make it alarming to find at home" (II, 276). Here one feels the shudder as if the room of one's own were already uncomfortably and uncompromisingly occupied.

Virginia Woolf is eager to find Jane Austen at tea. Although she deplores critics who make Austen domestic and ladylike—in a 1936 letter to R. W. Chapman she stresses Austen's coarseness and her own annoyance at "people who talk of her as if she were a niminy piminy spinster"—she frequently puts her behind the cups. She is watched sitting by the pot or picking out roses from the china. Woolf is never tempted, as she is with another artist, Christina Rossetti, to smash the teacup to reach her. In *Night and Day* Katherine Hilbury, pouring tea, reckons her activity occupies about a fifth of her consciousness.[12]

Henry James saw Austen as "the brown thrush who tells his story from the garden bough." Woolf makes the twittering image domestic: "Humbly and gaily she collected the twigs and straws out of which the nest was to be made and placed them neatly together" (I, 148–49). But the motherly housewife metaphor will not stick and, referring to a contemporary comment, Woolf exclaims in her predecessor's accent, "A wit, a delineator of character, who does not talk is terrific indeed!" (I, 144).

And she comments, "Sometimes it seems as if her creatures were born merely to give Jane Austen the supreme delight of slicing their heads off" (I, 149). The motherly domestic image fades before Medea in Hampshire.

When Woolf reads Jane Austen's letters, she decides that the reticence, the refusal to "talk" mars the fiction. Considering why Austen failed to be "much better than she was," she answers in her diary, "Something to do with sex, I expect; the letters are full of hints that she suppressed half of her in her novels."[13] We view her cozily at tea, then, because she refuses to let us see upstairs.

Virginia Woolf's irritation does not always take so open a form. Elsewhere she simply refuses to accept Jane Austen's secrecy. In her character sketches of women, she sought the typical moment or gesture that opened up the life and let in the critic. With Jane Austen she tries the same method, sometimes almost approaching success. In *A Room of One's Own*, she enters Jane Austen's circumscribed life: "If Jane Austen suffered in any way from her circumstances it was in the narrowness of life that was imposed upon her. It was impossible for a woman to go about alone. She never travelled; she never drove through London on an omnibus or had luncheon in a shop by herself. But perhaps it was the nature of Jane Austen not to want what she had not. Her gift and her circumstances matched each other completely."[14] Here Virginia Woolf veers off from her assessment and questions whether Jane Austen really belongs at all to the group of aspiring women—of Charlotte Brontë and herself, for instance—and empathy is lessened. Something in addition disturbs, for one is conscious that this need to break off, to swerve from empathy, may be due to Virginia Woolf's realization of her own smugness. For surely it is Virginia Woolf who traveled through London on an omnibus and had luncheon in a shop by herself.

A similar focus on the critic, not the criticized, comes from Woolf's decision to concentrate on Austen's juvenilia. Quoted in Virginia Woolf's prose, a passage renders Jane Austen a precocious child and her critic a kindly aunt reporting on her progress. " 'I die a martyr to my grief for the loss of Augustus. One fatal swoon has cost me my life. Beware of Swoons, Dear Laura . . . Run mad as often as you chuse, but do not faint. . . .' And on she rushed, as fast as she could write and quicker than she could spell to tell the incredible adventures of Laura & Sophia. . . ." (I, 145). Here the Austen quotation from *Love and Freindship,* one of the very few slightly extended examples, is distanced and made girlish by Virginia Woolf's own powerfully idiosyncratic prose.

Only in one respect does Virginia Woolf try for an extended time to make an Austen personality as woman. Significantly, it is not with the aid of the book always held up as the masterpiece—*Pride and Prejudice*—but through the last of Jane Austen's completed works, *Persuasion*, the one Virginia Woolf declared her favorite in a letter to David Cecil, and the only one not thoroughly revised by the author. Here, ignoring the irony that might reasonably connect this novel with Austen's other works and forgetting her own practice described by one critic as the rewriting of the same book "of which she has given us nine different versions,"[15] she insists on seeing the comment on Anne Elliot as entirely untinged with irony: "She had been forced into prudence in her youth, she learned romance as she grew older." The famous speech on female constancy, "All the privilege I claim for my own sex . . . is that of loving longest, when existence or when hope is gone," is likewise given a single tone and made to prove the biographical fact that Jane Austen had loved—and presumably lost (I, 152).

So if the poker spinster Austen repulses, a more sympathetic lovelorn lady, created by Woolf, can attract. The same tendency to make a sympathetic image to which the critic can respond is present in Woolf's efforts to turn Jane Austen, who died at forty-two, into a Keatsian tragic artist. For this image *Persuasion* becomes a kind of *Fall of Hyperion*, an unfinished transitional masterpiece, pointing toward radical change, and its author a nineteenth-century caterpillar about to emerge as a modernist butterfly. *Persuasion* turns into a new departure, with no links to its fictional predecessors. In this novel the sweet, sad influence of autumn, of suffering and sensibility, overwhelms the Austen fictional presence, and the sentimental leaves and dirty bottoms of *Sense and Sensibility* are forgotten.

Consideration of *Persuasion* leads Virginia Woolf to muse on what Jane Austen would have been had she lived, speculation employed also for Charlotte Brontë. In a letter of December 1932 she says confidently of Jane Austen, "she died at 42: the best to come." The "best," not surprisingly, is rather close to the fiction of Virginia Woolf herself. Jane Austen's admitted great strengths—her sure syntax and her concise dialogue—give way to reflections in the Woolfian manner. "Those marvellous little speeches which sum up, in a few minutes' chatter, all that we need to know of an Admiral Croft or a Mrs Musgrove for ever, that shorthand, hit-or-miss method, which contains chapter of analysis and psychology, would have become too crude to hold all that she now perceived of the complexity of human nature. She would have devised a method, clear and composed as ever, but deeper and more suggestive, for conveying not only what people say, but what they leave unsaid; not only what they are, but what life is" (I, 153). In other words, she would have become a kind of ur-Woolf.

The method of translation is employed not only in books Jane Austen did not write but also in those she did. Woolf, who professes organic form and savors works in their total integrity, rarely looks at an Austen book as a whole, trying instead in her criticism the method she used so bewitchingly in biography—the fictional investigation of a characteristic event. So *Mansfield Park,* that most hard-grained of novels, suddenly displays a Woolfian moment, and the critic insists that the reader follow her own code of female sensibility and ignore the comic:

> it is midday in Northamptonshire; a dull young man is talking to rather a weakly young woman on the stairs as they go up to dress for dinner, with housemaids passing. But, from triviality, from commonplace, their words become suddenly full of meaning, and the moment for both one of the most memorable in their lives. It fills itself; it shines; it glows; it hangs before us, deep, trembling, serene for a second, next, the housemaid passes, and this drop, in which all the happiness of life has collected, gently subsides again to become part of the ebb and flow of ordinary existence. (I, 150)

This is far from the effect of the Austen passage to which Woolf must be referring. The elements are certainly the same. Fanny Price, jealous of Mary Crawford's hold over her much beloved cousin Edmund, is walking upstairs when she is hailed by him. The cousins speak of Fanny's tiredness and Edmund's relationship with Mary, and he admits his misgivings about her character. They are interrupted by a housemaid. Yet the tone and treatment of the incident are profoundly at odds with the Woolf rendition. In Austen, conversation is rarely trivial without being comic, and the sentences are precise and full of surface significance. Silences are motivated; Fanny either struggles for conventional utterance against her deep emotions or she is silent while considering what to say and breaks off when embarrassed at the clarity of her own warning: "Excuse the liberty—but take care *how* you talk to me. Do not tell me any thing now, which hereafter you may be sorry for." Edmund, replying as precisely, assesses the two women and adequately conveys his dual emotion: "I can never be ashamed of my scruples; and if they are removed, it must be by changes that will only raise her [Mary's] character the more by the recollection of the faults she once had. You are the only being upon earth to whom I should say what I have said."

The interruption by the housemaid is not arbitrary, as in Woolf, but indicated by both Fanny and her comic novelist:

> They were now on the second floor, and the appearance of a housemaid prevented any further conversation. For Fanny's present comfort it was concluded perhaps at the happiest moment; had he been able to talk another five minutes, there is no saying that he might not have

talked away all Miss Crawford's faults and his own despondence. But as it was, they parted with looks on his side of grateful affection, and with some very precious sensations on her's.[16]

Virginia Woolf's Jane Austen is dreamy and word-obsessed, and the encounter of the cousins becomes a kind of epiphany, but its effect is strangely insincere, with the moment taking more symbolic weight than it needs or can bear. At the end of *The Waves,* Bernard remembers when he and his friend first heard of the death of Percival and how they had compared him to a lily: "So the sincerity of the moment passed; so it became symbolical. . . . Let us commit any blasphemy of laughter and criticism rather than exude this lily-sweet glue."[17]

The coopting of Jane Austen is only partial, and she can never enter the Woolfian prose completely. Most of the time the critic seems mildly irritated at the subject she cannot quite control. For example, she grumbles at Jane Austen's impersonality: "Her absence has," writes Virginia Woolf, "the effect of making us detached from her work and of giving it, for all its sparkle and animation, a certain aloofness and incompleteness" (II, 76). The text, inhuman and inhumane, is standoffish. It is an interesting judgment, when one considers not only Virginia Woolf's critical bias toward the impersonal in art but also the overwhelming presence of Jane Austen as narrator in all her books, including the much misused *Persuasion.* Other women Woolf chooses to probe do express themselves; Mary Wollstonecraft or Dorothy Wordsworth, for example. In an essay on "Aurora Leigh," she writes with a mixture of condescension and admiration, "Mrs. Browning could no more conceal herself than she could control herself" (I, 212).

Irritation is even clearer when Woolf contemplates Austen's lack of the polemics and passion which mark female texts from Charlotte Brontë to Virginia Woolf herself. Even the gothic novelist Ann Radcliffe, much mocked by male critics who venerate Austen, surpasses her great contemporary in feeling. "Jane Austen might have done worse than take a leaf from Radcliffe's book," Virginia Woolf considers and, concluding that Austen traveled too far from feeling, wrote, "I'm not sure I shan't lead a Radcliffe relief party."[18]

Although Ann Radcliffe and other writers are sometimes cited to counter the passionless Austen presence, the usual opposite is Charlotte Brontë, blamed, in *A Room of One's Own,* for disturbing the text with her intrusive pain. When only art is in question, Charlotte Brontë is rebuked for her crudeness by a Jane Austen made subtle and multifaceted, but when, as Charlotte Brontë herself might have said, it is "a question of the heart," then Jane Austen lacks the vehemence, the indignation, and the genius of Brontë. Interestingly, Virginia Woolf blames

Charlotte Brontë for her famous blindness to her great predecessor, while echoing it herself: "Vice, adventure, passion were left outside." By elevating suffering and sensibility, Charlotte Brontë's characteristics, Virginia Woolf makes Jane Austen seem tame and limited. In "On Rereading Novels," Charlotte Brontë lodges with the intoxicating novelists who surpass the cool Jane Austen in genius; only, Woolf admits, they can't quite express it all. Jane Austen "with less genius for writing than Charlotte Brontë . . . got infinitely more said." Her lack of passion and preaching is predicated on her tame, inscrutable life. "If Jane Austen had lain as a child on the landing to prevent her father from thrashing her mother, her soul might have burst with such a passion against tyranny that all her novels might have been consumed in one cry for justice" (III, 194).

Even in class stability, seemingly so much approved by Virginia Woolf, where Austen clearly overtops the ambiguous Brontë, she is sometimes disparaged. Virginia Woolf praises Jane Austen as a lady, and yet the praise is edged. Artistic judgments grow tinged with class and become trivialized. For example, Austen's values, like her social credentials, are termed "impeccable," and her discretion, although praised, is a matter of fictional care and social correctness. Morality becomes not feeling and judgment but upper-middle-class good breeding. Class limits her subjects and confines her plots: "There was the big house and the little house; a tea party, a dinner party, and an occasional picnic; life was hedged in by valuable connections and adequate incomes; by muddy roads, wet feet, and a tendency on the part of the ladies to get tired" (I, 149). Even her purity of form, a usual value in Woolf criticism, seems to concern class as much as artistry. Most of all, however, her class position connects with her lack of female feeling. In "Outlines," the Jane Austen type of lady is described as reticent and avoiding open passion. Ladylikeness comes to preclude womanliness.

In fact Jane Austen seems thoroughly unwomanly, despite her position in Virginia Woolf's pantheon of women, and her activity mocks the generalizations. In A Room of One's Own, Woolf judged the possession of a room essential for a woman artist, and yet she notes almost testily that Austen "had no separate study to repair to" and she quotes the remark of Austen's nephew, that "most of the work must have been done in the general sitting-room, subject to all kinds of casual interruption."[19] The female novel of the early nineteenth century is autobiographical, Virginia Woolf announces; yet Jane Austen, its greatest exponent, hides away her love life so resolutely not even Virginia Woolf can find it out. The sentence, once declared female in Jane Austen's hands, is forgotten when Virginia Woolf generalizes that writing is male and that women's use of it must be marked and marred by struggle and domination. Values, too, are patriarchal, inimical to a woman who must alter them and make new ones, which will, however, seem trivial and sentimentalized. But Jane Austen is not sentimental and she shows no embarrassment or discomfort at conventional values. About her art she is not vastly ladylike and she could not echo her admired Mary Brunton, who wrote of her horror of "being suspected of literary aims," "my dear, I would sooner exhibit as a ropedancer."[20] At the same time she does not tout her art or kick against the limits, accepting with proper pride her own "little bits . . . of Ivory." In short, Jane Austen seems hardly a woman writer. If Virginia Woolf has an androgynous vision, as Carolyn Heilbrun and Nancy Bazin believe, the sexes must be for her in some sense polarized, initially at least.[21] Jane Austen seems, annoyingly, quite oblivious of this scheme. She is not androgynous, merely devoid of gender. Her artistic novels prove it, for otherwise she would, like Mary Wollstonecraft, have subsumed them into one passionate cry.

Virginia Woolf praises Jane Austen as an artist and stresses her perfection. Yet the praise is often strangely negative and the perfection a matter of limits. Even in the review of the anecdotal book, all laudatory of Austen, Woolf admires her for saying nothing. So in the criticism of Brontë, Jane Austen succeeds by not having anger, and in the criticism of Gissing, by not expressing personal suffering. Even in the most extended and appreciative passage in "Phases of Fiction" there is the tendency toward negation:

> The talk is not mere talk; it has an emotional intensity which gives it more than brilliance. Light, landscape—everything that lies outside the drawing room is arranged to illumine it. Distances are made exact; arrangements accurate. It is one mile from Meryton; it is Sunday and not Monday. We want all suspicions and questions laid at rest. It is necessary that the characters should lie before us in as clear and quiet a light as possible since every flicker and tremor is to be observed. Nothing happens, as things so often happen in Dickens, for its own oddity or curiosity, but with relation to something else. No avenues of suggestion are opened up, no doors are suddenly flung wider; the ropes which tighten the structure, since they are all rooted in the heart, are so held firmly and tightly. For, in order to develop personal relations to the utmost, it is important to keep out of the range of the abstract, the impersonal; and to suggest that there is anything that lies outside men and women would be to cast the shadow of doubt upon the comedy of their relationships and its sufficiency. . . . But personal relations have limits, as Jane Austen seems to realize by stressing their comedy. Everything, she seems to say, has, if we could discover it, a reasonable summing up. (II, 75–76)

The phrases here are lined with dissatisfaction. Perfection, always allowed, is becoming a gloss for meanness and, as the passage goes on, the great sureness, Jane Austen's chief merit, is undercut by the tentativeness she inspires in the critic-respondent. Her emphatic "is" turns into "seems" in two adjacent sentences. The dissonant final comment with its double embedding, "she seems to say" and "if we could discover it," renders its subject limited, misled and misleading, above all prosaic. For, when the Austen smoothness is reduced to this roughness, nothing, Virginia Woolf "seems to say," is left.

Perfection is dull. In the essay "How It Strikes a Contemporary," Virginia Woolf laments the "unabashed tranquillity" of great books, found "in page after page of Wordsworth and Scott and Miss Austen which is sedative to the verge of somnolence" (II, 158). An example of the limits of perfection, which seems to preclude doubting subtlety and awareness, comes from Jane Austen's unfinished novel, *The Watsons:*

> From what, then, arises that sense of security which gradually and delightfully and completely overcomes us? It is the power of their belief—their conviction, that imposes itself upon us. . . . They know the relations of human beings towards each other and towards the universe. Only believe . . . that a nice girl will instinctively try to soothe the feelings of a boy who has been snubbed at a dance, and then, if you believe it implicitly and unquestioningly, you will not only make people a hundred years later feel the same thing, but you will make them feel it as literature. For certainty of that kind is the condition which makes it possible to write. (II, 159)

Jane Austen's artistic limitations are partly her own fault and partly the result of her position in history, for Virginia Woolf saw the novel as a progressive form taking in more and more of life. The limitations are expressed in metaphor, and the books are trapped in those same domestic and ordered images which Woolf used for Austen the woman and which the detractors have always employed for the prose. Sir Walter Scott, a partial admirer, started the tradition with his impression of Jane Austen's cottages and meadows, and Charlotte Brontë added hostility, making the Austen fictional world a "carefully-fenced, highly-cultivated garden, with neat borders and delicate flowers; but . . . no open country, no fresh air, no blue hill, no bonny beck."[22] Emerson irascibly saw Austen's novels in terms of an "English boarding house," pinched, narrow, sterile, and he judged suicide "more respectable."[23]

For Virginia Woolf, Austen's art is one of enclosure. It is a domestic garden beside the lighthouse of her own art. In *Between the Acts* there is a blue that never touched a garden, a vision that an Austen could never

catch. A passage in *To the Lighthouse* expresses something of the geo-
graphical effect: "It was all familiar; this turning, that stile, that cut across
the fields. Hours he would spend thus, with his pipe, of an evening,
thinking up and down and in and out of the old familiar lanes and commons . . . but at length the lane, the field, the common, the fruitful nut-
tree and the flowering hedge led him on to that further turn of the road
where he dismounted always, tied his horse to a tree, and proceeded on
foot alone. He reached the edge of the lawn and looked out on the bay
beneath."[24] Jane Austen knows the land but not the bay. Remove the
hedges from Austen's world, Woolf writes, and how much remains?

Even in small touches, Jane Austen's effect seems synonymous with
domesticity and limit. Her life is the residue of skimmed milk and, in a
letter of 1936, Virginia Woolf sees her lecture on Jane Austen as a new
fold to that so often neatly folded. Austen is clean linen and neatness, a
sorry fate for a writer who in *Northanger Abbey* mocked us all with her
laundry list.

So why is Virginia Woolf so ambivalent and uneasy? There are, no
doubt, many reasons, some to do with her own art, some with her life,
and a few, very few, to do with Jane Austen herself, who as the author of
the six novels largely disappears from Virginia Woolf's pages.

As noted, Jane Austen fails to fit in with Woolf's views on women
writers: women are marked by suffering and sensibility, and yet *Pride
and Prejudice* shows no signs that her circumstances have harmed Austen's work in the slightest. Indeed she seems annoyingly comfortable
within the patriarchy that gives Virginia Woolf and her sister authors so
much trouble.

Austen fails in particular to accord with Virginia Woolf herself, and the
criticism throws the reader back not only to Virginia Woolf's essay personality but also to her own life and fiction. Virginia Woolf rebukes Jane
Austen as woman and writer; so Jane Austen seems to rebuke Virginia
Woolf.

First is the matter of class. Here there is some ambiguity in Virginia
Woolf. Although securely upper middle class from her parents, and related through them to major administrators and writers of her time, she
would have to move only a generation or two backwards to remove the
"upper." In addition, her husband, being Jewish, was always slightly
outside the British class system, however intellectually aristocratic he
might have seemed.[25] In the matter of class, Virginia Woolf wished to
have her cake and eat it. Despite being found unladylike by Henry James,
she felt herself a lady and of high class through intellect and social standing.[26] In an embarrassing letter, published as "Middlebrow," she tries to

define class in intellectual terms, although the concept is shot through with social consideration. Insisting on the term "highbrow" for herself, she makes a personality of a woman who breakfasts in bed, derives from drunken, good-living forebears, and boasts an aunt who resides in India. She mocks the middlebrow and middle class who, like Jane Austen but without her breeding, pour tea and who reside in inferior parts of London: "If your reviewer, or any other reviewer, dares hint that I live in South Kensington, I will sue him for libel" (II, 203).

Woolf escaped into Bloomsbury, where hierarchy was to be based on merit and art, but she took along her social rank. So she can both fulminate against snobbishness and show all its marks. Her pronouncements are imbued with class, and her famous statement that "in or about December, 1910, human character changed" is entirely interpreted through social status: the Victorian cook in the depths of the house gives way to the Georgian servant, democratically in and out of the drawing room (I, 320). Jane Austen is as class-bound as her successor, but she knows nothing of it, and Virginia Woolf almost envies her this ignorance.

Jane Austen and Virginia Woolf share gender and childlessness; Jane Austen—Miss Austen, as Woolf tends to name her—went further by failing even to marry, so affronting D. H. Lawrence among others with her spinsterhood. Virginia Woolf was, it appears, happily married, and she seems both proud of and uneasy at her state. She admires married women like Mrs. Ramsay and is often merciless to single ones like Doris Kilman; yet she asks the question in *Orlando:* "If one still wished, more than anything in the whole world, to write poetry, was it marriage?"[27]

In addition, her relationship with Leonard was more or less sexless. According to her biographer Quentin Bell, she felt no physical attraction for him, and he was cold. Her choice of women for discussion may reflect a deep need to probe a companionable, not a sexual relationship: she writes on Swift and Stella, on Cowper and Lady Austen, and on William and Dorothy Wordsworth. In each there is the giftedness and subordination of the woman, and in each there is sexual refusal. In each of these relationships one of the partners went mad, as did Virginia Woolf herself beside Leonard in her companionable marriage.

Madness in women is a form of silencing. Other female writers Virginia Woolf chose to describe were silenced or overwhelmed, not by madness, but by fatherly images or marriages, rather as Virginia Woolf feared she might have been had her father lived: Dorothy Osborne, subsumed in Temple; Maria Allen, tamed by an exacting husband; and Sara Coleridge, endlessly editing her father. Jane Austen is not silenced, mad, or married. She is overwhelmed by no man.

But she did love her sister, although Virginia Woolf is strangely silent about this. Indeed Woolf tends, with the exception of the piece on Jane Carlyle and Geraldine Jewsbury, to underplay female ties, as she does in the essay on Mary Wollstonecraft, or concentrate on unequal ones like that of Selina Trimmer and her pupil. Yet her niece Angelica Garnett noted her desire to be loved by her sister Vanessa and her demand for "various kinds of kisses," and she describes the "very intimate, complicated and somewhat jealous relationship with Vanessa who was a second mother to her and whom she worshipped."[28] By what Jane Austen failed to do, then, and by what she did, Virginia Woolf seems strangely shadowed.

Jane Austen intrudes into Virginia Woolf's own writing. A review of Jane Austen's letters in the *Times Literary Supplement* of 1932 was thought by some to be by Virginia Woolf, for E. M. Forster, its author, had appropriated her style. A friend called the review her "very best," though Virginia Woolf testily pronounced it "feeble in the extreme."

More important, Austen invades the novels. An artist should be unpolemical, according to Woolf; yet she herself cannot be judged so if one considers the *Three Guineas*, the psychiatrists Holmes and Bradshaw of *Mrs Dalloway*, or Lily Briscoe crying out about her painting, "And it would never be seen; never be hung even, and there was Mr Tansley whispering in her ear, 'Women can't paint, women can't write. . . .' "[29] In her diary Woolf worried over the intrusion of the ego into her fiction; in 1920 she wrote: "Whether I'm sufficiently mistress of things—that's the doubt . . . I suppose the danger is the damned egotistical self." And she expresses her fear: "Have I the power of conveying the true reality? Or do I write essays about myself?"[30] Her novels were labeled works of sensibility; excessive sensibility was the butt of Jane Austen's six novels. Woolf distrusted the quality in theory—as her discussion of Sterne shows—yet the women she praises display excess of it and her diary and novels prove her fear of falling victim herself.

Virginia Woolf was conscious of writing modern fiction, but the elements of the traditional novel, however crude—precise plot, detail, character, and dialogue—pressed on her achievement. She was criticized for inattention to detail and she snapped back that one expects accuracy from Jane Austen—and, one might add, the precise biographer Leslie Stephen—but not from a writer like herself who was "trying to do something else." The traditional novel had to be fought; she called her books an elegy *(To the Lighthouse)*, a play-poem *(The Waves)*, and an essay-novel *(The Years)*. She avoided plot and character—"little snapshot pictures of people," she wrote contemptuously—where Jane Austen was supreme. By so doing she invited criticism, and E. M. Forster obliged:

"She dreams, designs, jokes, invokes, observes details, but she does not tell a story or weave a plot, and—can she create character? That is her problem's centre"; and again with the inevitable Austen slap, "She could seldom so portray a character that it was remembered afterwards in its own account, as Emma is remembered."[31]

The Austen image threatened the younger Virginia Woolf, who was mortified to find critics yoking them together. In 1919 she confided to her diary about Katherine Mansfield's review of *Night and Day* that she found the comparison with Jane Austen spiteful. "A decorous elderly dullard she describes me," Woolf complains, "Jane Austen up to date. Leonard supposes that she let her wish for my failure have its way with her pen."[32]

The comparison with Jane Austen seems to deliver failure, then. Unfortunately it is repeated. H. W. Massingham, writing on *Night and Day*, mocks its author's preoccupation with taxis and tea-drinking rather in the manner of Woolf on Austen, and he calls the four main characters "Four Impassioned Snails." Another reviewer answered Massingham's "cutting paragraph," as Virginia Woolf called it, by supporting the Austen comparison. And yet clearly it is one Virginia Woolf feared. "I had rather write in my own way of 'Four Passionate Snails' than be, as Katherine Mansfield maintains, Jane Austen over again."[33]

Certainly Woolf struggled to avoid the repetition, moving from the early Austen-invoking novels to the experiments of *To the Lighthouse* and *The Waves*. Yet Austen is always somehow there to mock; her perfection, so ambiguously appreciated in the criticism, rebukes the fiction, and her nineteenth-century sense sobers the twentieth-century sensibility:

> one must (we, in our generation must) renounce finally the achievement of the greater beauty: the beauty which comes from completeness, in such books as War and Peace, and Stendhal I suppose, and some of Jane Austen . . . Only now that I have written this, I doubt its truth. Are we not always hoping? . . . I was wondering to myself why it is that though I try sometimes to limit myself to the thing I do well, I am always drawn on and on, by human beings, I think, out of the little circle of safety, on and on, to the whirlpools; when I go under.[34]

Austen is to Woolf's text the context that limits and proves limits. Embraced imperfection is still simply imperfection, and the sensitive something Woolf seeks may indeed be "incompatible with the facts of human existence."

"Whatever 'Bloomsbury' may think of JA., she is not by any means one of my favourites," Woolf admitted. "I'd give all she ever wrote for half of what the Brontës wrote—if my reason did not compel me to see that she is a magnificent artist."[35] A diary entry is more plaintive; topics for discussion read: "Jane Austen, novels, pessimism."

*Janet Todd*
*Rutgers University*

# NOTES

1. Virginia Woolf, *Collected Essays* (London: Hogarth Press, 1966), I:204. References in the text are to these volumes.
2. Virginia Woolf, *A Room of One's Own* (London: Hogarth Press, 1929), p. 70.
3. For a discussion of this aspect of Virginia Woolf's biographies, see Josephine O'Brien Schaefer, "Moments of Vision in Virginia Woolf's Biographies," *Virginia Woolf Quarterly*, 2:294–303.
4. *Times Literary Supplement*, December 21, 1916, p. 623.
5. Henry James, *Essays in Modern Literary Criticism* (New York: Holt, Rinehart, 1961), p. 15.
6. For a description of Woolf's critical premises, see Mark Golman's *The Reader's Art: Virginia Woolf as Literary Critic* (The Hague: Mouton, 1976).
7. Harold Bloom, *The Anxiety of Influence* (New York: Oxford University Press, 1973), p. 26.
8. "When We Dead Awaken: Writing as Re-Vision," *Adrienne Rich's Poetry* (New York: Norton, 1975), p. 90.
9. See Noel Annon, *Leslie Stephen: His Thought and Character in Relation to His Time* (Cambridge, Mass.: Harvard University Press, 1952), pp. 249–55.
10. *A Room of One's Own*, p. 112.
11. *Times Literary Supplement*, October 29, 1920, p. 699.
12. *The Letters of Virginia Woolf* (London: Hogarth Press, 1946), VI:87; Virginia Woolf, *Night and Day* (London: Duckworth and Co., 1919), p. 1.
13. *Diary of Virginia Woolf*, ed. Anne Olivier Bell (London: Hogarth Press, 1977), V:127.
14. *A Room of One's Own*, p. 102.
15. Jean Guiguet, *Virginia Woolf and Her Works* (New York: Harcourt, Brace and World, 1965), p. 196.
16. Jane Austen, *Mansfield Park* (Harmondsworth: Penguin, 1966), pp. 275–76.
17. Virginia Woolf, *The Waves* (London: Hogarth Press, 1946), p. 188.

18. *The Letters*, III:418.
19. *A Room of One's Own*, p. 100.
20. Anne K. Elwood, *Memoirs of the Literary Ladies of England* (London, 1843), II:216.
21. See Carolyn Heilbrun, *Toward a Recognition of Androgyny* (New York: Knopf, 1973); Nancy Bazin, *Virginia Woolf and the Androgynous Vision* (New Brunswick: Rutgers University Press, 1973).
22. G. H. Lewes, "The Novels of Jane Austen," reprinted in B. C. Southam, ed., *Jane Austen: The Critical Heritage* (London: Routledge & Kegan Paul, 1968), p. 160.
23. *Journals of Ralph Waldo Emerson: 1856–1863* (1913), ed. E. W. Emerson and W. E. Forbes, IX:336–37.
24. Virginia Woolf, *To the Lighthouse* (Harmondsworth: Penguin), p. 51.
25. Claire Sprague, Introduction to *Virginia Woolf: A Collection of Critical Essays* (Englewood Cliffs, N.J.: Prentice-Hall, 1971), p. 3.
26. Leonard Woolf, *Sowing* (London: Hogarth Press, 1960), p. 107.
27. Virginia Woolf, *Orlando* (London: Hogarth Press, 1964), p. 238.
28. Quoted by Peter Lewis, *Sunday Telegraph*, January 24, 1982, pp. 6–7.
29. *To the Lighthouse*, p. 57.
30. *Diary*, II:14.
31. E. M. Forster, "Virginia Woolf," *Virginia Woolf: A Collection of Critical Essays*, p. 19.
32. *Diary*, I:314.
33. *Diary*, I:316.
34. *Letters*, II:599–600.
35. *Letters*, V:127.

# Sense and Silences
## Reading Jane Austen Again


$S$*ense and Silences* is the title of a
novel Jane Austen never wrote. Instead, it stands for that task of fantas-
tical yet reverential rewriting which is called literary interpretation. It is
*almost* the title of a novel Jane Austen did write. In that "almost" might
be measured the extent to which interpretation "differs from" and yet
"defers to"[1] its original. It is the measure of a certain risk.

But *Sense and Silences* is also a way of putting that now familiar choice
which presents itself to women seeking to claim a language and a literature of their own. The choice of *Sense and Silences* in its extreme form
becomes a choice of saying or not saying, writing or not writing, of
conforming or separating. Such a choice presents itself to me here and
now as one either of making a certain kind of academic Sense or else of
keeping Silent. To write about this opposition is already to have begged
the choice which it commands, and to have aligned myself with one side
rather than another. The apparent contradiction in my writing about
Silence is not, however, one which I want to resolve, or even one which I
regret. Quite the contrary. I want to make it obvious and critical. Thus
*Sense and Silences* is not only the title of this particular interpretation of
Jane Austen; it is also a title which makes of interpretation a dilemma.
My purpose is to show this dilemma at work in the literary text; to show
it, furthermore, as one of the pleasures of the text, which feminist theory
might usefully explore. I want to write about Sense and I want to write
about Silence, but mainly about Silence, in order to recover the Sense of
it. But is it possible to put Silence into words, as I need to do, without
betraying its essentially oppositional nature? Is there *any* Sense to Silence? The answer I want to give is—yes, many.

Of these Silences in the literary text, some are no doubt familiar. There
are, for instance, the *Silences* of which Tillie Olsen writes: those of

thwarted creativity, of "work aborted, deferred, denied."[2] To write in opposition to these kinds of Silences is to be a survivor,[3] and it is as an act of survival against the traditional "No-Voice" of women that much of our literature by female authors should be read. This is the Silence which greets Elizabeth Barrett Browning, for instance, when she writes "where are the poetesses? . . . I look everywhere for grandmothers, and see none."[4] The background of "Aurora Leigh" is one of missing female voices.

But there are other Silences which are not mute and inglorious like these, but which create from the limits of language another meaning, another Sense. These are the high Silences of mystical aspiration, of religious poetry in general, and perhaps most familiarly of Romantic poetry, with its celebration of the mysterious and divinely inspiring powers of the imagination. Here the height of creative power is very often marked by the ineffable, by that which lies on the further side of words, like light or darkness. Wordsworth's vision of the moon above a sea of mist in the last book of the 1850 *Prelude*, for instance, appears to him, in tranquil recollection, as

> the emblem of a mind
> That feeds upon infinity, that broods
> Over the dark abyss, intent to hear
> Its voices issuing forth to silent light . . . (XIV, 70–73)

Here the "voices" of a second genesis are transmuted into "light" which is "silent." In the distant reaches of the Romantic sublime we find this celebration of Silence, which requires a deliberate emptying of the "voices" of language before its own greater power and expressiveness.

There is yet another kind of literary Silence, which George Steiner discusses in his book *Language and Silence*, and which he sees as peculiar to the twentieth century. In the face of unimaginable political inhumanity, aesthetic language is shamed into "suicide."[5] " 'No poetry after Auschwitz,' "[6] he quotes from Adorno, and it is such a "failure of the word in the face of the inhuman"[7] that is enacted in the literature of the twentieth century. Thus, Sylvia Plath writes (after Auschwitz) of "The courage of the shut mouth, in spite of artillery," but also of the "black disks behind it, the disks of outrage."[8] In comparison to those of Romanticism, the Silences of the twentieth century might be described as a witness, not so much to the inexpressible as to the unspeakable.

But in both Romantic and twentieth-century literature we find this need to transgress the limits of the written word, in order to explore the peculiar resonance of what cannot be written. Fragments of language are shored up against the more difficult and strange expressiveness of Silence. However, what is significant is that these Silences always touch, at some point, the limit of language. They do not float freely, but remain in some kind of relation to words, to Sense. To write about Silence, toward Silence, is not the same as to *give up* writing, but it is to *go on failing* to resolve the choice which Silence offers. This is the dilemma that afflicts those most loquacious authors of Silence: the subjects of Beckett's novels. Thus "the Unnamable" struggles with his own story:

> I want it to go silent, it can't, it does for a second, then it starts again, that's not the real silence, it says that's not the real silence, and what can be said of the real silence, I don't know . . .'⁹

He speaks yearningly, despairingly, relentlessly, for the Silence which, like Godot, might resolve all his words.

However, there is another literary Silence, which is not that of failed creativity, or of the Romantic sublime, or of twentieth-century shame. Instead, this is the Silence of something which the text refuses to say openly, but which it allows, as a deliberate alternative to its own words. It is tempting to equate these escaping meanings with the Freudian unconscious, as Macherey does when he writes:

> The speech of the book comes from a certain silence . . . for in order to say anything, there are other things *which must not be said*. Freud relegated this *absence of certain words* to a new place . . . which he paradoxically *named:* the unconscious.¹⁰

However, I would argue that the alternative Silences of what is not said in the literary text are too much deliberated to be like the unconscious. In *The Language of the Self* Lacan writes:

> No doubt . . . we have to lend an ear to the "not-said" which lies in the holes of the discourse, but this does not mean that we are to do our listening as if it were to someone knocking from the other side of a wall.¹¹

However, in literature the " 'not-said' " makes itself heard very much like "someone knocking," and that "someone" very often a woman. Such Silences become evident where there are gaps or inconsistencies or ironies in the main text, but they become evident *as* voices knocking against the "wall" of the language which hides them. To recover the Sense of Jane Austen's Silences, then, is to hear the voices which her notoriously conservative and limiting language would conceal: the voice, in particular, of her younger, Romantic heroine, Marianne.

The story of Marianne, in *Sense and Sensibility*, is of one who, at the age of seventeen, falls romantically in love with a Byronic hero, Willoughby, is jilted, sinks into a mental and physical decline, comes close to death, and is finally married to a man eighteen years her senior, Colonel Brandon, who suffers from bouts of rheumatism, wears a "flannel waist-coat," and, in the course of the novel, scarcely finds one occasion to speak to her directly. As Marianne progresses from an early self-indulgent emotionalism to very real humiliation and despair, however, her story is heard, ever more silently, on the other side of what Austen rationally and censoriously chooses to tell. Her discreet, ironic, and finally dismissive style only makes more expressive those things which she leaves out, and by the end of the novel what she leaves out is the voice of Marianne herself. *Sense and Sensibility,* like all Austen's novels, is a drama of language in which her heroines *suffer* what can and cannot be said.

If the literary work is read as a palimpsest, in this way, where the surface text conceals and half reveals another, less obvious text, or where the narrative is deliberately complicated by secrets and enigmas, things unsaid and voices unheard, we may begin to hear in these Silences the sounds of women "knocking." For good as well as ill, the association of women with Silence has become a richly commonplace formula in con-temporary theory. Mary Jacobus writes, in her essay "The Difference of View," that

> femininity itself—heterogeneity, Otherness—becomes the repressed term by which discourse is made possible. The feminine takes its place with the absence, silence, or incoherence that discourse represses.[12]

Similarly, in an essay called "Is There Such a Thing as Women's Writing?" Xavière Gauthier writes that

> blank pages, gaps, borders, spaces and silence . . . emphasize the aspect of feminine writing which is the most difficult to verbalize because it becomes compromised, rationalized, masculinized as it explains it-self.[13]

Both passages imply a choice, where Silence entails a negation of speech. On the one hand, to make Sense of "spaces and silence" is to compromise them. On the other hand, if "spaces and silence" are not hedged about with rational and verbalized thought, they must remain unexplained and always on the outside of language. It seems that women are faced with a choice between two versions of an all too familiar defeat: they should either be Silent or come to their Senses.

However, Gauthier herself does suggest an alternative to making this choice when she writes:

> If . . . "replete" words *(mots pleins)* belong to men, how can women speak "otherwise," unless, perhaps, we can *make audible* that which

agitates within us, suffers silently in the *holes of discourse,* in the unsaid, or in the non-sense.[14]

It might be possible, in Gauthier's terms, to *"make audible"* without making "replete" that agitation and suffering which the "non-sense" of women bespeaks. It is necessary that the Silence which especially belongs to women be protected *by* them, even while they themselves refuse to be protected *in* it. The text which articulates this dilemma is a text which is in difficulty, a text which needs both to suppress and to protect its Silences.

*Sense and Sensibility* is a novel in which the Silences of two women are made powerfully *"audible."* The narrative is punctuated by their repeated but different refusals to speak. Elinor, on the side of Sense, withholds her words from considerateness for others, from a promise to keep their secrets, from admirable self-command, or occasionally from affronted intelligence, as when she refuses to pay Robert Ferrars "the compliment of rational opposition." Marianne, on the side of Sensibility, refuses to speak because she is careless of social proprieties, because she will not compromise the truth for politeness' sake, or because the strength of her feeling defies representation in words. Broadly, the Silences of Elinor are those of reserve and integrity; the Silences of Marianne are those of nonconformity and emotional powerlessness. While Elinor bravely suppresses the private language of her feelings, in order to engage in the public world of sometimes trivial and common Sense, Marianne retreats from that world into the serious and desperate privacy of her Sensibility. The main difference is that Elinor's Silences result from *self*-censorship— she listens "in silence and immovable gravity" to Robert Ferrars, for instance—but Marianne's do not. *Her* reticence is never resigned or heroic. It is either a sign of her indifference to the conversations of others, as when she refuses to give an opinion as to the respective heights of Harry Dashwood and William Middleton, because "she had never thought about it," or else it is a sign of the inexpressibility of her feelings. Marianne, after all, stands for the cause of Romanticism in this novel.

However, although both heroines retreat into Silence at various points, it is the Silence of Marianne which remains problematic, because it is not incorporated into the narrative, like Elinor's. Elinor's Silences have Austen's approval; they signify heroic reticence and control, and are contained by the language of Sense. Marianne's Silences signify emotions which have escaped control, and which are therefore in opposition to Austen's art. Marvin Mudrick writes that "Marianne represents an unacknowledged depth of her author's spirit."[15] I would add that this depth takes the form of a Silence which lies on the other side of the control of

Austen's language. Marianne's suppressed "scream" on receiving Willoughby's letter of repudiation, her growing depression and mental isolation, her decline into feverish raving and near-death—all these are covered by a fine veneer of understatement and qualification. By the end of the novel the divergence between the Sense of Austen's prose and the Silence of Marianne, which it throws into relief, has become painfully acute.

> Precious as was the company of her daughter to her . . . [Mrs Dashwood] . . . desired nothing so much as to give up its constant enjoyment to her valued friend; and to see Marianne settled at the Mansionhouse was equally the wish of Edward and Elinor. They each felt his sorrows and their own obligations, and Marianne, by general consent, was to be the reward of all.

The importance of what remains unspoken in Austen's works does not go unnoticed among critics. Barbara Hardy remarks that

> as we think of the busy social life in her novels and of the fully-occupied social lives of her characters, we also remember silence, solitude, isolation and privacy.[16]

However, with the possible exception of Tony Tanner,[17] they tend to concentrate on Elinor's self-censored story rather than on Austen's censorship of Marianne's. Gilbert and Gubar too stress the opposition between Marianne's shrill "indulgence in sensibility" and "Elinor's stoical self-restraint."[18] Somehow we are left with the impression that Sensibility makes more noise than Sense. But this is not entirely true. By a different reading, it is Marianne who retreats from social intercourse, refuses to pay polite visits, and is finally rendered speechless in misery and illness. Marianne, I want to claim, with a bias that goes contrary to the apparent sympathies of the author, is the place where the familiar dilemma of women, to speak or not to speak, is played out. The Silences of Marianne are those which her author most needs to censor and protect.

One of Austen's most interesting comments on the nature of the difference between her two heroines is given in the following passage:

> "What a sweet woman Lady Middleton is!" said Lucy Steele. Marianne was silent; it was impossible for her to say what she did not feel, however trivial the occasion; and upon Elinor therefore the whole task of telling lies when politeness required it, always fell.

*Sense and Sensibility* is usually interpreted as an argument of mind against heart, judgment against feeling, policy against spontaneity, Classicism against Romanticism, and, as a corollary of these, of reticence against self-expression. By this reading, Elinor's stoical reticence triumphs over

Marianne's naïve outbursts. But in this passage Austen seems to be saying something different. Here it is Elinor who has access to the language of polite "lies," while it is Marianne who remains silent. Sense has the privileges and powers of public speech, while Sensibility is a private and therefore powerless eloquence. The palimpsestic nature of this novel continually offers a choice of readings which depend on the angle of our gaze. In one light, Marianne's is merely an inconsequential adolescent drama, likely to be embarrassing for a time, but susceptible to cure. In another light, her long, if histrionic, misery challenges the conventions of polite lying.

The sensibility of Marianne, which, in its Romantic inheritance, represents what lies beyond the power of speech, is at once her prison and her weapon. Marianne defies the conventions of social intercourse because she is victimized by them, and her Silences speak against Sense because they are refused a hearing in the main text. This is not at first obvious, but it becomes so, as Austen's technique changes. At first her portrayal of Marianne relies on comic mockery and heavy irony. But as Marianne's feelings lose their fictionality and become true, Austen censors their expression by understating them, transferring them into mere physical illness, and finally by seeming to leave them altogether out of account.

At the start of the novel Austen's verbal exaggeration and irony serve to point the falsehood of the sentiments. Here she is still using the techniques of her earlier work, *Love and Freindship*, in which Laura is writing to one Marianne of the tragic events which cause her and her friend Sophia, who is "all Sensibility and Feeling," regularly to sigh and faint and rave and run mad. The ironic violence of this earlier work is echoed in some of the language used to describe the sensibility of Marianne in the later work. At the start, she is described as having an "excess" of "sensibility," and on having to leave Norland she and her mother encourage each other "in the violence of their affliction." Similarly, when Willoughby departs, Marianne is subject to a "violent oppression of spirits," and a "violence of affliction," which, the language clearly signals, are false. The idea of "violence" is usually too large for Austen's prose to contain it, and so it is presented only as exaggerated action or emotion. Violence such as Marianne's when Willoughby goes away is to be smilingly tolerated; Austen hedges it round with forbearing mockery. However, as Marianne's histrionic grief turns to very real humiliation, Austen ceases to use irony against her; she ceases to point out the comic disparities between her feelings and her reactions, and instead forces her heroine into a long retreat from language, as if to keep her protests at a safe distance. Marianne stifles her scream and at her lowest ebb raves incoherently. Her self-expression explores the furthest reaches from Sense.

The crisis of the novel is when Marianne receives Willoughby's cruelly explicit letter of repudiation. Elinor discovers her "stretched on the bed, almost choked by grief." Marianne thrusts a bundle of Willoughby's letters into Elinor's hands, and then, Austen writes, "covering her face with her handkerchief, almost screamed with agony." The word "almost," used twice in this short passage as a qualification of Marianne's actions, is crucial. It is as if the public language of Austen's prose can scarcely contain the violence of choking or screaming. But here, instead of mocking it with ironic exaggeration, she suppresses it. Marianne "*almost* screamed with agony." Such passion must be suppressed; her scream must not be heard. The language here acts out the actual event. The sound of screaming is stifled and silenced by polite understatement and circumspection and qualification. The word "almost" smothers the protest, imprisons the sound in the inarticulateness of mere Sensibility, and seems to assert the authority of rational control. The phrase magnificently enacts the whole drama of Marianne's rebellion in this novel. The more her protestations of grief must be concealed and contained by an enforced Silence of public propriety and passivity, the more eloquently violent does that Silence become.

This kind of linguistic censorship of Marianne's words and actions continues throughout the second part of the novel. When Mrs. Jennings hands Marianne a letter which for a moment she desperately believes to be from Willoughby, but quickly discovers to be from her mother, Austen writes of her:

> The cruelty of Mrs. Jennings no language, within her reach in her moments of happiest eloquence, could have expressed; and now she could reproach her only by the tears which streamed from her eyes with passionate violence. . . .

The authenticity of this later "violence" of feeling in Marianne is conveyed by the wordlessness to which it reduces her. There is no falsifying "eloquence" in her response. Instead, she is trapped in "Sensibility," in a prison which gives no access to the language of articulate protest, but the Silence of which is now resonant and violent. Such "passionate violence" is no longer of the surface but of the depths, and the sign of it is a kind of speechlessness which is not only Marianne's but also Jane Austen's.

The narrative turning point of the novel is Marianne's illness, which takes her to the brink of madness and death. But characteristically this event too is a drama of language. Marianne's speech during this illness becomes almost entirely unintelligible; it takes the form of "frequent but inarticulate sounds of complaint." The avenging specter of her long unhappiness is a language so alienated and private that it becomes almost entirely inaccessible to others. She shows a "feverish wildness," her "ideas" are "fixed incoherently on her mother," and Elinor fears never again to see her "rational." Such uncharacteristic melodrama in the main plot is not easily explained in ironic or moral terms, those two Senses for which Austen is famed. For Marianne's decline into near insanity and death is prompted by the trivial event of a solitary walk. The real cause of her decline is evaded in Austen's main plot, but it is hinted at in the language she uses to describe Marianne's escapade. Once again Austen's Sense seems to slant into Silences.

Here is the passage in which she describes the cause of Marianne's illness:

> Two delightful walks on the third and fourth evenings of her being there, not merely on the dry gravel of the shrubbery, but all over the grounds, and especially in the most distant parts of them, where there was something more of wildness than in the rest, where the trees were the oldest, and the grass was the longest and wettest, had—assisted by the still greater imprudence of sitting in her wet shoes and stockings— given Marianne a cold so violent . . .

Austen teasingly implies that Marianne's Romantic propensity for the superlative, for the "oldest" trees, the "longest and wettest" grass, is rightly punished by a cold. However, as that cold develops and worsens, bringing Marianne to the brink of death, this seemingly innocuous escapade acquires connotations that are perhaps not so trivial. It foreshadows a parallel occasion in *Mansfield Park* where Maria Bertram will not wait for Mr. Rushworth to bring his key, and with it "authority and protection," but instead, with Henry Crawford's help, negotiates the iron gate into the park. "I think it might be done," he urges, "if you really wished to be more at large, and could allow yourself to think it not prohibited." Here the event clearly foreshadows their more serious infringement of what is "prohibited" toward the end of the novel. In the case of Marianne, the analogy to some more serious crime is totally suppressed in terms of plot, but still hinted at in the language. Once again it is her characteristic "imprudence" which urges her to cross some hidden boundary and to trespass in that territory which lies beyond the social—"where there was something more of *wildness*." The boundary is internal and moral, of course, but it becomes evident in Austen's language as the boundary to excess. What Austen refuses to explain here, either in narrative or moral terms, is still "audible" if we are attuned to her Sense.

I suggest that this incident is related to another seemingly unexplained element in the book: that unnecessary and stagy subplot which tells of the fates of the two Elizas, and which is narrated by Colonel Brandon. Despite the unlikely melodrama of the two stories, their facts remain curiously unmemorable to the reader. One of the reasons for this might be Colonel Brandon's embarrassment and confusion when he tells them to Elinor. Another, I suggest, is Austen's own need to distance their implications from the main narrative. The first Eliza was "an orphan," brought up with Colonel Brandon; she is tricked on the eve of her elopement with him and forced to marry his brother, whom she subsequently leaves for another. Having been abandoned by this lover, and given birth to his child, she sinks into prostitution, debt, imprisonment, and death by consumption. The second Eliza is her child, who, in spite of Brandon's custody, is seduced and abandoned like her mother, by no other than Willoughby.

I suspect that these two stories are not interpolated just for the sake of contrast or sensation. Although Marianne is not in fact seduced and does not in fact die, her passion for Willoughby, and subsequent illness when he jilts her, are shot through with implications which Austen seems at pains to emphasize in the subplot. Marianne's own story begins with a fall, a fall which occurs on another imprudent walk, and she falls practically at Willoughby's feet—or, in Austen's own more tactful phrase, "within a few yards" of him. In the case of the first Eliza, the "fall" is figurative; it is a "fall" from virtue which results in the surprisingly explicit facts of pregnancy, prostitution, debt, imprisonment, and eventual death by consumption. But there are points at which Austen seems at pains to insure that her reader does not miss the connection:

> "Your sister, I hope, cannot be offended," said he, "by the resemblance I have fancied between her and my poor disgraced relation. Their fates, their fortunes cannot be the same. . . ."

Colonel Brandon generally protests too much, especially as he goes on to tell the tale of the younger Eliza, whose affection for Willoughby is "as strong, still as strong" as Marianne's own. Austen's purpose is not just to warn, or to emphasize Willoughby's unregenerate nature; it is also to suggest another writing of Marianne's story, for which her reader would have been prepared. As Marilyn Butler writes, "Mrs. West, Mrs. Hamilton, or the young Maria Edgeworth—would almost certainly have had Marianne seduced and killed off, after the errors of which she has been guilty."[19] (Austen's punishments, however, take a different form.) But an analogy between Marianne and the younger Eliza continues to link the two stories. Toward the end, the sight of Marianne laid low in sickness inevitably reminds Colonel Brandon yet again of "that resemblance between Marianne and Eliza already acknowledged, and now strengthened by the hollow eye, the sickly skin, the posture of reclining weakness, and the warm acknowledgment of peculiar obligation." The figure of the fallen woman seems to haunt the imagination of Colonel Brandon, and in the confusion of his mind's eye there might be written, behind the text as we have it, another story, another novel.

However, *Sense and Sensibility* purports to be a story of eventual recovery and happiness, a story which moves from innocent Sensibility to experienced Sense. Thus Austen's version of the female Awakening goes contrary to our post-Romantic expectations. Instead of coming to understand the thwarted sexual nature of her own sensibility, Marianne must grow out of her private and exclusive love for Willoughby and come to accept marriage based on "no sentiment superior to strong esteem and lively friendship." She awakens into a knowledge of herself which is that commanded by the society around her, and which is also that of Austen's curt and realist prose at the end. Marianne's development from love to "lively friendship," from illness to health, from egocentric Sensibility to conforming Sense, also takes the form of a development from private inarticulateness to public speech.

There is an interesting episode after Marianne's recovery, in which she and Elinor return to the place of her first fall. She says:

> "There, exactly there"—pointing with one hand, "on that projecting mound,—there I fell; and there I first saw Willoughby."

But the sign of her recovery comes a few lines later, where she admits to Elinor, "I *can* talk of it now, I hope, as I ought to do." While her fall has taken the form of a lapse into Silence, inarticulateness, and raving, her recovery and reintegration in society through marriage take the form of submission to the prescribed language of conventional morality: "I *can* talk of it now . . . as I ought to do." The reaction against sentimentalism and the novel of sensibility in the late eighteenth century, of which Austen is a prime example, usually works by a reassertion of "the ethical sense" against "unlimited toleration"[20] and sympathy. For Austen, however, "the ethical sense" is no more (and no less) than conformity to a certain public language. Unlike her two surrogates, Marianne *does* return to the public world of community, respectability, and Sense. She returns from Silences and learns to "talk." . . . Or does she?

As in so many of her novels, Austen's conclusion in *Sense and Sensibil-*

*ity* is perfunctory and swift. However, it is precisely in these last pages, in her *envoi* to her once Romantic heroine, in her detached and public tidying of events, and in her tone of realism and worldly wisdom, that Austen's Silences become deafening. At the point where she most ruthlessly claims the victory of Sense, she undermines that victory with a host of things unsaid. Let me quote once again those passages in which the future of Marianne becomes assured:

> . . . to see Marianne settled at the Mansion-house was equally the wish of Edward and Elinor. They each felt his [Colonel Brandon's] sorrows and their own obligations, and Marianne, by general consent, was to be the reward of all.
> With such confederacy against her . . . what could she do?
>
> . . .
>
> Colonel Brandon was now as happy as all those who best loved him believed he deserved to be; in Marianne he was consoled for every past affliction . . . and that Marianne found her own happiness in forming his was equally the persuasion and delight of each observing friend.

These last passages seem to be about the need for an affectionate, respectable, appropriate marriage; about Marianne's reconciliation with family and friends; about a "sensible" kind of happiness. But again, to read the text like a palimpsest, with an ear attuned to its Silences, is to begin to suspect that this tone of realism, like so much of the public speech of Austen's novel, only works as a polite lie. If Marianne is freed from the prison of her own sensibility at the end, it is only to be crowded out by the voices of all her well-wishing friends. We are told of *their* feelings, beliefs, persuasions, and delights. But behind this bustle of public opinion Marianne, it seems, has once more nothing to say. Having learned to "talk," it seems that at this crucial moment in her life she is to have no voice. Marianne has learned, through long trial and suffering, to be Silent.

It is this secretiveness which characterizes Austen's deceptive and ironic style. The point about irony is that it always tells either more or less than the truth, and therefore requires that the reader be constantly attuned to that meaning which slips the evidence of words. That which slips the evidence of these, Jane Austen's last words, is Marianne herself. Austen's irony forbids the reader to take any act or speech at face value, and is characteristic of an art that shows language itself to be a suspect social institution. For much of the dialogue of her novel has been a cunning exploration of how the spoken word does not quite match the speaker's intention, or else of how the commonly expressed opinion fails to match the truth. It forces us to read the text as many-leveled, rather than as linear. At the end, the truth of Marianne's feelings is totally ousted behind the convenience of happiness among friends and family. Once again Austen's language conceals and suppresses, as she linguistically impersonates their tyrannical wills and wishes. Their "persuasion and delight" are thinly disguised weapons, by which a "confederacy" of well-wishers enforces "happiness" on Marianne. She is victim to their "general consent," and her feelings are referred to Silence once more. This Silence, which in the past expressed her rebellion and defiance and uncompromising Sensibility, has now become the penalty which society exacts in order to proclaim its own common-Sense version of the happy ending. It seems, after all, that Marianne's story was only a choice of Silences.

Thus I return to the dilemma of "the feminine," which Mary Jacobus summarizes when she writes:

> The feminine takes its place with the absence, silence, or incoherence that discourse represses . . . [adding that] here again there's a problem for feminist criticism. Women's access to discourse involves submission to phallocentricity, to the masculine and the Symbolic; refusal, on the other hand, risks re-inscribing the feminine as a yet more marginal madness or nonsense.[21]

The answer must be not to choose, but to play out the choice: the choice of making Sense or keeping Silences. This is the choice which Austen's ironic and deceptive language continually dramatizes, and which is played out in the story of Marianne. For Marianne escapes from the marginalized language of Sensibility only to be tamed and punished by the public language of Sense. What appears to be, on the surface of the narrative, an escape from her own vulnerability, or a growth into knowledge and experience, is in fact only a more absolute affirmation of the social irrelevance of her voice. "With such confederacy against her . . . what could she do?" While for a time Marianne uses Silence as an outcry and a violation of proper speech, by the end it is used against her, to reaffirm the marginality of her place and of her speech: "that Marianne found her own happiness in forming his was equally the persuasion and delight of each observing friend." Silences, in this novel, represent the protest of "the feminine," but also, in the end, her punishment. Jane Austen's greatness lies in the fact that, beneath her artistic championing of Sense, she can make us *hear* those Silences that always lie on the other side of it.

*Angela Leighton*
*University of Hull*

# NOTES

1. Jacques Derrida, "Differance," in *Speech and Phenomena: And Other Essays on Husserl's Theory of Signs*, trans. David B. Allison (Evanston: Northwestern University Press, 1973), p. 129.
2. Tillie Olsen, *Silences* (London: Virago, 1980), p. 8.
3. Ibid., p. 39.
4. Frederick G. Kenyon, ed., *The Letters of Elizabeth Barrett Browning* (New York: Macmillan, 1899), 2 vols. in one, I:230.
5. George Steiner, *Language and Silence: Essays 1958–1966* (London: Faber and Faber, 1967), p. 69.
6. Ibid., p. 72.
7. Ibid., p. 71.
8. Sylvia Plath, "The Courage of Shutting Up," in *Winter Trees* (London, Boston: Faber, 1975), p. 20.
9. Samuel Beckett, *The Unnamable*, in *Molloy, Malone Dies, The Unnamable* (London: John Calder, 1959), p. 412.
10. Pierre Macherey, *A Theory of Literary Production*, trans. Geoffrey Wall (London, Henley, Boston: Routledge & Kegan Paul, 1978), p. 85.
11. Jacques Lacan, *The Language of the Self: The Function of Language in Psychoanalysis*, trans. Anthony Wilden (New York: Dell, 1968), p. 71.
12. Mary Jacobus, "The Difference of View," in *Women Writing and Writing about Women* (London: Croom Helm; New York: Barnes & Noble, 1979), p. 12.
13. Xavière Gautier, "Is There Such a Thing as Women's Writing?" in *New French Feminisms: An Anthology*, ed. Elaine Marks and Isabelle de Courtivron (Amherst: University of Massachusetts Press, 1980), p. 164.
14. Ibid., p. 163.
15. Marvin Mudrick, "Irony and Convention Versus Feeling," in B. C. Southam, ed., *Jane Austen: Sense and Sensibility, Pride and Prejudice and Mansfield Park: A Casebook* (London, Basingstoke: Macmillan, 1976), p. 114.
16. Barbara Hardy, *A Reading of Jane Austen* (London: University of London, Athlone Press, 1979), p. 21.
17. Tony Tanner, "Secrecy and Sickness in *Sense and Sensibility*," in *Casebook*, ed. Southam, pp. 131–46. I am indebted to this introduction for first analyzing the importance of silence in the novel.
18. Sandra M. Gilbert and Susan Gubar, *The Madwoman in the Attic: The Woman Writer and the Nineteenth-Century Literary Imagination* (New Haven and London: Yale University Press, 1979), p. 156.
19. Marilyn Butler, *Jane Austen and the War of Ideas* (Oxford: The Clarendon Press, 1975), p. 189.
20. Ibid., p. 23.
21. Jacobus, p. 12.

# The Language of Supposing
## Modal Auxiliaries in *Sense and Sensibility*

$G$iven Jane Austen's fondness for balanced verbal pairs—sense and sensibility, pride and prejudice—it is perhaps not inappropriate for me to propose another such set for discussion, namely, the actual and the hypothetical. The actual has to do with existing states of affairs, with the way the world in fact is as distinct from our wishes, desires, and suppositions. However much philosophers may argue about the external world, the actual is very real for Austen. Estates are unfairly entailed. Young men are engaged elsewhere. Uncles arrive unannounced to abort theatricals. Worse yet, uncles die (as in *Sense and Sensibility*) and leave their estates contrary to everyone's expectations. Every novel of hers turns at the beginning on a dislocation in the world, either a marriage or a death, an arrival or departure.

In addition, the books pulse with the small details of life. Think of the sides of pork and bushels of apples that go from Hartfield and Donwell Abbey to the Bateses. Think of the ribbons that are purchased, the wedding cake that is consumed. Consider Mrs. Allen's careful inventory of every new hat and gown that is to be seen in Bath, or Elizabeth Bennet's much remarked-upon muddy skirts. The sense of the circumstantial is so strong that critics have been tempted to see Jane Austen very much as the careful recorder of particulars, the acute historian of a world she knew so well. Caroline Mercer, for example, in the "Afterword" to the Signet edition of *Sense and Sensibility*, quotes from the *Letters* to underscore Austen's devotion to detail and desire to ground her fiction in fact:

> If you could discover whether Northamptonshire is a country of Hedgerows, I should be glad again.[1]

This view is not wrong. At the same time we know there is another Jane Austen, who is as much concerned with how people ought to behave

142

as she is with hedgerows. Presumably this is the Austen that F. R. Leavis had in mind when he cited her as the progenetrix of the Great Tradition, because of her "intensely moral preoccupation."[2] Leavis, too, is right. Although he is maddeningly evasive about what a "moral preoccupation" would entail, we recognize intuitively what he means about Austen. The question is how to put it into words.

Maybe one way to begin is with the hypothetical, with the world of supposition and desire as opposed to the world of hedgerows and apples. In this world we find the comic figures—like Mr. Woodhouse or Mrs. Jennings or Sir John Middleton—who are comic precisely because they are always busily remaking the actual to suit their assumptions. For Mr. Woodhouse, Mrs. Weston is forever "poor Miss Taylor." Mrs. Jennings is forever assuming that possible engagements are real ones, and Sir John insists that events "must and shall" be as he wishes them. They are incorrigible. But even misguided heroines fall into the same temptation, and the happy endings present us not only with suitable marriages but with a presumably reformed Catherine Morland or Emma Woodhouse or Marianne Dashwood now prepared to deal with things as they are. Yet who has not harbored the suspicion that young girls, even heroines, are not so easily rehabilitated? And what of the multitude of other fiction-makers in the novels? Who can assume that human nature is so malleable, so easily subdued to the exigencies of the actual? Certainly not Jane Austen.

The picture of Jane Austen as the judgmental narrator who delivers the main characters from error, leaving the minor ones forever mired in their delusions, and then steps in to tell us in a magisterial way how people ought to behave is no more adequate than the picture of her as an ironic miniaturist, simply sketching human foibles for our amusement. Yet, as everyone has noticed, her language *is* the language of judgment. There is scarcely a page that doesn't abound with "musts," "oughts," "shoulds," "coulds"—in fact, the whole range of modals, that peculiar set we were taught to call "helping verbs" in grammar school.[3]

If we begin, then, with her language and specifically with her use of modal auxiliaries, perhaps we can arrive at a more subtle, more modulated view of Austen. The etymology of the word "modal" is itself unclear but provocative. It comes either from the Old English *mod* for "mind" or from the Latin *modus* meaning "manner," or conceivably from both. The Old English and the Latin are not so different as to pose difficulties, for one could easily regard modals as reflecting the manner of the mind. They are the language of what I have called "the hypothetical"—of reflection, supposition, deliberation, judgment, in contrast to matters of fact.

The first question to consider is who uses modals in Austen. And the answer to that is easy: everyone uses modals,[4] Mr. Knightley as well as Emma, Elinor Dashwood as well as Sir John. There is hardly a conversation anywhere in the novels that doesn't revolve around what someone believes might be, should be, must be. And conversely, there is surprisingly little talk of the actual, of what was or is,[5] except as a point of departure for speculation, and that of course brings us back to the realm of the hypothetical (the modal).

Consider, for instance, the conversation between Mr. and Mrs. Dashwood in Chapter 2 of *Sense and Sensibility*. The actuality here is that John promised at his father's deathbed to take care of his stepmother and half-sisters. Now, at leisure, with the dead buried, Mr. and Mrs. Dashwood consider whether three thousand pounds would constitute reasonable care. Mrs. Dashwood is an expert at hypothetical deliberations of this sort.

> How *could* he rob his child, and his only child, too, of so large a sum?
> And what possible claim *could* the Miss Dashwoods . . . have. . . .[6]

John's answer—that it was his father's wish—is easily countered by her. He could not have meant them to give away half their fortune (which, needless to say, it is not). Yes, concedes John,

> "Perhaps it *would* have been as well if he had left it wholly to myself.
> He *could* hardly suppose I *should* neglect them. But as he required the
> promise, I *could* not do less than give it: at least I thought so at the
> time. The promise . . . *must* be performed. Something *must* be
> done." . . .

Mrs. Dashwood seizes the opportunity to remind him that money, once gone,

> never *can* return. . . . Your sisters *will* marry . . . the time *may* come
> [when] it *would* be a very convenient addition.

"It *would*," John echoes.

The discussion goes on like this for five pages, full of "woulds," "coulds," and "mays" with which Mrs. Dashwood sketches various possible scenarios, all of which augur doom for them and prosperity for Marianne and Elinor, only to conclude with a series of "cans," "wills," and "musts" which assert a happy ending for all if they do nothing. John is easily turned around. He never needed much convincing—a paragraph would have sufficed to disinherit the women—but who could cut short such a delicious scene of self-interest masquerading as disinterested deliberation?

I have focused on this scene because it provides the clearest example of what modals can do—not to mention what people can do with modals. They allow us to talk about the nonliteral, for they constitute the world of possibility, in this particular case the unsavory world of self-justifying fictions. And we do find in Austen, in *Sense and Sensibility* and elsewhere, that the foolish, the selfish, the manipulative are those most prone to fall into modal language, since they are forever reshaping the facts to match their desires. Sir John Middleton, for example, while miles beyond the Dashwoods in generosity, is just as bent as they upon remaking the world to conform to his will. Consider his response when it appears that the trip to Whitwell must be canceled because of Colonel Brandon's sudden departure.

> "We *must* go," said Sir John. "It *shall* not be put off when we are so near it. You *cannot* go to town till to-morrow, Brandon, that is all."

Here modals serve for what we surely read as imperatives. But whereas imperatives are direct expressions of will, the modals simply report *that* an imperative exists. Thus Sir John's "cannots" and "shall nots" and "musts" tend to mask (although very thinly in this case) the crudely willful nature of his outburst. They transform subjective desire into objective grounds, "I want you to stay" into "It is absolutely necessary that you stay." When Colonel Brandon proves recalcitrant, Sir John reluctantly assents to his going. Indeed, he could hardly do otherwise. But lest we should think that he has learned any lessons in submission, Sir John immediately begins planning the colonel's return. "He *must* and *shall* come back," he declares.

The covert willfulness expressed by modal language is not exclusively the mark of comic characters, however. We find even Elinor sounding very much like Sir John when, in reply to her mother's question about Willoughby, "Do you suppose him really indifferent to her?" she says, "No, I *cannot* think that. He *must* and does love her. I am sure." The certainty of that "I am sure" is illusory. We can be sure that there are or are not hedgerows in Northamptonshire, but our inferences about other minds are not similarly verifiable. Mrs. Dashwood is righter than she knows in asking "Do you suppose," for that is precisely what they are doing. And Elinor's answer is curiously evasive, for all its positiveness. After all, "I cannot think that" does not mean that she doesn't, and "He must love her" doesn't mean that he does. Binding as they are, "can" and "must" apply only to what is possible or necessary in an ideal world; they do not ensure the actual—in this case, the condition of Willoughby's heart. Finally, Elinor is invoking a hypothetical (and just) order in which lovers love where they ought, and appearances are not deceiving. She is as prone as Sir John or her contemptible brother- and sister-in-law to fictionalizing, creating scenarios in which events match her wishes.

The sensible characters, it turns out, are not much more immune to the charms of the hypothetical than the most self-indulgent wishful thinkers. One finds surprisingly little difference in the use or the frequency of their modals. Elinor, Edward, and Colonel Brandon use as many as Marianne or Sir John or Mrs. Jennings does, and all of them use modals to invoke nonactual worlds (some more pleasing or plausible than others) which instantiate and objectify their desires. Evidently, the distinction between Elinor and Marianne, or, for that matter, between Edward, the supposed literalist, and Marianne, the emotionalist, is less sharp than the contrastive "and" of the title suggests, at least insofar as their language is concerned.

Elinor is presumably the model of sense. She does none of the foolish things Marianne does in the name of love—no passionate letters or secret visits to ancestral houses for her. She never abandons herself to her feelings when her lover fails her, and, unlike Marianne, she is never publicly distraught. Moreover, Elinor doesn't seek out occasions for self-dramatization. She abjures poetical farewells and picturesque vistas, all opportunities for modal language. In contrast, Marianne savors such moments. "Oh! happy house," she exclaims on leaving Norland,

> "*could* you know what I suffer . . . I *may* view you no more . . . but you *will* continue the same. No leaf *will* decay . . . although we *can* observe you no longer . . . but who *will* remain to enjoy you?"

Marianne's posturing here is closely akin to her love of the picturesque, as becomes clear in her exchange with Edward about the picturesqueness of Barton Valley.

> "Look up at it and be tranquil if you *can*."
> "It is a beautiful country," he replied; "but these bottoms *must* be dirty in winter."
> "How *can* you think of dirt with such objects before you?"
> "Because," replied he, smiling, "among the rest of the objects before me, I see a very dirty lane."

Although this exchange appears to set up a clear-cut opposition between the literal and the imaginative, there is something more subtle going on: Edward is revealed to be less wooden and more fallible than one might guess. He sees the dirty road only partly, as he claims, because it's there. In fact, he, too, selects, focusing on the dirt because Marianne doesn't, and because he is low in spirits and in no mood to be shown the splendors of anything. So he offers his own projection to counter hers. His answer that the bottoms "must" be dirty in winter is no more an account of the actual than is her poeticizing. It is, rather, another hypothetical version, as the inferential "must" indicates.

In a slightly less fractious mood, Edward continues:

> "I shall call hills steep which *ought* to be bold; surfaces strange and uncouth which *ought* to be irregular and rugged; and distant objects out of sight which *ought* to be indistinct."

It is clear that Edward sees the picturesque as connected with a series of modal prescriptions, and the "oughts" of Marianne's doctrine offend him. What is less clear is the way in which Edward himself is using those same modals to argue unfairly. His characterization—hills that *ought* to be bold and surfaces that *ought* to be irregular—places the obligation squarely on the natural scene to behave as Marianne wishes, and although there is surely some truth in this parody, the "oughts" are, after all, Edward's misrepresentation and not hers.

Elinor herself is, in private, less sensible than one might expect. She is all too willing to construct arguments to rationalize Edward's behavior, which she continually contrasts favorably with Willoughby's. Looked at from the outside, it seems open to question whether there is so sharp a division between the two men as Elinor makes. If Willoughby makes love to Marianne and then drops her for a provident marriage, Edward too engages Elinor's affections although he cannot hope to wed her. Nor is he discreet. In his quiet way he makes his preference as public as Willoughby does his, with the additional consideration that Edward is *engaged,* while Willoughby is at least free. Yet rarely does Elinor seriously blame Edward. Quite the contrary. At the beginning of Book II, having heard Lucy's astonishing secret, she is "at liberty to think and be wretched." And liberty she takes. She cannot doubt the truth of the engagement, "supported as it was . . . by such probabilities and proofs, and contradicted by nothing but her own wishes." Nevertheless, she manages to envision a state of affairs very different from that described by Lucy. In a long introspective flight, full of hypotheses about how "it might have been," "it ought to be," she persuades herself that

> his affection was all her own. She *could* not be deceived in that . . . the youthful infatuation of nineteen *would* naturally blind him . . . but the four succeeding years . . . *must* have opened his eyes. . . .

Although Elinor tries hard to separate the reality from her own "wishes," she manages, against all internal warnings about persuasion, to persuade herself of what she wants to believe.

It appears that all of us, even Elinor, live rather more than we admit in modal rather than actual worlds. And one lesson of *Sense and Sensibility*, like that of *Northanger Abbey* or *Emma*, seems to be that we must give up these imaginary realms to take up firmer residence in the here and now. But Austen's view is not so simple, nor are modals so avoidable. Modals can be used to serve the ends of false reason precisely because they are fundamentally the language of all reasoning. And the most important lesson to be learned from Austen is not that some people are deluded, or even that all people are deluded, but that hypothesis, inference, supposition are what John Searle calls ground-floor properties of the human mind.

Almost everyone in *Sense and Sensibility* at some point considers the question of what would constitute right reasoning, even those least likely to act on that knowledge. The most amazing people invoke rationality. Marianne judges her mother's decision that they remain in London "to be entirely wrong, formed on mistaken grounds," and when Elinor assures Willoughby that Marianne "has long forgiven you," he objects, "Then she has forgiven me before she ought. . . . But she shall forgive me again, and on more reasonable grounds." Elinor criticizes her mother and Marianne because "with them, to wish was to hope, and to hope was to expect," only to have her own cautious skepticism called into question by Mrs. Dashwood, who asks, quite reasonably, "Are no probabilities to be accepted merely because they are not certainties?"

Accurate or not, the hypothetical is an inescapable mode (and inescapably modal) in a world where there are many more probabilities than certainties, and in actual life thought and discourse turn less on empirically verifiable statements like "The cat is on the mat" than on modal ones about unobservable things like causes, reasons, states of mind. Even as the talk ranges from trifling subjects like Mrs. Dashwood's intended remodeling to serious discussions of Edward's future, or Marianne's possible engagement, it involves the same processes of supposing and speculating about what someone might do, will do, ought to do. If Mr. and Mrs. Dashwood's vision of their own poverty on several thousands a year and their relations' affluence on several hundred serves as an ironic instance, other conversations equally full of modals need to be taken seriously.

As an illustration, here is Colonel Brandon speculating about what Edward will do now that he has offered him a living. Brandon does not

> suppose it possible that the Delaford living *could* supply such an income as any body in his style of life *would* venture to settle on . . . "This little rectory *can* do no more than make Mr. Ferrars comfortable . . . it *cannot* enable him to be married. . . . What I am now doing . . .

*can* advance him so little toward what *must* be his principal . . . object of happiness. His marriage *must* still be . . . distant . . . it *cannot* take place very soon. "

Brandon's assessment of the situation is not inaccurate, as Edward and Elinor later confirm when considering whether the income will suffice for them. (It won't.) Unlike the Dashwoods, Brandon is neither self-interested nor rationalizing reluctance in saying he would do more if he could. About Edward's actual eagerness to marry, both the reader and the colonel may harbor some doubts. But Brandon is reasoning theoretically; his argument rests not on Edward's real feelings, but on a (not incorrect) supposition about what men of his class should feel and would do, what Edward himself would undoubtedly have done if Lucy had not conveniently defected. In other words, Brandon is not discussing what the facts are (for Edward could easily choose to ignore all of the supposed difficulties and marry); he is outlining what *must* be the case if Edward behaves as he ought.

David Hume argued earlier in the century that it is impossible to derive an "ought" from an "is," that "oughts" occupy a separate realm derived from nonempirical premises, and Austen, in describing the way we reason, supports this. What one *does* is very different from what one might do, could do, or even must do. Conversely, "can" asserts global possibility without entailing its enactment. "I can call you" doesn't mean that I do; nor does "I might call" mean that I will; not even "must" entails necessity in the actual world. "If that's the noon whistle, it must be twelve o'clock" is a reasonable supposition, although the whistle may have gone off at eleven-thirty. Only in the mental realm of pure deduction, which exists independent of the empirical world, do "musts" hold absolutely—two and two must be four because we have priorly defined them that way, but that a man who is engaged ought to be in love is true only if we assume as the major premise that men always engage themselves honorably. Of course, that premise is not only a supposition, but one open, especially in Austen, to the gravest doubts.

The hypothetical and the actual, then, do not simply exist side by side in discrete realms; although distinct, they intersect, and we are constantly being asked to consider the connection (and often the disconnection) between the two. While surmising that it must be twelve o'clock because the noon whistle went off is legitimate enough, we need also ask whether the whistle went off when it ought—that is, we need to check the "ought" against the empirical question of whether it did. Now, figures like Mrs. Bennet rarely move from their fictive worlds into the actual. She never gives way on the subject of the entail and is saved from her refusal to acknowledge it only through the kindly offices of the novelist, who provides the rich suitors Mrs. Bennet has no reasonable right to expect. No one is quite so recalcitrant in *Sense and Sensibility* but, on the other hand, everyone is caught to varying degrees within the circle of his or her suppositions.

Consider, for example, how everyone in *Sense and Sensibility* handles one of the central questions in the book: Is Marianne engaged to Willoughby? No one seems to find it legitimate to cut the Gordian knot by asking Marianne how things stand. Elinor believes it is her mother's place to ask; Mrs. Dashwood feels that to ask would be an intrusion; Mrs. Jennings and Sir John simply assume an engagement; and Colonel Brandon is far too tactful to inquire—although perhaps he prefers speculation to certain knowledge.

Elinor, for one, works hard to shape her limited bits of information into a reasonable hypothesis and is the first to suspect that Marianne is not assured of Willoughby. After Willoughby's public rebuff, Elinor ponders the affair.

> That some kind of engagement has subsisted . . . she *could* not doubt . . . however Marianne *might* still feed her own wishes she *could* not. . . . Nothing but a . . . change of sentiment *could* account for it . . . absence *might* have weakened his regard, and convenience *might* have . . . overcome it, but that such a regard had . . . existed she *could* not bring herself to doubt.
>
> As for Marianne on the pangs, which so unhappy a meeting must . . . have given her, and . . . on those . . . which *might* await her . . . she *could* not reflect without deepest concern.

Elinor is quite correct in her suppositions; a change has taken place, and Marianne's suffering is real enough. Nevertheless, Elinor clings to a mistaken assumption in order to judge her sister less harshly, and both her sympathy and her inferences are founded on a false premise—that there was an engagement—a premise she surely knows enough of her sister's impetuous nature to question. She doesn't because she is reasoning less about the real Marianne than about what ought to be the case, supposing Marianne's behavior to be justified.

Elinor is clever and, like Emma Woodhouse later, she reasons well, but reasoning well is not enough, as Austen makes patently clear in *Emma* and suggests even in this earlier novel. At some point hypothetical constructs must touch base with the actual. If the literalness of the inexperienced Catherine Morland, who never speculates about anything until she is seduced by *Udolpho* and abused by the world, is no model for wisdom, neither is Emma's willful disregard of the actual lest it fail to confirm her scenarios. Elinor in contrast tries hard to avoid either of these extremes, and it is less her error than a mark of the fundamental fugitiveness of human knowledge that she too comes to imperfect assessments.

That reasonable sequences often turn out to be wrong is one of the great sources of irony in Austen's work, but it is important to understand that the irony derives less from faulty reasoning than from the collision between the smooth logic of hypothetical scenarios and the unpredictability of the actual world. For example, Miss Steele's account of Lucy and Edward's conversation realizes all of Colonel Brandon's earlier assumptions about money and marriage. Lucy has told Edward that "she *could* live with him upon a trifle and how little soever he *might* have she *should* be very glad . . ." They (Lucy and Edward) "talked for some time about what they *should* do and they agreed that he *should* take orders directly, and they *must* wait to be married. . . ." But of course none of this comes to pass, for Lucy is not about to wait or to be poor if she can help it.

Perhaps the highest comic dissonance between the hypothetical and the actual is achieved in those scenes where Lucy and Elinor play at being confidantes in a language filled with the politest and most tentative of modals, while each is very much aware of the other's real motives.[7] Elinor has surmised quite correctly that Lucy's revelations are directed at stinging her to jealousy while at the same time warning her to stay away from Edward. "What other reason for the disclosure . . . *could* there be but that Elinor *might* be informed . . . of Lucy's superior claims." Elinor on her part "*could* not deny herself the comfort of endeavoring to convince Lucy that her heart was unwounded." In a sequestered corner they chat. Lucy confesses that she feared she *might* have offended Elinor by her secret. "Offended me! How *could* you suppose so. . . . *Could* you have a motive for the trust that was not honourable and flattering to me?"—the answer to which, we all know, is yes, indeed, she can and does. Lucy proceeds to sketch a charming fictional version of her innocent and romantic attachment:

> I *could* give up every prospect . . . and *could* struggle with any poverty for him . . . we *must* wait, it *may* be for many years. With almost any other man . . . it *would* be an alarming prospect; but Edward's affection and constancy nothing *can* deprive me of, I know.

"That conviction *must* be everything to you" is Elinor's sweetly acid reply, while thinking to herself, "All this . . . is very pretty but it *can* impose on neither of us." The delicacy of these modals hardly needs to be demonstrated. If we substitute indicatives for the modals, we can see at once how the archness is lost as the insinuation becomes an assertion. We also see how dangerously confrontational the game becomes.

There is more than comedy to be gained by the modal language of supposition and more than wisdom about human reasoning to be learned. Society moves on these smoothly greased modal rails, and while hypothesis needs to be checked against the empirical world, acknowledging the actual too directly risks bringing the whole machine to a grinding halt. For instance, when Mrs. Jennings commits the ultimate gaucherie of openly referring to pregnancy, asking Colonel Brandon, "How does Charlotte do? I warrant you she is a fine size by this time," the colonel as a gentleman can only change the subject, hoping desperately, no doubt, that the size of a woman's belly is never again made the topic of polite conversation. With Elinor, too, the literal borders on the obscene when she defends Colonel Brandon against Marianne's charge of "infirmity." Taking the word in its literal, i.e., etymological sense, she assures Marianne that, aged as he "may appear . . . you can hardly deceive yourself as to his having the use of his limbs." These embarrassments of frankness only underscore the need for decorum and reticence, and among other things the indirect language of modals provides the very means of comfortable social intercourse.

The point is that modal language is neither the mark of the foolish and the willful nor strictly the sign of the self-reflective, although it certainly serves both of these functions. Beyond that, however, it is the language that binds human society together, the language that creates, both in the best and the worst sense, the fictions we live by. While reasoning rightly about others is at its best difficult, given our imperfect knowledge both of other minds and of our own, nevertheless, as Austen recognizes, human beings do (and probably must) make suppositions, perhaps even fictions, about the world in order to live in it, and that process, unideal yet inescapable, is reflected in the modal language of *Sense and Sensibility*. The gossip, the endless examination of trivia, the possible scenarios are all subcategories of deliberation. And deliberation is at the center of the novels—people reflecting on their own situations and those of others. Finally, it is the nature of thinking itself, hypothetical, suppositious, sometimes confusing desire with certainty, that we are being asked to consider, and I suspect this is what Leavis was responding to when he praised Austen's "intensely moral preoccupation," for her preoccupation is with the moral, not in the prescriptive sense of telling us (or her characters) what to believe or do, but in the wider sense of showing us how we come to decide these issues.

*Zelda Boyd*
*California State University, Hayward*

# NOTES

1. Jane Austen, *Sense and Sensibility*, with an afterword by Caroline G. Mercer (New York: New American Library, 1961), pp. 307ff.
2. F. R. Leavis, *The Great Tradition* (Garden City: Doubleday, 1954), p. 16.
3 Grammatically, modal auxiliaries constitute a finite syntactic set: "can"/ "could," "may"/might," "will"/"would," "shall"/"should," "must" and, with qualifications, "ought." These operate like the main auxiliaries, "be," "do," "have," in that the negative is attached directly to them and in the interrogative they are simply moved from the second to the first place in the sentence. But modals differ from the main auxiliaries (and are unique in English) because they are oddly morphologically defective. They don't inflect in the third person ("He eats," "He does eat," but not "He cans eat"); they have neither a present nor a past participle, nor a passive, nor an infinitive. Modals also form a semantic set, sharing the feature of what I have called the hypothetical, or nonactual. Where the other auxiliaries mark tense and/or aspect, modal auxiliaries mark certain nonindicative moods: possibility, necessity, obligation, permission. This is where philosophers pick up modals. Their concern is with conceptual notions like possibility or necessity, and while there are other ways of expressing these ideas (notably through adverbs— "maybe," "probably"—or through catenatives like "have to," or through subjective complements like "is possible" or "is a possibility"), the analysis of these concepts usually involves, especially in ordinary language philosophy, a discussion of the modal auxiliaries per se. Although one could certainly follow the philosophers and consider all kinds of modalized sentences, I have chosen to follow the traditional grammarians and consider specifically those sentences containing modal auxiliaries, partly as a convenient way of delimiting the topic, but, more important, because such sentences form so large a part of Austen's language.
4. Any writer who is much concerned with deliberation and possibility can be expected to use a highly modalized language. Henry James is an example. Conversely, the marked absence of modals also tells us something important about a writer's preoccupations. Hemingway, especially in the short stories, is in full flight from reflection and deliberation, and if we look at the places (there are not many of them) where modals do occur in his stories, we find that they are always connected with uncertainty and discomfort.
5. Notice that "will be" has been omitted from the temporal series, since the division hypothetical/actual places the future in the hypothetical domain. The etymology of the word "future"—from Latin "futūrus," meaning roughly "the about to be"—serves to corroborate this placement. Moreover, regarding the future as hypothetical is not only philosophically plausible, it also allows us to avoid the difficulties in English between "shall" and "will," both of which are used for the future, sometimes to make predictions about what is to come, sometimes to make declarations of intention about bringing it about. The conceptual distinctions between "shall" and "will" are real enough, but

for the purposes of this essay it is sufficient to see them both as expressions of the nonactual.

6. All quotations are from Jane Austen, *The Novels of Jane Austen*, ed. R. W. Chapman, 5 vols., 3rd edition (London: Oxford University Press, 1932–34, 1966). The italics here and hereafter are mine unless otherwise indicated.

7. It is hard these days to avoid the question of "women's language" when dealing with a woman writer. The fact that modals are sometimes used as politeness forms and/or to express tentativeness rather than assertion has invited speculation about whether modal language is not peculiarly feminine (if we think in terms of the traditional stereotypes). I do not think Austen offers support for this view. In the standard case, modals characterize not the language of reticence but the language of anyone concerned with reflection and deliberation, with what is possible or necessary. And this is certainly Austen's primary use of them. Moreover, her characters are, at their worst, more willful than polite; at their best, more deliberative than decorous. Not one of them exhibits "feminine" deference, either in language or behavior. In fact, unctuousness, the mark of fools like Mr. Elton or Mr. Collins or Miss Steele, is remarkably free from modals, not surprisingly, since the people never stop to think.

# "Pictures of Perfection" at Pemberley

## Art in *Pride and Prejudice*

In rewarding her heroine with Pemberley, Jane Austen certainly invites A. Walton Litz's theory that *Pride and Prejudice*[1] "supports the fine illusion that life itself can take on the discrimination and selectivity of art."[2] In fact, Austen uses the sister art of painting precisely to expose such an illusion. *Pride and Prejudice* laughs at perfection. To understand this we have to look at art in the novel, emblematized in its "pictures."[3] Austen not only makes informed use of the different symbolic suggestiveness of those two genres of portrait painting, the miniature and the full-size, but joins ranks with eighteenth-century English poets in clever exploitation of the technique of *ut pictura poesis* to structure an imaginary art gallery at Pemberley, and in Chapter III of Volume III to hang there a species of genre painting known as a "conversation piece." The corrective and consolatory function of these products of art, Austen with deliberate drama reserves for her last volume.

Chapter I of Volume III gives Elizabeth a fresh chance to form "first impressions," while correcting old ones. From the first sight of Pemberley, which Elizabeth views with a mind newly open to impressions, to her second meeting with the changed Darcy, she is bombarded with a series of stunning images, all expansive, lofty, elevating. Nature offers the "very large" park with its "great variety of ground," and the "beautiful wood stretching over a wide extent," through which Elizabeth and the Gardiners "ascended for half a mile" to find themselves "at the top of a considerable eminence"; architecture offers Pemberley House, itself "a large, handsome, stone building" placed advantageously "on rising ground, and backed by a ridge of high, woody hills," in front of which is "a stream of some natural importance . . . swelled into greater." As Darcy is forced into flexibility by Elizabeth's verbal resourcefulness, so

Elizabeth's mind is stretched by his aesthetic resourcefulness. At Pemberley she stops talking and looks with a new, finer receptiveness: "Elizabeth
was delighted," her "mind . . . too full for conversation" as "she saw and
admired every remarkable spot and point of view." At Rosings, Mr.
Collins had bored her by counting windows overlooking a bare prospect
at which Lady Catherine had exasperatingly forced her to look. At Pemberley, Elizabeth goes of her own volition "to a window to enjoy its
prospect"—and is accordingly rewarded.

Though Elizabeth had anticipated little worth seeing *in* the house, its
"large, well-proportioned" and "lofty, handsome rooms" prove to be an
art gallery of significant pictures, and views that compose themselves into
pictures. The latter is a painterly process A. Walton Litz has noted of
Jane Austen's technique in *Emma:* ". . . Emma stands for a moment at
leisure in the doorway of Ford's the draper, waiting for the scene to
compose itself like a picturesque sketch. . . ."[4] Studying the relationship
between the sister arts and eighteenth-century English poetry, Jean Hagstrum points to the poets' use of a "picture-gallery type of structure, in
which we move from scene to scene, tableau to tableau."[5] The"dining-
parlour" at Pemberley offers us tableau after tableau:

> They followed [the housekeeper] into the dining-parlour. It was a
> large, well-proportioned room, handsomely fitted up. Elizabeth, after
> slightly surveying it, went to a window to enjoy its prospect. . . . Every
> disposition of the ground was good; and she looked on the whole
> scene, the river, the trees scattered on its banks, and the winding of the
> valley, as far as she could trace it, with delight. As they passed into
> other rooms, these objects were taking different positions; but from
> every window there were beauties to be seen. . . . (p. 246).

The views are both Art and Nature, natural prospects composed into
pictures by the windows that frame them. The composition and recom-
position of these "pictures" corrects by expanding Elizabeth's point of
view. The painterly process is not solely the effect of her own movement
between the windows but results from the movement of the natural "objects" themselves as Austen actually animates them: "these objects were
taking different positions" so that "from every window there were
beauties to be seen."

Hagstrum suggests that in early prose romances "narrative form" came
to be "viewed as a series of tableaux. Reading a story would therefore be
like going through a gallery of paintings and statues. We move from scene
to scene, from image to image, from one plastic arrangement to another"
(pp. 32–33). This is precisely how Austen structures our reading process
in the Pemberley section of the novel, moving us from the "natural" art
gallery we have just been viewing (p. 246), into contemplation of an

arrangement of miniatures (pp. 247–249), to "the picture-gallery" with its "striking resemblance of Mr. Darcy" (pp. 250–51), and finally arresting us with a "conversation-piece" (pp. 267–68).

The miniatures form a central design which helps Elizabeth to correct her images of the two most "intricate" characters she has chosen to study. Austen here makes use of the commonly understood meaning of "miniature" as a "picture in little," to underscore the motif of shrinking and expanding images. But the very arrangement of the miniatures suspended on the mantel piece of the elder Darcy's room astonishes and puzzles Elizabeth, for it includes Wickham in intimate grouping with Georgiana and Darcy.[6] Hers is a silent drama of response in which no one else shares; since the others do not know the secret of the relationships between the "originals," they cannot suspect her emotions and necessary rearrangement of ideas. The author's own arrangement is to spread over several pages the discussion prompted by the viewing of the miniatures, thus achieving for Elizabeth a slow, believable process of forming new images:

> She approached, and saw the likeness of Mr. Wickham suspended, amongst several other miniatures, over the mantle-piece. Her aunt asked her, smilingly, how she liked it. The housekeeper came forward, and told them it was the picture of a young gentleman, the son of her late master's steward, who had been brought up by him at his own expense.—"He is now gone into the army," she added, "but I am afraid he has turned out very wild."
>
> Mrs. Gardiner looked at her niece with a smile, but Elizabeth could not return it. (p. 247)

After the expansive images of Darcy, Wickham's image at Pemberley has shrunk to miniature size. Mrs. Gardiner compounds the irony by unconsciously misplacing value on the wrong intimacy, diminishing Wickham with every smiling allusion meant to elevate him. To Elizabeth he is a disagreeable reflection of her own newly reduced self-image, reminding her of the indiscretion of her past partiality. Wickham's shrinking process is accelerated by the housekeeper's stressing his enormous debt to the family and his ingratitude for their intimacy in " 'turn[ing] out very wild.' "

Admitted into the intimacy of the elder Darcy's "favourite room," Elizabeth has learned that, despite Wickham's insinuations, Darcy has not tried to deny their relationship in his father's heart; he has kept the miniatures as they were during Mr. Darcy's lifetime. The miniatures, then, hang in a suggestive grouping, all together symbolic of Darcy's sustained respect for his father's feelings, separately rich in ironic suggestiveness about the relationships, past and present, of the three "originals." The miniature of Georgiana as a child reminds Elizabeth of Wickham's wicked design against her childish innocence, while Mrs. Reynolds' praise of Darcy as a good-natured child corrects her confirmed opinion that his is a "hateful" nature. For her private joke about Georgiana's Ramsgate escapade with Wickham, which their paired miniatures call to mind, she will be aptly punished when he seduces yet another fifteen-year-old child at another watering place, and it proves to be Lydia.

With unconscious irony, Mrs. Gardiner also calls for Elizabeth's opinion of Darcy's miniature (" 'But, Lizzy, you can tell whether it is like or not' "). Elizabeth both can and cannot. She can acknowledge the external likeness to be true: both miniature and man are "handsome." But she does not yet know the real Darcy the way she has come to know the real Wickham, and she no longer believes in what she so glibly suggested to Jane earlier, that for a young man to be handsome is sufficient. Now she will only admit to knowing him "a little." Mrs. Reynolds takes Darcy's character into her own hands. True to the aesthetic principles of the artist after whom she seems to have been ironically named, she disdains "the picture in little" and offers them "in the gallery up stairs . . . a finer, larger picture of him than this."[7] And not content with expanding her master's image through showing them the larger representation, Mrs. Reynolds "dwelt with energy on his many merits, as they proceeded together up the great staircase" toward the "picture gallery."

Making her way through ever increasing spaces, Elizabeth finds, in "reaching the spacious lobby above," the painting of Darcy:[8]

> At last it arrested her—and she beheld a striking resemblance of Mr. Darcy, with such a smile over the face, as she remembered to have sometimes seen, when he looked at her. She stood for several minutes before the picture in earnest contemplation, and returned to it again before they quitted the gallery. Mrs. Reynolds informed them, that it had been taken in his father's life time. (p. 250)

English writers had come to admire the painter's knowledge and techniques of rendering the psychology of character: Hagstrum observes that in England already in the seventeenth century "it was now widely acknowledged that the painter could . . . penetrate into the recesses of the heart and mind. It became highly stimulating to the literary artist to think that impalpable qualities could be represented instantaneously and economically (p. 122). If the "painter had but one moment of time" (p. 152) in which to communicate "psychological and moral reality" (p. 121), that moment, successfully rendered—and the artist of Darcy's portrait seems to have been successful—would have the dramatic power to "arrest" the viewer. Author and character in this novel seemingly have absolute faith in the truth-telling capacity of the portraitist. For though Elizabeth thinks that the language of art is not "intelligible" to the untaught, she has a naïve confidence in its power to make *character* intelligible. A novelist like Austen could exploit the power of the sister art through "inventing" such a psychologically resonant painting, one that could dramatically communicate in "several minutes" the correct alternative view to that which she has dramatized through two volumes. The smile on Darcy's face, in reminding us here of the many "smiling scenes" behind us, encourages a reinterpretation of the past.

In seeing that the "finer, larger picture" confirms the evidence of the miniature, we receive ironic confirmation of Mrs. Reynolds' principle that " 'they who are good-natured when children, are good-natured when they grow up.' " Something essential in character is not learned, but inherent, and persists through experience and design. Darcy had earlier hinted that every character has an ingrained flaw that resists being rooted out. What is here established is the consolatory side of that theory. Every character also has a *virtue* that no amount of design can flaw. What Elizabeth had thought to be an incurable evil in Darcy's character—"implacable resentment"—turns out instead to be an incurable virtue: good nature. The shrinking and expanding motif characteristic of the novel is sustained in the imagery and structure of the Pemberley episode. Miniature and full-scale portraits will forever emblematize for Elizabeth her opposing extremes—to shrink or to inflate—of subjective response to character.

Hagstrum suggests that "the increasing respect for pictorial expressiveness may have been related to the development in England of an indigenous school of portrait painting that was at once skillfully realistic and psychologically sophisticated. The presence in their midst of portraits by Van Dyck and Lely led poets to appreciate representations of the inner man on canvas" (p. 122). The discovery of the reality, the otherness of this "inner man" from her own creation for once shocks Elizabeth into the arrest of anticipation to deal with a present puzzle: "she stood for several minutes before the painting in earnest contemplation . . . and returned to it again before they quitted the gallery." In a refinement of her own inner state, she exchanges "a more gentle sensation towards the original" for the hardness of her habitual dislike and the keenness of her quick contempt. Newly generous, she "perfects" instead of depreciating, obscuring defects which before had riveted her critical attention—"remembered . . . warmth and softened . . . impropriety of expression." Under the stimulus of the painter's psychological skill, this is Elizabeth's first real study of character, "as she stood before the canvas, on which he was represented." Through art she is able for the first time to project another's point of view, indeed, to think about the process of someone else's viewing her.[9]

She now weighs Darcy's power to determine the quality of life. Pleasure or pain, good or evil, he can apparently choose, or even make, what she can only anticipate. Significantly, as she stands before his portrait, what she thinks of is Darcy's "power over happiness": "As a brother, a landlord, a master, she considered how many people's happiness were in his guardianship! How much good or evil must be done by him!" Measured by the real power for good of this smiling gentleman, her own schemes of guarded anticipation, with their superstitious, built-in defects to ward off evil designs have been but feeble fictions of control over present or future life. To be under such a guardianship is tempting. As she understands that other people's happiness has been bred into Darcy as a habitual responsibility, she finds it easier to forgive him for interfering in Bingley's affairs. Nina Auerbach has rightly pointed to this moment as concerned specifically with the *masculine* nature of Darcy's power.[10]

Very few gentlemen in eighteenth-century portraits smile—why does Darcy? Austen offers no other detail of comparable specificity to the smile in her portrait. What did she hope to accomplish through this extraordinary rendering of her hero? She establishes that the smile must be an essential part of Darcy's personality, for it is what the portraitist, looking for the individuating characteristic, chose to represent. And when Elizabeth admits the likeness of the portrait to the original in recognizing the smile, she confirms the soundness of the painter's insight.

This is preeminently a "social" portrait. Unlike the shy man of the ballroom who shrank proudly from an introduction, the man in the portrait seems so ready to enter into relationship that Elizabeth promptly responds by making him smile on *her*, for the first time exchanging good feelings with him. What nature had achieved earlier in making pleasing pictures for her, Elizabeth herself now advances when she attempts to make art become nature by making the man in the portrait smile on her. The trouble with the real Darcy had been that, having been made perfect through art, he had left that character, together with the responsibility for general smiling, at Pemberley, and grown unlike his own portrait.

The novel offers, in effect, a "Saturnine" and a "Jovial" portrait of Darcy,[11] the former primarily through the language and action of the first two volumes, the latter through Austen's use of the sister art of painting in the last volume. What is offensive in Darcy's behavior culminates in the Saturnine portrait. Elizabeth's verbal assault, prompted by Darcy's insultingly arrogant first proposal, is responsible for this angry portrait. He has come to her agitated, not because he fears rejection, but because he is confused by his own uncharacteristic excitement: " 'In vain have I struggled. It will not do. My feelings will not be repressed. You must allow me to tell you how ardently I admire and love you.' " The release from bounds is momentary. Darcy recovers his stateliness through the Van Dyck pose into which he arranges his limbs as he leans against the mantelpiece, complacently awaiting her response. It is violent. Elizabeth hurls her words at him as if they were missiles:

> Mr. Darcy, who was leaning against the mantle-piece with his eyes fixed on her face, seemed to catch her words with no less resentment than surprise. His complexion became pale with anger, and the disturbance of his mind was visible in every feature. He was struggling for the appearance of composure, and would not open his lips, till he believed himself to have attained it. The pause was to Elizabeth's feelings dreadful. (p. 190)

What we see through Elizabeth's eyes in the passage above is a species of living portrait contrasting dramatically with the actual portrait smiling at no one in particular at Pemberley. The passage demonstrates Austen's brilliant technique in the sister art: it is a speaking picture, the portrait of an aristocrat shocked from his conventional pose and assurance into immediate and intimate interaction with the viewer. Like the best of the eighteenth-century portrait-painters, Austen has been able on her canvas to capture the psychology of her subject through the rendering of his facial expression.

Of course, the angry portrait is partially created by the spectator's imperfect interaction with the subject: it is Elizabeth's rage that Darcy's face reflects. The "dreadful" moment while he struggles to internalize what he proudly thinks too painfully external frightens Elizabeth into doubt at the rightness of her open assault. But with her systematic rudeness she has succeeded in destroying his pose, forcing Darcy to "walk with quick steps" across the room, his control almost annihilated. Her influence on his physical as well as mental attitude has permanent consequences. When they next meet, at Pemberley, his behavior is dramatically plastic. Seeing her, "he absolutely started"; he addresses her "not in terms of perfect composure," but in a voice that "had none of its usual sedateness," and that betrays "the distraction of his thoughts."

The experimentation with the portrait is finally expressive of Austen's interest in the possibilities of her own art. For both author and character, the moment of contemplation, the device of the sister art is freeing. "As she stood before the canvas, on which he was represented, [Elizabeth] fixed his eyes upon herself" (p. 251); in viewing herself through Darcy's eyes, Elizabeth, in effect, moves into the picture, and from the temporal-linear into the spatial dimension. Darcy's portrait, in momentarily "arresting" Elizabeth, paradoxically liberates her, freeing her from the stress of continual anticipation. She has room to look back along the line of events that brought her here, to reconsider and reconstruct.

Pemberley seems a paradise, another country from that where artfulness rules. As a place it represents design of the happiest kind, perfectly realized. But such perfection, if generally diffused, would threaten the novel; it would arrest the development of the novelist's characters. Were they to deserve such a locale, Austen as a comic writer could have nothing more to do with them or tell of them. Fortunately, they do not, and the novel does not end here. The place may, indeed, as critics have asserted, be the product of the best in its owner's nature,[12] but its perfection is apparently not infectious, has not spread to human nature. Pemberley has not made Georgiana less shy, or Darcy more wise, judging from his behavior elsewhere. It has not, as Mansell has shrewdly pointed out, made of Wickham a good man.[13] In fact, attracted by the false perfections of that cad, Georgiana had once been content to abandon Pemberley. The place has not formed her taste in people. The rather ordinary group of people Darcy brings to Pemberley is not improved in manners by its perfections. Even Mr. Gardiner behaves badly there, allowing his wife to overtire herself in his selfish pleasure in the grounds.

Thus the pictures at Pemberley are not all of perfection. Once Elizabeth turns away from nature, from the windows that frame the only perfect subject at Pemberley, what she views are imperfect people in imperfect relationship. When in their awkward meeting Darcy addresses Elizabeth "if not in terms of perfect composure, at least of perfect civility," his is a perfection not yet achieved by the other inhabitants of Pemberley. Any tendency in her readers prematurely to idealize her characters—to endow them with the aesthetic value of Pemberley itself and of its art works—is corrected by Austen's satiric "droll" on the subject, the verbal painting she offers us in the "conversation" of women sipping tea in imperfect harmony.

In *Emblem and Expression,* Ronald Paulson establishes that a "conversation-piece" is "a portrait group of a family or friends in some degree of rapport seen in their home surroundings."[14] As a work of art in the genre, Austen's conversation piece is perfect; all the appurtenances of Pemberley lend themselves perfectly to its composition. But the scene pictured is morally and psychologically imperfect, and the genre of "conversation" is thus absurdly subverted. Citing Dr. Johnson as his authority, Paulson suggests that conversation is "etymologically derived from the Latin conversation . . . an abiding or living in a place with other people, which leads to the allied sense of conduct, behaviour, or social interchange, to 'familiar discourse' . . . opposed to formal coherence" (p. 121). Austen's conversation piece is centrally about conduct, as her heavy stress, in the passages surrounding and composing the "conversation," on the word "civility" expresses.

But how can we determine that the families and friends Austen collects together in imperfect civility for the "at home" of Pemberley constitute a *picture?* "For the eighteenth-century reader visualization of a full and proper picture was possible under the stimulus of a carefully selected detail," Jean Hagstrum argues, so that "the modern reader must learn the relevant iconographical context and respond to even slight visual stimulus" (p. 149). The iconography of a conversation piece conventionally includes a bowl of fruit signifying "family,"[15] and a tea table as the " 'means of establishing a natural relationship amongst' " the people gathered around it "conversing."[16] For *his* conversation pieces, William Hogarth, whose satiric paintings strongly influenced eighteenth-century novelists, invented "an incident or action of some kind. Something happens that brings the people together" as "one guest is introduced to another." He could, as Paulson points out, "by the placement and spacing, the relationships between people, room, doorways, windows [with] the outside glimpsed through the doorway, to the fruit associated with . . . women" define relationships between individuals and sexes, and between art and nature (pp. 128; 122–23).

Austen's utterly authoritative deployment of precisely such significant iconographical detail and compositional elements—the occasion, the significant arrangement of people, the fruit and teatable, the indoor/outdoor setting—is what makes possible the visualization of the conversation piece in *Pride and Prejudice* (pp. 267–68). She sets up her conversation piece by arranging to have Elizabeth and Mrs. Gardiner, in "an exertion of politeness" wait on Georgiana at Pemberley, where "they were received by Miss Darcy, who was sitting there with Mrs. Hurst and Miss Bingley, and the lady with whom she lived in London." The *composition* of the picture, then, as Austen carefully places its significant elements, is of this group of women gathered to converse around the teatable with its "cold meat, cake, and a variety of all the finest fruits in season"; they are sitting in the "saloon," its "windows opening to the ground" admitting "a most refreshing view" (pp. 267–68). The expressive function of the picture in *Pride and Prejudice* is characteristic of the genre: satiric, moral, and definitive.[17] Austen composes her artful characters into the art of the conversation piece to show that, ironically, they have nothing to say to each other. Silence, not art, is the inevitable absurd termination of their mutual linguistic designs, for the "degree of rapport" in this "conversation" is imperfect. Caroline and Mrs. Hurst are too hostile, Elizabeth too embarrassed, Georgiana too shy to talk:

> . . . On their being seated, a pause, awkward as such moments must always be, succeeded for a few moments. It was first broken by Mrs. Annesley, a genteel, agreeable-looking woman, whose endeavour to introduce some kind of discourse, proved her to be more truly well bred than either of the others; and between her and Mrs. Gardiner, with occasional help from Elizabeth, the conversation was carried on.
> (p. 267)

Only those characters outside the main design of the novel and never implicated in its marital schemes can carry out the straightforward theme of the "conversation." The *fruit*, brought in, thus becomes comically necessary to effect the composition:

> There was now employment for the whole party; for though they could not all talk, they could all eat; and the beautiful pyramids of grapes, nectarines, and peaches, soon collected them round the table.
> (p. 268)

Greed finally groups them as good will and good taste could not. Like the beautiful fruit, Pemberley attracts flies, exploiters of its goods. In this novel about the struggle of women for security and status through marriage, this is a powerful picture of their mutual aggression, prompted by competition for the riches of the fruit.[18] Those of the women not in direct conflict over the man and his possessions are frightened into silence by the hostility of the others. While Georgiana Darcy's reception of Elizabeth and Mrs. Gardiner has been very "civil," Mrs. Hurst and Caroline notice them only with a formal curtsy; "after sitting in this manner a quarter of an hour, without hearing Miss Bingley's voice," Elizabeth receives from her only a "cold inquiry" (p. 268). Caroline and Mrs. Hurst's bad conduct, their formal cold courtesies, violate an occasion specifically structured for the exchange of "familiar discourse"; they practice too much art in a situation calling for nature.

The "conversation" also establishes that poor Georgiana, the product of too much formal training on her stately brother's part, cannot cope with informality and is utterly undone when she must order tea or make the most ordinary kind of chitchat. Darcy's highly designed notion of the truly accomplished woman has kept her behind the pianoforte or easel, practicing with great industry everything but easy civility. She is stiff and shy, inhibited by her awkward formality. The gifts her brother sends her of musical instruments only isolate her further in a lonely, apparently proud perfection. In manners, Darcy's house has been governed by too much ceremony. Mr. Bingley's revealing remark about Darcy's being an "awful object on a Sunday at Pemberley" comes to mind.

"The basic categories of conversation settings are indoors and outdoors," Paulson establishes, "the former more conducive to the portrayal of a middle-class family and exact socio-personal definition, the latter to a kind of portrait group that displays an aristocratic family, garden imagery, and symbolism relating to art and nature" (p. 123). In her conversation piece, Austen cleverly unites the two categories by effecting a compositional synthesis of art and nature at aristocratic Pemberley. Darcy's art has already admitted nature. Though the women are sitting in the "saloon," its "windows, opening to the ground, admitted a most refreshing view of the high woody hills behind the house, and of the beautiful oaks and Spanish chestnuts which were scattered over the intermediate lawn." Darcy's skillful aesthetic arrangement of the trees distributed in the middle distance also extends art into nature, the "art" of the "indoors" thus carried "outdoors." Elizabeth is more attracted to exterior than interior life. Whether she is at Netherfield, Rosings, or Pemberley, she is anxious to get outside. In the northern "saloon," Austen offers her an "out," for here is the exterior in the interior, nature in art. Since the mind that has successfully achieved this happy accommodation is Darcy's, Elizabeth has found her haven.

By working with the symbolic distance between the members of this group portrait, Austen suggests that in the structure of the novel the synthesis of class has yet to be achieved.[19] Elizabeth would like to try to "reach" shy, aristocratic Georgiana but

> . . . soon saw that she was herself closely watched by Miss Bingley, and that she could not speak a word, especially to Miss Darcy, without calling her attention. This observation would not have prevented her from trying to talk to the latter, had they not been seated at an inconvenient distance. (p. 268)

A union of classes in the union of Elizabeth and Darcy is a prospect jealously guarded against by Caroline Bingley. Her resentment of Elizabeth seems to arise at least partially from the class prejudice of the newly arrived. Caroline has long made merry over Elizabeth's vulgar relations, suggesting that they make her contemptible. After she has lost Darcy to her, however, she persists in the connection. To sustain the privilege of elite association, she overcomes personal jealousy. We see from Austen's exact handling of spatial relationships in this little composition of women waging sexual and class warfare that even such ideal spaces as Pemberley can be abused by narrow and selfish human relationships. This party is in imminent danger of freezing under the influence of

Caroline's cold enmity. Even energetic Elizabeth gives up, rather than struggling to bridge the long distance to Georgiana.

In the subversive spirit with which she played the joke about "Reynolds," then, Austen uses the conversation piece as a necessary corrective to the idealizations, the "flaming character[s]" suggested by Darcy's smiling portrait and the smiling prospect of Pemberley.[20] She makes her commentary on sexual tension by eliminating men altogether from the composition and uniting the women only in their preoccupation with the absent man. Her attention solely on the conversation of women, she makes the dismal discovery that they have nothing to say to each other. The entrance of Darcy alters the composition of the picture. All the women at once turn their attention from each other to the man: "there was scarcely an eye which did not watch his behaviour when he first came into the room" (p. 269). Picture thus turns into scene as the lessons of art are achieved. Austen's literary pictorialism is so efficient that she has exploited "the three elements of greatest importance . . . the relationships between the people and between them and their milieu, and the function of these elements to define."[21]

In the beauty of Pemberley and in the discovery of beauty in Darcy's character, Elizabeth learns to anticipate some design with delight, but, lest the reader should submit to the illusion that life can "partake of the perfection of art," Austen herself paints satiric pictures of not very attractive subjects. The power of art to reveal the illusion is, of course, precisely its perfection. Further, Austen uses her own art ironically to suggest that aesthetic perfection can be pernicious. Georgiana and her brother are frozen in stateliness in their attempt to match the aesthetic perfection of their surroundings. Even the portrait of Darcy needed Elizabeth in all her human imperfection to bring it cheerfully to life, as picture and person exchanged glances and smiles.

At Pemberley, Darcy makes his most confident claim for Elizabeth's being a true beauty; Caroline attempts to prove him wrong by itemizing her rival's individual imperfections:

> "For my own part," she rejoined, "I must confess that I never could see any beauty in her. Her face is too thin; her complexion has no brilliancy; and her features are not at all handsome. Her nose wants character; there is nothing marked in its lines. Her teeth are tolerable, but not out of the common way; and as for her eyes, which have sometimes been called so fine, I never could perceive any thing extraordinary in them. . . ." (p. 270)

But these defects, faithfully recorded in Caroline's deliberately unflattering portrait, add up, for Darcy, to "'one of the handsomest women of my acquaintance' " (p. 271). Caroline is exposed as a bad portraitist be-cause she, unlike the artist who painted Darcy, does not see the spirit in the character of a face that transcends its imperfections—that renders its imperfections irrelevant. With consummate art, Austen shows Elizabeth a flattering, Darcy an unflattering portrait of the other at Pemberley; both discover as a consequence of comparing these with their former impressions that the truth of character lies somewhere in between such absolutes. The wisdom of the novel is located, finally, in the painter who portrayed Darcy smiling. It was her own smile she painted. Character and character, author and character, painter and original smile at each other in anticipation of mutual pleasure. Tony Tanner has observed that *Pride and Prejudice* is a "happy book,"[22] and, indeed, the lessons of art in this novel teach us that the appropriate expression to grace the face of the comic artist is a smile.

At Pemberley, under the influence of art and nature, Elizabeth and Darcy will slowly work on redesigning their characters. Pemberley is an art gallery in which we view portraits of characters in need of perfection; it is also a well-designed garden in which such characters can best attempt the process of self-perfection: its designer has not excluded the imperfect in Nature herself. At the conclusion of the novel Austen offers her heroine total gratification of romantic, aesthetic, and moral anticipation, but only because Elizabeth now knows the inevitable error in human speculation. Joyfully, she writes to her aunt that the utmost reach of the happiest imagination cannot transcend the real ideal of what will be achieved at Pemberley:

> "You supposed more than really existed. But *now* suppose as much as you chuse; give a loose to your fancy, indulge imagination in every possible flight which the subject will afford and . . . you cannot greatly err."(p. 382)

*Katrin R. Burlin*
*Bryn Mawr College*

# NOTES

1. The text I have used is R. W. Chapman's edition of the novel, 3rd edition (London: Oxford University Press, 1933), Vol. II. Page numbers are inserted in the text.

2. A. Walton Litz, *Jane Austen: A Study of Her Artistic Development* (London: Chatto and Windus, 1965), p. 103. But Samuel Kliger, "Jane Austen's *Pride and Prejudice* in the Eighteenth-Century Mode," *University of Toronto Quarterly*, 16 (July 1947): 357–70, reprinted in *Twentieth-Century Interpretations of* Pride and Prejudice: *A Collection of Critical Essays*, ed. E. Rubenstein (Englewood Cliffs, N. J.: Prentice-Hall, 1969), p. 52: "The governing idea of *Pride and Prejudice* is the art-nature antithesis; the perfection of form is achieved through relating each character and incident to the basic art-nature dialectic."

3. Tony Tanner's discussion of mental pictures and art in this novel does not seriously overlap with mine. Cf. his introduction to the Penguin edition of *Pride and Prejudice* (Harmondsworth, 1972).

4. " 'A Development of Self': Character and Personality in Jane Austen's Fiction," in *Jane Austen's Literary Achievement*, ed. Juliet McMaster (London: Macmillan, 1976), p. 69.

5. Jean Hagstrum, *The Sister Arts* (Chicago and London: The University of Chicago Press, 1958), p. 181. Wherever possible, all future references will be inserted in the text.

6. Darrell Mansell, *The Novels of Jane Austen* (New York: Barnes and Noble, 1973) argues that "Pemberley has been polluted from the beginning. [It] has never been quite free of Wickham. His picture may still hang there" (p. 107). I would argue that Darcy's keeping it there despite his own feelings transforms its negative symbolism into positive.

7. For an excellent discussion of the relationship between eighteenth-century English novelists and the sister art of painting, cf. Ronald Paulson, *Emblem and Expression: Meaning in English Art of the Eighteenth Century* (London: Thames and Hudson, 1975); Hagstrum, op. cit.; Sir Joshua Reynolds, *Discourses on Art* (New York: Collier Books, 1966), "Discourse Eight." Reynolds told his students that Du Piles was "undoubtedly right" in advising portrait-painters "to add grace and dignity to the characters of those whose pictures we draw" (p. 133). See also "Discourse Four," p. 67. Contemporary readers must have been amused when a "Reynolds" gives Darcy a "flaming character." Austen's readers would also have recognized the humor of Mrs. Reynolds' prejudice against the miniature and for the "finer larger picture." In this she conforms to the taste taught by such legislators of aesthetics as the Earl of Shaftesbury and Reynolds himself. This prejudice for the large picture is still unquestioningly rehearsed by modern critics who ought, perhaps, to be more suspicious, considering Austen's own choice of the miniature as metaphor for *her* art (cf. Tanner, pp. 24; 27). Austen, even in exploiting the sister art, was making fun of received prejudices in patriarchal art. For an

excellent discussion of how women writers subverted male genres, see Irene Tayler and Gina Luria, "Gender and Genre: Women in British Romantic Literature" in *What Manner of Woman,* ed. Marlene Springer (New York: New York University Press, 1977), pp. 97–121; Sandra M. Gilbert and Susan Gubar in *The Madwoman in the Attic: The Woman Writer and the Nineteenth-Century Literary Imagination* (New Haven: Yale University Press, 1979).

8. Among critics who study the significance of this confrontation between Elizabeth and the portrait are Alistair Duckworth, *The Improvement of the Estate* (Baltimore: Johns Hopkins University Press, 1971), pp. 122–23; Mansell, pp. 93, 96–97; Tanner, pp. 24, 27.

9. Duckworth sees the Pemberley scenes as exercises in the "perspectivist theme," *Improvement of the Estate,* pp. 124–25.

10. Nina Auerbach, *Communities of Women* (Cambridge: Harvard University Press, 1978), p. 52: "What compels her in the portrait is the awesomely institutionalized power of a man, a power that her own father has let fall. . . ."

11. For an identification of these two kinds of portrait-representation, cf. Theodore Meyer Greene, *The Arts and the Art of Criticism* (Princeton: Princeton University Press, 1940), pp. 301–302. In traditional iconography, the "Saturnian" portrait is "unsocial or morose," "taciturn," "entirely concentrated upon his own self"; the "Jovial" is "open to the world," "companionable," "interested in his fellow-beings" and "unlimitedly generous." Greene cites three portraits by Reynolds as expressive of the painter's interest in rendering both the "social" and the "reflective" subject.

12. Many critics have noted Austen's use of aesthetic Pemberley to redefine Darcy. The emblem of his fine, natural taste, it expresses also, as Litz establishes, his moral strength: *Jane Austen,* p. 103. Paulson points out that one kind of Dutch genre painting is the "portrait in which the sitter's status is emphasized by the presence of artifacts he has gathered, including his manor house, within a natural setting," *Emblem and Expression,* p. 123. Surely this is a technique Austen here deliberately borrowed from the sister art?

13. Mansell, op. cit.

14. Paulson, *Emblem and Expression,* p. 121. Wherever possible, all future references will be inserted in the text.

15. Paulson, p. 126.

16. Paulson, p. 122: "Around a table, for instance, is 'a means of establishing a natural relationship amongst' the people sitting around it."

17. Paulson, pp. 121ff.

18. Nina Auerbach offers a feminist reading of this passage: "We are given a chance, not so much to hear what the women say to each other during this excruciating period, as to have our attention called to the distrust and emotional pressure that forbid their saying anything." Darcy's "absent presence is the only emotional point of reference for all three women." Auerbach comments that "the 'pyramids' of fruit suggest both architectural and natural

power, neither of which is available in [Elizabeth's] mother's house," *Communities of Women*, pp. 38–44.

19. Kliger, p. 52. Paulson suggests that "in both painting and prose fiction the metaphor of social 'distance' has replaced traditional structures of analogy," p. 130.

20. Paulson, p. 121, points out that the conversation piece originated "as a reaction against such forms of 'high art' as . . . idealized portraiture."

21. Paulson, p. 121.

22. Tanner, p. 42; Mansell, p. 106.

# An Epistemological Understanding of *Pride and Prejudice*

## Humility and Objectivity

"She is beautiful considering we never saw her before."
—Mr. Woodhouse, *Emma*

There is a sense, then, in which seeing is a "theory-laden" undertaking. Observation of x is shaped by prior knowledge of x.
—Norwood Russell Hanson, *Patterns of Discovery*

The totality of our so-called knowledge or beliefs, from the most casual matters of geography and history to the profoundest laws of atomic physics or even of pure mathematics and logic, is a man-made fabric which impinges on experience only along the edges.
—Willard Van Orman Quine
"Two Dogmas of Empiricism"

In addition to the large number of dualities offered as interpretative frameworks of *Pride and Prejudice*, yet another disjunction leaps out from almost every page to a reader alert to the problems of knowledge.[1] The terms of this disjunction may be variously expressed as belief and knowledge, data and fact, perception and interpretation, or subjectivity and objectivity. The novel repeatedly reveals the salient gap between evidence and conclusion and the labyrinth of false paths and difficulties that lie between the two.

At times, explicit epistemological discussions occur with grandeur, as when they are the stuff of reconciliation between Elizabeth and Darcy, but more often as trivia in concerns about confirmation in the most prosaic exchanges. And the narrator's voice has an epistemological purview as she persistently refers to the ubiquity of differing and variable interpretation in describing everything from Georgiana to the flow of

171

public opinion. In short, comments and discussions about knowledge and understanding, and the erratic and variable interpretations on which they rest, not only supply the central subject of the book but also constitute the warp and woof of its fabric.[2]

The novel persistently points to the overwhelming problems of acquiring knowledge, the frustrating fallibility and insufficiency of evidence, the relativism of alternate interpretations, and the inevitable gap between what is believed and what is. The presuppositions inherent in *Pride and Prejudice* concerning the process of forming beliefs and gaining knowledge are susceptible to a general characterization.

The first implicit thesis is that beliefs are always based on other beliefs or bits of evidence, and nothing is ever known *simpliciter*. Conclusions and alleged facts are always presented together with the evidence on which they are based. Such a practice often, perhaps inevitably, serves to underline the fragility of the edifice of knowledge as the paucity of evidence upon which most people base their beliefs becomes apparent. When Mr. Darcy initially encounters the neighbors of Netherfield, the flimsy evidence on which he is first pronounced thoroughly admirable and then condemned is rather pointedly indicated. Echoes of this insight, the insignificant foundation on which public opinion changes, repeatedly sound in the text in isolated humorous sentences. Yet, in addition to being a source of levity, the structure of knowledge is a recognized and acknowledged concern of the main characters, reflected in their dialogue, as this speech by Jane to her sister demonstrates:

> ". . . I confess myself to have been entirely deceived in Miss Bingley's regard of me. But, my dear sister, though the event has proved you right, do not think me obstinate if I still assert, that, considering what her behavior was, my confidence was as natural as your suspicion. I do not comprehend her reason for wishing to be intimate with me, but if the same circumstances were to happen again, I am sure I should be deceived again. . . ."[3]

Jane claims that although she proved mistaken, she made the correct decision and held the correct belief on the basis of the evidence available to her. She is thereby explicitly making the rather sophisticated epistemological point that her belief was warranted if not true, appropriate to the evidence if not metaphysically certified.[4]

The introduction of Mr. and Mrs. Bennet appears as the ultimate illustration of the persistent implicit emphasis on the connection between evidence and judgment. At the end of Chapter I, the narrator gives an authoritative account of the personalities of Mr. and Mrs. Bennet. However, first, she has presented ample evidence on which such a judgment may be based. Since the work is literature, the evidence, appropriately enough, is not only substantive but stylistic as well. Certainly Mrs. Bennet and Mr. Bennet differ in terms of what they say, Mrs. Bennet discoursing at great length about trivial details, Mr. Bennet requesting concrete facts. However, their manner of presentation diverges as well. Initially, her long-winded conversations are reported verbatim, but his distance and coolness are indicated by means of the use of indirect discourse. Thus, the summary the narrator presents of the Bennets' character has first been richly inductively supported.[5] The reader, whose position in regard to knowledge has interesting similarities and dissimilarities with the characters in the book, in this instance understands the Bennets both through detailed demonstrations and authorial general statements.

The second tenet of this novel supposes that evidence-gathering and judgment-making are dependent upon the subject or perceiver. Susan Morgan, in her highly innovative book, *In the Meantime: Character and Perception in Jane Austen's Fiction*, expresses this insight: "In Austen's epistemology the observer is part of the process."[6] A multiplicity of instances, minor and major, establish that almost any evidence can be given two contradictory interpretations. After her bold walk alone over the countryside to inquire about the health of her sister, when Elizabeth makes her famous disheveled entrance, her reputation threatened by the shame of a muddy petticoat, the Bingley sisters and Mr. Bingley have radically different interpretations. Likewise, the letter written by Miss Bingley to Jane about Mr. Bingley's romantic interests is given divergent explanations by Elizabeth and Jane. The duality expressed here, the possibility of alternative conflicting explanations for the same sentences of a letter, presages Elizabeth's later painful ruminations about the proper interpretation of Darcy's crucial missive.

By what process, then, is one judgment or interpretation chosen? The answer lies in the strongly emphasized fact that interpretative schemes differ among individuals. For example, Jane's consistently beneficent mode of construing the world is particularly well delineated. In contrast, Elizabeth, although she prides herself on her realistic perception, often views the world with an amusedly cynical eye. She tells Darcy: "Follies and nonsense, whims and inconsistencies *do* divert me, I own, and I laugh at them whenever I can." And although she protests, "I hope I never ridicule what is wise and good" (p. 57), the weight of the text belies this hope.

Chapter IV of the first volume is really an illustrative study of different interpretative views at work. The reader learns how four different observers, Jane, Elizabeth, Bingley, and Darcy, perceive the ball. Jane's and

Bingley's ways of perceiving events are similar. Bingley, like Jane, has a mode of seeing the world suffused with his tractability and mildness of temper. Hence, for these observers, everything at the ball is pleasing and agreeable. Elizabeth and Darcy, although slightly less similar to each other than Jane and Bingley, still have analogous ways of viewing matters. Although they claim commitment to a reasonable and clear-eyed attitude, they have a naturally satirical eye. They reject charitable impulses to spotlight foibles and defects. Thus, at the ball, they see some disturbing elements.

Although Austen expansively exhibits these four characters' interpretative systems in the elegantly crafted Chapter IV, in Chapter III the ball serves to reveal the conceptual penchants of other characters as well. Mary's view of the world is recognized as egotistical, and Catherine's and Lydia's as undiscriminating, in a half-sentence apiece. Mr. Bennet's removal and aloofness from the world reveals itself in the fact that he alone among the main characters does not attend the ball but must be given an account of it. His lack of interest and satirical disposition are revealed: "He had rather hoped that all his wife's views on the stranger would be disappointed; . . ." (p. 12). Mrs. Bennet's unabashedly concrete and indiscriminate turn of mind is likewise captured by her faithful chronological recounting of Mr. Bingley's dance partners. Such a pattern often repeats itself. An event, major or minor, is an occasion which in its interpretation exhibits the modes of perception of the characters. Thus, the ball, an early major event of the novel, is typical of its other events; namely, the space devoted to its description is dwarfed by accounts of how its various elements are interpreted by different observers.

If the novel presupposes that every person has a conceptual framework through which he perceives reality, then it is legitimate to ask what framework the author encourages the reader to adopt. If follies and inconsistencies do divert Elizabeth, they seem to divert the author even more so. Hence, the reader is led to view the scenes that transpire with an amused, distant eye. The following description is typical of an often-assumed narrative stance:

> . . . A great deal more passed at the other table. Lady Catherine was generally speaking—stating the mistakes of the three others, or relating some anecdote of herself. Mr. Collins was employed in agreeing to everything her Ladyship said, thanking her for every fish he won, and apologizing if he thought he won too many. Sir William did not say much. He was storing his memory with anecdotes and noble names. (p. 166)

This ironic stance is all-encompassing. It is clear that the narrator, like Elizabeth, perhaps with more justification, takes pride in her intelligence and encourages the reader to do likewise. Both narrator and reader attend to the events of the novel, alert to the self-deception and foibles of its characters.

As the previous discussion has illustrated, characters in *Pride and Prejudice* may be explicated in terms of their conceptual frameworks. A character's mode of viewing the universe may, on occasion, even be collapsed into one privileged belief, so sacrosanct to the person who holds it that it shapes all else. This phenomenon of a central belief governing all other beliefs, Jane Austen repeatedly demonstrates. The idea has its most comic manifestation in Collins' proposal to Elizabeth. In spite of Elizabeth's hearty and copious refusals, he believes she is following the convention of a flirt because, for him, his own desirability is patently axiomatic.

Yet this very same process of altering evidence to salvage one fact receives very serious treatment in the discussion between Elizabeth and Jane concerning Charlotte's engagement to Mr. Collins. Although they both love Charlotte, Jane differs from Elizabeth in extending her affectionate feelings toward Charlotte to forestall any criticism of her engagement. However, Elizabeth recoils at such a violation of common sense:

> ". . . Mr. Collins is a conceited, pompous, narrow-minded, silly man; you know he is, as well as I do; and you must feel, as well as I do, that the woman who marries him cannot have a proper way of thinking. You shall not defend her, though it is Charlotte Lucas. You shall not, for the sake of one individual, change the meaning of principle and integrity, nor endeavor to persuade yourself or me, that selfishness is prudence, and insensibility of danger, security for happiness." (pp. 135–36)

Elizabeth thus declares distortion of evidence to be a moral evil, a position which anticipates her self-discovery speech as she reads Darcy's letter.

However, her righteous position is subtly undermined by the narrator's comment on Elizabeth's defense of the report that Wickham is marrying for money. The narrator thus alerts the reader, before Elizabeth herself can realize, that she is not the mistress of objectivity. The remark is part of a recurring narrative refrain, reminding the reader of the quintessential elusiveness of objectivity. It is even suggested that if a belief is held firmly enough, evidence may very well be imagined or invented to substantiate that belief. Mrs. Gardiner is guilty of this trait, and Elizabeth checks her own reactions to make sure that she is not.

This precept, that one belief can shape all else, actually is the epistemological preface of the novel. The opening words of the work are in the objective realm, and no words could be more epistemologically confident than these first four: "It is a truth . . ." Yet the next two words, "universally acknowledged," introduce the subjective. The six words together, "it is a truth universally acknowledged," constitute an ambiguity with striking metaphysical and epistemological ramifications. The phrase may be interpreted as designating an objective truth, which is universally acknowledged to be so, or as a subjectively held belief universally acknowledged to be true, but not necessarily so. The phrase is thus poised between the subjective and the objective. The second part of the sentence plummets the reader from the lofty plain of philosophical considerations and language to the mundane terrain of financial and nuptial matters. The descent is so precipitous that the reader is tempted to discard the abstract considerations raised in the first few words. However, of the many things Austen has accomplished with this opening sentence, one is surely the conflation of philosophical interests with sublunary, societal ones.[7]

Thus, in the first few sentences of *Pride and Prejudice*, the initial metaphysical fanfare of "It is a truth" begins, followed by the trumpeting assurance of "universally," and then the slight diminuendo of "acknowledged" precedes the *subito piano* of "a single man in possession of a good fortune, must be in want of a wife." The second sentence evokes the general epistemological tendency considered in the foregoing discussion. The last part of that sentence, " . . . this truth is so well fixed in the minds of the surrounding families, that he is considered as the rightful property of some one or other of their daughters," illustrates the effects of an idea steadfastly held. The next sentences, introducing the Bennets, particularize the general principles. Thus, the book begins with an epistemological prologue composed of two sentences, the first of which, however lightly, suggests the fissure between outer truth and inner belief, the second of which immediately insinuates the perverse and erratic process of the acquisition of knowledge.

If the principles thus far presented are truly the epistemological foundation of the novel, then inherent in *Pride and Prejudice*, in nascent form, is a philosophical view come to vogue in the last half of the twentieth century. Structuralism, the panoramic view, which has applications in science, anthropology, art, history, literary theory, and, it seems, all other areas of knowledge, states roughly that a person's mode, his system of perceiving and conceiving reality is creative. Understanding the world necessarily involves a system, and every system at least partially creates its object. No statement ever directly tests itself against reality, for a single statement is always embedded in a theory.

Willard Van Orman Quine has captured this phenomenon of human thought in a metaphor for science, which he interprets very broadly to include, for example, the hypothesis that there are physical objects:

. . . total science is like a field of force whose boundary conditions are experience. A conflict with experience at the periphery occasions readjustments in the interior of the field. . . . But the total field is so underdetermined by its boundary conditions, experience, that there is much latitude of choice as to what statements to reevaluate in the light of any contrary experience.[8]

The analogues of a much lower stratum are available in *Pride and Prejudice*. When Collins asks Elizabeth to marry him, since he rejects the truth of her answer, he alters his understanding of human exchange so that he no longer takes Elizabeth's "no" to be evidence that she does not want to marry him. Collins is a comic figure, but Jane often appears engaged in the same process. If the Bingley sisters act rudely to her, then she changes her view of human behavior to interpret these actions as efforts not to hurt her feelings.

This metaphysical view, which heeds Wittgenstein's dictum, "to treat of the net and not of what the net describes,"[9] has a striking overlap with the outlined presuppositions of *Pride and Prejudice*. Although the novel demonstrably deals with the processes of acquiring knowledge, more importantly, it exhibits the different interpretative models, the divergent theoretical structures, by which characters understand the world. In fact, characters are individuated by their mode of viewing reality. Moreover, no one of the characters' systems is clearly superior to all the others. Thus, as both Marilyn Butler and Morgan note, neither Elizabeth's nor Jane's schema is superior at acquiring truth.[10]

Does, then, *Pride and Prejudice* emphasize the creative, arbitrary, and essentially fictional nature of perception? Its unremitting concentration, alternately solemn and humorous, on the exquisite complexities and internal laws of human beliefs, pursued both in abstract disquisition and gossipy detail, favors this position. Its insistence on the shaping nature of beliefs bolsters the view.

However, there is another strain in *Pride and Prejudice*, long recognized by critics: the assurance of certainty in Jane Austen's world, the identification of knowledge with the good; as Alistair M. Duckworth proclaims, the belief that ". . . that which is good and true in life resists the perversions of the individual viewpoint. . . ."[11] Critics have labeled this current as Platonic; the elements to which they refer can be summarized in four cardinal propositions.[12] (1) Moral virtue is equivalent to knowledge.[13] The second principle is really a particularization of the first. (2) Those who are wisest are best; those who are not virtuous fail because they lack knowledge.[14] Further principles concern the nature of reason and its relation to other faculties. (3) Ideally, reason should control feelings.[15] The last principle concerns the processes involved in knowledge.

(4) Only when beliefs are subjugated to the painstaking test of reason do they result in knowledge.[16]

In addition to intellectual assumptions, there are Platonic motifs that run through the novel as well, particularly in the relationship between the two couples, Elizabeth and Darcy and Jane and Bingley. They are portrayed as existing on different planes of intelligence. The text forcefully establishes Darcy's and Elizabeth's intelligence. However, their intelligence has not been tested; like the alleged wise man of Socrates' time, they have not questioned their fundamental assumptions.[17]

The emphasis and testimony of the novel indicate that Elizabeth's happiness is superior to that of her less self-conscious sister, Jane. This novel, like Platonic philosophy, particularly in the *Republic,* makes the happiness of those who are less self-conscious dependent on those who are more so. Those who think and understand should be responsible for those who do not and cannot. As Marvin Mudrick characterizes the relationship, Bingley and Jane have their adult guardians.[18] The happy reunion of Jane and Bingley is a consequence of Darcy's and Elizabeth's change in understanding.

The Platonism in the novel assures the reader that there exists an objective order, truth knowable by a person who exercises her most acute faculties. Furthermore, truth attained by this rational means guarantees happiness. And indeed within the circumscribed world of the novel, happiness, in its highest sense, tinged with metaphysical grandeur, is equated with the good, the proper marriage.

Yet, as we have seen, beside the granite of the Platonism underlying the novel are the malleable surfaces of a structuralism shaping truth to viewpoint and collapsing if asked to support objective truth. By focusing on the plastic processes of human knowledge and the shifting, arbitrary shapes of human belief, the novel implicitly undermines the power of the human faculties to attain absolute knowledge of the world. A basic cleavage appears in *Pride and Prejudice* between pride in the power of the human mind to acquire objective truth and humility at the recognition of the fallibility, inevitable distortion, and prejudice of mental processes.

But fiction is fundamentally different from life. Ordinarily, if one were to accept the quasi-structuralist view demonstrably embedded in *Pride and Prejudice,* that all judgments about reality are dependent upon the conceptual structure of the perceiver, then one would have to accept the view that humans are unconditionally barred from an unbiased view of reality. Thus, in the actual human situation, the two views, (1) that beliefs about reality are necessarily filtered through somewhat arbitrary conceptual structures and (2) that objective truth is attainable, are completely irreconcilable. However, in fiction the two perspectives, the ontological and the epistemological, can be combined to provide metaphysical illumination. The author by virtue of her omnipotence and omniscience vis à vis her creation has two perspectives, objective truth and human interpretation, and thus can mend the rent between two such apparently discrepant viewpoints. But even so skilled an artisan as Austen leaves evidence of her stitches.[19]

Indeed, the last third of the book has always been a favorite target of the critics.[20] The usual reason cited for the abruptly appearing deficit and incongruity in the novel is Jane Austen's inability to incorporate sexual behavior into her ironic, literary world view.[21] However, whether or not this rather superficial observation has merit, deeper consideration must be invoked as well to account for the substantial shift within the text. The last third of the novel evidences nothing less than Austen's rather ambitious intellectual project of healing the split between the subjective and the objective. The author in this section is no longer content to share amusement with the reader over the eccentricities of the human personalities and the vagaries of the pursuit of knowledge, but instead insists on forcefully guaranteeing the seriousness and reality of the characters' moral concerns. By closing the ironic distance between narrator and character, Austen does what she had steadfastly refused to do before— metaphysically underwrites the validity of particular perceptions.[22]

Quite clearly, in the last part of the novel, a moral lesson is in evidence. In this section of the novel, for the most part, there is no space between, on the one hand, what the characters perceive, interpret, and ponder, and, on the other, what is; facts are presented baldly and indubitably.

It is not sufficient to explain this shift in narrative stance by repeating the obvious truth that Lydia's and Wickham's action, an illicit relationship outside of marriage, is absolutely impermissible and immoral for Austen. The more compelling level on which to consider the problem is why Austen introduces what, in the context of this novel, equating the good and proper marriage with happiness and fulfillment, is a clear paradigm of immorality. It apparently functions, as paradigms best can, to distinguish unmistakably good conduct from bad conduct and true beliefs from false ones. By conclusively displaying the rectitude and worthiness of Darcy's character, Austen certifies the validity of Elizabeth's processes of gathering evidence and of ultimately arriving at conclusions. By offering this extreme example of behavior, Austen puts the finishing touches on her gallery of portraits, illustrative of the alternatives in pursuit of marriage. Thus, the last part of the novel constitutes not only Austen's answer to the problem of knowledge but a justification for that answer. She declares that incorrigible knowledge is possible but also upholds a particular methodology of acquiring that knowledge. To understand why the author has chosen to endorse Elizabeth's methods and attempts to find truth, one must examine the presuppositions and epistemological structures of the other characters.

Critical opinion has frequently advanced the thesis that the characters as individuals and the couples clustered around Elizabeth should be taken as exemplars of moral evils and imperfections, so to speak, cautionary directional signals to warn Elizabeth of roads not to pursue and, as a consequence, to admonish likewise the reader. Interestingly enough, the characters mentioned in this regard vary with the critic.[23]

The obvious course under these circumstances is to examine the entire array of characters whose mental processes are accessible to the reader, with Austen's apparent presupposition in the foreground of investigation, that a person's mode of reaching judgment and belief is indicative of her moral status.

Lydia is the character most clearly morally condemned in the novel. Not only is she morally reprehensible, but what seems worse in the context of this novel, she is incapable of understanding her own mistaken and defective behavior. For her, the interchangeability of officers is as without consequence as that of bonnets. One strikes her notice, and therefore it is hers. Her total lack of discrimination, her total failure to see events within any sort of hierarchy of value, and her complete absence of priorities reflect themselves in the humorous letter she leaves before she runs off with Wickham. The principles, if one could call them that, regulating Lydia's interest and understanding are shamefully simple: she embraces whatever has an air of glamour and romance, whatever happens to flatter her, and she distinguishes among these things only by favoring what is most accessible.

Mrs. Bennet is, as a number of critics have remarked, an older version of Lydia.[24] She is as incapable of understanding and oblivious to moral principles as her irresponsible daughter. Both of their governing precepts are of the lowest and indiscriminate type: in one case to be admired by redcoats; in the other, to have her daughters married.

Although Jane's criterion of making judgments is, like that of almost all the other characters, statable in one phrase, "to see everything in the best possible light; not to think ill of anyone," the principle, unlike those of Lydia and Mrs. Bennet, is quite general, making no mention of any individual. Jane's difficulty in making judgments is not, as some critics have claimed, that she is led by feelings, but that, although relentlessly benign, the standard that governs her understanding is inflexible, almost totally excluding new data which would allow her to interpret something in a new way.

Mr. Collins is also driven by one simple motivation. In his case, it is egocentricity, which, for most of the book, is manifested in his slavish devotion to Lady Catherine de Bourgh's advice. Like Lydia and Mrs. Bennet, Collins is unintelligent and materialistic, but unlike them, he pontificates received principles with the air of belief. Whereas Lydia and Mrs. Bennet seem incapable of differentiation between physical details and more abstract concerns, Mr. Collins clings with equal assiduity to both, noting with equal care the details of Lady de Bourgh's breakfast room and the duties of a clergyman.

Mary, like Mr. Collins, is given to speaking in aphorisms, and her pronouncements also have no connection to either her observations or her behavior. Although she expresses a distillation of Austen's apparent ideas and concerns, because her statements have no contact with concrete reality, the reader regards her in much the same way as Elizabeth. "Elizabeth lifted her eyes in amazement, but was too much oppressed to make any reply" (p. 289).

Unlike Mary, who is pronounced to have "neither genius nor taste" (p. 25), Charlotte is introduced as a "sensible, intelligent young woman" (p. 18). Nevertheless, like Mary, she is given to pronouncements about human interaction, but unlike Mary, she is, much to the astonishment of Elizabeth, capable of acting upon them. Because Charlotte is an acknowledgedly intelligent character, her thought processes are of interest to the reader and a source of outrage to Elizabeth. Nevertheless, in spite of her intelligence, she rejects the significance of all human variables except material advantage, and thus, it is assumed, deserves the fate that must await the intelligent person living with silly, pretentious Mr. Collins. It is not that Charlotte cannot make distinctions in the real world; she simply chooses not to. She chooses to subsume all other considerations to the economic one.

Sharing Charlotte's reductive view of the world, and no doubt surpassing her intelligence, Mr. Bennet has his own perspective on the rest of humanity, in his case, a comedic, voyeuristic one: "For what do we live, but to make sport for our neighbors, and laugh at them in our turn?" (p. 364). Indeed, his distanced, mocking vision knows no bounds; from nearly every encounter or conversation, he extracts the intellectual pleasure of ridicule. However, his derisive stance is, in its own way, as completely indiscriminate as, say, Charlotte's economic perspective or Mrs. Bennet's matrimonial view. The reader sympathizes when he is the baiting and sarcastic counterpoint to the banality of Mrs. Bennet. However, when he feels triumph in Charlotte's announced marriage to Mr. Collins, when he pokes fun at even the beneficent Jane, the reader's smile fades. Mr. Bennet sees situations acutely but selectively, eliminating all that is moving, poignant, and serious. Thus, his epistemological vista is as distorting and depreciating of situations and other human beings as that of Charlotte, if somewhat more appealing.

With this discussion of Mr. Bennet, the review of the array of epistemological options present in *Pride and Prejudice* concludes. Other characters, whose minds are closed to the reader, may be assumed to have thought processes similar to those of the characters known.[25] It is clear, then, why Austen underwrites Elizabeth's epistemological stance in preference to that of any other character. The others' structures of understanding are rigid, composed of discrete entities without play or intersection among theories and beliefs and data.

Although Elizabeth has many of the epistemological foibles of the characters discussed, she has the capacity to test her beliefs against her experience and form new beliefs on that basis.[26] Contrary to the appearances of the early part of the novel, she holds no belief so strongly that it is not corrigible in the face of new evidence.

The plot and its resolution depend not only on Elizabeth's reevaluation of her beliefs, but also on her realization of the defects of her previous procedures for evaluating evidence. According to her own testimony, she perceives her former errors in making judgments about the truth as a crucially enlightening experience in her understanding of self. For Elizabeth, knowing herself is tantamount to knowing her prejudices in making judgments and in acquiring knowledge about the world. The reader has learned in detail the painful processes by which Elizabeth has come to change her mind. She weighs possibilities; she thinks what counts in favor of one hypothesis, then another. She collects evidence. She has learned how difficult acquiring knowledge really is; consequently, besides renouncing her former belief, she renounces, too, her former brash sense of confidence in her own insight. Thus, one might conjecture that it is not for her opinions about the world that Austen metaphysically rewards Elizabeth, but for her comprehension of the structure of knowledge.

In her detailed portrait of the conceptual proclivities of all the characters, particularly Elizabeth, Austen is engaged in work parallel to that of Samuel Johnson, her admiration of whom is well known, namely, that of practical morality, ridding each person of his natural adverse proclivity. Elizabeth, after her epistemological purification, has been cured of her most prevalent negative intellectual tendency, her arrogance about knowledge, and, as a consequence, cured of her ironic detachment as well.

The narrator and the reader must be chastened from their natural temperamental epistemological biases also. Indeed, as if Austen were taking heed of her own inherent epistemological lesson, the ironic attitude which presumes certainty lapses as the evils of the assumption of certainty become more apparent. The intelligent reader, missing in the last part of the novel Austen's detached, acerbic humor, must give up her own comfortably aloof position as well and thus, like Elizabeth and the narrator, become swept up in the seriousness of human concerns. However, there is another irony, an irony parallel to that associated with Socrates, whom the oracle identified as the wisest of men just because, as he came to discover, he knew that he knew nothing. There is a reward for the epistemologically modest. To her now humbled readers, Austen offers, after exposing them to all the perils that prevent knowledge, the hope that if one is modest enough, alert enough to one's own predispositions of mind, and open enough to new information, one can, in spite of everything, attain knowledge and gain the happiness that follows. Even the least among us, by correction of foibles, may know more and thereby gain more. This lesson is evidenced by the fate of Kitty, who throughout the book is portrayed as the intellectual and moral twin of Lydia.

The final irony concerns the author Jane Austen. Although the narrator of *Pride and Prejudice* retreats from her ironic, subtly audacious perspective, the author herself, by foisting on her reader, in spite of all the evidence to the contrary, a metaphysically and morally certified view of knowledge, projects a supreme arrogance about what is true, thereby ultimately contradicting the fabric of the entire novel. Thus, the schism Austen has bridged within the text ultimately reemerges between reader and text.

*Martha Satz*
*Southern Methodist University*

# NOTES

1. A few might be mentioned: art and nature (for example, Samuel Kliger, "Jane Austen's *Pride and Prejudice* in the Eighteenth-Century Mode," *University of Toronto Quarterly*, 16 [1947]: 357–70); the individual and society (for example, Dorothy Van Ghent, *The English Novel: Form and Function* [New York: Rinehart & Company, 1953], p. 100, and Lionel Trilling, "Emma," *Encounter*, 8 [1957]: 49–59); feelings and reason (for example, Van Ghent,

p. 107, Barbara Hardy, *A Reading of Jane Austen* [London: Peter Owen
Ltd., 1975], pp. 37–65, and Juliet McMaster, "The Continuity of Jane Austen's Novels," *Studies in English Literature 1500–1900*, 10 [1970], pp. 729–
30); satire and charity (for example, Marilyn Butler, *Jane Austen and the War
of Ideas* [Oxford: The Clarendon Press, 1975], p. 212); economic conservatism and liberalism (for example, Leonard Woolf, "The Economic Determinism of Jane Austen," *New Statesman and Nation*, XXIV [1942]: 40; D. J.
Greene, "Jane Austen and the Peerage," *PMLA*, LXVIII (1953): 1017–31,
and Alistair M. Duckworth, *The Improvement of the Estate* [Baltimore:
Johns Hopkins Press, 1971], pp. 116–43); and freedom and determinism (for
example, Marvin Mudrick, *Jane Austen: Irony as Defense and Discovery*
[Princeton: Princeton University Press, 1952], pp. 124–26.

2. Mudrick, pp. 116ff., comments about one of the manifestations of Austen's
skill in this area: ". . . Jane Austen shows an almost Jamesian awareness of
the multiple ways of reading a man's behavior. She conveys her sense of the
possibility of very different interpretations of the 'same' action, as James
often does, through dialogues which look trivial and which are extremely
ambiguous." Reuben Brower (*The Fields of Light* [New York: Oxford University Press, 1951], pp. 167–70) detailedly analyzes this artfulness in connection with the dialogues between Elizabeth and Darcy.

3. Jane Austen, *Pride and Prejudice*, in R. W. Chapman, ed., *The Novels of
Jane Austen* (London: Oxford University Press, 1923; 3rd ed., 1932, 6th
impression, 1952), p. 148. All further references to this work appear in the
text.

4. Richard McKeon ("*Pride and Prejudice:* Thought, Character, Argument, and
Plot," *Critical Inquiry*, 5 [1978]: 517) takes note of the epistemologically
reflective tendency of the main characters: ". . . their judgments turn reflex-
ively on the creditability of their judgments." Philip Drew ("Jane Austen and
Bishop Butler," *Nineteenth Century Fiction*, 35 [1980]: 127–149) appreciates
a parallel distinction Jane Austen consistently draws between the reasons for
a moral judgment and its subsequent consequences. Chiefly on the basis of
this distinction, he broadly concludes that Austen is an intuitionist closer to
Butler than Shaftesbury, as Gilbert Ryle ("Jane Austen and the Moralists,"
*Oxford Review*, 1 [1962]: 5–18, reprinted in *English Literature and British
Philosophy*, ed. S. P. Rosenbaum [Chicago: University of Chicago Press,
1971]) had claimed. However, in so doing he largely ignores both the epistemological difficulties inherent in ethical intuitionism to which, by focusing
on the individuality of perception, Austen sensitively attends, and Shaftesbury's ethical aestheticism, which Ryle subtly characterizes and then traces in
Austen's novels.

5. Norman Page (*The Language of Jane Austen* [Oxford: Basil Blackwell,
1972]) discusses these points on pp. 115 and 121.

6. Susan Morgan, *In the Meantime: Character and Perception in Jane Austen's
Fiction* (Chicago: University of Chicago Press, 1980), p. 6. Her work, published after I had presented ideas similar to the ones enunciated in the present
article in a paper at the International Association for Philosophy and Litera-

ture (Case Western Reserve, May 1978), declares that "Austen's subject is the problem of perception" (p. 3). However, as becomes obvious later in this article, although our ideas independently begin at a similar origin, they diverge considerably.

7. Compare this interpretation with McKeon's rather sweeping statements on this topic: "Justification for reading *Pride and Prejudice* as a philosophical novel may be found in its much cited and variously interpreted opening sentence. . ." (p. 513).

His various renderings of the first sentence are imaginative and his philosophic interpretations cosmic:

The New Academic skepticism chooses a low place on those ladders, which is excellently named in the opening sentence of *Pride and Prejudice:* knowledge is based on self-evident truths, opinion can rise no higher than "a truth universally accepted," "possession of a good fortune" is a dubious degradation of vision of the ideal Good to possession of material goods, and "want of a wife" is a transformation of charity of *agape* or love of the good in itself to concupiscence or eros *or* matrimony.

This is a skeptical philosophy which credits what is generally accepted but doubts everything. It reduces knowledge to opinion, being to becoming, reality to appearance, aspiration and will to need and want, love to desire and concupiscence and cupidity. (p. 514)

8. Willard Van Orman Quine, "Two Dogmas of Empiricism" in *From a Logical Point of View*, 2nd ed. (New York: Harper and Row, 1961), p. 42.

9. ". . . handeln vom Netz, nicht von dem, was das Netz beschreibt," Ludwig Wittgenstein, *Tractatus Logico-Philosophicus*, and German text *Logisch-philosophische Abhandlung*, trans. D. F. Pears and B. F. McGuiness (London: Routledge & Kegan Paul, 1961), 6: 35.

10. Butler, p. 216, and Morgan, p. 99.

11. Duckworth, p. 125.

12. McKeon, for example, says: "The thought of *Pride and Prejudice* may be uncovered by interpreting it in accordance with any of a variety of philosophies, but it is peculiarly appropriate and enlightening to recognize its Platonizing echoes . . ." (p. 513).

13. Reginald Farrer, "Jane Austen," *Quarterly Review*, CCXXVIII (1917): 12; van Ghent, p. 103.

14. Richard Simpson, "Jane Austen," *North British Review*, LII (1870): 136.

15. Everett Zimmerman ("Pride and Prejudice" in *Pride and Prejudice*, *Nineteenth Century Fiction*, 23 [1968–1969]: 106) and Andrew E. Wright (*Jane Austen's Novels: A Study in Structure* [London: Chatto and Windus, 1964], p. 66) agree; however, Barbara Hardy, pp. 51 and 59, and McMaster, p. 729, see an opposite tendency as well.

16. Brower (p. 92) agrees, but Morgan (p. 92) objects.

17. McKeon agrees here, pp. 514–15.

18. Mudrick, p. 106

19. Drew, focusing on the ethical system in Jane Austen, identifies a moral disjunction within her novels, bridged at their end, which he thinks is ". . . the gift of the author to the readers, and as such is recognized as marking a point at the end of the story where the fiction and the world outside the fiction follow different paths . . ." (p. 148). He interprets this conjoining not only as a bow to the comic convention but as a persuasive moral device as well. This ethical stance, introduced into the aesthetic of her novel, he claims is a reason for her philosophic greatness: ". . . I am prepared to assert, Jane Austen, wishing to convince her readers of the existence of a world in which benevolence and private virtue, though distinct, were not incompatible but approached the harmony which is the ideal of every ethical system, displayed the distinctness and the coincidence through the medium of fiction. If this is true, it is not without reason that she has been given a place among the British moralists" (p. 149).
20. See, for example, Butler, p. 217, Brower, p. 180, and Mudrick, p. 111.
21. See, for example, Mudrick, p. 111.
22. Both Mansell (*The Novels of Jane Austen* [London: Macmillan, 1973], pp. x–xi) and Mudrick (p. 11) suggest that the inconsistency in the last part is due to Austen's determination to follow an intellectual plan.
23. Wright (p. 33) proposes Charlotte and Wickham in this connection. Zimmerman (pp. 66–67) mentions Mary, Mr. Collins, and Mr. Bennet; Morgan (p. 11), Mr. Bennet and Charlotte. Laurence Lerner (*The Truthtellers: Jane Austen, George Eliot, D. H. Lawrence* [New York: Schocken Books, 1967], p. 156) suggests even Jane.
24. Zimmerman, p. 66, and Mudrick, p. 99.
25. Wright (p. 33) points out that Wickham has much in common with Charlotte. Bingley's understanding of the world resembles Jane's.
26. Like Lydia and Mrs. Bennet, in her encounter with Wickham, her vanity obscures her sense and powers of observation. Like them also, she can dismiss the significance of whatever she believes not to be of immediate interest. She is as capable as Mr. Collins or Mary of disjoining a general principle from a concrete instance. Although she condemns Charlotte in the strongest possible terms for marrying for economic advantage, she defends Wickham's plan to do the same. She admits in a conversation with Darcy to having the same weakness as Mary and Mr. Collins of desiring to pronounce notable generalizations. Her statement that "Follies and nonsense, whims and inconsistencies *do* divert me" (p. 57), and Bingley's observation that she is a "studier of characters" (p. 42), to which she readily assents, tie Elizabeth to her father.

# Pride and Prejudice
## The Eyes Have It

When devoted readers of Jane Austen's fiction try to visualize the author, I imagine that, like myself, they recall the portrait-sketch by her sister Cassandra and perhaps also Hoppner's painting, believed to depict Jane as a girl.[1] The most striking feature on both canvases is the pair of large eyes, which, in the first, glance skeptically yet wistfully away from the spectator, while, in the second, they embrace the onlooker with what seems a wide-eyed yet sly ingenuousness. It is, of course, the stereoscopic vision of what her nephew James E. Austen-Leigh called those "bright hazel eyes"[2] that projects upon her fictional canvases her ironically detached yet sympathetically involved perceptions of life. And this is never more true than when the author's eyes view, from both without and within, the eyes of her characters.

Some readers feel, however, that though her vision is certainly accurate, it is by no means very penetrating or comprehensive. As Charlotte Brontë argues, "Her business is not half so much with the human heart as with the human eyes. . . ."[3] But this thrust by Austen's most celebrated critic not only sums up the still repeated indictment of her novels as finely wrought yet small in scope, but also provides an unintentional clue to the Braille-like sensitivity that lines the visible fabric of her best work. This is especially true of *Pride and Prejudice* (1813), which she described as that "little bit (two Inches wide) of Ivory on which I work with so fine a Brush."[4] Here "human eyes" become windows to the inmost depths of "the human heart"; and though Miss Austen, like Miss Dickinson, never *saw* a moor, her provincial romantic comedy also dramatizes a universal theme—the clash between appearances and reality, between proud and prejudicial *First Impressions* (the novel's original title) and tolerant and forgiving hindsight, which promotes mature foresight. By reviewing what probable causes led to the frequent appearance of eyes in *Pride and Prejudice* and by analyzing the optical contributions to character presentation, plotting, theme, and technique, we can further understand the insightful perceptiveness of Jane Austen's "bright hazel eyes" and perhaps expand that ivory from two inches to two leagues.

Before tracing the influences on Austen and reviewing the drama of eyes in *Pride and Prejudice*, however, we need to hear other comments on this area of her art. Frederick R. Karl, for example, while discussing the courtship ritual between Austen's heroines and suitors, remarks that "contact between them must therefore be made through the glance of an eye or the nuance of a word."[5] In a passing reference, David P. Demarest Jr. is more penetrating: "A good deal of the pleasure the reader finds in an Austen novel derives from a kind of detective story motif (recalling the novel's reiteration of eyes, sight, seeing, etc., one might say with a flash of thoroughly un-Austenian wit, that she writes about the 'private-eye')."[6] More comprehensively, Hugh L. Hennedy's "Acts of Perception in Jane Austen's Novels" offers a serious and deliberate examination of sight (and sound) in *Northanger Abbey* and *Persuasion*.[7] Finally, and most relevantly, Leslie H. Willis has briefly treated the sexual overtones of the "watcher watched" theme in *Pride and Prejudice*. The general implications of Willis's sexual reading, which I had not seen until after the original completion of this essay, certainly reinforce and complement the views presented here: "The act of looking plays a considerable part in the development of mutual awareness and reciprocal feeling between the principal characters, and its increasing complexity parallels the growing intricacy of personal relationships within the book."[8]

I

A glance at the probable influences at work, stimulating Austen's visual cues, suggests a very large frame indeed for those two inches of ivory—a frame composed of British empiricism, the Romantic revolution, the origin and demands of the novel as a genre, and the fictional (if not cultural) role of the Englishwoman. Although the limits of this essay allow only a general sketch of each influence and its impact, still such a survey is relevant not only to the understanding of visualization in *Pride and Prejudice*, but also to the composition of English fiction in general.

From Robinson Crusoe's sighting of human footprints in the sand to Stephen Dedalus's watching his ashplant score trails on the beach of Sandymount in the "Proteus" chapter of *Ulysses*, the English novel has historically been a product of the empirical spirit. For our purposes, this tradition of logical induction can be traced from Bacon's *The New Orga-*

*non* (1620), through Locke's *Essay Concerning Human Understanding* (1690), Newton's *Opticks* (1704), and Hartley's *Observations on Man* (1749), to Burke's *A Philosophical Inquiry into the Origin of Our Ideas of the Sublime and Beautiful* (c. 1756–1757). For example, Bacon writes in *The New Organon:* "All depends on keeping the eye steadily fixed upon the facts of nature and so receiving images as simply as they are."[9] Thus, the cornerstone of British empiricism is the acceptance of the primacy of perception as catalyst to ideas, or even as precondition of existence itself—Bishop Berkeley's *esse est percipi* on the one hand, and on the other, to turn Descartes around, *video ergo sum.* For as Ernest Tuveson has remarked apropos of post-Lockean aesthetics, empiricism and induction especially favored sight as the key to understanding: "From the nature of the mind as described by Locke, we could expect a new poetry to be highly visual in nature, for the faculty of sight came to monopolize the analysis of intellectual activity. Since ideas are images, since even complex ideas are multiple pictures, and since understanding itself is a form of perception, the visual and intellectual would tend to become amalgamated."[10] Howard O. Brogan is certainly correct in relating this tradition to Jane Austen, but just as surely wrong in failing to stress her thematic acceptance of truth and beauty as residing, at least partially, in the eye of the beholder: "Austen seems to reconstruct a kind of human experience which is permeated with the theoretical assumption that the material world exists objectively in what Newton described as 'absolute, true, and mathematical' space and time, quite apart from our relative and mutable subjective psychological impressions of it. . . ."[11]

In his "Biographical Notice" of Jane, her brother Henry explains that "her reading was very extensive in history and belles lettres; and her memory extremely tenacious."[12] Thus, although it is impossible to verify the specific influence of the empirical tradition, it seems a safe guess to assume that one existed, especially given her historical place in the pre-Romantic and Romantic milieus. Edmund Burke's essay on "the Sublime" illustrates just how indigenous sight and eyes were to the late eighteenth-century intellectual climate and helps suggest how pertinent the visible and visual are to the world of *Pride and Prejudice.* Not only does Burke describe the literal and metaphoric sources of ocular beauty in his section on "The Physical Cause of Love," he also relevantly reports that when the beloved is observed, "the eyelids are more closed than usual, and the eyes roll gently with an inclination to the object."[13] Furthermore, Burke explicitly links the visual and the intellectual: "The eye affects, as it is expressive of some qualities of the mind, and its principal power generally arises from this."[14] In one instance, he even goes so far as to assert that "there is no difference" between the eye and the mind.[15]

Similar allusions repeatedly appear in the drama of eyes in *Pride and Prejudice*.

But the general effect of this empirical spirit on English fiction, and here especially on Jane Austen, is that it helps arrest the shifting sands of mutable and chaotic experience through the capturing vision of the protagonist. Ironically, this visual capture, the multiple or unified point of view of the novel, is both relative to the perceiver and universal for each individual reader, since it repeatedly sustains the unique authority of private perception.[16] But cognition must begin with sight—Robinson Crusoe induces the presence of fellow human beings and, just as assuredly, Stephen Dedalus opens his eyes after experimenting with feigned blindness and reasons that life is "what you damn well have to see." Similarly, Elizabeth and Darcy must both learn to consecrate visible fact instead of fabricating untested fantasies. Yet (and it is here that Austen begins to flirt with Romantic epistemology) both must also learn to see through the phenomenological mirage, which sensible appearances sometimes conjure up, to inner truths.

Romanticism, of course, took this original sensory bias of British empiricism and used it as a magical open sesame to unlock the doors to the interior self. Although it would be misleading to argue that Jane Austen is a wholehearted Romantic (self-schooled as she was in neoclassic aesthetics), still it would be equally misleading to forget that the same forces from the cult of sensibility which shaped Romanticism also served as her favorite reading fare. For example, Henry Austen reports that, "her favorite moral writers were Johnson in prose, and Cowper in verse";[17] and though Johnson places one of her feet firmly in the Enlightenment, Cowper, with lines like the following from *The Task*, stretches the other just as firmly to pre-Romanticism with its penchant for the more dynamic "speculative" vision: "now roves the eye;/And, posted on this speculative height,/Exults in its command." Moreover, the polarity between sense and sensibility in Austen's fiction is not always so distant as some contend; in isolation both responses, as Austen often demonstrates, have their blind spots. Thus, as we will see, *Pride and Prejudice* generally shares Blake's condemnation of "single vision and Newton's sleep" and echoes his celebration of "double vision" (in his verse epistle to Thomas Butts). In other words, the novel affirms the Coleridgean ideal of the balance of opposite or discordant qualities, both external and internal reality, both vision and insight.

Henry even provides a relevant source of Austen's Romanticism: "She was a warm and judicious admirer of landscape, both in nature and on canvass. At a very early age she was enamoured of Gilpin on the Picturesque; and she seldom changed her opinions either on books or men."[18]

Significantly, William Gilpin, in his *Three Essays* (1792) on the picturesque, constantly denies the absolute authority of individual perceptions: "Ideas of beauty vary with the object, and with the eye of the spectator."[19] Furthermore, like Cowper and anticipating Austen's handling of perspective during the tour of Pemberley, he urges the spectator to approach a picturesque subject from as many different viewpoints as possible. In true Romantic fashion, Gilpin ultimately celebrates the epiphanic power of visual perceptions: "We are most delighted, when some grand scene, tho perhaps of incorrect composition, rising before the eye, strikes us beyond the power of thought . . . and every mental operation is suspended. . . . We feel rather than survey it."[20] Such early Romantic notions provide the substance of Henry Tilney's lectures to Catherine in *Northanger Abbey;* but more than that, they can generally help us appreciate the visual themes and aesthetic techniques of *Pride and Prejudice.* And obviously they helped Jane Austen in her own drawing and sketching, another probable influence on her penchant for visualization. Thus Wordsworth's boast in his Preface to *Lyrical Ballads* that "I have at all times endeavored to look steadily at my subject" could almost as easily have been written by Jane Austen.

As a genre, the novel itself, originating as a model for correct letter-writing and thereafter often dependent upon epistolary conventions, presupposes a creative scenario whose opening act normally recites visual first impressions and whose last act provides a mental soliloquy reflecting upon such visual data. More particularly, the prescribed epistolary format is: "I saw such-and-such . . . but I think this-and-this about it"; later, nonepistolary fiction simply compresses this format into a spontaneous meditation upon the visual, the immediacy of which epistolary fiction had been at a loss to effect. As far as I know, however, only Reva Stump in her *Movement and Vision in George Eliot's Novels*[21] has comprehensively traced the impact of *seeing* through a novelist's canon; and yet optical vocabulary, and its ultimate concern with correct point of view, pervades English fiction perhaps more than any other kind of trope. And whether or not *Pride and Prejudice* was originally written in epistolary form, as many critics believe, we will see that it toys incessantly with what aesthetic ophthalmologist Stephen Dedalus calls the "ineluctable modality of the visible."

One prevalent theme in English fiction which has not received enough scholarly attention is the lady-in-waiting, or lady-in-watching, syndrome. Most clearly mythologized in "The Lady of Shalott," this theme provides many of the most memorable moments in the British tradition—Pamela peering out the window for Mr. B's dreaded/desired arrival in Lincolnshire; Catherine Earnshaw's peeping from outside the window of

Thrushcross Grange at the "other world" of polite society; Eustacia Vye on Rainbarrow, scanning Egdon with a telescope for the approach of Wildeve; and Clarissa Dalloway watching through her window as the old woman next door retires for the night. In brief, I think there are two interesting points to be made regarding this theme: one, the window is usually metonymic for the woman; and two, female novelists, as Marilyn Butler has also generally recognized,[22] seem most sensitive to the theme. Three of the above examples serve to testify to the reappearance of the window in this tradition; and its symbology need not be read in any Freudian sense since, as Shakespeare's Sonnet XXIV expresses, windows have often represented eyes: "Mine eyes have drawn their shape, and thine for me / Are windows to my breast." But more simply and accurately, the window is both the limiting frame for the woman's watchful waiting, usually for the man, and the separation between interior or feminine domesticity—waiting on the male—and exterior or masculine adventure—working toward a goal. Perhaps Anne Brontë's *The Tenant of Wildfell Hall* best describes the general *waiting* theme when Helen Huntingdon notes in her diary her husband Arthur's portrait of a wife: "Judging from appearances, his idea of a wife, is a thing to love one devotedly, and stay at home—to wait upon her husband, and amuse him and minister to his comfort in every possible way, while he chooses to stay with her; and when he is absent, to attend to his interests, domestic or otherwise, and patiently wait his return" (Chapter 29). Interestingly, portrait-painting, and especially that genre which Mario Praz calls *Biedermeier,* or scenes of bourgeois, and often melancholic, domestic tranquillity,[23] depicts again and again interiors with a single woman sitting by a window with a book on her lap and a setter at her feet, each waiting for her / its master to return. Perhaps, though, John Everett Millais' wistful portrait (minus the window) of a watchful woman individualized by only her red bonnet and dwarfed in middle distance by the framing stone wall and surrounding natural landscape, most insightfully captures the melancholy vigilance of the *waiting* theme. Appropriately, it is simply titled *Waiting* (1854).

At any rate, as a woman writer, Jane Austen is intimately familiar with window-watching. For instance, the Bennet sisters' first sight of Bingley is from "the advantage . . . of an upper window."[24] And Elizabeth, similarly, after her climactic meeting with Darcy at Pemberley, "resolved not to be out of sight of the inn"; and when he finally arrives, "she retreated from the window, fearful of being seen" (p. 260). Mrs. Bennet's "period of anxiety and fretfulness" by the window, while awaiting the arrival of Bingley and his long-hoped-for proposal to Jane, provides a comic commentary on this theme, but also brings the happily-ever-after reunion of Elizabeth and Darcy: "But on the third morning after his arrival in Hertforshire, she saw him from her dressing-room window, enter the paddock, and ride towards the house. . . . Elizabeth, to satisfy her mother, went to the window—she looked—she saw Mr. Darcy with him and sat down again by her sister" (p. 332).

But what makes the woman writer so natively predisposed to watching—like Jane Eyre, whom Rochester, disguised as the old gypsy fortuneteller, describes as habitually "sitting in that window-seat" (Chapter 19)? The answer is not difficult: one who, like a child, should be seen but not heard must *ipso facto* keep her eyes and ears open to hear but especially to see so that, as a cultural have-not, she can gain every possible vantage point. And a young woman like Fanny Burney, one of Austen's favorite authors, whose diaries depicting eighteenth-century drawing rooms illustrate the value of such silent observation and whose *Evelina* probably influenced the plot of *Pride and Prejudice*, is just one example of such a silent vantage point. Jane Austen herself is another example; as her brother admits, "Though the frailities, foibles, and follies of others could not escape her immediate detection, yet even on their vices did she never trust herself to comment with unkindness. . . . Where extenuation was impossible, she had a sure refuge in silence."[25] The significance of her contemplative observation is, however, loudly proclaimed in the visual message and method of *Pride and Prejudice*.

## II

Generally, eyes are an index to character in three overlapping ways: descriptive epithets applied specifically to eyes and the closely related position or attitude of the eyes; the act of looking at someone or being looked at by someone; and the manner in which individual country homes are visualized or provide visualization. For example, early in the novel Elizabeth reveals the delicate poise between gullibility and tolerance in her sister Jane's outlook toward others: "You never see a fault in anybody. All the world are good and agreeable in your eyes. . . . With *your* good sense, to be so honestly blind to the follies and nonsense of others!" (p. 14). As so often occurs with the visual imagery, Elizabeth's barb here is ironically double-edged, since she at this point is herself "honestly blind" to the fact that Jane's wide-eyed tolerance, which is parallel to Bingley's "blind partiality" (p. 90) toward Darcy, is exactly that saving grace which she herself sadly lacks. On the other hand, Lydia's dishonest blindness in distinguishing between appearances and reality and her irrepressible narcissism both preview her headlong but unplanned fall from honor at Brighton: "She saw with the creative eye of fancy, the streets of that gay bathing place covered with officers. She saw herself the object of attention, to tens and scores of them at present unknown" (p. 232).

Similarly, the matchmaking and fortune-making designs of Mrs. Bennet are twice almost identically revealed when Bingley's friendly attentions to the Bennets become first apparent: "Mrs. Bennet's eyes sparkled with pleasure" (pp. 30, 61). Mr. Collins' marriage-making designs (he considers proposals to three different young ladies in the course of a few days) and lack of self-insight are comparably illustrated when, after Elizabeth's almost rude unwillingness to be left alone with him, this eyesore blithely counters with: "You would have been less amiable in my eyes had there not been this little unwillingness" (p. 105). Fittingly enough, Elizabeth uses visual vocabulary to portray Collins' third choice, Charlotte Lucas, as a spinster ready to accept anybody's proposal: "she had chosen it with her eyes open" (p. 216). Finally, in their private interview, Darcy's aunt, Lady Catherine de Bourgh, exclaims to Elizabeth: "Unfeeling, selfish girl! Do you not consider that a connection with you, must disgrace him in the eyes of everybody?" (p. 357), thus indicating the normative value for her of the public viewpoint. But the actual moral blindness of the public view is clear from its visual fascination with Wickham: "Mr. Wickham was the happy man towards whom almost every female eye was turned" (p. 76).

As most readers might suspect, however, the most spectacular drama of the eyes is staged between Darcy and Elizabeth. Darcy, first of all, betrays his pride in his first impression of Elizabeth: "Though he had detected with a critical eye more than one failure of perfect symmetry in her form, he was forced to acknowledge her figure to be light and pleasing" (p. 23). For Darcy such a begrudging compliment is a major step toward falling in love, as Mr. Bennet's later appraisal implies: "Mr. Darcy, who never looks at any woman but to see a blemish" (p. 363). But Elizabeth herself is aware of this inclination; and her awareness provokes the half-conscious coquetry that wins Darcy and reveals her own interest: "He has a very satirical eye, and if I do not begin by being impertinent myself, I shall soon grow afraid of him" (p. 24). It is, of course, this same "very satirical eye," the testimony of false pride in his own discernment, which prompts Darcy to persuade Bingley of Jane's apparent lack of interest in him, thus producing his later soul-searching and humbling honesty in the letter to Elizabeth and finally his reconciling contrition. During that first "evening's scrutiny," though, Darcy's "eyes were directed with a very serious expression towards Bingley and Jane, who were dancing together" (pp. 92–93). Still, it is Darcy's visual preoccupation with Elizabeth that most frequently labels his fortunate fall from

Lady Catherine's brand of class superiority. More will be said about this warfare of the eyes in the discussion of plotting in the novel; here we need simply observe one early skirmish, which indicates the convoluted complexity of eyes eyeing eyes in *Pride and Prejudice:*

> Occupied in observing Mr. Bingley's attentions to her sister, Elizabeth was far from suspecting that she was herself becoming an object of some interest in the eyes of his friend. Mr. Darcy had at first scarcely allowed her to be pretty; he had looked at her without admiration at the ball; and when they next met, he looked at her only to criticize. But no sooner had he made it clear to himself and his friends that she had hardly a good feature in her face, than he began to find it was rendered uncommonly intelligent by the beautiful expression of her dark eyes. To this discovery succeeded some others equally mortifying. (p. 23)

It is impossible to trace the pedigree of the innumerable references to Elizabeth's bright, dark eyes—Burke may be one such source. But their appearance as well as their viewpoint is certainly a major focus in the novel. For example, when Darcy tells the conniving Caroline Bingley that "I have been meditating upon the very great pleasure which a pair of fine eyes in the face of a pretty woman can bestow," she "immediately fixed her eyes on this face" (p. 27). Her basilisk stare continues throughout the novel as she jealously watches Darcy watch Elizabeth's eyes. She repeatedly offers caustic "witticisms on *fine eyes*" (p. 46), trying to provoke him by her sarcasm, and finally at Pemberley loses both composure and Darcy when her public ridicule ironically exposes her own inferiority: "As for her eyes, which have sometimes been called so fine, I never could perceive anything extraordinary in them. They have a sharp, shrewish look, which I do not like at all" (p. 271). Consequently, whether Elizabeth's "bright eyes are . . . upbraiding" (p. 92) Sir William Lucas's gallantry, whether there appear "tears in her eyes" (p. 283) upon discussing Lydia's downfall with the Gardiners, or whether "betwitched" Darcy is musing that "it would not be easy, indeed, to catch their expression, but their colour and shape, and the eye-lashes, so remarkably fine, might be copied" (pp. 52–53), these enchanting orbs capture the attention of everyone.

Furthermore, their gaze is often clearsighted and penetrating. For example, Elizabeth "had never been blind to the impropriety of her father's behavior as a husband. She had always seen it with pain" (p. 236). The prejudice in these same eyes, however, keeps them "less clear-sighted" (p. 149) to Bingley's feelings for Jane and totally closed to the real worthlessness of Wickham and worth of Darcy. When Jane's letter reporting

Lydia's disappearance with Wickham confirms Darcy's earlier indictment of him, though, Elizabeth's "eyes were opened to his real character" (p. 277). Here their physical beauty is finally matched by their moral insight.

Moreover, the reader's initial response to the foil relationships among Bingley, Wickham, and Darcy is conditioned by visual vocabulary; and here first impressions are often accurate—only later in the novel do appearances begin ironically to mask the truth. Thus, Bingley's innocuous vanity, which his friend gently exposes as "the appearance of humility" (p. 48) in their early debate on epistolary excellence, is first hinted at when Bingley in his fine "blue coat" pretends to visit Mr. Bennet, while actually entertaining "hopes of being admitted to a sight of the young ladies" (p. 9). That evening, however, it is rather "his friend Mr. Darcy" who "soon drew the attention of the room by his fine, tall person, handsome features, noble mien . . . and he was looked at with admiration for about half the evening" (p. 10). The deceiving Wickham, though, purposely confuses appearances and reality by ridiculing Darcy to Elizabeth in the same manner that Miss Bingley ridicules Elizabeth to Darcy. Protesting too much and thus revealing his own inadequacies, like Caroline, Wickham charges that "the world is blinded by his fortune and consequence, or frightened by his high and imposing manners, and sees him only as he chuses [*sic*] to be seen" (p. 78). Wickham's evaluation is doubly ironic since it not only provokes Elizabeth's assent, thereby exposing her initial blindness to the real worth of the two gentlemen; but also this apparently false statement is actually correct since the world is "blinded" by Darcy's self-imposed appearance, which cloaks, however, his real, deeper merit, not the lack of it.

The point of view or "prospect" afforded to and by each of the country homes in *Pride and Prejudice* also provides a visible and visual symbol of the personality inhabiting the home.[26] For example, Netherfield, the temporary estate of shilly-shally, "charming" Bingley, simply overviews "a charming prospect over that gravel walk" (p. 42). Lady Catherine's criticism of the Bennets' home is equally telling, since in stressing the blinding sunlight from the setting sun it connotes the moral blindness of both shortsighted Mrs. Bennet and detached, longsighted Mr. Bennet: "This must be a most convenient sitting room for the evening, in summer; the windows are full west" (p. 352). Likewise, Mr. Collins' parsonage at Hunsford allows ample opportunity for this watchdog's favorite hobby—"looking out of window [*sic*] in his own book room, which fronted the road" (p. 168) before Lady Catherine's country estate, Rosings. Thus his house becomes a symbol of the sycophant himself, who "wished for" nothing more than "the power of displaying the grandeur of his patroness to his wondering visitors, and of letting them see her civility towards himself and his wife" (p. 160). In fact, "of all the views which his garden, or which the country, or the kingdom could boast, none were to be compared with the prospect of Rosings, afforded by an opening in the trees that bordered the park nearly opposite the front of his house" (p. 156). And what of this "handsome modern building, well situated on rising ground" (p. 156)? Appropriately, we are never told that the elevated structure looks out upon anything, but only that everything else looks up to it. Like its inhabitants, Rosings consequently is one of those "instances of elegant breeding" usually observed only "about the court" (p. 160)—at least so thinks Sir William Lucas. As a matter of fact, the only observable bits of landscape reiterated by the text are private, sheltered walking-paths, and palings, or fences, both of which screening devices are emblems of aristocratic elitism and its mania for privacy from lower-class observation. Inside, Mrs. Jenkinson's only duties seem to be listening to Miss de Bourgh, Lady Catherine's daughter, and "placing a screen in the proper direction before her eyes" (p. 162).

Contrasting significantly with Rosings' closed point of view and life-denying artifice, however, the visible blending of both Nature and Art at Pemberley discloses the true character of its owner: "the eye was instantly caught by Pemberley House. . . . It was a large, handsome, stone building, standing well on rising ground, and backed by a ridge of woody hills;—and in front, a stream of some natural importance was swelled into greater, but without any artificial appearance. Its banks were neither formal nor falsely adorned. Elizabeth was delighted. She had never seen a place for which nature had done more, or where natural beauty had been so little counteracted by an awkward taste" (p. 245). And, of course, as famously noted by Walter Scott, and humorously by Elizabeth herself, the heroine's love for Darcy first appears, in her words, upon "seeing his beautiful grounds in Pemberley" (p. 373). At any rate, Pemberley certainly transcends the claustrophobic atmosphere of Rosings, for it "gave the eye power to wander" over its "many charming views" (p. 253). These liberating views, however, are more than simply physical; they are also mental since, although Elizabeth "seemed to direct her eyes to such objects as they [the Gardiners] pointed out, she distinguished no part of the scene. Her thoughts were all fixed on that one spot of Pemberley House, whichever it might be, where Mr. Darcy then was" (p. 253).

Once inside the house, Elizabeth discovers that, unlike the one-eyed narcissism of Rosings, "its windows opening to the ground, admitted a most refreshing view" (p. 267). Moreover, her visual perceptions of the interior, besides again contrasting with those of Rosings, further confirm her new impression of Darcy: "Elizabeth saw, with admiration of his taste, that it was neither gaudy nor uselessly fine; with less of splendor, and more real elegance, than the furniture of Rosings" (p. 246). Finally, upon visiting the picture gallery, Elizabeth's newfound vision of Darcy is complete. Interestingly, their visual drama, which is specifically reviewed in the next section on plotting, here reaches a climax when Elizabeth very willingly believes Darcy's portrait is making eyes at her: "As she stood before the canvas, on which he was represented, and fixed his eyes upon herself, she thought of his regard with a deeper sentiment of gratitude than it had ever raised before; she remembered its warmth, and softened its impropriety of expression" (p. 251).

### III

The plot of *Pride and Prejudice* relies so consistently on the body language of the eyes that identifiable patterns and postures of watching develop, which in turn clarify the different stages of the unfolding love story of Elizabeth and Darcy. This structure provides three general movements symbolizing their initial distorted vision of each other, their counter di-vision, and finally their corrected and correct re-vision. More specifically, it suggests that, blinded by the early impressions of love at first sight, Darcy, with increasing frequency and fervor, stares at uninterested Elizabeth, herself plagued by a prejudicial kind of tunnel-vision. Next these visual postures reverse themselves, and Elizabeth curiously and attentively spies on Darcy, while he looks away. Finally, the roles grow more flexibly interchangeable as both can look and look away with equal ease and dis-ease.

As suggested, the lengthy first act of their ocular drama presents Darcy, somewhat against his will, voyeuristically fascinated by the mere physical sight of Elizabeth, and Elizabeth, against her own willfulness and while continuously disclaiming any interest whatsoever, piqued at his visual attentions. Thus, Darcy must learn to see through mere physical appearances in order to gain insight to Elizabeth's interior beauty. Furthermore, as Elizabeth later playfully charges, he must not "disguise" (p. 380) his own true self, but honestly and openly reveal it to her sight. And finally, he must relinquish his voyeuristic posture to act positively in Elizabeth's behalf and thereby become more than a mere spectator of life and love. Elizabeth, in contrast, must not be duped by the misleading appearances of Darcy's visual interest; only in this way can she achieve the clear vision and self-insight necessary for the kind of love match her father's visual metaphor predicts would insure her happiness: "I know your disposition, Lizzy. I know that you could be neither happy nor respectable, unless you truly esteemed your husband; unless you looked up to him as a superior" (p. 376). At the outset during their stay at Netherfield, however, it is Darcy who looks up, while Elizabeth condescendingly looks down and, in effect, away: ". . . Elizabeth could not help observing as she turned over some music books that lay on the instrument, how frequently Mr. Darcy's eyes were fixed on her. She hardly knew how to suppose that she could be an object of admiration to so great a man; and yet that he should look at her because he disliked her, was still more strange. . . . [His apparent rudeness] did not pain her. She liked him too little to care for his approbation" (p. 51).

Interestingly, in a variation of these visual postures, Darcy repeatedly insists to himself that he can hold command over his eyes and not look at all toward Elizabeth. Such a comical *volte-face* protests too much and is an even clearer indication of his growing preoccupation with her, as his implied Spartan agony suggests: "Steady to his purpose, he scarcely spoke ten words to her through the whole of Saturday, and though they were at one time left to themselves for half an hour, he adhered most conscientiously to his book, and would not even look at her" (p. 60). In a similar humorous reversal of ocular form, after her observance of the curious meeting between Darcy and Wickham and after the latter's false description of their past history together, Elizabeth fantasizes seeing herself watch Darcy's torment as he beholds her dancing with his enemy. Again, her "pleasure" ironically betrays more delight than disdain: "Elizabeth thought with pleasure of dancing a great deal with Mr. Wickham, and of seeing a confirmation of everything in Darcy's looks and behaviour" (p. 86). Later at the ball, while her mother rudely insults the eavesdropping Darcy, she tries to realize her earlier fantasy as "she could not help frequently glancing her eye at Mr. Darcy" (p. 100). During the pivotal scene of Darcy's first proposal, however, the two engage in a rare confrontation, the momentary honesty of which is mutually cathartic and prepares for the subsequent therapeutic and tranquil review of their emotion: "Mr. Darcy, who was leaning against the mantle-piece with his eyes fixed on her face, seemed to catch her words with no less resentment than surprise. His complexion became pale with anger, and the disturbance of his mind was visible in every feature" (p. 190).

After the faulty vision between Darcy and Elizabeth in the first act of their courtship, there follows a brief counter act of di-vision, or devaluation of first impressions and subsequent reevaluation of each other, based upon memory. The two scenes in this act consist of the interlude of their separation, while Elizabeth is still on stage and Darcy is off, and their reunion at Pemberley. During this period, Elizabeth views and "review[s]" (p. 193) the proposal scene; but not until her reading of Darcy's eye-opening letter does she understand the scene's real import,

Darcy, or (almost) herself. Her self-analysis is crucial, not only because its thematic significance rests upon visual "discernment" and blindness, but also because its irony reveals that Elizabeth does not understand that she is falling in love and hence still does not totally "know myself": "She grew absolutely ashamed of herself.—Of neither Darcy nor Wickham could she think, without feeling that she had been blind, partial, prejudiced, absurd. 'How despicably have I acted!' she cried.—'I who have prided myself on my discernment! . . . How humiliating is this discovery!—Yet, how just a humiliation!—Had I been in love, I could not have been more wretchedly blind. But vanity, not love, has been my folly. . . . Till this moment, I never knew myself' " (p. 208).[27]

As we have already observed, visual gestures reverse themselves in this act's second scene at Pemberley, and "out of sight" in no way signifies "out of mind" for Elizabeth. She now "walked in quest of the only face whose features would be known to her"; and the face does fix "his eyes upon herself" (p. 251)—but Darcy's "eyes" are only oil paint on canvas. In fact, throughout these chapters preceding the news of Lydia's disgrace, Elizabeth's eyes more and more seek out Darcy's; while he, playing the perfect host and tour guide, points out things and people of interest, for example his sister, but does not play his old game of eyewitness to Elizabeth's every move and look. Presumably, this indicates that Darcy, once burnt and twice shy, is recovering from erroneous (because built primarily upon the mirage of physical infatuation) first impressions and is recoiling from again provoking false impressions in Elizabeth. In fact, the only mention of his eyeballing occurs when Darcy cannot help it during their first, unexpected meeting at Pemberley. Here the honest emotional release is a photocopy of the visual catharsis of the first proposal, with the exception that mutual anger is replaced by mutual, though slightly suppressed, admiration: "So abrupt was his appearance, that it was impossible to avoid his sight. Their eyes instantly met, and the cheeks of each were overspread with the deepest blush" (p. 251).

The last brief act in this visual courtship parallels the second in that it too consists of a separation during which distance increases mutual desire, and then another, and this time final, revision and reunion. The separation (following Elizabeth's abrupt departure for Longbourn) significantly occurs after "one serious, parting, look" (*sic*, p. 279) from Darcy and allows the heroine to throw a wistful "retrospective glance over the whole of their acquaintance, so full of contradictions and varieties" (p. 279). During this tranquil recollection of her past emotional vicissitudes, Elizabeth thematically reviews the central love-at-first-sight problem, "so often described as arising on a first interview with its object" (p. 279), and concludes that her first nearsighted impressions of

Darcy and Wickham were indeed distorted. This crucial insight reinforces her earlier admission of being blinded by appearances and blind to realities as she now exclaims regarding Wickham: "When *my* eyes were opened to his real character.—Oh! had I known what I ought, what I dared, to do! But I knew not—I was afraid of doing too much. Wretched, wretched, mistake!" (pp. 277–78). Again, here, a more farsighted visual sense provides a more reliable sensibility, and Elizabeth's displacement of pride and prejudice by humility and tolerance previews her happily-ever-after reunion with Darcy. But what of Darcy, who is again offstage? Significantly, his "parting look" is his last visual gesture for some time as he most conclusively relinquishes his passive voyeurism and initiates positive action to effect Wickham's marriage to Lydia and thereby earn his own to Elizabeth.

In the last scene of the novel, both are able to look and look away with equal spontaneity, control, and curiosity and thus achieve the new vision, or re-vision, which heralds their united maturity. Furthermore, their embarrassed and hesitant glances, which begin the scene, are almost look-for-look mirrored in the identical visual confusion between Jane and Bingley. This is especially true in chapters 11 and 12 of Volume III, where Jane, waiting for Bingley's appearance, fluctuates between "a smile of delight which added lustre to her eyes" (p. 334) and "striving to be composed . . . without daring to lift up her eyes" (p. 335). Elizabeth, flustered by Darcy's noncommittal appearance, reacts similarly: "When occasionally, unable to resist the impulse of curiosity, she raised her eyes to his face, she as often found him looking at Jane, as at herself, and frequently on no object but the ground" (p. 336). And yet at other times, for example upon her mother's rambling about Lydia's marriage, "Elizabeth dared not lift up her eyes. How Mr. Darcy looked, therefore, she could not tell" (p. 336). As Bingley's attentions and intentions to Jane become embarrassingly obvious to all, "his eyes . . . turned towards Mr. Darcy, with an expression of half-laughing alarm" (p. 340). And during the card game, Darcy's attentions to Elizabeth are equally humorous and visually telling: "His eyes were so often turned towards her side of the room, as to make him play as unsuccessfully as herself" (p. 342). Finally, after the helpful interference of Lady Catherine, Elizabeth and Darcy take that momentous walk during which the eye's vision is replaced with the heart's insight: "Had Elizabeth been able to encounter his eye, she might have seen how well the expression of heart-felt delight, diffused over his face, became him; but, though she could not look, she could listen, and he told her of feelings, which, in proving of what importance she was to him, made his affection every moment more valuable" (p. 366).

## IV

It remains for us to discuss the thematic and technical importance of visual perception in *Pride and Prejudice*. In the Preface to *Jane Eyre*, Charlotte Brontë warns her reader that "appearance should not be mistaken for truth"; and this simple but universal nostrum lies at the core of Jane Austen's masterpiece. Moreover, she provides two guides to clear visual understanding: accuracy of perception and variety of perception, and both control the novel's theme and technique. Both define the well-rounded individual as one who can see through optical illusions to the real truth.

When Elizabeth considers her walking tour with the Gardiners, she stresses accuracy in a way reminiscent of Gilpin's *Three Essays:* "Oh! what hours of transport we shall spend! And when we do return, it shall not be like other travellers, without being able to give one accurate idea of anything. We *will* know where we have gone—we *will* recollect what we have seen" (p. 154).[28] In more emotional matters, however, the three detours of pride, prejudice, and early love, or infatuation, retard accurate recollection "of what we have seen." Pride, whether Darcy's or Elizabeth's, makes one hypermetropic, or longsighted, able to see only in terms of one's own magnified perspective. Prejudice, conversely, makes one myopic, or shortsighted, able to see only in terms of one's own narrow bias. As Elizabeth teases Darcy: Do you "never allow yourself to be blinded by prejudice?" (p. 93). Consequently, Everett Zimmerman is quite right in observing that ". . . pride and prejudice are qualities which thwart any moral perspective on events."[29] Finally, as Shakespeare's Sonnet CXXXVII indicates, love, or better infatuation, results in total loss of external sight: "Thou blind fool, Love, what dost thou to mine eyes/ That they behold, and see not what they see?" In a real sense, all three distortions of accurate sight can be diagnosed as symptoms of narcissism—impaired vision due to a subjective blind spot—and all three plague Elizabeth especially. The only cure for her impaired vision is added experience, the increasing accumulation of a wide variety of different perceptions. Even the sententious Mr. Collins can ironically draw attention to this limited "scope" of Elizabeth's knowledge: "I have the highest opinion in the world of your excellent judgement in all matters within the scope of your understanding. . . . Pardon me for neglecting to profit by your advice, which on every other subject shall be my constant guide, though in the case before us [addressing Darcy without an introduction] I consider myself more fitted by education and habitual study to decide on what is right and wrong than a young lady like yourself" (p. 97). After accurately observing the inconstancy of Bingley, but even before her eyes are so opened to Wickham, Elizabeth ironically employs a visual metaphor which previews the final scope of her full vision: "The more I see of the world, the more am I dissatisfied with it; and every day confirms my belief in the inconsistency of all human characters, and of the little dependence that can be placed on the appearance of either merit or sense" (p. 135). When she finally resolves her cynicism and penetrates through "the appearance" of things, thereby viewing the real truth with tolerance and forgiveness, Elizabeth's character is complete. And an interesting analogue to this development of Elizabeth's mature vision is the similar maturation of the critically neglected Mary Bennet, who grows from an avid and pretentious reader, eyeing and then spouting "new observations of threadbare morality" (p. 60) to being, at the very end of the novel, "obliged to mix more with the world" (p. 386), and thus presumably accumulating a more varied vision of reality.

## V

If the reader is to earn Mary's and especially Elizabeth's wider vision, he or she must pay special attention to Jane Austen's visual manipulation of point of view; for technique most persuasively yet also most imperceptibly argues for the revolving dialectic between the eye and the I. Perhaps Austen's preoccupation with contrasting points of view stems from her love of Samuel Richardson's epistolary variety; at least her brother tells us that Richardson's different characters "gratified the natural discrimination of her mind."[30] On the other hand, perhaps the influence is Gilpin and the Picturesque School's[31] demand for multiple spatial frames of view, for as we have heard Henry report, "She was a warm and judicious admirer of landscape, both in nature and on canvass."[32] At any rate, the nineteenth-century mania for what Morse Peckham calls the "drive for orientation,"[33] and what we can simply describe as the need to collect and absorb as many frames of epistemological reference as possible, assuredly is reflected in the conflicting demands Jane Austen's technique places upon her readers. Thus, as her focus changes, we, like Elizabeth herself, are constantly asked willingly to suspend our disbelief or belief, to reserve judgment and sympathy while we sift through all the visible evidence. As Howard Babb declares, "In *Pride and Prejudice* there is no one on whom we can depend for a true account. Rather, we are for the most part confined to Elizabeth's deeply biased perceptions, and Jane Austen tempts us to accept her heroine's view of Darcy at every turn, though just as consistently leaving the door open to a more favorable interpretation of his behavior."[34] But, we must still ask, how exactly are Elizabeth's and the reader's visual problems identical, and how, then, do accuracy and variety of vision relate to technique?

In the celebrated irony of the novel's opening passage, Jane Austen juxtaposes the "little known . . . views" of a "single man in possession of a good fortune" against the preconceived "truth . . . so well fixed in the minds of the surrounding families" (p. 3). And, of course, it is the "little known views" of Darcy and Wickham, more especially than Bingley, which collide against the prejudged "truths" of Elizabeth and, by extension, the reader, both of whom base their first impressions upon circumstantial, visual evidence. Depending upon the visual metaphor, Wayne Booth's description of early reader involvement in *Emma* is useful in understanding our similar participation in *Pride and Prejudice:* "We learn much of what we know from the narrator, but she turns over more and more of summary to Emma as she feels more and more sure of our seeing precisely to what degree Emma is to be trusted."[35] However, and as we have repeatedly seen, in *Pride and Prejudice* the controlling point of view is much more mobile and flexible than this; and the reader is aware of multiple and extremely diverse spatial-temporal frames of visual reference. Such awareness is not granted to Elizabeth or the reader of *Emma.* For example, Elizabeth's and Darcy's debate over the merits of living at relatively short or long distances from one's family (pp. 178–79) suggests the need to observe an object from many different spatial distances in order to know its total reality. Thus, from different angles and distances at Pemberley, the reader is able to screen Elizabeth's second impressions of Darcy through the more distant and normative eyewitness vision of the Gardiners. This provides the reader with a pair of ironic bifocals and sometimes even trifocals, while he or she watches the Gardiners watch Elizabeth watch Darcy. Because of such multiple visual advantages, the reader's vision fairly early outgrows Elizabeth's more limited and slower-developing perspective. By the time of her marriage to Darcy, however, Elizabeth too has been able to see from all the different points of view in time and space presented in the novel. Thus, as irony against her decreases and she learns to laugh at her own past blindness to other perspectives (pp. 380 ff.), the narrative perspective melts into Elizabeth's own. Heroine, reader, narrator, and author finally share one unified vision.

In retrospect, we have observed throughout this essay how significant the act of seeing is to the world of Jane Austen in general and to her created world of *Pride and Prejudice* in particular. Predictably, her emphasis on sight places her in the firm neoclassic tradition of British empiricism; somewhat unpredictably, however, it also demonstrates her more subtle affinities with the Romantic revolution and thus urges us to reconsider or at least qualify the usual tendency to label Austen as a literary conservative if not reactionary. Thus, *Pride and Prejudice* provokes its reader to look before and after in literary history. We recall earlier heroines whose limited domestic purview is captured by the talismanic window frame. But, on the other hand, we may also want to consider whether Austen's concern with modulating perspectives even anticipates the more radical examination of multiple frames of reference in a modern work like *To the Lighthouse*.[36] Our ultimate experience of the novel is probably less venturesome, but presumably more vital because it focuses on our growing delight in watching Elizabeth and Darcy make eyes at each other. In repeating this characteristic and universal act of human signification, they do no more nor less than reflect their creator's own delight in making eyes.

*Mark M. Hennelly, Jr.*
*California State University*

# NOTES

1. For photographs of both portraits, see Peter Quennell, *A History of English Literature* (Springfield, Massachusetts: G. & C. Merriam Co., 1973), pp. 329–30.
2. J. E. Austen-Leigh, *A Memoir of Jane Austen*, 2nd ed. (1871), ed. R. W. Chapman (Oxford: The Clarendon Press, 1926), p. 87.
3. Quoted in Mark Schorer, "Pride Unprejudiced," *Kenyon Review*, 18 (1956): 76.
4. Letter to J. Edward Austen, December 16, 1816, quoted in Donald J. Gray, ed., *Pride and Prejudice: An Authoritative Text, Backgrounds, Reviews and Essays in Criticism* (New York: W. W. Norton & Co., Inc., 1966), p. 284.
5. Frederick R. Karl, *A Reader's Guide to The Nineteenth Century British Novel* (New York: Noonday Press, 1964), p. 31.
6. David P. Demarest, Jr., "Legal Language and Situation in the Eighteenth Century Novel: Readings in Defoe, Richardson, Fielding, and Austen," Dissertation, University of Wisconsin, 1963, p. 191.
7. *SNNTS*, 5 (1973): 22–38.
8. Leslie H. Willis, "Eyes and the Imagery of Sight in *Pride and Prejudice*," *ESC*, 2 (1976): 156.

9.  In M. H. Abrams, *Natural Supernaturalism: Tradition and Revolution in Romantic Literature* (New York: W. W. Norton & Co., Inc., 1971), p. 62, where he also relevantly suggests the visual links between Bacon and Wordsworth. There have been a number of other studies relating empiricism and literature. See, for example, Abrams, *The Mirror and the Lamp: Romantic Theory and the Critical Tradition* (New York: W. W. Norton & Co., Inc., 1958), p. 36 and following; Kenneth MacLean, *John Locke and English Literature of the Eighteenth Century* (New York: Russell & Russell, Inc., 1962); Marjorie Hope Nicholson, *Newton Demands the Muse: Newton's "Opticks" and the Eighteenth Century Poets* (Princeton: Princeton University Press, 1946); Nicholson, *Mountain Gloom and Mountain Glory: The Development of the Aesthetics of the Infinite* (New York: W. W. Norton & Co., 1963), *passim,* but especially chapter 8; Walter Jackson Bate, *From Classic to Romantic: Premises of Taste in Eighteenth Century England* (New York: Harper & Row, 1961); Ernest Tuveson, *The Imagination as a Means of Grace: Locke and the Aesthetics of Romanticism* (Berkeley: University of California Press, 1960); Patricia Meyer Spacks, *The Poetry of Vision* (Cambridge: Harvard University Press, 1967); and finally the more specialized essay, Howard O. Brogan's "Science and Narrative Structure in Austen, Hardy, and Woolf," *Studies in English Literature,* 11 (1957): 276–87, especially 276–79.
10. Tuveson, pp. 72–73.
11. Brogan, 276–77.
12. In *Pride and Prejudice, An Authoritative Text. . . ,* p. 309; the "Biographical Notice" originally appeared as a Preface to the volume containing *Persuasion* and *Northanger Abbey,* which was published after Jane Austen's death.
13. Edmund Burke, "On the Sublime and Beautiful," in *On Taste, On the Sublime and Beautiful, Reflections on the French Revolution, A Letter to a Noble Lord,* The Harvard Classics, ed. Charles W. Eliot, XXIV (New York: P. F. Collier and Son Co., 1909), p. 111.
14. Ibid., p. 119.
15. Ibid., p. 111.
16. For a discussion of privacy in Jane Austen's novels, see Francis R. Hart, "The Spaces of Privacy: Jane Austen," *Nineteenth-Century Fiction,* 30 (1975): 305–34.
17. *Pride and Prejudice, An Authoritative Text . . . ,* p. 309.
18. Ibid.
19. In William D. Templeman's *The Life and Work of William Gilpin* (Urbana: University of Illinois Press, 1939), p. 136.
20. Ibid., p. 142.
21. Reva Stump, *Movement and Vision in George Eliot's Novels* (Seattle: University of Washington Press, 1959).
22. Marilyn Butler, "The Woman at the Window: Ann Radcliffe in the Novels of Mary Wollstonecraft and Jane Austen," *W&L* n.s., 1 (1980): 128–48, especially 144ff.
23. Mario Praz, *The Hero in Eclipse in Victorian Fiction,* tr. Angus Davidson

(London, Oxford, New York: Oxford University Press, 1969), see especially pp. 117–18, note 4.

24. *Pride and Prejudice* from *The Novels of Jane Austen*, The Text Based on Collation of the Early Editions by R. W. Chapman, 3rd ed. (London, New York, Toronto: Oxford University Press, 1932), II. All future citations will be taken from this edition and noted within the text.

25. *Pride and Prejudice, An Authoritative Text . . .*, p. 308.

26. There have been several discussions of the Nature-Art dialectic and the related symbol of the country home in *Pride and Prejudice*. See, for example, Samuel Kliger, "Jane Austen's Pride and Prejudice in the Eighteenth Century Mode," *UTQ*, 16 (1947): 357–70, and Charles J. McCann, "Setting and Character in *Pride and Prejudice*," *Nineteenth-Century Fiction*, 19 (1964): 65–75.

27. See Kenneth L. Moler, *"Pride and Prejudice:* Jane Austen's Patrician Hero," *ELN*, 7 (1967): 491–508, for a discussion of Elizabeth's gradual awakening, or eye-opening. For example, Moler reports that "With her eyes thus opened, Elizabeth comes to see in the novel that Darcy's position and fortune, and his pride in them, can be forces for good as well as sources of snobbery and authoritarianism" (p. 505).

28. For a discussion of the "picturesque" landscape around Pemberley, see Martin Price, "The Picturesque Moment," in *From Sensibility to Romanticism: Essays Presented to Frederick A. Pottle*, ed. Frederick W. Hilles and Harold Bloom (London, Oxford, New York: Oxford University Press, 1965), pp. 266–68.

29. Everett Zimmerman, "Pride and Prejudice in *Pride and Prejudice*," *Nineteenth-Century Fiction*, 23 (1968): 67.

30. *Pride and Prejudice, An Authoritative Text . . .*, p. 309.

31. Again, see the Price essay, pp. 259–92, for a thorough discussion of the picturesque.

32. *Pride and Prejudice, An Authoritative Text . . .*, p. 309.

33. Morse Peckham, *Beyond the Tragic Vision* (New York: George Braziller, 1962), *passim*. See also my *"Dracula*: The Gnostic Quest and Victorian Wasteland," *English Literature in Transition*, 20 (1977): 13–26, for a discussion of this mania for an epistemology.

34. Babb, p. 115.

35. Wayne Booth, *The Rhetoric of Fiction* (Chicago and London: University of Chicago Press, 1961): p. 257.

36. For a discussion of this visual concern in *To the Lighthouse*, see my "Romantic Psyche and Symbol in *To the Lighthouse*," forthcoming in *Journal of Evolutionary Psychology*.

# Jane Austen's Dangerous Charm
## Feeling as One Ought about Fanny Price

$A$lone among masters of fiction, Jane Austen commands the woman's art of making herself loved. She knows how to enchant us with conversational sparkle, to charm our assent with a glow of description, to entice our smiles with the coquette's practiced glee. No major novelist is such an adept at charming. Samuel Richardson, her greatest predecessor, disdained gentlemanly amenities in his revelations of the mind's interminable, intractable mixture of motives when it engages itself in duels of love; George Eliot, her mightiest successor, rejected charm as an opiate distracting us from the harsh realities her knobby, convoluted books explore. These majestic truthtellers could not write winningly if they tried, for they are too dismally aware of the dark side of enchantment; while even in her harshest revelations, Jane Austen is a maestro at pleasing.

Yet, from the cacophony of marriages with which it begins, to the depressed union which ends it, *Mansfield Park* is unlikable. When so knowing a charmer abrades her reader, her withdrawal from our pleasure must be deliberate. She herself studied the gradations of liking *Mansfield Park* inspired, something she had not troubled to do with her earlier books, as we know from her meticulously compiled "Opinions of *Mansfield Park*": "My Mother—not liked it so well as P. & P.—Thought Fanny insipid.—Enjoyed Mrs. Norris.— . . . Miss Burdett—Did not like it so well as P. & P. Mrs. James Tilson—Liked it better than P. & P.,"[1] and so on. We do not know whether these carefully measured dollops of liking amused Jane Austen or annoyed her, but we do know that she was intrigued by the degree to which her unlikable novel was liked. Her apparent withdrawal from the reader's fellowship suggests a departure from the community and the conventions of realistic fiction toward a Romantic and a dissonant perspective. If we examine this difficult novel, with its particularly unaccommodating heroine, in relation to contemporaneous genres beyond the boundaries of realism, we may better understand Jane Austen's withdrawal from a commonality of delight.

The silent, stubborn Fanny Price appeals less than any of Austen's heroines. Perhaps because of this, she captivates more critics than they. "Nobody, I believe, has ever found it possible to like the heroine of *Mansfield Park*,"[2] Lionel Trilling intoned in 1955, and few would contradict this epitaph today. Yet Trilling goes on to apotheosize this literary wallflower, transfiguring her into a culturally fraught emblem who bears on her scant shoulders all the aches of modern secularism. Such later interpreters as Avrom Fleishman[3] similarly embrace Fanny as emblem if not woman, wan transmitter of intricate cultural ideals. It seems that once a heroine is divested of the power to please, she is granted an import beyond her apparently modest sphere, for, unlike Jane Austen's other, more immediately appealing heroines, Fanny has been said to possess our entire spiritual history as it shapes itself through her in historical time. Elizabeth and Emma live for readers as personal presences, but never as the Romantic, the Victorian, or the Modern *Zeitgeist*. Failing to charm, Fanny is allowed in compensation to embody worlds.

But readers who have been trained to respect the culturally fraught Fanny still shy away from her as a character. Living in uncomfortable intimacy with her as we do when we read the novel, we recall Kingsley Amis's taunt that an evening with Fanny and her clergyman husband "would not be lightly undertaken."[4] We may understand our heritage through Fanny Price, but ought we to want to dine with her? The question is important because, for theorists like George Levine, the more bravely realism departs from the commonality of fellowship, the more radically it tilts toward a monstrosity that undermines the realistic community itself.[5] In the very staunchness of her virtue Fanny Price seems to me to invoke the monsters that deny the charmed circle of realistic fiction. Though she uses the word "ought" with unyielding authority, she evokes uncertainty and unease. Though we learn more about her life, and participate more intimately in her consciousness, than we do with Jane Austen's other heroines, the bothering question remains: How ought we to feel about Fanny Price?

*Mansfield Park* tilts away from commonality in part because it breaks the code established by Jane Austen's other novels. Few of us could read *Pride and Prejudice*, *Persuasion*, or even *Emma*, without liking the heroines enough to "travel with them," in Wayne Booth's charming phrase.[6] *Mansfield Park* embodies a wryer literary perception, one especially congenial to Jane Austen's poetic contemporaries: the creator of Fanny Price assumes that one may live with a character one doesn't like.

One motive power of Romantic poetry is the fascination of the unconge-
nial. In "Resolution and Independence," Wordsworth can be possessed
by a deformed and virtually nonhuman leech-gatherer, although the poet
is too remote from the old man to absorb a word of his exhortation; an
unkempt sinner, Coleridge's Ancient Mariner, can snatch our imagination from a wedding, that great congenial sacrament of human community. These gnarled figures lure us out of fellowship to adopt the
perspective of the monstrous and the marginal.

Fanny captures our imaginations in this same Romantic way, by wel-
coming the reader into her solitary animosity against the intricacies of the
normal: "Fanny was again left to her solitude, and with no increase of
pleasant feelings, for she was sorry for almost all that she had seen and
heard, astonished at Miss Bertram, and angry with Mr. Crawford."[7] The
compelling, blighting power of Fanny's spectatorship at Sotherton is
characteristic: morality dissolves into angry and unpleasant feelings
whose intensity is an alternative to community. For while Fanny's Romanticism suggests itself in her isolating sensibility, her stylized effusions
to nature, she is most Romantic in that, like Wordsworth's leech-gatherer
or Coleridge's Mariner, there is something horrible about her, something
that deprives the imagination of its appetite for ordinary life and compels
it toward the deformed, the dispossessed.

This elevation of one's private bad feelings into a power alternate to
social life associates Fanny not merely with early Romantic outcasts, but
with such dashingly misanthropic hero-villains as Byron's Childe
Harold, Mary Shelley's Frankenstein, and Maturin's Melmoth. Their
flamboyant willfulness may seem utterly alien to this frail, clinging, and
seemingly passive girl who annoys above all by her shyness, but like
them, she is magnetically unconvivial, a spoiler of ceremonies. During
the excursion to Sotherton, the rehearsals of *Lovers' Vows*, the game of
Speculation, her baleful solitude overwhelms the company, perhaps because it expresses and exudes their own buried rancor. In families ranging
from Sir Thomas Bertram's stately authoritarianism to the casual disorder
of her father's house, Fanny exists like Frankenstein as a silent, censori-
ous pall. Her denying spirit defines itself best in assertive negatives: "No,
indeed, I cannot act" (p. 168).

Fanny's credo resonates beyond her particular disapproval of staging
*Lovers' Vows*, for, even when the play is not in question, Fanny refuses
to act. Instead, and consistently, she counteracts; a creed which seems a
high-minded elevation of her own honesty against the dangerous deceit of
role-playing is also resistance to the comic, collective rhythms of realistic
fiction itself. The joyless exercises of her delicate body tacitly condemn
not only acting, but activity in general; Mary Crawford's elation at horse-

back riding is as antagonistic to Fanny as is her flair for acting. At Sotherton, Fanny stations herself beside the dangerous ha-ha as a still bulwark against the mutual serpentine pursuit of the other characters; playing Speculation, she alone will not take the initiative that will advance the game. Fanny's refusal to act is a criticism not just of art, but of life as well. Her timidly resolute denial of acting includes activity and play, those impulses of comedy which bring us together in ceremonial motions where fellowship seems all. Her refusals are her countercharm against the corporate and genial charm with which Jane Austen's comedies win love.

Fanny's role as counteractive genius and spirit of anti-play is anomalous in a romantic heroine, but not in a hero-villain. Like Frankenstein and his monster, those spirits of solitude, Fanny is a killjoy, a blighter of ceremonies and divider of families. It is precisely this opposition to the traditional patterns of romantic comedy that lends her her disturbing strength. Her misery amid the bustle of the play is the stigma of her power:

> She was full of jealousy and agitation. Miss Crawford came with looks of gaiety which seemed an insult, with friendly expressions towards herself which she could hardly answer calmly. Every body around her was gay and busy, prosperous and important, each had their object of interest, their part, their dress, their favourite scene, their friends and confederates, all were finding employment in consultations and comparisons, or diversion in the playful conceits they suggested. She alone was sad and insignificant; she had no share in any thing; she might go or stay, she might be in the midst of their noise, or retreat from it to the solitude of the East room, without being seen or missed. (p. 180)

But though she is stricken in the midst of play, unable and unwilling to act, Fanny never retreats from activity. Finally, her "jealousy and agitation" seem to take concrete shape in the angry intruder, Sir Thomas Bertram, who lends authority to Fanny's bad feelings and ends the play. Sir Thomas's interruption seems only the culmination of Fanny's silent, withering power over performance, for before he appears she has already drawn control to her watching self. Backstage, she alone is in possession of each actor's secret grievance; watching and prompting from her isolation, she alone knows everybody's lines. A center of fierce inactivity, Fanny broods jealously over the play until she masters both its script and the secret designs of its actors, at which point Sir Thomas's return vindicates her silent obstructive power. Fanny abdicates from stardom to assume a more potent control over the action: she appropriates to her solitude the controlling omniscience of the rapt audience.

As her novel's sole and constant watcher, the controlling spirit of anti-play, Fanny relinquishes performing heroism to become the jealous reader, whose solitary imagination resurrects the action and keeps it alive. In her own delicately assertive phrase, "I was quiet, but I was not blind" (p. 358). As quietly seeing spectator of others' activities, Fanny plays a role as ambiguous as the reader's own: like Fanny, we vivify the action by our imaginative participation in it, while we hold as well the power to obstruct it by our censure. The anomalous position of the watcher more than justifies Mary Crawford's perplexed question: "Pray, is she out, or is she not?" (p. 81). Withholding herself from play, Fanny ingests the play of everyone she silently sees. As omniscient spectator of all private and public performances, Fanny remains "out" of the action, while her knowledge seeps into its subtlest permutations. Our discomfort at her, then, may incorporate our discomfort at our own silent voyeurism; as a portrait of the reader as a young woman, she is our unflattering if indelible reflection. Her fierce spectatorship forces our reluctant identification.

As omniscient watcher and anti-comic spirit linked in uncomfortable community to the solitary reader, Fanny possesses a subtler power than we find in brighter and livelier heroines of fiction. That dynamic misreader Emma Woodhouse is forced by her own misconstructions into the limited position of actor in the comedy she is trying to control from without, while Fanny's role as omniscient outsider thrives on her continued abstention. In her role as controlling, anti-comic watcher, Fanny moves beyond the sphere of traditional heroism to associate herself with a host of dashing British villains. Like them, this denying girl will not, perhaps cannot, eat; her abstinence makes her a spectral presence at the communal feast. Reunited with her family at Portsmouth, instead of feasting with them, as any of Dickens' or Charlotte Brontë's waifs would gladly do, she is repelled by the very suggestion of food, by "the tea-board never thoroughly cleaned, the cups and saucers wiped in streaks, the milk a mixture of motes floating in thin blue, and the bread and butter growing every minute more greasy than even Rebecca's hands had first produced it" (p. 428). Family food induces only a strangely modern nausea. Fanny's revulsion against food, along with her psychic feasting on the activities of others, crystallizes her somewhat sinister position as outsider who strangely and silently moves into the interior. Her starved incapacity to eat familial food is suggestive of that winsome predator the vampire, an equally solitary and melancholy figure who haunts British literature in his dual role as dark abstainer from a comic dailiness of which he is secretly in possession. Like Fanny, the vampire cannot eat the common nourishment of daily life, but he feasts secretly upon human vitality in the dark.

In adopting the role of traditional literary villains, Fanny infects our imaginations in a way that no merely virtuous heroine could do. Her hungry exclusion seems unappeasable and triumphant. Insofar as she draws sustenance from her role as omniscient outsider at family, excursion, wedding, play, or feast, she stands with some venerable monsters in the English canon. Not only does she share the role of Mary Shelley's creature, that gloomy exile from family whose vocation is to control families and destroy them, but there is a shadow on her even of the melancholy Grendel in the Anglo-Saxon epic *Beowulf*. An exile from common feasting, Grendel peers jealously through the window of a lighted banquet hall. He defines his identity as outsider by appropriating the interior; he invades the lighted hall and begins to eat the eaters. At the end of *Mansfield Park*, Fanny too has won a somewhat predatory victory, moving from outsider in to guiding spirit of the humbled Bertram family. Fanny's cannibalistic invasion of the lighted, spacious estate of Mansfield is genteel and purely symbolic, but, like the primitive Grendel, she replaces common and convivial feasting with a solitary and subtler hunger that possesses its object. In this evocation of an earlier literary tradition, Fanny is Jane Austen's most Romantic heroine, for she is part of a literature newly awakened to ancient forms and fascinated by the monstrous and marginal. In the subtle streak of perversity that still disturbs readers today, she shows us the monsters within Jane Austen's realism, ineffable presences who allow the novels to participate in the darker moods of their age.[8]

Fanny's jealous hunger, which can be assuaged only by private, psychic feasting, isolates her in comedy while it associates her with such venerable predators as the Ancient Mariner, the vampire, the Byronic hero-villain, and, in a far-off echo, *Beowulf*'s Grendel. Her initiation is not that of the usual heroine, whose marriage reconciles us to the choreography of comedy; instead, like the hero-villain, she proclaims her uniqueness through possessive spectatorship. The implications of Fanny's refusal to act are more richly glossed in Romantic poetry and fiction than in early nineteenth-century realism, but Romantic criticism also illuminates the complex genesis of a Fanny Price: her stubborn creed, "I cannot act," recalls some problematic characters of Shakespeare, in whom such critics as Coleridge and Hazlitt discovered new significance.

Like *Mansfield Park*, Shakespearean drama characteristically pivots upon the performance of a play within a play; like Jane Austen, Shakespeare increasingly pushes to center stage the character who refuses to act. Thus, in his early *A Midsummer Night's Dream*, all the rustics lumber through their parts in the thoroughly comic "Pyramus and Thisbe," but by the time we reach *Twelfth Night*, the play is marred: the austere Malvolio is made to perform in a cruel drama not of his making, posturing for the delectation of the raucous plotters just as he thinks he is being most sincere. This humiliation of an upright, if unlikable, character by the cruelty of play anticipates the complex tone of *Mansfield Park*, though Fanny's sharper eye for traps forbids her seduction by the players.

Malvolio abandons his part in outrage, bellowing as he exits, "I'll be revenged on the whole pack of you!" Perhaps in his revenge he returns as Hamlet, our most famous star who refuses to act. Like Fanny, Hamlet casts himself as a jealous and melancholy death's head in a gay, if false, company. His stern creed—"Madam, I know not seems"—epitomizes, like hers, refusal to act. Nonactive in the complex political drama of his family life, Hamlet likewise takes no part in the microcosmic play within the play, though, like Fanny, he hovers hungrily around its periphery, knowing all the parts. His avid spectatorship ultimately upstages the actors and spoils the performance, replacing communal play with rage and slaughter; at the end of her novel, Fanny too reigns at Mansfield in consequence of a family havoc begun at the ruin of the play.

Of course, Fanny is not Hamlet, nor was she meant to be. She is not a doomed prince, but a pauper, a woman, and a survivor; she neither rages nor soliloquizes, revealing her power and her plans only haltingly and indirectly. Still, in her complex relation to the play which epitomizes her novel's action, Fanny has more in common with Hamlet than she does with the helpless women he excoriates when they cross his path. For Hamlet is Shakespeare's supreme anti-actor and counteractor, the avid and omniscient spectator of the game, who fascinates us as Fanny does because he expresses his virtue by the characteristics of conventional villainy. Jane Austen's contemporaries were obsessed by this troubling sort of hero: Samuel Taylor Coleridge reconceived Hamlet as a paragon of nonactivity, deifying for the modern age a character too pure to act, whose doom and calling are the destruction of play. Fanny Price may be one feminized expression of this new, Romantic fascination with Hamlet as a modern type. As Jane Austen's Hamlet, scourge and minister of a corrupted world, the perfection of the character who won't play, Fanny Price in her unyielding opposition, her longing for a purified and contracted world, gains majesty if not charm. She is as sternly denying as Hamlet, banishing in turn her cousins Maria and Julia, her parents, and the rakish, witty Crawfords from her own finer sphere. These multiple banishments align her with one type of Romantic hero, while denying her the warmth readers want in a heroine. Confronted with so richly disturbing a figure, we would insult her to sentimentalize her when *Mansfield Park* itself does not. For, as we shall see, Fanny's anti-human qualities are stressed in the text of the novel as well as in its contexts. In her progress toward power, her charmlessness only increases her efficacy as Mansfield's scourge and minister.

"Nobody falls in love with Fanny Price," Tony Tanner warns us (p. 8). We have seen that few readers have done so; Jane Austen further confounds our emotions by making clear that none of the characters within the novel falls in love with her either, though most heroines exist to win love. She wins neither the affection nor the interest of her parents, though they are not always unresponsive; the charm of a Henry Crawford evokes an answering charm in them, but when Fanny's penitential visit to Portsmouth is over at last, her parents seem as relieved to see her leave as she is to go. Kinship is equally unappetizing to all.

Within Mansfield, the gracious adoptive family to which Fanny returns with such ardor, she wins love in proportion to her cousins' shame, receiving emotional interest they failed to earn. Fanny, despised by all, is embraced as a last resource when Sir Thomas's natural children disgrace themselves in turn. Jane Austen is coolly explicit about the cannibalistic undercurrents of this, and perhaps of all, requited love:

> My Fanny indeed at this very time, I have the satisfaction of knowing, must have been happy in spite of every thing. She must have been a happy creature in spite of all that she felt or thought she felt, for the distress of those around her . . . and happy as all this must make her, she would still have been happy without any of it, for Edmund was no longer the dupe of Miss Crawford.
>
> It is true, that Edmund was very far from happy himself. He was suffering from disappointment and regret, grieving over what was, and wishing for what could never be. She knew it was so, and was sorry; but it was with a sorrow so founded on satisfaction, so tending to ease, and so much in harmony with every dearest sensation, that there are few who might not have been glad to exchange their greatest gaiety for it. (p. 446)

In this redemption from her usual depression, Fanny's only available happy ending is the predator's comedy; surely there is deliberate irony in Jane Austen's pitiless repetition of "happy" amid this household of collapsed hopes. Never in the canon is the happy ending so reliant upon the wounds and disappointments of others; though we leave Fanny ministering avidly to these wounds, they will never heal. The love she wins from her adoptive family is not a free tribute to her beauty, her character, or her judgment, but the last tender impulse of a stricken household.

The love of her two suitors, Henry and Edmund, is similarly undermined. Everything about Henry Crawford, that mobile and consummate actor, calls his sincerity into question. He stages his love scenes before select audiences, all carefully chosen to put the greatest possible pressure on Fanny, only to humiliate her flamboyantly by his elopement with Maria once she has begun to respond. As Fanny and we know, his passion for her repeats more grandly his pattern of behavior with her silly cousins, so that only the most sentimentally credulous reader could find this new performance credible. The watcher Fanny knows his love is play, and thus by definition the medium of her humiliation; but in exposing the ardor of the romantic hero as a sadistic game, Jane Austen undermines the reader's own impulse to fall in love with Fanny by undermining love itself.

Readers of *Sense and Sensibility, Pride and Prejudice,* and *Emma* expect Edmund Bertram, Fanny's proper husband and sober soulmate, to redress the balance; the probity of this good suitor's love should define the sham of Henry's. But if for Henry love is another variant of private theatricals, a series of ritual attitudes staged for an audience, Edmund's love is so restrained as to be imperceptible. Like Mr. Knightley, he is exemplary as Fanny's tender mentor, proud of his pupil's right feelings and right attitudes, but he has none of Mr. Knightley's life as an incipient lover. Sexual jealousy fuels the latter's sternly protective manner and his indignant disapproval of Frank Churchill, while Edmund hints of no passions beyond what we see, showing not a glimmer of jealousy when Henry Crawford makes demonstrative love to Fanny. Edmund's impeccably clerical conscience interprets his future wife's prospective marriage as a convenience to facilitate his own engagement to Henry's seductive sister. Jane Austen is a sharp observer of men struggling with powerful feelings; like Knightley, Darcy and Wentworth fight to repress, through prudence or anger, a love that proves too strong for them; but she withholds from Edmund Bertram any feelings worth denying. The unlocated and undramatized conversion that leads to his marriage carries as little emotional weight as it could do: "I only intreat every body to believe that exactly at the time when it was quite natural that it should be so, and not a week earlier, Edmund did cease to care about Mary Crawford, and became as anxious to marry Fanny, as Fanny herself could desire" (p. 454).

This clipped, perfunctory summary, together with the fact that no earlier hints have prepared us for an outbreak of passion on Edmund's part, seems deliberately designed to banish love from our thoughts. The final marriage is as stately and inevitable as Edmund's ordination will be; the ritual is performed, though neither love nor guardianship quite joins the marrying couple. The narrator's reiterated appeal to nature—"what could be more natural than the change?"—is a further symptom of the hopelessness of love, for, as we shall see below, nature is a feeble contender in the manipulated world of *Mansfield Park*. Though Edmund marries the woman he ought, the stern hope he husbands is a loveless strength.

A romance from a writer of marriage comedies that so unremittingly denies love to its heroine is a brave novel indeed, particularly when this heroine is ready to love both her emotionally desiccated suitors. If two wooing men cannot manage to love Fanny, with the true suitor proving as hollow as the false, then surely the reader never will. Austerely alone in a community of fictional heroines for whom love is their chief talent and reward, Fanny is further isolated from affection by her radical homelessness. This waiflike attribute may lead us to associate *Mansfield Park* with such Victorian orphan-myths as *Jane Eyre:* Jane, like Fanny, is an unprepossessing orphan, "a discord" in her corrupted foster family, who grows into an iron-willed little savior. But like most of her orphaned analogues in Victorian fiction, Jane is baptized into strength by the recovery of family: it is not her love for Rochester, but her healing interlude with her recovered cousins, the Rivers family, that allows her identity and her destiny to cohere.[9] The more radical Fanny similarly recovers her family during a romantic crisis, only to discover her total absence of kin. Her ideal home is her utter homelessness. She belongs everywhere she is not: "When she had been coming to Portsmouth, she had loved to call it her home, had been fond of saying that she was going home; the word had been very dear to her; and so it still was, but it must be applied to Mansfield. *That* was now the home. Portsmouth was Portsmouth; Mansfield was home" (pp. 420–21).

The word may be very dear, but the thing eludes her as she eludes it. Victorian orphan-fiction typically begins with the loss of home and ends with its recovery, but here, home is palpable to Fanny only by its absence. Mansfield itself is no true home. The vacuum at its heart is evident not only in the flights of all its members except the supine Lady Bertram, but in the chilling ease with which it can be transformed into a theater. Upon her return, Fanny compels the gutted Mansfield to be her home by an act of will, but in its shrunken regenerate state it bears little resemblance to the place in which she grew up. Fanny's dual returns, to her natural and then to her adoptive origins, prove only the impossibility of self-discovery through return. Thus, though she may resemble later orphan-heroes, Fanny is a more indigestible figure than these wistful waifs, for whom embracing their kin is secular salvation. In the tenacity with which she adheres to an identity validated by no family, home, or love, she denies the vulnerability of the waif for the unlovable toughness of the authentic transplant. Her fragility cloaks the will to live without the traditional sanctions for life. Underlying her pious rigidity is a dispossession so fundamental that, among nineteenth-century English novelists, only the tact of a Jane Austen could dare reveal it in a lady.

Readers are right, then, to find Fanny a relentlessly uncomfortable figure in a domestic romance and to wonder nervously where Jane Austen's comedy went. This uncompromising novel never dissolves its heroine's isolation; she merely passes from the isolation of the outcast to that of the conqueror. Her solitude is rarely alleviated by pathos; instead, she hones it into a spectator's perspective from which she can observe her world and invade it. In this above all, she is closer to the Romantic hero than to the heroine of romance: her solitude is her condition, not a state from which the marriage comedy will save her. In her relentless spectatorship, Fanny may be Jane Austen's domestic answer to Byron's more flamboyant and venturesome Childe Harold, exile from his kind, passing eternally through foreign civilizations in order to create elegies to their ruins. Though Fanny travels only to Sotherton and Portsmouth, her role too is alien and elegiac, as it is at Mansfield itself; like Byron's persona, she is a hero because she is sufficiently detached to see the death of worlds. Fabricating an identity from uprootedness, she conquers the normal world that acts, plays, and marries, through her alienation from it. In the text of her novel, she is a being without kin, but in its context, she exudes a quiet kinship with the strangers and the monsters of her age.

Like other literary monsters, Fanny is a creature without kin who longs for a mate of her own kind. The pain of her difference explains a longing in *Mansfield Park* that is common to much Romantic literature and that, in its obsessed exclusiveness, may look to modern readers unnervingly like incest: the hunger of sibling for sibling, of kin for kind. Seen in its time, the ecstatic, possessive passion Fanny divides between her brother William and her foster brother Edmund, her horror at the Crawfords' attempt to invade her emotions, seem less relevant to the Freudian family romance than to the monster's agonized attempts to alleviate his monstrosity. Mary Shelley's monster asks only that Frankenstein create for him a sister-wife; Bram Stoker's Dracula experiences his triumphant climax when turning his victims into fellow members of the Undead, thus making of them sisters as well as spouses. Fanny yearns similarly in isolation for a brother-mate, repelling the Crawfords above all because they are so different as to constitute virtually another species: "We are so totally unlike . . . we are so very, very different in all our inclinations and ways, that I consider it as quite impossible we should ever be tolerably happy together, even if I *could* like him. There never were two people more dissimilar. We have not one taste in common. We should be miserable" (p. 345).

This rage of self-removal extends itself to Mary Crawford as well, above all perhaps in the emotional spaciousness with which Mary reaches out to Fanny as her "sister."[10] Mary's quest for sisters of gender rather than family, her uncomfortably outspoken championship of abused wives, her sexual initiative, and her unsettling habit of calling things by their names, all suggest the pioneering sensibility of her contemporary, Mary Wollstonecraft; but Fanny cannot endure so universal an embrace, clutching only the shreds of kinship. The novel ends as it ought, with Mary's expulsion into a wider and sadder world, while Fanny, still isolated, clings jealously to her conquered family.

Fanny as Romantic monster does not dispel our discomfort in reading *Mansfield Park*, but may explain some of it. Until recently, critics have limited their recognition of the monsters that underlie Jane Austen's realism to the peripheral figures whose unreason threatens the heroine, while the heroine herself remains solidly human.[11] Yet Fanny excites the same mixture of sympathy and aversion as does Frankenstein's loveless, homeless creature, and the pattern of her adventures is similar to his. Frankenstein's monster begins as a jealous outcast, peering in at family and civic joys. His rage for inclusion makes him the hunted prey of those he envies, and he ends as the conqueror of families. Fanny too is a jealous outcast in the first volume. In the second, she is besieged by the family that excluded her in the form of Henry Crawford's lethal marriage proposal; finally her lair, the chilly East room, is hunted down like Grendel's and invaded by Sir Thomas himself. In the third volume, Fanny, like Mary Shelley's monster, becomes the solitary conqueror of a gutted family. This movement from outcast within a charmed circle to one who is hunted by it and then conqueror of it aligns Jane Austen's most Romantic, least loved heroine with the kin she so wretchedly seeks.

Modern readers may shun Fanny as a static, solitary predator, but in the world of *Mansfield Park* her very consistency and tenacity are bulwarks against a newly opening space that is dangerous in its very fluidity: even Sir Thomas Bertram's solid home is made vulnerable by economic fluctuations in far-off Antigua.[12] Though the large and loveless house that gives it its name has made many readers feel that *Mansfield Park* is Jane Austen's most oppressive novel, its dominant emotional atmosphere induces a certain vertigo, evident in the apparent rocklike solidity, but the true and hopeless elusiveness, of the word "ought." "Ought" tolls constantly, its very sound bringing a knell of absolutism, and nobody uses it with more assurance than the hero and heroine. Fanny can dismiss Henry Crawford simply because "he can feel nothing as he ought," while Edmund freights the word with religious and national authority: "as the clergy are, or are not what they ought to be, so are the rest of the nation" (p. 121). As a barometer of feelings, morals, and institutions, the word seems an immutable touchstone, but in fact it has no objective validation. Its authority in the novel is entirely, and alarmingly, self-generated. The great houses Mansfield and Sotherton scarcely institutionalize the "ought" that resounds in the novel's language; the Portsmouth of the Prices and the London of the Crawfords are equally ignorant of its weight. It has no echo in the world of households and institutions.

Yet this lack of official authority does not prevent the novel's misguided characters from using the word with the same assurance as Fanny and Edmund do. Sir Thomas says of a Fanny who is brewing rebellion, "She appears to feel as she ought" (p. 230); for Mary, the party with which Maria Rushworth inaugurates her miserable marriage finds everything "just as it ought to be" (p. 406); Maria herself avoids only the word in seeing her mercenary marriage as "a duty" (p. 72). Even Edmund, who has transmitted its value to Fanny, abuses the word throughout the novel, beginning with his myopic pressure on Fanny to live with her hated Aunt Norris: "She is choosing a friend and companion exactly where she ought" (p. 60). The incoherence underlying Edmund's authoritative vocabulary tells us that the word recurs anarchically, for there is no objective code to endow it with consistency. Fanny, for example, longs for a loving reunion with her indifferent mother, hoping that "they should soon be what mother and daughter ought to be to each other" (p. 366), but as usual the novel provides no objective image of this "ought": in *Mansfield Park* and throughout Jane Austen's canon, mothers and daughters are at best indifferent and at worst antagonistic, depriving the commanding word of validation. Fanny is repeatedly hymned as the only character who feels consistently as she ought, but in a world where the word changes its meaning so incessantly, her role as a walking "ought" merely isolates her further. Whatever authority Fanny has comes magically from herself alone. Though she can control the inchoate outside world, it is too lacking in definition to claim kinship with her.

For though Fanny possesses a quasi-magical power over the action, she represents less a moral than a shaping principle, assuming the author's prerogatives along with the reader's: the novel's action happens as she wills, and so her emotions become our only standard of right. In its essence, the world of *Mansfield Park* is terrifyingly malleable. Jane Austen detaches herself from her Romantic contemporaries to reveal both inner and outer nature as pitifully ineffectual compared to what can be made. Mrs. Price grows listless toward Fanny because the "instinct of nature was soon satisfied, and Mrs. Price's attachment had no other source" (p. 382). The gap between Mrs. Price and Mrs. Bertram can never heal because "where nature had made so little difference, circumstances

[had] made so much" (p. 400). Mary Crawford's nature, like Maria's and Julia's, is similarly helpless against the constructive, or the deconstructive, power of her medium: "For where, Fanny, shall we find a woman whom nature had so richly endowed?—Spoilt, spoilt!—" (p. 441). By contrast, we know that Susan Price will survive, not because of her natural qualities, but because she is "a girl so capable of being made, every thing good" (p. 409). Nature's insufficiency may explain the deadness of Fanny's effusions to stars, trees, and "verdure," for though she laments improvements, Fanny is the most potent of the novel's improving characters. In so malleable and so defective a world, Fanny is polite to the stars, but she turns her most potent attention on the vulnerable, that which is "capable of being made."

In Mary Shelley's *Frankenstein* as well, family, nature, and even the Alps pall before the monster who is capable of being made. The monstrosity of *Mansfield Park* as a whole is one manifestation of its repelled fascination with acting, with education, and with landscape and estate improvements: the novel imagines a fluid world, one with no fixed principles, capable of awesome, endless, and dangerous manipulation. The unconvivial stiffness of its hero and heroine is their triumph: by the end, they are so successfully "made" by each other that he is her creature as completely as she has always been his. The mobility and malleability of *Mansfield Park* is a dark realization of an essentially Romantic vision, of which Fanny Price represents both the horror and the best hope. Only in *Mansfield Park* does Jane Austen force us to experience the discomfort of a Romantic universe presided over by the potent charm of a charmless heroine who was not made to be loved.[13]

*Nina Auerbach*
*University of Pennsylvania*

# NOTES

1. Jane Austen, *Minor Works*, ed. R. W. Chapman (1954; reprinted London: Oxford University Press, 1969), p. 432.

2. Lionel Trilling, *"Mansfield Park,"* reprinted in Ian Watt, ed., *Jane Austen: A Collection of Critical Essays* (Englewood Cliffs, N.J.: Prentice-Hall, 1963), p. 128.

3. Avrom Fleishman, *A Reading of Mansfield Park* (1967; reprinted Baltimore: The Johns Hopkins University Press, 1970), pp. 57–69.

4. Kingsley Amis, "Whatever Became of Jane Austen?" (1957), reprinted in Watt, p. 142.

5. "Keeping the monster at bay is one part of the realist enterprise. The other is to keep him, or her, alive," George Levine, *The Realistic Imagination: English Fiction from Frankenstein to Lady Chatterley* (Chicago: University of Chicago Press, 1981), p. 80. Judith Wilt, *Ghosts of the Gothic: Austen, Eliot, and Lawrence* (Princeton: Princeton University Press, 1980), pp. 121–72, provides an eerily suggestive discussion of the terror that infuses Jane Austen's vision of commonality.

6. Wayne Booth, *A Rhetoric of Fiction* (Chicago: University of Chicago Press, 1961), p. 245.

7. Jane Austen, *Mansfield Park* (1814; reprinted Harmondsworth: Penguin, 1966), p. 127. Future references to this edition will appear in the text.

8. George Levine speculates about the monstrous potential of Jane Austen's more inquisitive heroines, though he assumes, overhastily in my opinion, that Fanny's passivity exempts her from monstrosity (p. 41). Sandra M. Gilbert and Susan Gubar are more catholic in their definition: "[Austen's] heroines, it seems, are not born like people, but manufactured like monsters, and also like monsters they seem fated to self-destruct," Gilbert and Gubar, *The Madwoman in the Attic: The Woman Writer and the Nineteenth-Century Literary Imagination* (New Haven: Yale University Press, 1979), p. 129. For more capacious examinations of Jane Austen's dark Romanticism, see Wilt, pp. 121–72, and my "Jane Austen and Romantic Imprisonment," in *Jane Austen in a Social Context*, ed. David Monaghan (London: Macmillan, 1981), pp. 9–27.

9. See Maurianne Adams, *"Jane Eyre:* Woman's Estate," in Arlyn Diamond and Lee R. Edwards, eds., *The Authority of Experience: Essays in Feminist Criticism* (Amherst: University of Massachusetts Press, 1977), pp. 137–59; and Fleishman, p. 72, for more discussion of Fanny as orphan. For a broader discussion of the subversive implications of fictional orphanhood, see my "Incarnations of the Orphan," *ELH* 42 (Fall 1975): 395–419.

10. See Janet Todd, *Women's Friendship in Literature* (New York: Columbia University Press, 1980), pp. 246–74, for a provocative analysis of Fanny's, and Jane Austen's, rejection of female friendship and the radical autonomy it provides.

11. See, for instance, Donald Greene, "Jane Austen's Monsters," in John Halperin, ed., *Jane Austen: Bicentenary Essays* (Cambridge: Cambridge University Press, 1975), pp. 262–78. Amis, in Watt, p. 144, and Julia Prewitt Brown, in *Jane Austen's Novels: Social Change and Literary Form* (Cambridge, Mass.: Harvard University Press, 1979), p. 100, do in passing call Fanny Price a monster, but this appellation seems more a cry of horror than an expression of sustained literary interest.

12. See Fleishman, pp. 36–42.

13. A somewhat shorter version of this paper was presented as the keynote address of the 1980 meeting of the Jane Austen Society. Their kind invitation to speak made me wonder for the first time how I ought to feel about Fanny Price.

# What Fanny Knew
## A Quiet Auditor of the Whole

As Lionel Trilling has suggested, *Mansfield Park* looks more gravely than any other Austen novel at the dangers to society of self-expression.[1] Its heroine, Fanny Price, will not express herself and is a new kind of Austen heroine in that she embodies (in a disembodied sort of way) those who will not and do not act, on stage or off. Despite her industriousness, she is a center of nonenergy, a heroine who will demonstrate that personal energy in pursuit of social mobility· is a punishable offense. Fanny solves the dilemma of self-expression through the mode of passivity—in Austen's words, by resisting "the temptation of immediate pleasure"[2] (p. 467); in our words, by the deferral of gratification.

Ellen Moers reports that before the writing of *Mansfield Park* Austen is rereading a little-known (to us) novel, Mary Brunton's *Self Control*, of which she says in a letter to her sister that she means to write ". . . a close imitation. . . . I will improve upon it."[3] In fact, Fanny's self-control is so strong a force in the novel that it emerges to modern readers as a form of passive aggression, with indirectness of discourse as its source of power.

The central tension of the novel is this process of deferral. Trilling has noted the extraordinary preference in *Mansfield Park* for rest over motion.[4] Those who move (and improve) are dangerous, in the sense perhaps that a lady was later defined by the Victorians as someone who did not move. "I must move," says Mary Crawford. "Resting fatigues me" (p. 96). At chess she exclaims to William Price:

> "There, I will stake my last like a woman of spirit. No cold prudence for me. I am not born to sit still and do nothing. If I lose the game, it shall not be from not striving for it." (p. 243)

224

Alas for Mary Crawford, such words ring in our heads; they seal her fate, even in the first half of the book.

Fanny's absence of energy, the physical weakness that everyone remarks on, is not of course fatigue, or the inertia that Austen derides in Lady Bertram, for Fanny is not inert. She is the moral presence who watches and listens, especially listens. Austen says she is a very courteous listener, and "often the only listener at hand" (p. 164), the one to whom the others, the actors, bring their complaints and distresses. "*She* knew. . . . She knew . . . she knew . . . she knew" (p. 164). She is "a quiet auditor of the whole" (p. 136), saved from partaking in the sin of acting in the play, saved from the sin of wishing Sir Thomas dead in Antigua (she merely grieves to herself that she cannot grieve his absence). Listening and observing, without speaking, are the sources of her character, and they will outdo background, breeding, and money as the reasons for her success. She even contrives to be unseen as well as unheard, in Austen's sly inside joke, that Fanny "had edged back her chair behind her aunt's end of the sopha, and, screened from notice herself saw all that was passing before her" (p. 185). It is the moment in which Sir Thomas has called them all to account.

Fanny's apparent passivity has made her unattractive to many readers, especially to women readers who are often suspicious of those of their sisters who seem to be what men want women to be, but her passivity is more symbolic than personal and reflects the energy going on around her in the "improvements." Tony Tanner suggests that Fanny represents an eighteenth-century England holding fast against the encroachments of the industrial revolution.[5] The energetic ones are going to bring down the house, and only those drained of all but religious energy can preserve the past.

Fanny's silent acquiescences are contradicted in two longish speeches (really outbursts) on the subject of nature. They are quite unlike her, and they stand out because sustained verbal expression is so rare for Fanny. Perhaps the subject of nature arouses her, when in Volume 2, Chapter 4, she utters some 350 words to Mary Crawford as they walk in Mrs. Grant's gardens. Perhaps she is defending herself against the "fascination" (p. 208) that draws her into Mary's company every two or three days.

Now it is Mary Crawford's sin that she sees "no wonder in this shrubbery equal to seeing myself in it" (pp. 209–210). But Fanny too seems to see herself in the natural world, if somewhat less directly than Mary. Her view of nature is a view of mutability, tied in part to the improvements.

Her thoughts on nature turn rapidly into a disquisition on the nature of change and on the human "powers for recollecting and forgetting" (p. 210). It is a strange speech, not only for its length; the words trouble us, and the irony—that Fanny's view of nature shows up the shallowness of Mary's—is not quite achieved.

> "This is pretty—very pretty. . . . Every time I come into this shrubbery I am more struck with its growth and beauty. Three years ago, this was nothing but a rough hedgerow along the upper side of the field, never thought of as any thing, or capable of becoming any thing; and now it is converted into a walk, and it would be difficult to say whether most valuable as a convenience or an ornament; and perhaps in another three years we may be forgetting—almost forgetting what it was before. How wonderful, how very wonderful the operations of time, and the changes of the human mind!" (p. 208)

Perhaps Fanny is commenting unconsciously on the changes within herself: perhaps it is her growth and her conversion into something else and her being valuable as either convenience or ornament. At any rate, she will become so by natural means, since Mansfield has released in her her natural delicacy, and in three years' time she too will have forgotten how it was done that she came from Portsmouth to Mansfield. The speech, then, is not really about shrubbery in the gardens; it is about Fanny seeing herself in nature.

Her words in this section are remarkable in their contrast to what Fanny is not saying in the rest of the novel. If we look closely at what Fanny actually says, certain patterns emerge. We have a new construct in *Mansfield Park*, thirteen years after the *sprezzatura* of Elizabeth Bennet, and before the art of *Persuasion* is painfully relearned by Anne Elliot, as Jane Bowman Swanson has recently shown.[6] We have a heroine in flight from speech, but she is not a heroine like Elizabeth or Anne. She is mythic, a Cinderella, a foundling, as many critics have seen, and she is the only Austen heroine we see as a child, almost a Victorian waif in the making. Fanny is Griselda, too, a type unchanged since Chaucer's time, patient, voiceless, controlling emotion before others, a quiet center of duty—in short, a prefiguration of the Angel in the House. Her part of the house, in fact, is described in elaborate detail: she is the child in the attic whose wicked stepmother (Aunt Norris) allows her no fire to keep her warm.

Fanny's speeches and impulses to speech expand in the last quarter of the novel, as she grows stronger and prettier. Actually, her speeches lengthen as her social status rises, but even in the last quarter of the book a central metaphor for personal energy is apparent: a remarkable hostility to language competency, especially but not exclusively in women, often an extension of the immorality of performing the play. If those who move are dangerous, so are those who talk, talk to no purpose, who squander talk. Fanny talks to purpose. She is "more inclined to silence when feeling most strongly" (p. 369), and we watch with some dismay the possible disappearance under her hand of those freewheeling verbal exchanges that had animated rainy country afternoons and evenings.

Fanny is described throughout as strangled by speech. She is unable to speak; she will not talk; she is overcome with emotion; she ventures speech to no avail; she starts and stops endless sentences; she gasps, murmurs, mutters in undertones (just managing, with Sir Thomas, to be overheard sufficiently to contribute to the downfall of Aunt Norris). She colors and says nothing. She talks to herself, but even when she is alone, her speeches are usually fewer than three lines. If solicited by Edmund for an opinion, she is seen "shrinking from such a compliment" (p. 153). When he appeals to her judgment, she insists that she can be only a listener; she urges him to be careful how he talks to her since she is not qualified to be an adviser (p. 269). When her brother turns to her after a tiring social evening, it is for quiet. He says, "I have been talking incessantly all night, and with nothing to say. But with *you*, Fanny, there may be peace. You will not want to be talked to. Let us have the luxury of silence" (p. 278).

Her actual discourse falls into distinct patterns. There is general naysaying, part of the rituals of self-denial; she will not allow, for instance, that she is tired when it is plain to Edmund that she is exhausted, for there is "no spirit of murmuring within her" (p. 280). Saying too much is doing wrong (p. 354). She speaks in defense of principles, religious principles in particular, since this is a novel, after all, about ordination. Here she is often described as "crying out," that is, forced into speech as a last resort against evil, for example, when she defends Edmund's taking orders (pp. 86, 109). She conducts joyful tête-à-têtes with her brother, although most of the time only his speeches are reported, and he does all the information giving. (In fact, when he visits Mansfield, he seems to speak for both Fanny and himself to Sir Thomas; he has the authority of his sex despite her long residence there.) She speaks (or listens) as a kind of moral sounding board, or nondirective control, first for Edmund, then for Henry Crawford, who, interestingly, loves her, he says, because he can "so wholly and absolutely confide in her" (p. 294). And, finally, she says "no" to males who wish to force her into morally indefensible acts. In the passages in which she refuses Henry Crawford and refuses her uncle—the set pieces of the novel—her oral spasms are three and four to the page. After a 13-line, 134-word speech to her uncle, she is exhausted, "she could say no more; her breath was almost gone" (p. 315).

Silence is eloquence for Fanny, and the verbal-oral inhibition extends to her letter-writing. The only letter we see of hers (in a novel originally planned in epistolary form, according to Q. D. Leavis)[7] is, Fanny says, "excessively ill-written, that the language would disgrace a child" (p. 108). That talker Mary Crawford is of course a consummate letter-writer, as is her brother, and "Miss Crawford's style of writing, lively and affectionate, was itself an evil, independent of what she (Fanny) was thus forced into reading from the brother's pen. . . ." (p. 376).

Hostility to language performance brings with it a doubleness of attitude. Henry is very attractive to Fanny when he is talking, as an actor, although the influence of his voice is felt by all of them at Mansfield. His ability to release speech is charged for her and for the others, giving us our conscious sense that speech is eroticized in *Mansfield Park*, equated with play, with *the* play, and with the disturbing sexuality of the Crawfords. The attempt on Fanny's sexuality is also tied to talk. Henry Crawford wishes to crack her careful, composed self to find the warmth underneath. He cannot bear her indifference: it tempts him.

> A little difficulty to be overcome, was no evil to Henry Crawford. He rather derived spirits from it. He had been apt to gain hearts too easily. His situation was new and animating. (p. 327)

He is especially aroused by her affection for her brother, himself a brother. As Austen readers know, "even the conjugal tie is beneath the fraternal" (p. 235). He speaks of wanting Fanny in language that hints of assault upon the young:

> He was no longer in doubt of the capabilities of her heart. She had feeling, genuine feeling. It would be something to be loved by such a girl, to excite the first ardours of her young, unsophisticated mind! She interested him more than he had foreseen. A fortnight was not enough. (pp. 235–36)

To charm her, Crawford discourses on the beauty of the church liturgy, although in hope of forcing her into speech. He confesses that he sometimes grows weary in church:

> "Did you speak?" stepping eagerly to Fanny, and addressing her in a softened voice; and upon her saying, "No," he added, "Are you sure you did not speak? I saw your lips move. I fancied you might be going to tell me I *ought* to be more attentive, and not *allow* my thoughts to wander. Are you not going to tell me so?" (p. 340)

Later, she is "wearied at last into speaking" to him; "Crawford, delighted to get her to speak at any rate, was determined to keep it up" (p. 343).

Fanny is so silent at age eighteen, when the Crawfords first meet her, that they cannot discover if she is "out" or not. To be out is to be sexually and maritally available, and to be sexually available is to talk. ". . . she says so little," says Mary, "that I can hardly suppose she *is* [out]" (p. 48). "A girl not out, has always the same sort of dress . . . looks very demure, and never says a word" (p. 49). Silence here is chastity, and although Fanny escapes quite narrowly acting in the play, she is untainted by too early talk. Indeed, as she grows up and becomes attractive, both Edmund and her uncle want her to talk more (p. 198).

Fanny and Mary, "the Jane and the anti-Jane," as Lawrence Lerner calls Austen's fragmentation of heroines,[8] divide, then, along linguistic lines, the talkative and the silent. But Mary is more than "other" for Fanny. She and her brother pose a real threat to Mansfield's values in the quality of their talk, in its license. Even Edmund calls Mary's conversation "indecorous" (p. 64). Had the Crawfords been entirely impersonators, as Tanner states,[9] then Austen should not have given us so much information on the depths of the feelings that Crawford discourse arouses in Fanny and Edmund. At the end, when Henry and Mary have understood that the other two might have saved them from chaos, they fall silent at last.

Awareness of language extends to extreme sensitivity to voices. Lady Bertram does not offend by loudness, but Austen will bring her in for comment that is entirely appropriate: ". . . she never took the trouble of raising her voice; her voice was always heard and attended to" (p. 16). Despite her lassitude, however, she is deemed a better person for Fanny to grow up with than is Mrs. Norris, for "one could hide behind others at Mansfield, but with Aunt Norris Fanny will be forced to speak for herself" (p. 25). Her father's voice is loud, and when Fanny returns "home" she is deeply pained by his coarse language. The farther from Mansfield, the more unpleasant the sounds, for "Mansfield was home" (p. 436). Portsmouth is impossible because of the noise, the very "abode of noise, disorder, and impropriety" (p. 388):

> The living in incessant noise was to a frame and temper, delicate and nervous like Fanny's, an evil which no super-added elegance or harmony could have entirely atoned for. It was the greatest misery of all. At Mansfield, no sounds of contention, no raised voice, no abrupt bursts, no tread of violence, was ever heard. . . . Here, every body was noisy, every voice was loud (excepting perhaps, her mother's, which resembled the soft monotony of Lady Bertram's, only worn into fret-

fulness.)—Whatever was wanted, was halloo'd for, and the servants halloo'd out their excuses from the kitchen. The doors were in constant banging, the stairs were never at rest, nothing was done without a clatter, nobody sat still, and nobody could command attention when they spoke. (Pp. 391–92)

In separating herself from the noises of Portsmouth, Fanny completes her passage home to Mansfield.

What did Fanny know? How to listen. And at the end of the novel, in the rush of elopements, marriages, adulteries, the flurry that "other pens will dwell on" (p. 461), my Fanny's "soft light eyes" will be preferred to "sparkling dark ones" (p. 470), Fanny and Edmund will be wed at last. With Fanny at his side, Edmund will become a most excellent neighborhood clergyman, not a fancy preacher who drops in three or four times a year to touch parishioners' hearts with glib talk. And in a novel with so much talk about talk, what is to be our last view of Fanny and Edmund? He will be "always with her and always talking confidentially" (p. 470).

*Marylea Meyersohn*
*City College of the City University of New York*

# NOTES

1. Lionel Trilling, in *"Mansfield Park,"* Ian Watt, ed., *Jane Austen: A Collection of Critical Essays* (Englewood Cliffs, N.J.: Prentice-Hall, 1963) pp. 124–40.
2. *Mansfield Park*. All references to *Mansfield Park* are to R. W. Chapman, ed., *The Novels of Jane Austen: The Text Based on Collation of the Early Editions*, vol. III, third edition (London: Oxford University Press, 1934).
3. Ellen Moers, *Literary Women* (Garden City, N.Y.: Doubleday & Co., 1976).
4. Trilling, p. 127.
5. Tony Tanner, ed., *Mansfield Park* (Baltimore: Penguin, 1966), p. 10.
6. Jane Bowman Swanson, "Toward a Rhetoric of Self: The Art of *Persuasion*," *Nineteenth-Century Fiction*, 36 (June 1981).
7. Q. D. Leavis, "A Critical Theory of Jane Austen's Writings (II): 'Lady Susan' into 'Mansfield Park,'" *Scrutiny*, 10 (October 1941):123.
8. Lawrence Lerner, *The Truthtellers: Jane Austen, George Eliot, D. H. Lawrence.* (London: Chatto and Windus, 1967), p. 161.
9. Tanner, p. 12.

# Feminist Irony and the Priceless
# Heroine of *Mansfield Park*

" 'I do not quite know what to make of Miss Fanny. I do not understand her.' " So says Henry Crawford (*Mansfield Park*, p. 230).[1] What to make of Miss Fanny is the central moral puzzle Jane Austen presents to her anti-hero. He fails to discover the correct solution. It is also the central puzzle presented to the reader, testing the soundness of his moral attitudes and the quickness of his wits. It may be that the author misjudged what could be expected of her readers, for they have not, by and large, solved the riddle of Miss Price satisfactorily. Even Henry Austen took a bit of time over it (*Letters*, nos. 92–94). He had the advantage of familiarity with contemporary works to which allusion is made, as well as a knowledge of the author's point of view, and yet he found this puzzle a difficult one. No wonder, then, that later readers, lacking his privileged knowledge, have sometimes blundered.

In this essay, I shall try to show that Jane Austen teases us about Miss Fanny. Irony, far from being suspended in *Mansfield Park*, is turned upon the reader. We are given a heroine who, in some respects, looks like an exemplary conduct-book girl, but this is deceptive. Fanny is not a true conduct-book heroine and, insofar as she resembles this ideal—in her timidity, self-abasement, and excessive sensibility, for example—her author mocks her—and us, if we mistake these qualities for virtue. Jane Austen hated "unmixed" characters in general, and "unmixed" heroines in particular, a point on which she disagreed with the Dr. Johnson of *Rambler* 4. Writing to her niece Fanny Knight (the one with a weakness for Evangelical gentlemen), she discusses the opinions of an aptly named Mr. Wildman, who had not found her novels to his taste:

> Do not oblige him to read any more.—Have mercy on him. . . . He and
> I should not in the least agree of course in our ideas about Heroines;

pictures of perfection as you know make me sick and wicked—but there is some very good sense in what he says, and I particularly respect him for wishing to think well of all young Ladies; it shows an amiable and delicate Mind—And he deserves better than to be obliged to read any more of my Works.[2]

If Jane Austen created a conduct-book heroine, it cannot have been without an ironic intention of some kind. A clue to what it was occurs in an unsigned article on the "Female Novelists" published in *New Monthly Review* in 1852: "Then again, in *Mansfield Park*, what a bewitching 'little body' is Fanny Price . . ."[3] This Victorian writer sees in Fanny, not a paragon of virtue, but a little enchantress, and it is important to notice that, when Crawford falls in love, he too sees her in this way. Fanny's apparent saintliness is closely connected with her sexual desirableness, as Crawford shows in Chapter XII of the second volume, where he tells his sister that he is in love. His appreciation of "Fanny's graces of manner and goodness of heart," as well as his recognition of her "being well-principled and religious," is mingled with his dwelling on her "charms" (p. 294), "her beauty of face and figure," her beautifully heightened color, as she attends to the service of that stupid woman, her Aunt Bertram, and the neat arrangement of her hair, with "one little curl falling forward . . . which she now and then shook back" (pp. 296–97).

Crawford is incapable of understanding that the "religious principles" he admires in Fanny are formed, as Providence intended rational beings to form moral principles, out of rational reflection upon experience. His view of her is deeply sentimental, for he sees her as something like the ideal woman of Rousseau's *Émile*, innocent, virtuous, tractable, and crying out for protective love, which her prettiness and gentleness excite in him. By Volume Three, he discovers that she has "some touches of the angel" in her (p. 344). Henry Austen must have seen at that point, if he had not seen it before, that his sister would not allow her heroine to marry Crawford, for Austen's objection to the comparison of young women to angels is so consistently maintained that this blunder of Crawford's could not pass unnoticed. Elizabeth Bennet once says, jokingly and critically, that her sister Jane has angelic characteristics (*Pride and Prejudice*, p. 134); otherwise, from the *Juvenilia* to the mature works, only fools or villains make this analogy. It is pointedly avoided by all the Austen heroes, but used to define the defects of the more complex anti-heroes, notably Willoughby and Crawford, and to define Emma's disillusion with Frank Churchill (*Emma*, p. 479).

The point is of great importance to a right understanding of Fanny Price and *Mansfield Park*, because it directs us to the criticism of the conduct-book ethos which is the essential irony of Miss Price's characterization. It may seem strange to us that physical weakness, or lassitude, should be thought to enhance a girl's sexual attractiveness, nor do we think religiosity alluring, but it was not always so. The conduct-book ideal of young womanhood was deeply sentimental, and the genre included works in which salaciousness was mixed with moral advice.

Two examples, quoted and proscribed by Mary Wollstonecraft in *A Vindication of the Rights of Woman,* are of especial interest. Wollstonecraft berates James Hervey, whose *Meditations and Contemplations,* written between 1745 and 1746, were "still read" in 1792. Hervey told his readers (mostly female) that:

> Never, perhaps, does a fine woman strike more deeply, than when, composed into pious recollection, and possessed with the noblest considerations, she assumes, without knowing it, superior dignity and new graces; so that the beauties of holiness seem to radiate about her, and the bystanders are almost induced to fancy her already worshipping among the kindred angels.

Mary Wollstonecraft could not stand that sort of thing. "Should," she asks, "a grave preacher interlard his discourses with such folleries? . . . Why are girls to be told that they resemble angels: but to sink them below women." Like Jane Austen, she has no patience either with Dr. Fordyce, whose *Sermons to Young Women* (1766) contain a remarkable passage in which the awfulness of abusing young angels is discussed with salacious relish:

> Behold these smiling innocents, whom I have graced with my fairest gifts, and committed to your protection; behold them with love and respect; treat them with tenderness and honour. They are timid and want to be defended. They are frail; oh do not take advantage of their weakness! Let their fears and blushes endear them. Let their confidence in you never be abused. But is it possible, that any of you can be such barbarians, so supremely wicked, as to abuse it? Can you find in your hearts to despoil the gentle, trusting creatures of their treasure, or do anything to strip them of their native robe of virtue? Curst be the impious hand that would dare to violate the unblemished form of chastity! Thou wretch! thou ruffian! forbear; nor venture to provoke Heaven's fiercest vengeance.

Mary Wollstonecraft says, not unreasonably:

> I know not any comment that can be made seriously on this curious passage, and I could produce many similar ones; and some, so very sentimental, that I have heard rational men use the word indecent when they mentioned them with disgust.[4]

It will be remembered that it was Fordyce's *Sermons* that Mr. Collins chose, after having turned down a novel, to read aloud to the ladies at Longbourn. Perhaps it was at just such a passage that Lydia Bennet, no angel, but "a stout well-grown girl of fifteen," interrupted his "monotonous solemnity" to tell her mother an interesting bit of gossip about the regiment quartered nearby. At all events, Mr. Collins' approbation of Fordyce is a clear indication that Jane Austen disapproved of him.

There is good reason to think, in the light of her novels and letters, that this was a disapproval founded in sympathy with rational, post-Enlightenment feminism. This is not to suggest that Austen was in agreement with Wollstonecraft on anything more than these fundamental ideas: (a) that women, being possessed of the same "powers of mind" as men, have the same moral status and the same moral accountability; (b) that girls should be educated in a manner appropriate to this view of the female sex; (c) that a "respectable" marriage is an "equal" marriage, in which man and woman are "partners," and must therefore rest on "friendship and esteem," and (d) that literary works in which any other view is endorsed are objectionable. Modern feminists may find these very tame, but around 1800 they were the essential convictions of rational feminism. We need not be put off because Austen is "a moralist" after the Johnsonian fashion; so, in many respects, is Wollstonecraft, especially in the *Vindication,* itself a sort of conduct book. The moral argument upon which Wollstonecraft bases her feminist case derives very largely from Bishop Butler's *Analogy of Religion* (1796) and from Richard Price's *Review of the Central Question in Morals* (1758). Butler was a bishop of the established church, whose views accord to a large extent with Johnson's. Price was a Dissenter and, through his influence upon progressive Dissent, associated not only with Wollstonecraft herself but with many of the radicals of his time. His ambience was thus quite different from Butler's, but the essential character of his view of morals was not, as he himself acknowledges.

So far as late-eighteenth-century feminism went, Butler and Price could both be seen as laying down principles upon which a feminist moralist could found her argument. This is crucial to a right understanding of the relationship between the first well-known English feminist theorist, Mary Wollstonecraft, and the first major woman novelist in English. Thinking of them, as we do, as totally different in their religious and political affiliations, lifestyle, and temperament, we may easily miss what connects them as feminist moralists, whose roots lie in a common tradition of ethical discussion. There is no need to assume that Austen was an undercover Jacobin because she is so close to Wollstonecraft as a feminist moralist.

Austen's implicit demand that men and women be judged, and judge themselves, by the same, somewhat strict, standard in sexual matters, should not be seen as a sign of her commitment to anti-Jacobin fervor. It is no more than the mark of her convinced feminism. Among the radicals, as both Gary Kelly[5] and Marilyn Butler show, feminist feeling went hand in hand with emphasis upon the need for reason and restraint in sexual matters. Butler is impatient with them about it: "In sexual matters, the Jacobins thought and behaved (whatever their opponents claimed) like forerunners of the Evangelicals." Believing in the power of reason to liberate mankind, they renounced the example of "Rousseau, Goethe and Kotzebue . . . when they refused to exploit sexual passion as a powerful natural ally against a moribund society and its repressive conventions." Butler contrasts the English Jacobins unfavorably in this respect with their Continental counterparts, including Madame de Staël.[6]

A feminist point of view is not only compatible with the argumentative style of an eighteenth-century moralist, but may be positively connected with it. Were *Mansfield Park* primarily about political and social questions *other* than feminist ones, the conservative character of the moral argument which it embodies would justify us in supposing it to be fundamentally conservative in outlook, but, if the feminist issues are the central ones, it may be that the orthodox, rather old-fashioned character of the argument indicates feminist radicalism rather than orthodoxy. An example may be useful here. In attacking the education commonly provided for middle-class girls, Mary Wollstonecraft says:

> Though moralists have agreed that the tenor of life seems to prove that *man* is prepared by various circumstances for a future state, they consistently concur in advising *woman* to provide only for the present.[7]

She refers to the belief, best exemplified in Bishop Butler's *Analogy of Religon*, and popularized in many sermons and moralistic works, that the world is so ordered as to teach us moral principle through secular experience. Even without a belief in God, the order of nature, including human nature, of which rational powers are a part, insures that we are rewarded when we act well and punished when we act badly. It was an orthodox belief of established moralists that this was so, but, in applying it to women, Mary Wollstonecraft is able to use it to attack existing practices in education and social custom, which rule out one half of mankind from the benefits of exercise in the moral gymnasium designed to teach moral principles.

In the Austen novels the heroines learn about morals through the application of rational reflection to experience. This is how they are shown to acquire principle. They never learn it from clerical advisers. The process by which they acquire understanding of duty, and of right courses of action, is entirely secular, as Ryle noted.[8] The way in which they are shown as becoming morally accountable may look a little old-fashioned, if we forget that they are young women, not young men. If we remember it, and see it in relation to contemporary feminist discussion, we may see that Jane Austen is sometimes a radical wolf when she pointedly adopts orthodox moralists' sheep's clothing.

It is time to return to Miss Fanny, and to show further that her characterization is to be illuminated by Mary Wollstonecraft. The implication of this must be that either Austen had read Wollstonecraft or that she was familiar with her works through the filtering through of their arguments and examples to other, less controversial writers. I do not mean to argue the case for direct influence here. During the five years she spent in Bath, with its well-stocked bookshops and circulating libraries, by no means confined to fiction,[9] Austen had access to the works of Mary Wollstonecraft. In the absence of direct biographical information, the case must stand upon the probability implied by closeness of point of view and, in some instances, of allusion and vocabulary.

*Vindication* is not primarily about the political and constitutional rights of women, but about the ideas referred to above as constituting the essence of post-Enlightenment rational feminism. It is largely an attack upon Rousseau, especially the Rousseau of *Émile,* and upon those sentimental moralists and divines who had followed him in denying women the moral status of rational, adult, moral agents. With them are coupled imaginative writers of both sexes, including Madame de Staël, who, by emphasizing the sensibility of women at the expense of their powers of reason, have "Rendered them Objects of Pity, Bordering on Contempt" (p. 173). Wollstonecraft's animus against Rousseau arises from his having made Sophie—his ideal mate for Émile, the ideal man—a different kind of moral creature. Whereas Émile is to enjoy bodily and mental exercise, Sophie is to be confined to bodily weakness and to obedience. This, Rousseau thought, was in accordance with the nature of the two sexes and with their purposes in life. It was for the man to enjoy the advantages of a free, experiential life; it was for the woman to please him, to arouse his sexual passion, to enjoy his protection, and to obey him. All this was anathema to Wollstonecraft and, to Austen, a fit subject of ridicule.

Take first the question of health and strength, which is of particular importance to the characterization of Miss Fanny. Wollstonecraft objects to Rousseau's belief that genuine weakness and the affected exaggeration of weakness are natural to women and a means by which they gain an ambiguous power over men. She quotes with disgust a passage from *Émile* in which it is asserted of women:

So far from being ashamed of their weakness, they glory in it; their tender muscles make no resistance; they affect to be incapable of lifting the smallest burdens, and would blush to be thought robust and strong. (p. 174)

Wollstonecraft declares that

. . .the first care of mothers and fathers who really attend to the education of females should be, if not to strengthen the body, at least not to destroy the constitution by mistaken notions of female excellence; nor should girls ever be allowed to imbibe the pernicious notion that a defect can, by any chemical process of reasoning, become an excellence. (p. 126)

She then attacks such conduct-book authors as have taken their cue from Rousseau and encouraged girls to cultivate either real or affected weakness and low spirits. Among these she reluctantly places Dr. John Gregory, whose *A Father's Letters to His Daughters* (1774)

actually recommends dissimulation and advises an innocent girl to give the lie to her feelings, and not dance with spirit, when gaiety of heart would make her feel eloquent without making her gestures immodest. In the name of truth and common sense, why should not one woman acknowledge that she has a better constitution than another? (pp. 111–12)

Austen did not admire physical weakness or ill-health or ignorance in young women, but a lot of people, including those who ought to have known better, did. The relevance of this to Miss Price is obvious. Austen created in her a heroine whom the unwary might take for something like the Rousseauist ideal of the perfect woman, but she expects her more discerning readers to see through it, and gives them a good many indications that this is not a proper reading. The most important of these is, of course, the category mistake of the anti-hero, but there is a good deal else. The true hero is never shown as encouraging Fanny in her partly self-imposed fragility and timidity, although he is kind to her when he observes her genuine tendency to tire easily. He gets her a horse, encourages her to ride regularly, and tells her to speak up for herself, even to her uncle. But the major comic emphasis, through which Austen shows that she does not admire hypochondria in women, even beautiful ones, comes through the splendid portrait of pampered indolence in Lady Bertram.

Fanny is quite different from her aunt in that she has, both as a child and as a very vulnerable adolescent, experienced both neglect and hardship. Given Mrs. Price's predilection for sons and her slatternly housekeeping, there is little reason to think that the health (whether of body or mind) of her eldest daughter had ever received much attention. At Mansfield, the somnolence of Aunt Bertram, the sadism of Aunt Norris, and the false regard for wealth and status of Sir Thomas Bertram, his elder son, and his daughters, have all combined to ensure that Fanny's mental and physical health are put in jeopardy. She has not a strong constitution, but she was not as a child devoid of normal impulses to active life. She did not enjoy such freedom as Catherine Morland, rolling down green slopes with her brothers, and it is never positively established that she preferred cricket to dolls or nursing dormice, as Catherine did, but Fanny, in her early years at Portsmouth, was important as *"play-fellow,"* as well as "instructress and nurse" to her brothers and sisters. The single instance of remembered childhood activity which Austen mentions concerns dancing. William recalls how he and Fanny used to dance together as children. It is what prompts him to ask Sir Thomas if his sister is a good dancer, Sir Thomas being forced to reply that he does not know. William says, "I should like to be your partner once more. We used to jump about together many a time, did not we? when the hand organ was in the street?" (p. 250). Fanny's excessive fragility of body and lack of self-confidence are the result of inconsiderate, and sometimes humiliating, treatment by her illiberal, selfish aunts, but it has not quite stamped out of her an impulse to life which is to be seen in her continued love of dancing. At her first ball, "she was quite grieved to be losing even a quarter of an hour . . . sitting most unwillingly among the chaperons . . . while all the other young people were dancing" (pp. 116–17). Later, when a ball is given in her honor, the narrator tells us, "She had hardly ever been in a state so nearly approaching high spirits in her life. Her cousins' former gaiety on the day of a ball was no longer surprising to her; she felt it to be indeed very charming" (p. 273). And she actually practices her steps in the drawing room, when she is sure Aunt Norris won't see. She gets tired later at this ball, partly because she is jealous of Miss Crawford, but it is three o'clock in the morning, and she is up earlier than anyone else, apart from William, next day, in order to see him off.

Fanny Price's feebleness is not a mark of Clarissa Harlowe-like saintliness, as Lionel Trilling thought, nor is it to be dismissed, as Marilyn Butler dismisses it, as "quite incidental." It is essential to the play of anti-Rousseauist, feminist irony upon Miss Price and those who seek to interpret her. Once her cousins leave Mansfield, prolonged ill-treatment is seen to have curious effects. The affectation of fragility, which it took an expensive education to achieve, Fanny lacks, but a genuine fragility now makes her seem something like the Rousseauist ideal, and by this Crawford is, as he puts it, "fairly caught." But, if Fanny's physical frailty amounts to more than it seems, the strength of her mind, despite the physical and emotional deprivation she has endured, is truly formidable. Housed within the "bewitching little body," lurking behind the "soft light eyes," is a clear, critical, rationally judging mind, quite unlike the tractable, childlike mind of the true conduct-book heroine. Wollstonecraft says, "The conduct of an accountable being must be regulated by the operation of its own reason; or on what foundation rests the throne of God?" (*Vindication*, p. 121). Just before Fanny offends her uncle by insisting upon her right to regulate her conduct, by the operation of her own judgment, in a matter of great moment, he is made to say, though without understanding what it implies, "You have an understanding, which will prevent you from receiving things only in part, and judging partially by the event.—You will take in the whole of the past, you will consider times, persons, and probabilities" (p. 313). He is talking about Aunt Norris's past behavior, but he describes exactly what Fanny does in forming her opinion of Crawford.

The moral and comic climax of *Mansfield Park* occurs at the start of Volume Three, in the East room, when Fanny confronts her august uncle and defies him. Sir Thomas, once he is able to make out that she intends to refuse Crawford, thunders away at her about ingratitude, selfishness, perversity, and sheer obtuseness as to her own interest. He is forced to wonder if she does not show "that independence of spirit, which prevails so much in modern days, even in young women, and which in young women is offensive and disgusting beyond all common offence" (p. 318). Austen expects us to laugh at him, but she does not spare her heroine either. Returning from her walk in the shrubbery, Fanny finds that a fire has already been lighted, on Sir Thomas's orders, in the bleak East room. She does not say, as a creature wholly regulated by reason might have done, "Well, wrongly though he has judged and acted, he has kind and benevolent aspects." She says—and it is truer to life, as well as to the comic spirit—"in soliloquy," ' "I must be a brute indeed, if I can be really ungrateful. . . . Heaven defend me from being ungrateful!' " (pp. 322–23).

Jane Austen laughs at Fanny when she herself acquiesces, as she often does, in the submissive role in which an unjust domestic "order" has cast her. She exposes, with a more bitter ridicule, the foolishness which has all but stamped out of Fanny her ability to laugh, dance, play, or to act—in any sense. But she does not despair. Reason, and the will of a less insane God than that invoked by such clerics as Fordyce and Mr. Collins or Dr. Grant, will prevail, where men have such sense as Edmund and women such sense as Fanny. "Good sense, like hers, will always act when really called upon" (p. 399), and so it does. Fanny becomes "the daughter that

Sir Thomas Bertram wanted," that is, *lacked*, and, together with Edmund, is shown as capable of establishing at the parsonage a more liberal and more securely based domestic order than that of the Great House.

Fanny does not, as some critics, more concerned with mythic elements of plot than sound moral argument, have thought, "inherit" Mansfield Park. She marries the younger son, not the heir (who is pointedly restored to health), and she goes to live at the parsonage, where an enlightened, rational, secular Christianity is likely to be the order of the day. It is, perhaps, unlikely that the next Lady Bertram will waste so many years in a state of semiconsciousness, devoid of mental or physical life, upon a sofa, with a lapdog and a tangled, useless, meaningless bit of needlework, as the former Miss Maria Ward has done. But it is at the parsonage, not the Great House, that there is to occur that "unspeakable gain in private happiness to the liberated half of the species; the difference to them between a life of subjection to the will of others, and a life of rational freedom," of which J. S. Mill was later to write. [10]

In *Mansfield Park*, Austen shows some sympathy with points made in the *Vindication* and anticipates Mill *On the Subjection of Women*. It looks to me as though she may also have profited from a critical reading of Wollstonecraft's two novels. There is no direct evidence that she read them, but Godwin's publication of his *Memoirs of the Author of a Vindication of the Rights of Woman* in 1798 caused a great deal of interest in its subject. The "Advertisement" to *Mary* (1788) tells us that its heroine is "neither a Clarissa, a Lady G. [randison] nor a Sophie." In it, "the mind of a woman who has thinking powers" is to be displayed. Mary, its heroine, had "read Butler's *Analogy*, and some other authors: and these researches made her a Christian from conviction" (p. 23). Austen would not have countenanced the pretentious tone of this, but, in her own ironic way, she shows us that much the same could be said of Fanny. By the time *Maria* was written—it was still unfinished in 1797, when Wollstonecraft died—the author had become a Deist, rather than a Christian, but this does not prevent her from applying Butler's argument about how we learn moral principles in her new work. She says that in most novels "the hero is allowed to be mortal, and to become wise and virtuous as well as happy, by a train of events and circumstances. The heroines, on the contrary, are to be born immaculate . . ." (p. 73).

Both in Wollstonecraft and Austen, the language of law and property as well as the language of capture and captivation are shown as improperly applied to marriage and to decent sexual relationships. *Mansfield Park* opens with the *captivation* by Miss *Ward* of *Hunting*don, of a baronet to whom her uncle, "*the lawyer, himself,* . . . allowed her to be at least three thousand pounds short of any *equitable claim*" (my italics).

Wollstonecraft's Maria talks about "the master key of property" (p. 157). Austen, in the Sotherton episode, makes use of the lock and key image in connection with Rushworth and his property. Wollstonecraft's Maria says, "Marriage had bastilled me for life" (p. 155). Maria Bertram, flirting with Crawford while her intended husband has gone off to look for the key to the iron gate, which gives her "a feeling of restraint and hardship," alludes to the starling which Yorick found caged in the Bastille, and which sang incessantly, "I can't get out, I can't get out" (p. 99). She also refers to Sotherton as a prison, "quite a dismal old prison" (p. 53). Wollstonecraft's anti-hero declares "that every woman has her price" (p. 161). Austen borrows, as the name for her heroine, that of Crabbe's in one of *The Parish Register* tales. Crabbe's Fanny Price is a refuser of the captive-captivate game; Austen's is shown as unfit, by her nature, to become a commodity in the marriage market, though capable of paying the price of enduring wrongful abuse and misunderstanding, which secures her "right to choose, like the rest of us."

Jane Austen does not, like Mary Wollstonecraft, present us with an innocent heroine imprisoned in a marriage for which she is not regarded as bearing a responsibility. Austen's Maria chooses her own fate, though neither Sir Thomas nor the moral standards of the society of which he is a pillar are held blameless. Fanny, who avoids an imprisoning marriage, since she enters a partnership based on affection and esteem, does so not because she is "innocent," but because she is what Milton called "a true wayfaring Christian." Hers is not "a fugitive and cloistered virtue, unexercised and unbreathed," but one that has been put to "trial . . . by what is contrary."[11]

Once the irony at work in the characterization of Miss Price is recognized, the way is open to consideration of what is shown as truly valuable in the right ordering of domestic society and in the world beyond it. Jane Austen did not believe that individuals had to create their own morality; she believed that moral law was objectively enshrined in the nature of the world itself. To that extent, she supposes that human beings are required to be obedient to moral laws or principles, but she is perfectly clear that the individual human being has the right, and duty, of determining, by the operation of his or her own reason, what these principles are and how they are to be applied in the personal regulation of conduct. By showing that Sir Thomas's niece and his younger son are better to be relied upon in judging correctly, an implicit criticism of "birthright and habit," which debar women and younger sons from influence, even when their superior abilities are known, is made. It is quite in line with Wollstonecraft's attitude to "the Pernicious Effects which Arise from the Unnatural Distinctions Established in Society" (part of the title of Chapter 9 of *Vindica-*

*tion*). When Mary Crawford says that Edmund ought to have gone into Parliament, he replies, "I believe I must wait till there is an especial assembly for the representation of younger sons who have little to live on" (p. 214). Sir Thomas is a Member of Parliament, as, presumably, his elder son will also be. It is suggested (p. 161) that Mr. Rushworth will also enter the House when Sir Thomas is able to find him a borough. A rotten borough is not specified but would undoubtedly be appropriate. The case for the recognition of the *equality* of women with men is implicitly allied with the case against such unnatural distinctions and inequalities as are inherent in the law of primogeniture and in the unrepresentative character of Parliament.

*Mansfield Park* is also pointedly concerned with *fraternity*. What ought to be, and sometimes is—as in the relationship between Fanny and her brother William—the paradigm of equal, affectionate relationships between men and women is always held up as an ideal, having implications beyond the literal meaning of "brother" and "sister." Edmund Bertram treats his inferior little cousin as a sister early in Volume One. He does not fall in love with her until the final chapter, in which this is treated cursorily and ironically. This is not because Jane Austen had suddenly and unselfconsciously become interested in incest; it is because the marriage which provides the necessary happy ending of a comic work carries implications about the right relationships between men and women, both in marriage as a social institution and in society at large. As Mill was to say some fifty or more years later:

> The moral regeneration of mankind will only really commence, when the most fundamental of the social relations is placed under the rule of equal justice, and when human beings learn to cultivate their strongest sympathy with an equal in rights and cultivation.

Austen, in *Mansfield Park*, shows that such an ideal is more readily to be found, in contemporary society, between brothers and sisters than husbands and wives, though she seeks a transference to the marriage relationship of the ideal. With William, Fanny experiences a "felicity" which she has never known before, in an "unchecked, equal, fearless intercourse" (p. 234).

It is, however, with liberty, and the moral basis upon which individual liberty must be founded, that *Mansfield Park* is clearest and boldest. Women, in the Midland counties of England, like servants, were not slaves. Even a *wife*, not beloved, had some protection, "in the laws of the land, and the manners of the age." So Catherine Morland had learnt, under the tutelage of Henry Tilney. "Murder was not tolerated . . . and neither poison nor sleeping potions to be procured like rhubarb, from every druggist" (*Northanger Abbey*, p. 200). But what of an indulged wife? And a falsely respected one? In the Midland counties of England, murder might not be necessary where a wife could retain all the advantages of outward respect, rank, precedence, and "respectability," while passing her days in a state of partly self-induced semiconsciousness. Lady Bertram had "been a beauty, and a prosperous beauty, all her life; and beauty and wealth were all that excited her respect" (p. 332). She values herself on her possession of these things and, in the corrupt social order of which she is part, is valued for them. Never shown as going outside, or breathing fresh English air, Lady Bertram represents the slavery to which women who accede to such ideas reduce themselves, with the unwitting connivance of those, like Sir Thomas, who see nothing disgraceful in their condition. Not literally a slave and not suffering from the effects of a literal sleeping potion, what is she as a human being? What is she morally, as a rational, accountable one?

It is well known that in America the movement for women's rights was accelerated by the part women played in the movement for the emancipation of the slaves. As they heard, and put, moral arguments against slavery, they made an analogy between the moral status of a slave and of a woman, especially a married woman. This analogy is made in the *Vindication* and implied in *Mansfield Park*. Wollstonecraft says that a "truly benevolent legislator always endeavours to make it the interest of each individual to be virtuous; and thus private virtue becoming the cement of public happiness, an orderly whole is consolidated by the tendency of all the parts towards a common centre" (p. 257). Women, however, are not taught to be virtuous in their domestic life and so are not to be trusted in either private or public life. They learn to be subject to propriety, "blind propriety," rather than to regulate their actions in accordance with moral law as "an heir of immortality" ought. She asks, "Is one half of the human species, like the poor African slaves, to be subjected to prejudices that brutalise them, when principles would be a surer guard of virtue?" (p. 257).

In England, agitation against the slave trade had gone on all through the last quarter of the eighteenth century. The arguments against it were rehearsed widely in the early nineteenth century, leading up to the passing of the Act of Abolition, which became effective in 1808. Jane Austen must have been familiar with them and, in a letter of 1813, speaks of having been in love with Thomas Clarkson's writings (*Letters*, p. 292). In 1808, Clarkson published *The Abolition of the African Slave Trade:*

> We have lived in consequence of it to see the day when it has been recorded as a principle of our legislation that commerce itself shall have its moral boundaries. We have lived to see the day when we are likely

to be delivered from the contagion of the most barbarous opinions. Those who supported this wicked traffic virtually denied that man was a moral being. They substituted the law of force for the law of reason. But the great Act, now under our consideration, has banished the impious doctrine and restored the rational creature to his moral rights.

It is easy to see here that a woman who rejoiced that the slave trade had been ended might ask whether it had yet been recorded "as a principle of our legislation that commerce itself shall have its moral boundaries"—so far as women were concerned. Was it universally accepted that woman was "a moral being"? Had the rational creature been restored to *her* moral rights?

Clarkson goes over the history of the anti-slavery movement and refers to a particularly famous legal judgment, which established that slavery was illegal in England. This was the Mansfield Judgment, given by the Lord Chief Justice of England in 1772, in a case concerning a black slave, James Somerset, the question being whether, having been brought to England, he could still be held to be "owned" by his master. Arguing that he could not, counsel for the defence, referring to an earlier judgment given in the reign of Queen Elizabeth, said:

> . . . . it was resolved that England was too pure an air for slaves to breathe in . . . and I hope my lord the air does not blow worse since—I hope they will never breathe here; for this is my assertion, the moment they put their feet on English ground, that moment they are free.

Lord Mansfield found in favor of Somerset and, by implication, of this view of English air.

In *Mansfield Park* the English patriarch is also the owner of Antiguan plantations and of the slaves who work them. When he returns to England, his niece puts a question to him about the slave trade (p. 198). We are not told what the question was, nor what answer was given, but, through her title, the making of Sir Thomas a slaveowner abroad, and the unstated question of Miss Fanny, *her* moral status in England is implicitly contrasted, yet also compared, with that of the Antiguan slaves. Since it is often assumed that Jane Austen could not have thought much about anything which did not impinge upon her domestic life and familial relations, or else been said by Dr. Johnson, it may be worth noting that at the house of her brother Edward she met Lord Mansfield's niece on a number of occasions, and that Boswell reported Johnson's view on another slavery case, *Knight* v. *Wedderburn*, as follows: "No man is by nature the property of another. The defendant is therefore by nature free!"[12]

Slaves have masters but cannot truly be said to have a country, since they are neither protected by its laws nor accorded those rights which belong to freeborn citizens. That this was true in England of women is a point made by Wollstonecraft in *Maria,* where the heroine has no redress in "the laws of her country—if women have a country" (p. 159). Austen, not doubting that even such an unpromising feminist as Fanny Price "speaks the tongue that Shakespeare spoke" and, apart, no doubt, from a small difference about Adam and Eve, holds "the faith and morals . . . which Milton held," assumes that enlightened readers will know that she has the same "titles manifold" to British freedom as anyone else. She assures us that the soil at Mansfield is good, especially at the parsonage, and she makes a great point of the wholesomeness of English air, which is frequently associated with health and liberty. At Sotherton, with its prisonlike atmosphere, all the young people share "one impulse, one wish for air and liberty." Fanny's need for fresh English air is stressed again and again, often in ironic contexts. After berating her for not accepting Crawford, Sir Thomas tells her to get some exercise outside, where "the air will do her good," and Henry Crawford says of her, that she "requires constant air and exercise . . . ought never to be long banished from the free air and liberty of the country" (pp. 410–11). Of course, he means the countryside, but does not Austen expect the intelligent, enlightened reader to see a bit further?

Finally, we come to *Lovers' Vows.* It has been thought that, because this play had been attacked in anti-Jacobin circles, Austen's choice of it must be taken as a sign of her reactionary political viewpoint. However, it is quite directly associated with the main feminist themes of this novel. For a start, as its title shows, it is about the sentimental treatment of lovers' promises and is used to point the contrast between the lack of commitment involved in such promises as Baron Wildenhaim made to Agatha before he seduced her, or as Crawford half-makes to Maria, and the binding nature of the marriage contract. *Lovers' Vows* is a work in that tradition of Rousseauist literature which Mary Wollstonecraft objected to as rendering women objects of pity bordering on contempt. Agatha, having endured twenty years of poverty and humiliation because Wildenhaim broke his promise to her, makes a grateful, tearful acceptance of his eventual offer (following their son's intervention) to marry her. The curtain comes down on the following tableau:

> Anhalt leads on Agatha—The Baron runs and clasps her in his arms—supported by him, she sinks on a chair which Amelia places in the middle of the stage—The Baron kneels by her side, holding her hand.
> BARON. Agatha, Agatha, do you know this voice?
> AGATHA. Wildenhaim.
> BARON. Can you forgive me?
> AGATHA. I forgive you *(embracing him).*

FREDERICK *(as he enters)*. I hear the voice of my mother!—Ha! mother! father!
(Frederick throws himself on his knees by the other side of his mother—She clasps him in her arms.—Amelia is placed on the side of her father attentively viewing Agatha—Anhalt stands on the side of Frederick with his hands gratefully raised to Heaven.) The curtain slowly drops.

Anyone who doubts whether Jane Austen laughed at this had better reread *Love and Freindship*, but we have good reason to suppose that she thought the "happy ending" morally objectionable, not because the baron was letting his class down by marrying a village girl, nor the honor of his sex by marrying the girl who had lost her virtue through his agency, but because Agatha should have had more respect for herself, and too much contempt for him to have him at any price.

*Mansfield Park* remains a puzzling novel, partly, I think, because Jane Austen enjoyed puzzles and thought it both amusing and instructive to solve them. She asks a great deal of her readers—sound moral attitudes, derived from rational reflection upon experience; quick-wittedness and ingenuity in making connections; and a belief in the wholesomeness of laughter. It would be possible to make of *Mansfield Park* something like a piece of feminist propaganda, in which regulated hatred predominates, but it would be false. It is a great comic novel, regulated by the sane laughter of an implish, rational feminist. The pricelessness of Miss Price is its heart—and head.

*Margaret Kirkham*
*Bristol Polytechnic*

# NOTES

1. Page references to *Mansfield Park* and to other Austen novels are to R. W. Chapman, ed., *The Novels of Jane Austen* (London: Oxford University Press, 1931–34).
2. R. W. Chapman, ed., *The Letters of Jane Austen* (London: Oxford University Press, 1932).
3. Item 31 in B. C. Southam, ed., *Jane Austen: The Critical Heritage* (London: Routledge & Kegan Paul, 1968).

4. Mary Wollstonecraft, *Vindication of the Rights of Woman*, ed. Miriam Kramnick (Harmondsworth: Penguin, 1973), pp. 192–94.
5. Gary Kelly, *The English Jacobin Novel* (London: Oxford University Press, 1976), p. 8.
6. Marilyn Butler, *Jane Austen and the War of Ideas* (Oxford: The Clarendon Press, 1975), p. 45.
7. Wollstonecraft, p. 118.
8. Gilbert Ryle, "Jane Austen and the Moralists," in B. C. Southam, ed., *Critical Essays*.
9. W. J. Kite, "Libraries in Bath 1618–1964," thesis for a Fellowship of the Library Association, 1966, pt. 2, *passim*.
10. "On the Subjection of Women," in Richard Wollheim, ed., *John Stuart Mill: Three Essays* (Oxford: The Clarendon Press, 1975).
11. *Areopagitica* in *Milton's Prose*, ed. H. W. Wallace (London: Oxford University Press, 1925), p. 290.
12. James Boswell, *The Life of Samuel Johnson*, ed. Croker, p. 562.

# Two Faces of Emma

L̲et me recite two case histories, or character sketches, of certain young persons already well known to readers of English literature and other students of human nature.

The first subject I shall call "M.A."—not the initials of her name but her designation in a riddle, in which she is marked by "two letters of the alphabet . . . that express perfection."[1] But this young lady is far from perfect, by some measures of analysis. Briefly, the case history runs as follows: Born to a gentry family in England in the late eighteenth century; lost her mother at age five; father retired and elderly (of whom more to follow); raised by a governess "who had fallen little short of a mother in affection" (I.i.5) but whose "mildness of . . . temper had hardly allowed her to impose any restraint," so that the child was always "doing just what she liked . . . directed chiefly by her own [judgment]."

We find here the standard ingredients for the creation of an *overindulged child* syndrome. By age twelve, M.A. is "mistress of the house and of . . . all. In her mother she lost the only person able to cope with her. She inherits her mother's talents, and [would] have been under subjection to her" (I.v.37).

Even more shattering than the loss of a parent as intelligent as herself, Miss A. is burdened by the care of a semi-invalid father. It's often assumed by the layman that people with evident *hypochondria* are really well, but M.A.'s father, though not organically, is clearly mentally ill. The diagnosis of his illness is probably *premature senility*, featuring acute anxiety. His precise age is not known, but with an adult daughter he may be anything from his forties upward; he is not, however, necessarily a "senior citizen," in our current euphemism. From his daughter's point of view, indeed, he is as much a permanent lover as a parent: " 'Never, never could I expect to be so truly beloved and important; so always first and always right in any man's eyes as I am in my father's' " (I.x.84). A contemporary assessment of his condition runs as follows:

248

His spirits required support. He was a nervous man, easily depressed; fond of every body that he was used to, and hating to part with them; hating change of every kind. Matrimony, as the origin of change, was always disagreeable; and he was by no means yet reconciled to his own daughter's [i.e., M.A.'s sister's] marrying, nor could ever speak of her but with compassion . . . ; [finally, there are] his habits of gentle selfishness and of being never able to suppose that other people could feel differently from himself. . . . (I.i.7–8)

Now this may sound quite normal, considering the egocentrism of much of the behavior we see every day; but the incapacity to adjust to changes, especially in the maturation of his daughters, and the tendency to melancholy are telltale signs of neurosis, if not worse.

Everyone treats M.A.'s father with the mingled solicitude and irony due a defective mind, e.g., when M.A. playfully calls him "a fanciful, troublesome creature." Entirely lacking in self-irony but full of self-pity, he sighs, "I am afraid I am sometimes very fanciful and troublesome," so that his daughter is forced to retreat into disclaimers ("a joke—it is all a joke" [I.i.10]). He characteristically has "unsafe subjects" which must be avoided, especially those having to do with death and illness. Yet he can be depended upon to fail to understand most subjects of conversation: M.A. can talk around him, for "the entire deficiency in him of all such sort of penetration or suspicion, was a most comfortable circumstance" (II.v.193).

As in most psychological studies, the significance of parental descriptions lies in accounting for traits in the offspring. In the present case, Mr. "A" passes on to his daughter one of his neurotic modes of behavior, that known to science as *projection*. Mr. A has a druggist-physician named Perry, to whom he consistently refers his own hysterical hypochondria: "his friend Perry, to whom he had, in fact, though unconsciously, been attributing many of his own feelings and expressions" (i.xii.107; the precision of this contemporary report, and its employment of modern technical terminology, bear mention in passing).

It is, then, no wonder that his daughter employs this very psychic mechanism in most of her social relations, especially those charged with that threatening subject, sex. Time after time in her young life, M.A. becomes attracted to a man (or becomes the object of his desire) and projects her feelings onto her friend Harriet. First she tries to marry her friend off to the local minister, in the willful illusion that he's attracted to her, but he turns out to be more interested in herself, and she's overcome with sexual revulsion. Then a young playboy comes to town and M.A. thinks of the prestige involved in winning him, but she doesn't follow this up for long and begins thinking of Harriet as someone to fob him off on (it turns out that he's already engaged). Finally, an older man in the neighborhood begins to take a guarded but pronounced interest in her as she comes to marriageable age, and she readily thinks of Harriet again—though the absurdity of trying to pair those two off is too great even for her hyperactive imagination. Reality begins to break through when she's seriously disturbed by the suspicion that there's really something going on between her displaced lover and her factitious surrogate. Only jealousy—or "mediated desire," as it has been elegantly titled—can put her in touch with her own sexuality.

These psychic mechanisms are very well known, and only the ambivalence with which M.A. employs them both as bars to sexual involvement and as instruments of her sexual claims marks them as neurotic behavior. There is, it may be deduced, a *homosexual component* in M.A.'s tendency to projection that goes far to account both for her guarded virginality and her aggressive matchmaking for others. When M.A. first thinks of employing Harriet in her psychosexual schemes, we find her thinking in explicit terms: "She was a very pretty girl, and her beauty happened to be of a sort which [M.A.] particularly admired. She was short, plump and fair, with a fine bloom, blue eyes, light hair, regular features, and a look of great sweetness; and before the end of the evening [M.A.] was as much pleased with her manners as her person . . ." (I.iii.23). Further, when she tries to talk Harriet out of accepting a proposal by a highly eligible man who loves her, she wages what seems like a struggle for possession. After making it clear that if Harriet takes Mr. Martin, she loses her, M.A., she is highly pleased when Harriet gives up the idea: "Thank you, thank you, my own sweet little friend. We will not be parted. A woman is not to marry a man merely because she is asked, or because he is attached to her . . ." (I.vii,54). She is, moreover, fully aware that "at present I only want to keep Harriet to myself" (I,viii,66).

M.A. has a mature friend who sees there's something peculiar in her behavior, calls her relationship to Harriet "infatuation," and labels her defense of her conduct "madness" (I.viii.60–61). But in the limited psychological knowledge of the time these unconscious mechanisms were not well understood. There is, however, explicit discussion of such phenomena as the *unconscious* (as in the quotation about the father projecting his feelings onto Perry); *dreams* (a long conversation is recorded [III.v.345–47] in which M.A.'s friends discuss the presence and distortion of people we know in our dreams); and *free association* (one of M.A.'s friends seems to be suffering from compulsive volubility, in which she says whatever comes into her mind, but her very sophisticated friends merely humor her—indeed, when M.A. says something nasty about this babbling, she is made to feel criminal). In addition, people in this society know what it is to be *depressed;* as one of her friends says, "I am fatigued; but it is not the sort of fatigue—quick walking will refresh me. . . . We all know at times what it is to be wearied in spirits. Mine, I confess, are exhausted" (III.vi.363).

Now, all this evidence should lead M.A. into the psychiatric literature as a case study in *projective neurosis, repressed homosexuality,* and associated *phobic delusions.* The result of her attempting to live by means of *inauthentic psychic devices* and *manipulative personal relations* is that she thoroughly entangles those around her (and, most of all, herself) in near-disastrous complications. I leave the details of her *perceptual distortions, elaborate rationalizations,* and *emotional exploitation of others* to those who have studied the full report.

What is perhaps most worrisome in this young woman is the risk she runs of denying her own sexuality and thus preventing any lasting heterosexual relationship. When there's a possibility that her friend—the older man who's growing interested in her—might marry another, she *rationalizes* instead of competing: he "must not marry" (II.viii.224) because that would lead to his siring an heir and would cause her own nephew to lose his inheritance. She is willing to acknowledge a relation to this attractive man only as that of "brother and sister" (III.ii. 331).

What brings Miss A. into active competition and acknowledgment of her own sexuality is the so-called "mediated desire." As soon as she thinks her lover interested in her sweet young friend, "It darted through her, with the speed of an arrow, that Mr. Knightley must marry no one but herself!" (III.xi.408). This sudden passion is mere anxiety at the threatened loss of sexual objects of both sexes. But with the breakdown of her repressive mechanisms it is little wonder that she falls into a profound self-loathing: "She was most sorrowfully indignant; ashamed of every sensation but the one revealed to her—her affection for Mr. Knightley.—Every other part of her mind was disgusting" (III.xi.412).

One way of dealing with such troublesome feelings is to defuse or *castrate* her prospective husband's sexual powers by conceiving of him as a brother or as someone like her father: "From family attachment and habit, and through excellence of mind, he had loved her, and watched over her from a girl, with an endeavour to improve her, and an anxiety for her doing right, which no other creature had at all shared" (III.xii.415). This sounds even better than her own father, and carries a note of reproach toward the literal parent which she has hitherto been unwilling to indulge. But M.A. knows another way to use her father, to interpose him between herself and a lover: "Marriage, in fact, would not do for her. It would be incompatible with what she owed to her father, and with what she felt for him. Nothing should separate her from her father" (III.xii.416). This is designed to render her asexual, of course, but Miss A. requires the neutralization of her lover as well—in behalf of her *sadomasochistic* interests. She wishes for "his remaining single all his life. Could she be secure of that, indeed, of his never marrying at all, she believed she should be perfectly satisfied" (III.xii.416).

Gradually, this appalling negativity (with hints of the *death-wish*) is broken down. Miss A. is led to consent to an engagement, if not to a marriage, with "the most solemn resolution of never quitting her father.—She even wept over the idea of it, as a sin of thought. While he lived, it must be only an engagement; but she flattered herself, that if [the engagement were] divested of the danger of drawing her away, it might become an increase of comfort to him" (III.xiv.435). Her sense of the sinfulness of sexual maturity is assuaged by the curious notion that an unconsummated engagement would provide an increased piquancy to her father's declining years—perhaps to herself, as well. Fortunately, M.A.'s father is not as sick as all that, and can be manipulated into feeling the need for a man around the house to offer protection from burglars. So they marry, and the husband is domesticated to the role of an auxiliary nurse.

Nevertheless, Miss A. is bitter over the fate of women, and when her former governess bears a daughter, she is heavy with the woes of womankind: "Poor child! . . . what will become of her?" (III.xvii.461). It remains for her wise friend to reply: "Nothing very bad.—The fate of thousands. She will be disagreeable in infancy, and correct herself as she grows older. I am losing all my bitterness against spoilt children, my dearest Emma" (III.xvii.461).

Now I have let the name out of the bag; but I am not ready to be as indulgent as Mrs. Weston, her substitute for a mother, for Emma has shown herself to be not merely a "spoilt child" but a danger to herself and to those closest to her—an incurable neurotic who sows confusion wherever she goes, an unfortunate but unappealing victim of her orphaned state and of her father's inadequacy.

What can we say to make Emma seem less helpless if not less reprehensible? We may, of course, recommend her as a functional neurotic, one who learns to live with her disabilities and who comes to adjust to the constraints of life with/without father. Indeed, Emma wins a prize: not merely a surrogate father figure and the chief proprietor of Highbury, but a keen and honest observer who will help her to catch herself in acts of misperception and distorted judgment. Knightley is aware that he must seem a bitter pill, but a salutary one: "If I loved you less, I might be able to talk about [love] more. But you know what I am.—You hear nothing but truth from me.—I have blamed you, and lectured you, and you have borne it as no other woman in England would have borne it.—Bear with the truths I would tell you now, dearest Emma . . ." (III. xiii. 430). After this, Emma is able to accept "that Harriet was nothing [to him]; that she was every thing herself; that what she had been saying relative to Harriet had been all taken as the language of her own feelings; and that her agitation, her doubts, her reluctance, her discouragement, had been all received as discouragement from herself" (III. xiii. 430–31). With these telling revelations of the limited effectiveness of her pattern of projection, taking a lover like Knightley is as good as having a therapist in the bargain.

Yet there are other grounds to commend Emma, "handsome, clever, and rich," but gamely plugging along in life with her severe handicaps. If we tend to become judgmental, we might remember to consider what those around her are like. We know them from their conversation for hundreds of pages, and though we aren't entirely bored with the fumblings of Emma's father and the flow of Miss Bates's free association, or the insipidities of Harriet, or the social-climbing crassness of the Eltons, or the *hausfraulich* simplicity of Emma's sister, or the depressive Jane or the manic Frank, we begin to wilt under the weight of their banalities. In this temper, we have one recourse: to close the book for a while and return to the commonplaces of our own lives. But Emma has to live with these people. (I moot here the mimetic distinction between a literary character and a human being, and refrain from comparisons between Emma's society and Jane Austen's, remarking only that Emma has to endure it in a book, while her author may well have had to endure it in life.)

The most oppressive trait in this humdrum existence is *repetition;* people are always saying the same things—sometimes each in his own little round of characteristic utterances, sometimes all together in the voice of the common man, the group mind. It is this voice that Emma is able to hear as no other can; e.g., when her governess bags a wealthy widower, Emma exults in having predicted it: "Every body said that Mr. Weston would never marry again. Oh dear, no! Mr. Weston, who had been a widower so long, and who seemed so perfectly comfortable without a wife. . . . Oh, no! Mr. Weston certainly would never marry again" (I. ii. 12). Emma is boasting of her own perceptiveness, of course, and lording it over others, as is her habit. But who else can claim her mimetic voice, her comic perception not merely of the foibles but of the *rhythms* of other minds?

Nor is Emma immune from seeing herself in the same light, as the victim of human limitation and folly. The law of life is eventually laid down by Jane Austen: "Seldom, very seldom, does complete truth be-

long to any human disclosure; seldom can it happen that something is not
a little disguised, or a little mistaken; but where . . . though the conduct is
mistaken, the feelings are not, it may not be very material" (III. xiii. 431).
This is the voice we associate with the comic spirit, which sees the lit-
tleness of men with sharp-eyed attention to the absurd, but laughs without rancor, knowing that we are all implicated in the common fate. It is
Emma who shares this awareness with Jane Austen: "She walked on,
amusing herself in the consideration of the blunders which often arise
from a partial knowledge of circumstances, of the mistakes which people
of high pretensions to judgment are for ever falling into . . ." (I. xiii. 112).
This comic sense of others doesn't help her much (as it doesn't here)
when she blunders from her own "partial knowledge of circumstances,"
and performs pratfalls from her "high pretensions to judgment." But her
errors are those of a lively mind; she exhibits not the absurdity of ignorance but rather the *humor of intelligence*—of the keenest eye blinded and
the sharpest wit missing the point.

Nor does Emma long miss the point; when it turns out that Mr. Elton
is after her and not Harriet, she goes over their conversations to catch the
mistaken interpretations she has placed on his words: "She had taken up
the idea [of his liking Harriet], she supposed, and made every thing bend
to it" (I. xvi. 134). And the resulting blow to her ego tempts her to refrain
from making *any* interpretations or inferences. This course, too, is denied
her: "It was rather too late in the day to set about being simple-minded
and ignorant; but she left . . . with every previous resolution confirmed of
being humble and discreet, and repressing imagination all the rest of her
life" (I. xvii. 142). We know how long such a resolution can last for an
imaginative mind—but that is precisely the point about Emma. She is a
person of imagination, and even knows how to give herself a categorical
name: "Could a linguist, could a grammarian, could even a mathe-
matician have seen what she did [without thinking as she did]?—How
much more must an imaginist, like herself, be on fire with speculation
and foresight!" (II. iii. 335). An imaginist—that's the word that labels
Emma, far more firmly pinning her than do the diagnostic terms of any
science.

There are comparisons to be made, of course, between this and other
methods of describing character and behavior, for literary imagination—
and a literary character's imaginativeness—are not entirely incommensurate with the well-worn paths of psychopathology and illusion in
everyday life. Emma is, to be sure, a "great dreamer" (II. v. 345), as
somebody calls her; but she is not quite what Knightley is called, a
"humourist" (III. vi. 355)—someone with so independent a mind that the
petty creatures around them think they are somewhat deranged, or at best

crotchety. For all her follies, Emma is too socially competent ever to appear ridiculous; nor will she ever allow her dreams—unconscious desires or daydreams of an impossible gentility—to come to the surface so as to mark her as quixotic. Yet she has a way of seeing the ideal and the real together that only novelists of the tribe of Miguel de Cervantes have been able to record; though Emma is no artist, lacking the control of her own language, she sees as they see. After a detailed account of innocuous activity and inactivity on the main street of Highbury, to which she is patiently attentive, we are told: "A mind lively and at ease, can do with seeing nothing, and can see nothing that does not answer" (II. ix. 232).

One more trait we must allow her: she can see the comedy in herself. An inveterate matchmaker, she sarcastically joins a flirtatious young man in characterizing herself as a paragon: " 'Find somebody for me [he says]. I am in no hurry. Adopt her, educate her.' 'And make her like myself [she readily agrees]. I undertake the commission. You shall have a charming wife' " (III. vii. 373). And when her schemes are undone and her mistakes exposed, she has no difficulty in satirizing herself as "one who sets up as I do for Understanding" (III. xiii. 427). Miss Understanding we might name her, and her story might be subtitled, a comedy of mis-understanding.

Now that we have given her a third name, what shall we say of M.A. / Emma that would compose these views of her into a totality of fictional character—more or less resembling a human being? I think we can agree that the psychological view, especially when pushed to its limit in the move to psychoanalyze a character, must tend to reduce that subjectivity to object status. A psychiatrist has, I suspect—though the professional society would be sure to deny it—his natural impulse to see the limits and errors of his patients as somewhat disgusting. But he has, I hope, a well-trained resistance to his own reactions, and a caring attitude toward the suffering human being before him. The psychological critic has no such compunctions; indeed, his impulse must be to place himself at a superior vantage-point, looking down at the evidence with a lofty detachment and delivering judgment as he sees fit. Fortunately, there is no living person there to suffer from his contempt.

From the literary standpoint, we observe a reverse phenomenon; instead of belittling the character and magnifying the observer, the study of fictional characters tends to confirm us in our suspicion that we don't know very much. And this may be to our advantage, after all: if we readers are subject to the same limitations of vision that characters exhibit in novels, we are well placed to exercise our imaginative sympathy with them. We can understand because we've been there—are there ourselves. Like the friendly therapy delivered by Emma's interpreter, Knightley, this critical standpoint is based on love: "I could not think about you so much without doating on you, faults and all; and by dint of fancying so many errors, have been in love with you . . ." (III. xvii. 462).

*Avrom Fleishman*
*Johns Hopkins University*

# NOTES

1. All quotations are from R. W. Chapman, ed., *The Novels of Jane Austen* (London: Oxford University Press, 1931–34). Subsequent citations are parenthetical, by volume, chapter, and page number.

# *Emma* and Its Critics
## The Value of Tact

Criticism of Jane Austen's novels has generally been a rather conservative enterprise. There is an apparent reluctance to understand her novels within contexts too alien, too remote from the novels themselves, or to express that understanding in language too technical, too modern or fashionable. Especially now, when trendy critical systems from France and elsewhere have been so thoroughly popularized that they are available to all who care to employ them, the reticence of Austen criticism to venture much beyond its traditional historical and New Critical confines has become all the more manifest—and all the more questionable. It is as if her critics, by the very tenderness of their touch, would suggest a corresponding tenderness, fragility, or even a brittleness in the novels themselves. Like frail china jars, they are easily broken, easily violated, and the critic takes care not to do so.

It is not obvious to me that this conservatism should occasion either indignant complaints that Austen criticism has opted for a valetudinary traditionalism, or self-congratulation at its having escaped modishness. The critic has a double allegiance. As a reader of Jane Austen, a certain fidelity to the novels is required of him, an assurance that he is in fact reading Jane Austen and not something else. Yet insofar as the critic is not only a reader but also a writer, he owes a second allegiance to those of his own time by whom he himself expects to be read. To assume that there is no tension between these two claims is to assume that nothing important has happened since the early nineteenth century—at least nothing of which the critic need take account in addressing a modern audience. But this implies that we need be only readers, for nothing more than Jane Austen wrote needs now to be written. On the other hand, to suppose that the twin demands placed on the critic as reader and as writer are irreconcilable suggests that so much has happened of late, so significantly has the world altered, that the truths now most necessary to be known are modern truths, incommensurate with old ones. Thus there is no reason to read Jane Austen at all. The critic unaware of his historical difference writes about Jane Austen's novels—just as the critic unaware of his similarity reads them—in vain.

This is to say that Austen criticism, like all criticism, must adjudicate between competing claims. "To require the classic to speak to us directly in our time, rather than demand of ourselves the effort to speak to the classic in *its* time, is an instance of what Eliot calls 'overestimation of the importance of our time' and of ourselves."[1] Yet since there is possible a corollary overestimation of past times and underestimation of our own, the fundamental success of criticism consists in denying the importance of neither. Ideally, the critic of Jane Austen brings both times into dialogue and also into jeopardy by establishing points of tangency between Jane Austen and the modern reader. This requires that the critic exercise a certain diplomacy, a certain tact, in separating or bringing together, for their mutual benefit, two parties that apparently have nothing to say to one another because they understand each other all too well or not at all. To this end what is required of the interpreter is not a double neutrality but a double commitment.

All Jane Austen's novels are novels of interpretation, but none more than *Emma*. Here interpretation, successful and unsuccessful, is most explicitly thematized. All of the characters, and Emma most of all, interpret and are themselves interpreted not only by each other and by the author but also by the novel's readers. The question I would raise is whether this coincidence is important, whether the fact that what happens *in* the novel prefigures what happens *to* the novel is significant. It may be merely a quirk of linguistic history that the process of understanding other people and of understanding novels can both be called "interpretation"; but if it is a mistake to identify these two senses of the word, it is a mistake fostered by *Emma* itself. In this novel to understand others is to read them. Emma's idea of Frank Churchill, in Mr. Knightley's words, is "the great man—the practised politician, who is able to read everybody's character" (p. 150).[2] Emma does think of Frank as the perfect reader to whom all others are open books—because she conceives of herself too as one for whom every riddle, every charade must be immediately transparent. Frank's illiteracy and Emma's own, however, are disclosed as he is about to reveal his engagement to Jane: " 'In short,' said he, 'perhaps, Miss Woodhouse—I think you can hardly be quite without suspicion'—He looked at her, as if wanting to read her thoughts. She hardly knew what to say" (p. 260). Frank perfectly misreads Emma's thoughts, and she his. The point of these two passages, it may seem, is that books are a good deal easier to read than people; but that is too easy a reading. *Emma*, at least, is a book no less dense and opaque than life itself, and for the same reason: seldom, very seldom does complete truth belong to any human disclosure, *Emma* included.

Insofar as human disclosure is also a concealment, interpretation is always necessary; and if in novelistic as well as personal and critical communication something is usually a little disguised, a little mistaken, then interpretation needs always to be tactful—open but reticent, straightforward while acknowledging the possibility of misunderstanding. This tact, defined as clarity and discretion, is a standard of interpretation within the novel and, I propose, it is a criterion for judging interpretation of the novel as well. It is not enough that interpretation be clear. Emma's interpretation of the pianoforte as an expression of Dixon's illicit love is clear, too clear. The fault of her interpretation is not even that it is false; rather its culpability lies in the crudity and presumption of its content and the fact that it is communicated at all. "I am half ashamed," Emma admits, "and wish I had never taken up the idea" (p. 216). Frank, on the other hand, because he is himself Jane's benefactor, interprets the gift quite correctly: "True affection only could have prompted it." The accuracy of his interpretation does not vindicate it, however, since, if perfectly correct, his interpretation is also perfectly obscure. When Emma replies to him, "You speak too plain," we feel the irony that it is her own fault that she reproves here, not Frank's. While Frank's concealment is misguided, nevertheless Emma's garrulous openness is culpable as well. It is not the case in this novel that plain dealing is *always* best (p. 341). Often, very often, something ought to remain a little disguised and a little mistaken.

The problem is to determine the particular occasions when complete truth should not belong to human disclosure. As a rule, plain dealing is a value worth striving for; but as a rule, discretion is no less valuable. The difficulty consists in applying these general rules, because neither is universally or a priori applicable. One must know the principles and standards of right conduct, but it is not enough to know them without being able to apply them in appropriate circumstances. Tact is this ability. It is given many names in *Emma*—taste, propriety, judgment, understanding—and what all these terms point to is not some happy medium between conflicting values but rather a capacity to apply rules aptly, without any superior rule that dictates their application. There is no rule to prescribe the concrete occasions when the rule of clarity or of discretion obtains; and in the absence of such a rule for applying rules, tact becomes a capacity more valuable than the knowledge of any rule, for it governs them all.

I will turn in conclusion to a closer examination of tact as it functions in *Emma;* but if tact is not only a personal and novelistic merit, if it is an aptitude valuable in criticism as well, it may be instructive at this point to consider a few recent and, I hope, representative attempts to write tactfully about *Emma*, the novel of tact. The task for critics of the novel is the same as for characters in the novel: we need to decide which rules are applicable to *Emma*, our occasion, just as the characters must determine which rules fit theirs. If the idea of applying rules to the interpretation and assessment of the novel seems too reminiscent of an outdated neoclassicism, we can rephrase the issue. Which of all the possible contexts available to us—contexts philosophical, psychological, religious, sociological, critical, literary, biographical; contexts originally predating the novel, coinciding with it, or postdating it—which of these various contexts shall we accept as appropriate to this novel, this occasion? Or should we combine several of them, or adopt none at all?

This last option is immediately alluring in the face of such plenitude. There seems no good reason to delimit our expectations of what *Emma* can be and mean by specifying a context of interpretation or choosing a point of view. On the contrary, the establishment of a sphere of possible significance for *Emma* is precisely what is to be avoided, since it always amounts to a Procrustean bed, to which everything must willy-nilly be fitted. Barbara Hardy's *Reading of Jane Austen* apparently aims at this kind of context-free neutrality. It belongs to the English commonsensical tradition of criticism, and one consequence of this fact is that (as commonsensical) the book requires no theoretical introduction, no special elucidation of its principles of interpretation, for to all appearances it gets along without any. This strategy of naturalness is designed to allow Jane Austen to speak for herself, without the intrusion of the critic. "Of course she is a novelist, not a social psychologist," Hardy writes, and adds in a footnote: "I have avoided the use of obviously applicable modern terminology in describing her social groups."[3] One might take this avoidance as an instance of tact, a laudable reluctance to impose an extraneous pattern of relevance: Jane Austen is not a social psychologist, and modern jargon must therefore be irrelevant. But such is not the case: we read that such terminology is "obviously applicable." Why not apply it, then? Because it is modern? Because it is terminology? If it were applied, would it be so clearly a matter "of course" that Jane Austen is not a social psychologist? There may be something slightly patronizing in the strategy of naturalness—patronizing either to Jane Austen, since she is denied the possibility of addressing social psychologists by being protected from them, or else to the readers of this *Reading*, who may be thought not quite up to grasping modern terminology. Or it may be that modern psychology is in fact applied, though without the terminology and without acknowledgment.

One isn't informed which psychologists are being avoided here. Let me propose an unlikely candidate: Jacques Lacan. Professor Hardy characterizes Mrs. Elton as "a combination of matrimonial patronage and residual predatoriness." What would be gained or lost by citing in this connection Lacan's elucidation of "the aggressive motives that lie hidden in all so-called philanthropic activity"? With respect to Jane Fairfax, would it obscure matters or rather clarify them to remark with Lacan, "Only saints are sufficiently detached from the deepest of common passions to avoid the aggressive reactions to charity"?[4] For anyone convinced that Lacan represents the best of current psychology, the gain to be won by aligning *Emma* with his pronouncements is a demonstration of the fact that Jane Austen has nothing to fear from modernity or its terminology. More, Lacan may open to our view possibilities that we could not otherwise have seen.

What can be lost by such a contextualization becomes evident in *Character and Conflict in Jane Austen's Novels* by Bernard Paris. In this book the approach is perfectly explicit: "Readers who are familiar with my previous work will recognize that this book is a further application of the methodology which I developed in *A Psychological Approach to Fiction*"[5]—that is, a further application of Karen Horney's *Neurosis and Human Growth*. If Hardy's *Reading* is none the better for its unselfconsciousness and obscurity about the general context within which Jane Austen is there valued and understood, *Character and Conflict* is none the worse for being decided and open. There is no way, at least that I am aware of, to determine a priori that Horney's psychology is inapplicable to *Emma*. Paris is cognizant of the dangers that beset his project:

> Psychological theory is quite reductive compared to the concrete portrayals of experience in literature. There is a reciprocal relationship, I propose, between psychological theory and the literary presentation of the phenomena which it describes. The theory provides categories of understanding which help us to recover the intuitions of the great writers about the workings of the human psyche. These intuitions . . . amplify the theories which have helped us to perceive them and give us a phenomenological grasp of experience which cannot be gained from theory alone.[6]

Psychological theories, Paris rightly suggests, offer categories that help us perceive what would otherwise be invisible; conversely, the concrete experience portrayed in the novels fleshes out the theory's abstractions.

This is the reciprocal relationship of text and context as Paris conceives it; but in fact, full reciprocity, given this program, is rather precluded than enabled. Jane Austen's novels can amplify Horney's theories, exemplify and illustrate them with particulars; but the instance cannot contradict the rule, for the theories of personality here employed have already been accepted as incontrovertible. Thus, instead of reciprocity between text and context, we find programmatic subordination.

What we need in order to establish the possibility of real dialogue is evidence of the possibility that Horney is in jeopardy from Austen, but such evidence is not here forthcoming. Paris focuses on Emma's "narcissism," her "compulsive goodness"—especially in relation to her father.

> She is compelled, much of the time, to repress her resentment, to disguise her feelings, and to act a part. In her father's presence, her lack of spontaneity, congruity, and transparence is striking and nearly complete. . . . As a result, she is almost always, to some extent, insincere. The burdensomeness of this becomes clear when she begins to look forward to a relatively frank relationship with Knightley. . . . Mr. Woodhouse remains, however, and it is not pleasant to imagine the constant hard labor of pretending which living with him will entail.[7]

No, it is not pleasant; but it is plain enough, as Paris acknowledges, that Jane Austen "approves of Emma's hypersensitivity to [her father's] needs and wishes," and if we are to judge duty in this novel by appeal to the pleasure principle, then Frank must represent the apex of virtue. In *Emma* the constant hard labor of pretending, of repression, of disguise is one remedy for narcissism and thus no less a moral prerequisite than its contrary.[8]

This failure in *Character and Conflict*, I suggest, is best understood as a failure of tact. Specifically it consists in the assumption that Horney's theories are true, complete, and universally valid. There is no need to determine the specific occasions to which they are applicable, no need for the exercise of tact, because the theories are universally applicable. *Emma*, however it fills out Horney's taxonomy of character, can be no more than an instance, a case subsumed under that fixed and incorrigible system of rules; and when Jane Austen deviates from them, her fictions are merely falsehoods.

My objection to Paris's method, then, is not that it applies modern psychology to *Emma* but that it applies it indiscriminately. It may be that Austen is mistaken in overvaluing self-restraint, but we will never know until she is given a full hearing. Stuart Tave offers that hearing in *Some Words of Jane Austen*. In this study her words, assumptions, and intentions are accorded an authority comparable to those of Horney in *Character and Conflict*. Tave writes:

It is not helpful to say, with one critic of many, that [Jane Austen] "feels compelled to tidy up life's customary messiness," because to say that is to make an assumption about life that is not hers. . . . Life is not a disorder to be ordered, a given mess on which those of tidy compulsions impose a tidiness. It is not a meaningless heap from which meaning is extracted by reduction and exclusion. Meaning is the first fact.[9]

This, in my estimation, is an insight of the first magnitude. It does seem to me that Jane Austen assumes meaning is the first fact. But what if her assumption were false? Would it then be a sufficient rebuttal of wayward critics to show that they make an assumption that is not hers? To have done so would seem rather their merit.

That meaning is the first fact is not an indisputable and incontrovertible proposition, and we cannot assume its validity merely because Jane Austen does so. Indeed the long tradition of empiricism in the seventeenth and eighteenth centuries, and of positivism in the nineteenth and early twentieth—not to mention absurdism of later date—militates against accepting this proposition. So far from presuming the priority of significance to fact, we now need some help even to take the idea seriously.

By assuming the obviousness of Jane Austen's assumption, Tave underestimates the differences between our world and hers. Perhaps rightly so, but we need some proof that the differences are more apparent than real. We may need to summon assistance from our own time, from someone who has thought long and deeply on the question of fact and meaning—not in order to validate Jane Austen's assumption, but to give it the credibility for a modern audience that the critic's voice alone cannot. Jane Austen, let us agree, does not view the world as a disorder to be ordered, a heap of insignificance on which significance needs to be imposed. Neither does Heidegger: "In interpreting, we do not, so to speak, throw a 'signification' over some naked thing which is present-at-hand, we do not stick a value on it; but when something within-the-world is encountered as such, the thing in question already has an involvement which is disclosed in our understanding of the world, and this involvement is one which gets laid out by the interpretation."[10] Is it clear that these words of Martin Heidegger would be inappropriate or tactless in *Some Words of Jane Austen*?

In one sense the answer must be yes; but that answer has more to do with the context—the rule of interpretative expectation—that Tave selects for the novels than with the novels themselves. That context is historical.

If Jane Austen had a special liking for Emma, one reason is that her own special subject, early and late, was the eighteenth-century problems and pleasures of imagination. . . . The contrasting of "imagination" or "fancy" or "wit" with "judgment" or "understanding" or "reason"—all the terms are used and all are important in *Emma*—is a commonplace in the writers of the eighteenth century.[11]

If we are in a quandary about the context in which to understand Jane Austen's novels, it seems natural and obviously right to locate them in their own context. We know that Jane Austen read, admired, and imitated Johnson; and Tave cites him frequently as a commentator on the novels. This practice will appear perfectly unobjectionable unless we recall that Tave's historical relativism is as alien to Johnson and Austen as ethical relativism.[12] Though principles and standards of expectation are difficult of application, it is nonetheless necessary to have them; and they cannot be deduced from the situation (literary or moral) to which they are to be applied. To suppose that the occasion itself decides which rules are appropriate to it precludes the operation of tact just as surely as the contrary notion that a given rule is universally valid. The general rule cannot determine whether it applies in a particular situation; nor can the particular situation determine whether a general rule applies to it. Only tact can do so.

Even those who suspect that Heidegger's existential phenomenology is an inappropriate context (because it is not Austen's own) may not be convinced that the moral psychology of Dr. Johnson fares any better. In her book *In the Meantime*, Susan Morgan reminds us: "Some important facts about *Emma* are that it was published in 1816, written after *Mansfield Park*, after *Lyrical Ballads*, after the revolution in France. In other words, Austen wrote *Emma* well into what literary historians call the English romantic period. . . . It is time to accept that Jane Austen belongs in the romantic age and that her subject is perception as an epistemological as well as a moral question."[13]

As a student of Tave, Morgan is aware how much her point of view differs from his, and how little. It is the same historical relativism, though the novels are here situated in a different history. "This book," Morgan informs us, "offers an analysis of Austen's ideas which originated in reading her through Shelley's epistemological interests."[14] It matters little that Austen never read him; filtering her novels through Shelley rather than Johnson makes for some remarkably fine insights. But the very fact that Morgan situates Jane Austen in her own time—precisely her own time, among romantics she never read—reveals with exemplary clarity that Jane Austen's own context is not inherently natural or appropriate to understanding her. Shelley's epistemology, however obviously contemporaneous, is in fact no more (or less) relevant than Locke's epistemology a century earlier or Heidegger's a century later. Only tact can decide whether Jane Austen's own context is apropos, for it is not automatically applicable.

From the viewpoint of Shelley's skeptical epistemology, "When we look for continuity in the novels we see immediately that Austen has no pure truths to tell."[15] Thus Morgan contrasts Richardson's moral absolutism to its contrary in Austen:

> The difference between *Clarissa* and *Emma* can be best seen by asking if Emma is virtuous—assuming that virtue means something other than simple virginity. The question is clearly inappropriate because we cannot think of Emma in Richardson's terms. *Emma* is cast in a relativistic world. . . . Characters and situations differ in ways that matter, and therefore how one ought to think and act will differ too. Moral vision grows out of relations to people and experiences. It is a process, rather than a definable standard asserting general truth.[16]

Morgan's comment on the variability of situation and conduct is the kind of insight that makes her book worth reading. But the problem in this passage originates in the dichotomy it erects. From the fact that the world of *Emma* is not absolutistic, it does not follow that it is relativistic. From the fact that appropriate action differs in differing circumstances, it does not follow that there are no definable, general standards—only that they are not universally applicable. "Like most of her poetic contemporaries," we read, "Austen's commitment is to particulars. The forms of thought which often blind us begin as generalities." From here it is but a short and predictable step to Blake's idiotic generalization: " 'To Generalize is to be an Idiot.' This is such a central truth about Austen's novels that we can use it to locate many of her characters and to describe a major thematic continuity in her work."[17] Blake's self-contradiction seems to have been contagious, for Morgan concludes that the general truth of Jane Austen's novels is that there is no general truth.

As epistemology—even as literary criticism—this will not do. If it is the case (and I think it is) that Jane Austen's "subject is perception as an epistemological . . . question," why not read her through a real, tough-minded, honest-to-goodness, philosophical epistemologist? And if, further, Jane Austen "belongs in the romantic age," why not do her the justice of invoking the Romantic epistemologist par excellence? When one wants to know about the relation of particulars to generals in early-nineteenth-century epistemology, there is no excuse for not turning to the *Critique of Pure Reason*. Like Blake, Kant knew that general conceptions without particular intuitions are empty; but he recognized further that intuition without conception is blind. Simply put, if you don't have a general idea of what you are looking for, you will never find it; but if you never find it, you will never know whether your general idea referred to anything. Whether in literary criticism, or in natural science, or in Highbury, both conception and perception are necessary—and equally so. The conjunction of the two constitutes meaningful knowledge, in Kant's view; and although that may not be the last word in epistemology, yet it has earned a respect so solid that no apology is needed for introducing the *Critiques* into any discussion of epistemology—let alone Romantic epistemology.

Without apology, then, let me offer a passage from the first *Critique* that I consider relevant to *Emma* and the criticism of it. The problem Kant addresses here is this: given that we must have a general idea in order to locate some particular thing, how can we know when we have found it? How can we know that this particular is in fact an instance of the relevant rule, or that the rule is applicable to it?

> If understanding in general is to be viewed as the faculty of rules, judgment will be the faculty of subsuming under rules; that is, of distinguishing whether something does or does not stand under a given rule. General logic contains, and can contain, no rules for judgment. . . . If it sought to give general instructions how we are to subsume under these rules, that is, to distinguish whether something does or does not come under them, that could only be by means of another rule. This in turn, for the very reason that it is a rule, again demands guidance from judgment. And thus it appears that . . . judgment is a peculiar talent which can be practised only, and cannot be taught. It is the specific quality of so-called mother-wit; and its lack no school can make good. For although an abundance of rules borrowed from the insight of others may indeed be . . . grafted upon a limited understanding, the power of rightly employing them must belong to the learner himself; and in the absence of such a natural gift no rule that may be prescribed to him for this purpose can ensure against misuse. A physician, a judge, or a ruler may have at command many excellent pathological, legal, or political rules, even to the degree that he may become a profound teacher of them, and yet, none the less, may easily stumble in their application. For, although admirable in understanding, he may be wanting in natural power of judgment. . . . Sharpening of the judgment is indeed the one great benefit of examples . . . and those who are lacking in the natural talent can never dispense with them.[18]

In the space remaining I clearly cannot provide anything like a full reading of *Emma* through this passage, but perhaps such completeness is unnecessary to suggest its relevance. Kant's thesis is that judgment governs the application of rules but is governed by none; it can be learned by example but not taught by precept; or it may be a natural talent, not learned at all.

The question is, what should be the rule of Harriet Smith's marital expectations? " 'She is, in fact, a beautiful girl,' " Emma tells Mr.

Knightley. " 'I am very much mistaken if your sex in general would not think such beauty, and such temper, the highest claims a woman could possess.' 'Upon my word, Emma, to hear you abusing the reason you have, is almost enough to make me think so too. Better be without sense than misapply it as you do' " (pp. 63–64). Emma is not without reason, rather she has abused it; she is not without sense, she has misapplied it. The point is worth insisting on: it is the application, not the principle, that is at fault. In fact, Emma's conception fits Frank Churchill quite exactly: 'Did you ever see such a skin?' he exclaims of his fiancée (p. 478). Emma's generalization about men is a good one—but not so universal as to obviate the need for what Kant calls judgment in its application. The same fault appears in her interpretation of the charade: " 'That is *court*. . . . That is *ship;* plain as can be . . .—and then follows the application' " (p. 73), which is a good deal more obscure.

Emma's failure to apply "courtship" to herself, we can say with Mrs. Weston, is what most impedes her happiness throughout the novel: " 'I should like to see Emma in love, and in some doubt of a return; it would do her good' " (p. 41). The good it does her, finally, is that the love is returned. Mrs. Weston predicts Emma's destiny precisely (though paired with the wrong suitor), and that fact should not go unnoticed. The prophecy comes true. But even if it had not, as so often happens in *Emma,* the solution is not to avoid prediction altogether. "I only name possibilities," says Mr. Knightley. "I do not pretend to Emma's genius for foretelling and guessing" (p. 38). But though not pretending to genius, he does pretend to foretelling. "Depend upon it," he predicts. "Elton will not do. Elton is a very good sort of man . . . but not at all likely to make an imprudent match" (p. 66). There are two questions here. Like Emma, Mr. Knightley must establish the general rule: What sort of man is likely to make an imprudent match? To this question Emma answers, "Every man" (p. 64). By contrast Knightley proceeds from the universal to the particular: Is Elton that sort of man? The answer establishes not only what Elton is, but what he is likely and unlikely to do. Mr. Knightley joins the general and the specific; he thereby makes a prediction, determines a possibility, even a likelihood; and he depends on it.

Generality (whether of rule, principle, law, or context) always has a predictive force; and however often one's expectations are disappointed, there is no getting along without them. Not to generalize is to be an idiot. "What is before me, I see," Miss Bates confesses (p. 176). Hers is the mind "lively and at ease" that "can do with seeing nothing, and see nothing that does not answer" (p. 233). Like Harriet, "she will give you all the minute particulars" (p. 472). Seeing what is before her, Miss Bates sees everything in detail and nothing in general. Her mind is like her huswife, full of oddments, full of particulars, where things keep getting lost. But not everything. "What is before me, I see. At the same time, nobody could wonder if Mr. Elton could have aspired—" (p. 176). It would scarcely be surprising, all quite predictable—to the imaginative mind of Miss Bates, at least. To Emma it was otherwise: "I am very much astonished, Mr. Elton. This to *me!*" (p. 130).

We know why Emma, the imaginist, has not the slightest premonition of Elton's impending proposal. She was "too eager and busy in her own conceptions and views to hear him impartially, or see him with clear vision" (p. 110). But if this is a fault of imagination, only by imagination can it be rectified. "Are you imagining me to be Mr. Elton's object?" Emma asks John Knightley. He replies, "Such an imagination has crossed me, I own" (p. 112). Or again, "Between Mr. Frank Churchill and Miss Fairfax?" Emma asks the older brother. He replies, "I have lately imagined that I saw symptoms of attachment between them" (p. 350). Emma's fault is not the exuberance of "her own conceptions" but their deficiency. There are certain possibilities that she cannot imagine, certain eventualities she cannot conceive; and this narrowness of expectation no accumulation of facts, no mere perception can remedy. The facts go "unnoticed, because unsuspected" (p. 410). How does it happen that Mr. Knightley observes Frank Churchill with such acuteness of penetration? "Mr. Knightley, who, for some reason best known to himself, had certainly taken an early dislike to Frank Churchill, was only growing to dislike him more. He began to suspect him of some double dealing in his pursuit of Emma . . . [and] to suspect him of some inclination to trifle with Jane Fairfax" (p. 343).

"Prejudiced! I am not prejudiced," he protests (p. 150). But the fact is the contrary, and ironically Mr. Knightley's suspicion and prejudice—his general conception of his supposed rival, formed before they have ever met, and his own secret love for Emma—assist him to understand Frank the more clearly. "Natural enough!—his own mind full of intrigue, that he should suspect it in others.—Mystery; Finesse—how they pervert the understanding! My Emma, does not every thing serve to prove more and more the beauty of truth and sincerity in all our dealings with each other?" (p. 446).

We are sorely tempted to interpret this pronouncement as the moral of the novel, a generalization without exception and hence in need of no tact, no judgment in its application. But as I have already suggested, in *Emma* intrigue, mystery, and finesse sometimes assist the understanding. Is it the case, then, that truth and sincerity are the ideal of *all* our dealings with each other? "Emma agreed to it, and with a blush of sensibility on

Harriet's account, which she could not give any sincere explanation of"
(p. 446). Hers is not a sincere agreement because she can be neither
truthful nor sincere to Mr. Knightley about Harriet. And in this case, on
this occasion, in this particular instance, Emma's insincerity and concealment are precisely right. She is willing to bear "the pain of being
obliged to practice concealment towards him" (p. 463).

The obligation to conceal is not a duty much discussed in criticism of
*Emma,* but it is precisely this social rule that is applicable at Box Hill.
Emma's nasty quip is both true and sincere, but it is hardly beautiful and
it should have been repressed. Further, it is not for an unlicensed tongue
in general that Mr. Knightley reproves Emma but for its exercise on this
occasion. Were Miss Bates "a woman of fortune, I would leave every
harmless absurdity to take its chance, I would not quarrel with you for
any liberties of manner. Were she your equal in situation—but, Emma,
consider how far this is from being the case. . . . Her situation should
secure your compassion" (p. 375).

The situation of Mrs. Elton, by contrast, secures no compassion, and
thus she is fair game for the insolence of Mr. Knightley's wit. "I wish we
had a donkey," she says. "The thing would be for us to all come on
donkies, Jane, Miss Bates, and me." Mr. Knightley obligingly replies,

> "Come on a donkey . . . if you prefer it. You can borrow Mrs. Cole's. I
> would wish every thing to be as much to your taste as possible."
> "That I am sure you would. Indeed I do you justice, my good friend.
> Under that peculiar sort of dry, blunt manner, I know you have the
> warmest heart." (p. 356)

Under that dry, blunt manner, he conceals a rapier so sharp that Mrs.
Elton cannot feel the wound; and Mr. Knightley is indebted more to the
event than to kindness of intention for his acquittal.

That seems to be the case in his dealings with Emma as well. If there is
also a warm heart under that blunt manner, he conceals it well. "I have
been a very indifferent lover," he admits to Emma (p. 430). He courts her
in the "true English style, burying under a calmness that seemed all but
indifference, the real attachment" he feels (p. 99). So deeply buried is his
affection that Emma no more anticipates his proposal than Elton's. Jane
is reserved, Frank duplicitous, but Mr. Knightley is inscrutable. He is
"the last man in the world," Emma tells Harriet, "who would intention-
ally give any woman the idea of his feeling for her more than he does"
(p. 411). But intentions alone are not good enough. He is so busy with his
owns plans for Harriet that, even gazing into her moony eyes at Donwell
Abbey, at least one possibility never occurs to him. Thus unwittingly he,
like Emma, encourages affections of which he is totally unsuspecting

because, like her, he fails to apply courtship to himself. For the apparent warmth of his attentions to Harriet, as for the apparent indifference of his love for Emma, Mr. Knightley is acquitted only by the event.

Patterns of expectation are ineluctably necessary to the characters of *Emma*. They act most responsibly when they possess the knowledge—necessarily multiple and various—of what is likely to occur generally. Even when that knowledge of probabilities originates in not entirely laudable emotions (Mr. Knightley's jealousy or Emma's vanity), it is nonetheless preferable to ignorance. The knowledge of general rules alone, however, is inadequate; and it even risks obscuring what is required of a particular situation, unless they are applied judiciously. Judgment and tact are needed to apply the rules; and for that application no rules, as Kant contends, are available or possible. In this sense, tact is not merely the reticence that lets pass what should remain concealed but also the bluntness that opens up what should be disclosed. Tact is not merely the knowledge of general possibility but the wisdom that can employ it in particular and actual situations.

Frank does not possess it. Yet, Mr. Knightley says, "I am very ready to believe his character will improve, and acquire from [Jane's] the steadiness and delicacy of principle that it wants" (p. 448). Example, Kant remarks, sharpens judgment while precept cannot. Frank does not lack principles but rather steadiness and delicacy in applying them. As he is without natural judgment, his only hope of acquiring it is Jane. Similarly, given Mr. Knightley's continued tactful and blunt reproofs, he seems Emma's only hope. She thinks so: "I had the assistance of all your endeavours to counteract the indulgence of other people. I doubt whether my own sense would have corrected me without it." But, as Kant reminds us, the power of rightly employing rules "must belong to the learner himself; and in the absence of such a natural gift no rule . . . can ensure against misuse." Emma has that gift, Mr. Knightley asserts: "Nature gave you understanding:—Miss Taylor gave you principles. You must have done well. My interference was quite as likely to do harm as good" (p. 462). "Sharpening of the judgment is indeed the one great benefit of examples. Correctness and precision of intellectual insight, on the other hand, they more usually somewhat impair. For only very seldom do they adequately fulfill the requirements of the rule." Even Mr. Knightley, as we have seen, is not perfectly exemplary.

If one function of criticism—as of literature itself—is to provide an example of applied rules, a paradigm of how to relate a general context to particular circumstances, the danger is that such critical interference will do as much harm as good. The novel may not adequately fulfill the requirements of the rule, or the rule those of the novel. Should the reader of this essay have already determined that the Kantian context that I have applied to *Emma* is irrelevant—or, if not, then tactlessly applied—the conclusions I wish to draw from it will be superfluous. But if, on the contrary, this reading has seemed productive or at least suggestive, the implications for Austen criticism are worth making explicit. Though students of Jane Austen feel a proper reluctance to clothe the novels in each new critical fashion, though they rightly feel no urgency to go running after Lacan and Heidegger, such contexts are not a priori inappropriate. They open up vistas of general possibility, and whether these possibilities are realized in individual authors or novels can be determined only by tact, not by rule. The fact that Immanuel Kant is Jane Austen's contemporary does not make his epistemology intrinsically applicable, nor does the fact it is pure philosophy make it obviously irrelevant. Whether and how it applies must be decided by the judgment that Kant himself discusses.

Yet the very lack of obvious relevance of Lacan, Heidegger, and Kant to Jane Austen may explain their attractiveness at this juncture in the history of Austen criticism. Timidity is always in danger of being mistaken for tact. Perhaps it is only appropriate that criticism of her novels remain a conservative enterprise. Yet we need to be as wary of inflexible diffidence as of inflexible openness, for Jane Austen's limitations are always, in part, our own.[19]

*Joel Weinsheimer*
*Texas Tech University*

# NOTES

1. Frank Kermode, *The Classic* (London: Faber and Faber, 1975), p. 43.
2. Parenthetical notations refer to R. W. Chapman, ed., *The Novels of Jane Austen*, vol. 4, *Emma* (London: Oxford University Press, 1933).
3. Barbara Hardy, *A Reading of Jane Austen* (London: Peter Owen, 1975), p. 113.
4. Both quotations appear in Jacques Lacan, "Aggressivity in Psychoanalysis," *Écrits*, trans. Alan Sheridan (New York: Norton, 1977), p. 13.
5. Bernard Paris, *Character and Conflict in Jane Austen's Novels: A Psychological Approach* (Detroit: Wayne State University Press, 1978), p. 11.

6. Ibid.
7. Ibid., p. 82.
8. I have discussed Emma's relation to her father at length in "In Praise of Mr. Woodhouse: Duty and Desire in *Emma*," ARIEL: *A Review of International English Literature*, 6 (1975): 243–51.
9. Stuart Tave, *Some Words of Jane Austen* (Chicago: University of Chicago Press, 1973), p. 33.
10. Martin Heidegger, *Being and Time*, trans. John Macquarrie and Edward Robinson (New York: Harper and Row, 1962), pp. 190–91.
11. Tave, *Some Words of Jane Austen*, pp. 206–7.
12. "Johnson is unlike most modern . . . relativists primarily because he goes ahead to pass explicit moral judgment upon the alien standards by invoking his own values as superior." Paul Kent Alkon, *Samuel Johnson and Moral Discipline* (Evanston, Ill.: Northwestern University Press, 1967), p. 30. I argue against the notion of Austenian relativism below.
13. Susan Morgan, *In the Meantime: Character and Perception in Jane Austen's Fiction* (Chicago: University of Chicago Press, 1980), p. 43.
14. Ibid., p. 3.
15. Ibid., p. 12.
16. Ibid., p. 48.
17. Ibid., pp. 10–11.
18. This and all subsequent quotations from Kant appear in the *Critique of Pure Reason*, trans. Norman Kemp Smith (London: Macmillan, 1961), pp. 177–78.
19. Lest I seem to arrogate to myself a breadth of knowledge I do not possess, I should not close this essay without confessing that I am not so familiar with Kant as to cull from him at will passages of relevance to Jane Austen. I came across a sentence of the passage cited while reading *Truth and Method*, ed. Garrett Barden and John Cumming (New York: Seabury, 1975), p. 37. In this section of the book, Gadamer establishes the terminology of interpretative tact that I have applied throughout.

# Anne Elliot, the Wife of Bath, and Other Friends

Debate fills the penultimate chapter of *Persuasion*. Faced with Captain Harville's accusation about the inconstancy of women, with his threat to call up "fifty quotations in a moment on my side the argument" from histories, stories, songs, and proverbs, Anne Elliot replies firmly, "If you please, no reference to examples in books." All of them are written by men, who, she says, "have had every advantage of us in telling their own story. Education has been theirs in so much higher a degree; the pen has been in their hands. I will not allow books to prove anything." It is a grand moment for women, but haven't we cheered before at sentiments like these? Indeed we have, and the one who uttered them was Chaucer's Wife of Bath. Driven to distraction by Jankyn's collection of stories and proverbs about wicked women, the Wife takes a stand for the honor of women. She too declares stoutly that it all depends upon who tells the story:

> By God! if wommen hadde writen stories,
> As clerkes [learned men] han withinne hire oratories,
> They wolde han writen of men moore wikkednesse,
> Than al the mark of Adam may redresse.[1]

Anne Elliot and the Wife of Bath might seem a capricious, even ludicrous pairing, given that they are so very unlike. But this close similarity of argument might well suggest that Jane Austen had read Chaucer with attention.

What are we to do with such allusions? It is evident that Jane Austen, whenever she was taken by a novel, a play, or a poem, read it until she knew it virtually by heart, entering into its imagined world until it was as real to her as life itself. Her first edition copy of her favorite novel,

Samuel Richardson's *Sir Charles Grandison*,[2] she read so often that the characters were as familiar to her, J. E. Austen-Leigh says, "as if they had been living friends."[3] According to Henry Crawford, the same thing happens with Shakespeare. "One gets acquainted with [him] without knowing how. It is a part of an Englishman's constitution . . . one is intimate with him by instinct." Edmund agrees: one is familiar with Shakespeare from one's earliest years.[4]

If she did have a peculiarly retentive mind, assisted by the habit of rereading, it need not surprise us if the works Jane Austen knew so well served not merely as embellishments but as direct inspirations to her own. I have already found this to be so for *Mansfield Park, Pride and Prejudice*, and *Emma*,[5] where other books seem to have played a part in feeding her mind, however much of a metamorphosis they subsequently underwent. And if, say, Richardson or Shakespeare were important to her in this way, why not any other author that she read closely? With any of the books that she or her family owned we are on fairly safe ground when we think we hear echoes of something we know. Where the evidence is not direct but circumstantial, one must beware of free association, be cautious in claiming too much. But we have full lists neither of her collection nor of her borrowings from the circulating libraries, only of the books she mentions or books that have happened to turn up in sales. We can thus at least explore the possibility that an apparent allusion like this one to the Wife of Bath is more than a remembered scrap of the kind that Edmund says most people know Shakespeare by, and if her own work seems to be deeply informed by the same issues and ideas, pursue the seam as long as it will hold.

Chaucer is someone she could scarcely miss, just as, if we had no proof of her reading Shakespeare, we could safely invent it. Thomas Tyrwhitt's edition of Chaucer, first published in 1775–1778, was reprinted in 1798. Illustrators seized on the pilgrims as a topic, notably Thomas Stothard, who also illustrated Richardson, and William Blake, whose painting of 1809 was published as an engraving in 1810. She is unlikely to have read Blake's account of the Wife of Bath as a scarecrow to warn young readers in his rare *Descriptive Catalogue*. Did she, however, know Stothard and Hoppner's prospectus, where, says Blake disgustedly, they "think that the Wife of Bath is a young, beautiful, blooming damsel, and H——says, that she is the Fair Wife of Bath, and that the Spring appears in her Cheeks"? These are conventional images enough, but she used both "bloom" and "spring" to characterize her own fair woman of Bath. If she had perhaps read this, or Dryden's affectionate and generous praise of "the Father of *English* poetry" prefacing his *Fables Ancient and Modern*, she could well have been fired to read Chaucer's own words for herself.

Dryden's version of the Wife's Tale and Pope's of the Prologue were widely available in early nineteenth-century collections of poetry, but on those occasions where she appears to be drawing on Chaucer for *Persuasion*, she seems closer to the original than to those distinguished but often free translations. It is intriguing to think that Jane Austen might have read Chaucer's English, especially a Prologue too immodest, wrote Dryden, to translate.

How far, then, may we pursue the Wife into *Persuasion*? When the two are laid together, significant similarities do spring to the eye. I shall suggest that from the Wife's Tale she could have drawn not only the story of the Loathly Lady herself, but her ideas of "gentillesse" defined as rank, wealth, outward finery, and deeds, while the Wife's Prologue may have provided her with ways to characterize "maistrie," and the means to defend women's constancy.

### The Loathly Lady

The Wife tells of a knight who marries in exchange for her help a repellent old woman. Given the choice as to whether his wife will be old and faithful or young and untrue, the knight sighs deeply and says the decision is hers. He is instantly rewarded, for the lady is at once both fair and young and promises to be always faithful.

Anne Elliot likewise changes from a loathly lady to a lovely young woman in the course of *Persuasion*, but Jane Austen could scarcely use magic to do the trick. Instead she uses loss of health and its restoration, an idea she probably found in the book from which she had already derived so many good ideas, *Sir Charles Grandison*. Richardson's heroine, Harriet Byron, pines away in the course of the novel because the man she loves, Sir Charles, will apparently marry Clementina della Porretta. Only his return restores her health. Jane Austen's heroine, Anne Elliot, pines away because she has lost Captain Wentworth eight years before, and she too must watch him court another. Harriet's heart being a "wedded heart,"[6] she refuses another suitor; Anne too refuses Charles Musgrove out of faithfulness to Wentworth (p. 28). Anne is surely Harriet's sister, for their cases are similar and their symptoms are the same. The comprehensive account of Harriet in the second letter of *Grandison* in particular contains details corresponding to Anne's being a model of female excellence (p. 159), with an elegance of mind and sweetness of character, an original bloom, prudence, and mild eyes (pp. 5–6). When Harriet believes she has lost Sir Charles her cheek fades and her health languishes (II.546), to the grief of her loving family: "And must Harriet Byron, blessed with beauty so unequalled; health so blooming; a temper so even; passions so governable; generous and grateful, even to heroism!—Superior to every woman in frankness of heart, in true delicacy; and in an understanding and judgment beyond her years—Must *she* be offered up, as a victim on the altar of hopeless Love!" (II.542). Harriet's faded cheeks, pale lips and changed complexion, her swelled eyes, her sighing, her resignation, all give the impression that she is not built for duration (II.659). She remains cheerful for fear of giving concern, playing the harpsichord as soon as she is asked and joining in any private ball that her grandmother decides to give (II.516).

Anne at the start of *Persuasion* is, like the Loathly Lady, foul and old— Sir Walter thinks her haggard (p. 6). Twenty-seven years old (she had bloomed at fifteen, p. 153), she is, like Harriet, "faded and thin," her bloom vanished early (pp. 6, 28). She sighs as she walks in her favorite grove (p. 25), but, like Harriet, conceals her grief—not out of concern for her loving family, however, but in the knowledge that they are too selfish to care. At any "unpremeditated little ball" Anne also is the pianist (p. 47), playing for as long as she is wanted, her eyes sometimes filling with tears (p. 71).

Anne, then, begins as a blooming Harriet and from loss of love alters like her into a Loathly Lady by the time *Persuasion* begins. How she is restored (like Harriet) to youth and beauty (like the Loathly Lady) is the story of the novel. Chaucer's knight had been appalled that his lady looked so "foule," and she had chidden him for being "dangerous," disdainful, not courteous. Wentworth is equally "not very gallant" when he thinks Anne so altered he should not have known her again, confirming Anne's sense of the destruction of her youth and bloom. "He had thought her wretchedly altered," says the narrator (pp. 60–61), while Anne imagines him looking at her "altered features . . . the ruins of the face which had once charmed him" (p. 72). The way to restore her features is the same as for Harriet, the restoration of affection. Sir Charles Grandison, proposing to Harriet, compliments her on her "restored complexion [I did indeed feel my face glow]" (III. 76), and after this her health is never again in doubt. "Glow" is Jane Austen's word also for a blush, a sensibility, an erotic awareness, and like Richardson she uses "complexion" again and again as a sure indication of Anne's condition. At Lyme the narrator repeats the same words: her features "having the bloom and freshness of youth restored by the fine wind which had been blowing on her complexion" instantly impress Mr. Elliot, and Wentworth's look seems to say, "Even I, at this moment, see something like Anne Elliot again" (p. 104). Anne's remarkable improvement in plumpness and looks brings hopes that she may be blessed with a second spring of youth and beauty (p. 124). Even her father thinks her "less thin in her person, in her cheeks; her skin, her complexion, greatly improved, clearer—fresher" (p. 145). Although he puts it down to Gowland, the baronet is not all wrong; complexion is the key to beauty, for it reveals the condition of its owner. Soon she is generally acknowledged to be very pretty (p. 177), and encouragement about Wentworth's feelings makes her eyes brighten and her cheeks glow (p. 185). Walking with him after his proposal, Anne finds that "cheeks which had been pale now glowed" (p. 240); she is "glowing and lovely" (p. 245). Wentworth in the blindness and forgetfulness of his love earnestly assures her that "even if you were personally altered . . . to my eye you could never alter," and Anne lets it pass, knowing that it is something for a woman to be assured, in her eight-and-twentieth year, that she has not lost one charm of earlier youth (p. 243). When Chaucer's knight sees how fair and young the lady is, "for joye" he seizes her in his arms, "his herte bathed in a bath of blisse." And, says the Wife, they lived to their lives' end "in parfit joye." So too Anne and Wentworth, exquisitely happy, their "spirits dancing in private rapture," pace the gradual ascent, and the author promises them a future in which to number this moment among their happiest (p. 240). Thus Jane Austen turns her lady from a loathly to a lovely one as Chaucer has done, calling on Richardson's more plausible and realistic method to do so.

## Gentillesse as Rank, Wealth, and Beauty

Chaucer's knight, wallowing and tossing in his bed beside his new wife, complains bitterly of her age, her ugliness, her lowly degree. She responds briskly, attacking the notion that "gentillesse / As is descended out of old richesse" inevitably makes men noble. "Swich arrogance is nat worth an hen." The greatest gentleman, she says, is he who does all the gentle deeds he can; gentillesse comes from Christ alone. She quotes from Dante's *Purgatorio* (VII. 121–23) to the effect that true goodness comes from God, not through the "branches" of a family. Virtuous living is not to be bequeathed like wealth; the fact that man may hurt and maim temporal things indeed proves in another way that "genterie / Is nat annext to possessioun." A lord's son may do shame and villainy even when born of a gentle house and noble and virtuous elders; conversely, if he does not do gentle deeds "he nis nat gentil, be he duc or erl; / For vileyns sinful dedes make a cherl." In short, she concludes, "he is gentil that dooth gentil dedis." Dryden neatly sums it up: the Wife's Tale shows "the silly Pride of Ancestry and Titles without inherent Vertue, which is the true Nobility."

One can see at once how like this is to the principal theme of *Persuasion*. Jane Austen is as forthright as Dryden or the lady when she talks of

Anne's "conceited, silly father" (p. 5), his belief in the importance of beauty and inherited rank, his attachment to his "possessioun" Kellynch Hall, his vanity in thinking that his position in life is his by just desert. Captain Wentworth by contrast does noble deeds by land and sea in a profession distinguished by its domestic virtues as well as its national importance (the lady speaks of deeds "privee and apert," private and public) and thus proves himself a gentleman (p. 252). Mr. Elliot, though of noble blood, proves a churl, an undutiful "branch . . . dismembered . . . from the paternal tree" (p. 136), exactly as Chaucer, echoing Dante, had said. Incidentally, commentators here agree that Chaucer's translation is not altogether clear, and Jane Austen, who knew something of Italian,[7] may well have checked for herself what Dante actually said. In the original the stanza is indeed made up of "inverted, transposed, curtailed Italian lines" such as William Elliot admires Anne for being able to translate (p. 186).

Pride of descent is linked in *Persuasion*, as in the Tale, with wealth and vanity of outward appearance. All three are embodied in Sir Walter Elliot, admiring, as the book opens, his own ancient and respectable lineage. Jane Austen's tone is consistently attacking whenever she speaks of Sir Walter (why Auden could ever have thought her preoccupied with "brass" in any simple kind of way is unimaginable):

> Vanity was the beginning and the end of Sir Walter Elliot's character; vanity of person and of situation. . . . Few women could think more of their personal appearance than he did; nor could the valet of any new made lord be more delighted with the place he held in society. He considered the blessing of beauty as inferior only to the blessing of a baronetcy; and the Sir Walter Elliot, who united these gifts, was the constant object of his warmest respect and devotion. (p. 4)

Pride of descent made Sir Walter forbid the "degrading" alliance of Anne to the base-born Wentworth, "a stranger without alliance or fortune" (pp. 26–27). (Dryden's Preface had pointed to his translation of Boccaccio's *Sigismonda and Guiscardo* as being similar in theme to the Wife's Tale. Here, as in *Persuasion*, a tyrant father separates his noble daughter from a "Plebian Mate.") Lady Russell and the Musgrove girls provide variations on the central theme of "rank, people of rank, and jealousy of rank" (pp. 11, 46); Mrs. Clay flatters Sir Walter, and Sir Walter is proud to walk behind the broad back of privilege belonging to Lady Dalrymple (p. 185). She and her daughter, Miss Carteret, wonderfully prove the Tale's contention that to be born of noble blood is not necessarily to be noble. "There was no superiority of manner, accomplishment, or understanding. Lady Dalrymple had acquired the name of 'a charming woman,' because she had a smile and a civil answer for every body. Miss

Carteret, with still less to say, was so plain and awkward, that she would never have been tolerated at Camden-place but for her birth" (p. 150). When the little flea Mrs. Clay deserts Sir Walter, he finds that "to flatter and follow others, without being flattered and followed in turn, is but a state of half enjoyment" (p. 251).

Anne is the only Elliot to stand out against pride of rank. " 'Well,' said Anne, 'I certainly am proud, too proud to enjoy a welcome which depends so entirely upon place' " (p. 151). Charles Musgrove's warm outburst that he will not fawn on the Dalrymples and Mr. Elliot— " 'I am not one of those who neglect the reigning power to bow to the rising sun. If I would not go for the sake of your father, I should think it scandalous to go for the sake of his heir' " (p. 224)—allows Anne to show Wentworth that she agrees, and so helps on the match.

"Possessioun" is to Sir Walter the second sign of a gentleman. Wentworth's brother had no property and so is nobody (p. 23); Charles Musgrove, the eldest son of a man of landed property and general importance, is a somebody (p. 28). But, as the Lady says, nobility must deserve its riches, and Sir Walter is foolish and spendthrift, without "principle or sense enough to maintain himself in the situation in which Providence had placed him" (p. 248). He is so distressed for money that he must retrench (p. 9), and his response is all the funnier when it is recognized as a swift and accurate parody of that other proud old man, King Lear. " 'What! Every comfort of life knocked off! Journeys, London, servants, horses, table,—contractions and restrictions every where! To live no longer with the decencies even of a private gentleman! No, he would sooner quit Kellynch-hall at once, than remain in it on such disgraceful terms ' " (p. 13). Sir Walter stalks off, not to the tempestuous heath but to rainy Bath, and his daughters are not so much his tormentors as his companions in vanity. Anne, however, does resemble Cordelia (her voice, too, is gentle and low, an excellent thing in a woman), for even when it harms her she does what she sees as her duty, whether in obeying Lady Russell or in clearing away the claims of creditors (p. 12). It is she, like Cordelia, who is the true defender of her father's honors when William Elliot plots, Edmund-like, to gain the very ranks and titles he despises in their present owner (p. 206). Anne-Cordelia's true worth is recognized in the midst of her self-seeking family by Wentworth-France, and although Sir Walter "could give his daughter at present but a small part of the share of ten thousand pounds which must be hers hereafter," he recognizes her at the end, and is indeed a very fond and "foolish" old man (p. 248).

Sir Walter never understands how much his importance depends upon Kellynch Hall. Only Anne must sigh that her father should feel no degradation in his change; should see nothing to regret in the duties and dignity of the resident land-holder; should find so much to be vain of in the littlenesses of a town; and she must sigh, and smile, and wonder too, as Elizabeth threw open the folding-doors, and walked with exultation from one drawing-room to the other, boasting of their space, at the possibility of that woman, who had been mistress of Kellynch Hall, finding extent to be proud of between two walls, perhaps thirty feet asunder. (p. 138)

By contrast, the naval officers cut through dependence upon place by having no home at all. The Crofts are happy to be tenants merely of Kellynch Hall; Captain Harville by "ingenious contrivances and nice arrangements" turns the small rooms of their lodgings to "excellent ac-commodations" (pp. 98–99); women on ships, says Mrs. Croft, may be "as comfortable on board, as in the best house in England" (p. 69). It is not the nature of the accommodation that matters but the busyness and merit of the occupants. Anne's "raptures of admiration and delight on the character of the navy—their friendliness, their brotherliness, their open-ness, their uprightness . . . they only knew how to live, and they only deserved to be respected and loved" (p. 99) have much to do with the fact that their characters, not their quarters, give them consequence.

Most important of all, the seafaring people are noble by reason of their hospitality. Hospitality as a mark of gentility one finds not in the Tale, but in Pope;[8] it pervades his *Odyssey* as well as his poems about his own hospitable house at Twickenham. "Horace II. ii, To Mr. Bethel," which shrugs off the loss of property into other hands, is a particularly apt rebuke for Elizabeth Elliot.

> My lands are sold, my Father's house is gone;
> I'll hire another's; is not that my own,
> And yours my friends? thro' whose free-opening gate
> None comes too early, none departs too late;
> (For I, who hold sage Homer's rule the best,
> Welcome the coming, speed the going guest). (155–60)

Elizabeth knows she ought to ask the Musgrove party to dine with them in their hired lodgings, but is held back by her awareness that she must betray a difference from the style at Kellynch Hall, rationalizing to her-self, " 'Old fashioned notions—country hospitality—we do not profess to give dinners—few people in Bath do' " (p. 219). Even in hired lodgings the Harvilles, however, are "kindly hospitable." Anne, who sees "such a bewitching charm in a degree of hospitality so uncommon, so unlike the usual style of give-and-take invitations, and dinners of formality and display" (p. 98), that is "heartless elegance" (p. 226) like Timon's, might well conclude with Pope,

Let Lands and Houses have what Lords they will,
Let Us be fix'd, and our own Masters still.

Anne alone of all her family has never believed that property makes the gentleman. She is easily able to resist the temptation of returning to Kellynch as its mistress and William Elliot's wife, and when she does visit it again "she could not but in conscience feel that they were gone who deserved not to stay, and that Kellynch-hall had passed into better hands than its owners.'" She has "no power of saying to herself, 'These rooms ought to belong only to us. Oh, how fallen in their destination! How unworthily occupied! An ancient family to be so driven away! Strangers filling their place!' No, except when she thought of her mother, and remembered where she had been used to sit and preside, she had no sigh of that description to heave" (pp. 125–26). Instead of gaining their importance from the "richesse" of property, the naval men, forever on the move, derive their nobility from the noble deeds of their profession, their national importance, and their domestic life. For them indeed "genterie is nat annext to possessioun."

Poverty, says the Loathly Lady, is not to be despised. Answering the knight's complaint that she is not only old and ugly but poor, she argues (pointing to the example of Jesus) that whoever is content with his poverty is in fact rich, even if he is without a shirt. He who is poor but not covetous is rich indeed, for all that the knight may think him a menial. Poverty is a hateful good, she says, being a great incentive to a livelihood; it improves the wisdom of those who take it patiently, for the poor man discovers both God and himself, and finds out who his true friends are. These arguments surely inform the Mrs. Smith episode in *Persuasion*. Sir Walter, also reviling women for being ugly, old, and poor, particularly attacks Anne's friend for being "a poor widow, barely able to live," "old and sickly." This is choice, because he, who despises a Mrs. Smith for being poor, has frittered away his own fortune, and (forgetting his toady Mrs. Clay) does not recollect that Mrs. Smith is "not the only widow in Bath between thirty and forty, with little to live on" (pp. 157–58).

To this ungentle knight Anne makes the same reply as the Loathly Lady to hers. Mrs. Smith, she observes, has allowed neither sickness nor sorrow to close her heart or ruin her spirit. Although she has lost everything, husband and influence both, and has neither child, relations, nor health (compare Chaucer's "al hadde he nat a sherte"), poverty *has* been a hateful good to her, it *has* set her upon a livelihood, making and selling knickknacks through her friend Nurse Rooke. As Anne says, expanding upon Chaucer's lady, "a submissive spirit might be patient, a strong understanding would supply resolution, but here was something more; here was that elasticity of mind, that disposition to be comforted, that power of turning readily from evil to good, and of finding employment which carried her out of herself, which was from Nature alone." This, thinks Anne, is the choicest gift of Heaven, an instance where, "by a merciful appointment, it seems designed to counterbalance almost every other want" (p. 154). And if poverty is, as the Lady says, "a spectacle . . . Thurgh which he may his verray freendes see," Mrs. Smith from the vantage of her poverty sees that there is "little real friendship in the world" (p. 156). William Elliot, once a most intimate friend of her husband, betrayed him in his poverty. Like the loving friend Antonio in *Twelfth Night,* who complains that the apparent Sebastian denies him his own purse freely lent, Mr. Smith treated Mr. Elliot like a brother: having the "finest, most generous spirit in the world," he "would have divided his last farthing with him; and I know that his purse was open to him" (pp. 199–200). Mr. Elliot's "cold civility," his "hard-hearted indifference" make up for Anne, as for Amiens in *As You Like It,* "a dreadful picture of ingratitude and inhumanity," making her feel that "no flagrant open crime could have been worse" (pp. 209–10).

Mrs. Smith finds a friend in Anne and another in Wentworth, who, taking on the task of executor relinquished by Mr. Elliot, brings her some financial relief. But, says the narrator, "these prime supplies of good," her "cheerfulness and mental alacrity," were still as they had been when she found contentment in the Wife's "glad poverte"; indeed, she says, giving it one final turn, "she might have been absolutely rich and perfectly healthy, and yet be happy" (p. 252).

## Gentillesse as Outward Appearance

Sir Walter Elliot believes that nobility inheres in rank, wealth, and beauty, but is not himself ennobled by any of the three. In the fixity of his conviction he is easy prey to those who fasten on the vulnerable vanity of place—a Mr. Shepherd, shepherding his client wherever he likes, or a Mrs. Clay, common as clay and as malleable as it, changing allegiance from the old king to the new. In his personal vanity, too, he is easily deceived by an apparent nobility of outward appearance. Here, to develop her characterization of the theme in Mr. Elliot, Sir Walter, and Captain Wentworth, Jane Austen turned again, I think, to Richardson.

William Elliot seems at first to be like Sir Charles Grandison as described in I, letter xxxvi. His manners are "so polished, so easy" (p. 143): Sir Charles shows "ease and freedom of manners"; "though not handsome, [William Elliot] had an agreeable person" (p. 105): Sir Charles is "thought (what is far more eligible in a man than mere beauty) very agreeable." Like Richardson's hero, William Elliot claims to have "strong feelings of family-attachment and family-honour," and lives with the "liberality of a man of fortune, without display" (p. 146). Sir Charles dresses "rather richly . . . than gaudily," and his equipage is "not so much to the glare of taste, as if he aimed either to inspire or shew emulation." Mr. Elliot judges "for himself in every thing essential, without defying public opinion in any point of worldly decorum" (p. 146); Sir Charles lives "to himself, and to his own heart; and . . . tho' he had the happiness to please every-body, yet made the judgment or approbation of the world matter but of second consideration."

Like Sir Charles, Mr. Elliot values all the felicities of domestic life (p. 147), and his first marriage has produced "no unhappiness to sour his mind" (the good sense of Sir Charles is not "rusted over by sourness, by moroseness"). His "air of elegance and fashion" produces a "very gentle-manlike appearance" (Sir Charles "dresses to the fashion"), together with his well-shaped face (the face of Sir Charles is "a fine oval") and his sensible eye (the eye of Sir Charles shows "sparkling intelligence"). No wonder that everyone should be fooled when he corresponds so closely to Richardson's perfect hero. And yet one might be warned by Sir Walter's lament that he is very much under-hung (p. 141).

Sir Walter for once is right. William Elliot is not Richardson's virtuous Sir Charles Grandison but his rakish Sir Hargrave Pollexfen, who courts the reluctant heroine. When Mr. Elliot claims longer acquaintance with Anne than is physically possible, arguing that " 'I knew you by report long before you came to Bath. I had heard you described by those who knew you intimately. I have been acquainted with you by character many years. Your person, your disposition, accomplishments, manner—they were all described, they were all present to me' " (p. 187), he is particu-larly like Sir Hargrave seeking to ingratiate himself with Harriet Byron: " 'And are at last my eyes bless'd with the sight of a young Lady so celebrated for her graces of person and mind? Much did I hear, when I was at the last Northampton races, of Miss Byron: But little did I expect to find report fall so short of what I see' " (I.43). No more than Harriet Byron does Anne wish to marry her unwelcome suitor—he is nothing to her, she says (p. 196), as casually as Harriet says, "He does not hit my fancy." She thus provokes Mrs. Smith's accusation that she is being cruel in pretending to delay, just as Harriet, accused of cruelty by Sir Har-grave, decides not to indulge in "female trifling" (I. 83).

The abrupt revelation of Mr. Elliot's villainy has puzzled many readers; it seems such an uncharacteristically clumsy way for Jane Austen to resolve her plot, and one wonders what she might have done with it if she had revised it as she revised the ending. It is, then, of some interest to realize that Mrs. Smith's melodramatic sketch of the man's true character and the terms that she uses echo closely the scene in which Richardson arbitrarily introduces a character into *Grandison* to warn his heroine of the iniquities of Sir Hargrave. Harriet knows of the rake's ungentle deeds before she ever meets him; Anne's shock is the greater for having liked the man before she knows him. But the device is unsatisfactory in either case. Sir Hargrave, says Harriet's informant, is "a man of malice; of resentment; of enterprize; a cruel man"; he is "a very dangerous and enterprising man . . . malicious, ill-natured, and designing; and sticks at nothing to carry a point on which he has once set his heart." He has "ruined" three young creatures (I.63). Mr. Elliot, says Mrs. Smith, is a man "without heart or conscience; a designing, wary, cold-blooded being, . . . who . . . would be guilty of any cruelty," one who leads others into "ruin" (p. 199). Thus Jane Austen conflates two of Richardson's characters, his hero and his villain, into one—and her conflation makes possible the unfolding of the plot.

Sir Walter ought by his station in life to be a Sir Charles Grandison, but Admiral Croft makes a better landlord than he, a better example to the parish and kinder to the poor (p. 125). In his vanity Sir Walter is more like Sir Hargrave. When the admiral remarks, "He must be rather a dressy man for his time of life.—Such a number of looking-glasses! oh Lord! there was no getting away from oneself" (p. 128), the mind leaps to the foppish Sir Hargrave, who

> . . . forgets not to pay his respects to himself at every glass; yet does it with a seeming consciousness, as if he would hide a vanity too apparent to be concealed; breaking from it, if he finds himself observed, with a half-careless, yet seemingly dissatisfied air, pretending to have discover'd something amiss in himself. This seldom fails to bring him a compliment: Of which he shews himself very sensible, by affectedly disclaiming the merit of it; perhaps with this speech, bowing, with his spread hand upon his breast, waving his head to and fro—By my Soul, Madam (or Sir) you do me too much honour. (I. 45)

Just so Sir Walter precipitates a compliment when he pretends that all eyes must be on Colonel Wallis. "Modest Sir Walter! He was not allowed to escape, however. His daughter and Mrs. Clay united in hinting that Colonel Wallis's companion might have as good a figure as Colonel Wallis, and certainly was not sandy-haired" (p. 142). For Sir Walter and his sacred rites of pride the watch from "The Rape of the Lock" might well strike eleven with its silver sounds (p. 144).[9]

Taken to extremes, concern for outward appearance actively disables; as Fielding wrote in the *Covent-Garden Journal*, no. 4 (14 January 1752), the word "fine" in phrases such as "*fine* Gentleman, *fine* Lady . . . is to be understood in a Sense somewhat synonymous with useless." Convention's power to fetter is what Mrs. Croft protests about to Wentworth: "I hate to hear you talking so, like a fine gentleman, and as if women were all fine ladies, instead of rational creatures" (p. 70)—that is, sensible women who cope, like her (like Anne), with adversity and hardship.

Captain Wentworth alone is a true Sir Charles Grandison, for only in him appears that Platonic correlation between outward beauty and inner worth, that fine appearance that neither deceives the spectator nor disables the possessor. Sir Charles is "a real fine gentleman," best valued "not so much for being an handsome man; not so much for his birth and fortune" but "for being, in the great and yet comprehensive sense of the word, a *good man*" (I. 182). Richardson is here struggling to characterize realistically the Christian Hero, one whose deeds are both traditionally heroic and socially valuable. The Wife's public and private spheres of action reappear in the remark that Sir Charles is "one of the busiest men in the kingdom . . . and yet the most of a family-man" (I. 279). He rescues the heroine, he delivers his friends, he performs all those social duties relative to other people that the domestic conduct books recommend. Captain Wentworth's deeds are conditioned by their setting in Regency not Arthurian England, but his rescue of Anne from the suffocating embraces of the child, his concern that she ride in the carriage when fatigued, are knightly and gentle enough, while his dashing naval career provides substantial evidence of the martial hero. In private he is most like Sir Charles when he helps the Harville family, succors his friend Benwick, or acts as executor for Mrs. Smith. The "domestic virtues" and "national importance" of his profession are the last, resounding words of the novel, summing up Wentworth's true standing as a Christian Hero. Sir Walter, eyeing his new son-in-law more closely by daylight, is "very much struck by his personal claims" and feels that such superiority of appearance might be not unfairly balanced against Anne's superiority of rank (p. 248). When he enters the marriage in the volume of honor, he ennobles Wentworth as he ought, for here is a man gentle not by rank or wealth but by virtue of his deeds, as the Loathly Lady prescribes.

## Maistrie

Whether or not the Wife's Tale and her Prologue were originally both designed for her, each deals with the same thing—that is, who has control, or "maistrie," in marriage. The Loathly Lady and the Wife are older women married to young men, and have thus lost the power once automatically granted them by youth. As soon as sovereignty is given back to the women, they are immediately loving—and young as well, in the case of the Lady. Both stories are self-referential, self-fulfilling; by acting out his theoretical knowledge that the thing women love best is "maistrie," the knight wins a wife miraculously restored to youth; Jankyn, by giving the Wife the reins, insures she will be loving and true.

The Wife fights to get what she wants; violence ends her Prologue when she attacks Jankyn for gloating over his book. Dramatically she tears out a leaf (or three), throws it in the fire, and hits him backwards into the fire. He smites her on the head so that "in the floor I lay as I were deed." Suddenly the story looks very like that of the determined Louisa Musgrove jumping down from the Cobb at Lyme in Chapter 12. She too falls down on the pavement, severely bruising her head, and is "taken up lifeless!" "Her face was like death . . . 'She is dead! she is dead!' screamed Mary." The Wife, only pretending to die, feigns to wake out of her "swogh"; Louisa "once opened her eyes, but soon closed them again, without apparent consciousness . . . a proof of life." Jankyn, "agast" when he sees "how stille that I lay," is stricken by remorse and kneels down beside her; Wentworth, seeing Louisa's closed eyes, her lack of breath, her pallid face, "knelt with her in his arms, looking on her with a face as pallid as her own, in an agony of silence." Jankyn asks forgiveness of his "Deere suster Alisoun," promising "As help me God! I shall thee nevere smite." He adds, though, "That I have doon, it is thyself to wite [blame]." In very similar words Captain Wentworth says, "Oh, God! that I had not given way to her at the fatal moment! Had I done as I ought! But so eager and so resolute! Dear, sweet Louisa!" Like Jankyn, he blames himself but her too.

The Wife thus wins mastery over Jankyn, but Jane Austen, by giving her story to Louisa, shows Anne (and Wentworth) that such one-sided "maistrie" will not do. And yet just as the Wife "condescended to be pleas'd" (in Pope's version) when she gains "by maistrie, al the soverainetee," Anne feels "a pleasure . . . a great pleasure" that Wentworth shows a "deference for her judgment" in the emergency at Lyme. Jane Austen's first volume thus ends just where the Prologue does, in triumph for the woman's point of view. That the Wife's Prologue belongs to Anne as well as Louisa is in fact shown when Mary, dimly perceiving there is something up between Anne and Wentworth, assures herself "with some anxiety, that there had been no fall in the case; that Anne had not, at any time lately, slipped down and got a blow on her head" (p. 238). Anne too, after all, is a woman of Bath.

Chaucer-like, Admiral Croft seizes on the creative possibilities of the exciting event: "A new sort of way this, for a young fellow to be making love, by breaking his mistress's head! . . . This is breaking a head and giving a plaister truly!"[10] Is Jane Austen actually revealing her opinion of

Chaucer and not just of Admiral Croft when she adds that his "manners were not quite of the tone to suit Lady Russell, but they delighted Anne. His goodness of heart and simplicity of character were irresistible" (pp. 126–27)? And is she expanding on her critique when she praises Nurse Rooke, Mrs. Smith's friend, as a shrewd, intelligent, sensible woman who has "a line for seeing human nature . . . a fund of good sense and observation which, as a companion, make her infinitely superior to thousands of those who having only received 'the best education in the world' know nothing worth attending to . . . she is sure to have something to relate that is entertaining and profitable, something that makes one know one's species better"? When Anne agrees that Nurse Rooke witnesses "varieties of human nature" (pp. 155–56), she seems to echo Dryden's Preface ("a perpetual Fountain of good Sense," "the various Manners and Humours . . . of the whole *English* Nation"). One can certainly see the appeal that a woman author denied formal education might find in Chaucer as a fellow observer of human nature. Indeed, she may possibly extend Dryden's observations on Chaucer to her own characters. Where Dryden thought Chaucer "a rough Diamond" who "must first be polish'd e'er he shines," Sir Walter thinks naval men "rough and rugged to the last degree" (p. 20), but allows that he might not be ashamed to be seen with Admiral Croft "if his own man might have had the arranging of his hair" (p. 32).

If the Wife's final struggle pertains to Louisa and to Anne, her appearance as described in Chaucer's General Prologue is transferred rather to Mrs. Croft. The Wife, bold and red-faced, with wide-set teeth and broad hips, has "passed many a straunge strem" in her wanderings. Mrs. Croft, though neither tall nor fat, had a "squareness, uprightness, and vigour of form, which gave importance to her person." She has "good teeth" and a "reddened and weather-beaten complexion, the consequence of her having been almost as much at sea as her husband" (p. 48). "In felaweship" the Wife was well able to laugh and talk; Anne delights to watch the Crofts talk together, or to see "their eagerness of conversation when occasionally forming into a little knot of the navy, Mrs. Croft looking as intelligent and keen as any of the officers around her" (p. 168). Jane Austen seems to protect Mrs. Croft from being thought too like the Wife, however, when she adds of her open and decisive manner, "without any approach to coarseness, however, or any want of good humour" (p. 48). Neither does Mrs. Croft seek for "soverainetee," but goes "shares with him in every thing" (p. 168). Where the Wife gets "al the bridel in myn hond" (Pope has it "receiv'd the reins of absolute command"), Mrs. Croft only takes the reins to save them both from common danger:

"My dear admiral, that post!—we shall certainly take that post."
   But by coolly giving the reins a better direction herself, they happily passed the danger; and by once afterwards judiciously putting out her hand, they neither fell into a rut, nor ran foul of a dung-cart; and Anne [felt] some amusement at their style of driving, which she imagined no bad representation of the general guidance of their affairs. (p. 92)

Such equality of "maistrie" is what Anne and Wentworth will seek. Not sovereignty, not weakness, but a sense that they are both "more equal to act." Wentworth has learnt, after Lyme, "to distinguish between the steadiness of principle and the obstinacy of self-will, between the darings of heedlessness and the resolution of a collected mind" (p. 242); he has learnt to criticize Louisa (and by implication the Wife of Bath) and to appreciate a more balanced equality like the Crofts'. Like Admiral Croft, he will hand over the reins to Anne on important issues, and is prepared to forgive Lady Russell and be in charity with her; later, in spite of her "former transgressions, he could now value [her] from his heart. While he was not obliged to say that he believed her to have been right in originally dividing them, he was ready to say almost every thing else in her favour" (p. 251). He comes as close as can be fairly expected to admitting that Anne was right: "Perhaps I ought to have reasoned thus . . . but I could not. I could not derive benefit from the late knowledge I had acquired of your character" (pp. 244–45). Jane Austen at least seems to think that Anne was right when she suggests that they are "more exquisitely happy, perhaps, in their re-union, than when it had been first projected; more tender, more tried, more fixed in a knowledge of each other's character, truth, and attachment; more equal to act, more justified in acting" (pp. 240–41). The Wife and Jankyn never argue again, she being as loving and faithful to him as he to her. Anne too we learn is "tenderness itself, and she had the full worth of it in Captain Wentworth's affection" (p. 252). By deferring to her judgment both at Lyme and at the end, Wentworth, like the knight, like Jankyn, exchanges some of his sovereignty for lifelong happiness with his wife.

## The Constancy of Women

   True valor, sings Bunyan, may be seen in one who is constant, come wind, come weather. So too Jane Austen in *Persuasion* celebrates the real heroism of constancy. Anne's relationship with Wentworth is in effect a contest in constancy, for which the revised ending provides a soaring cadenza. Anne, who has consistently turned to literature to illustrate her feelings, does so here more than ever in the contemplation of constancy and alteration. The density of allusion of this chapter is remarkable, as the speakers take on the voices of characters in other literary works, voices that add up to a "book" to answer Jankyn's list of treacherous women in the Wife of Bath's Prologue.

Early on (p. 30), Anne guesses that Wentworth may be constant, and she is right. The clues eventually point to his "eternal constancy" (p. 192), allowing her to hope that "Surely, if there be constant attachment on each side, our hearts must understand each other ere long" (p. 221). Wentworth can write with some justice, "Dare not say that man forgets sooner than woman . . . I have loved none but you. Unjust I may have been, weak and resentful I have been, but never inconstant" (p. 237). Proof of their true constancy in love shows in the refusal of each to see alteration in the other. Eight or nine years have not robbed him of one personal grace (p. 179), thinks Anne; when Wentworth, anxious to discover if Anne has changed, remarks pointedly, "Time makes many changes," Anne cries out, "I am not yet so much changed" (p. 225). The change in Anne is of course only temporary; rapidly Wentworth observes as little alteration in Anne as she in him. Both are in effect saying, like Shakespeare in Sonnet CXVI, that love is not love that alteration finds. To the marriage of these true minds impediments disappear; the preventing crowds that cluttered the rooms and spaces where they met transform into an animated frieze, their power to hurt gone.

Opposed to the constant pair Wentworth and Anne stand the fickle couple Benwick and Louisa. Benwick's inconstancy to the dead Fanny Harville, strikingly shown in his having his portrait reset for Louisa, appalls Captain Wentworth (p. 183). When Captain Harville, arguing for the constancy of men, thinks of Benwick, his tongue is tied (p. 236). Louisa, once so resolute and determined, alters her personality to suit her new lover, sitting quiet all day and starting and wriggling like a dabchick when the door shuts a little too hard (p. 218).

Jane Austen wrote two different endings to *Persuasion*. The original, discarded one is dull, functional, bathetic, with the lovers' *éclaircissement* occurring almost comically through the agency of Admiral Croft. The revised ending, however, astonishes with its power to move. This is partly because Anne and Captain Harville debate issues central to the whole book (the openness to persuasion of men and women, their constancy or alteration), but also because its rich and persistent allusiveness expands these issues out into a much larger world, the world of Jane Austen's literary predecessors.

In her final speech, Shakespeare's Katherine implicitly praises the "painful labour" of men above the passivity of women, who lie "warm at home, secure and safe." Anne, arguing that women forget less, turns this distinction another way: "We cannot help ourselves. We live at home, quiet, confined, and our feelings prey upon us. You are forced on exertion. You have always a profession, pursuits, business of some sort or another, to take you back into the world immediately, and continual occupation and change soon weaken impressions."[12] Katherine argues that the "soft conditions" of women's external parts make them "unapt to toil and trouble in the world," a point repeated by Sir Charles Grandison in Volume VI, Letter lv: "Why gave [nature] delicacy, softness, grace, to . . . the woman . . . strength, firmness, to men: a capacity to bear labour and fatigue; and courage, to protect the other?" This, he says, is a "temporary difference" in the "design of the different machines" that enclose our souls. Admiral Croft similarly argues in return to Anne for a "true analogy between our bodily frames and our mental; and that as our bodies are the strongest, so are our feelings; capable of bearing most rough usage, and riding out the heaviest weather." Anne replies generously in the language of Sir Charles Grandison (he had said, "We . . . travel and toil for them; run through, at the call of Providence, or of our King and country, dangers and difficulties"), adding, however, that to comprehend both kinds of suffering, men's and women's at once, would be intolerable:

> "Your feelings may be the strongest . . . but the same spirit of analogy will authorise me to assert that ours are the most tender. Man is more robust than woman, but he is not longer-lived; which exactly explains my view of the nature of their attachments. Nay, it would be too hard upon you, if it were otherwise. You have difficulties, and privations, and dangers enough to struggle with. You are always labouring and toiling, exposed to every risk and hardship. Your home, country, friends, all quitted. Neither time, nor health, nor life, to be called your own. It would be too hard indeed . . . if women's feelings were to be added to all this."

Anne maintains that it is man's very nature that made Captain Benwick inconstant. Her "authority" could be the Duke in *Twelfth Night*, admitting to Viola,

> For, boy, however we do praise ourselves,
> Our fancies are more giddy and infirm,
> More longing, wavering, sooner lost and won,
> Than women's are.

Even more likely is the song in *Much Ado*, that men were deceivers ever, one foot on sea and one on shore, to one thing constant never—particularly when Anne is kindly prepared to blame Benwick's business at sea for weakening impressions, and Captain Harville retorts that the peace has in fact turned him on shore.

But it is to their own experience, not to the authority of books, that both the Wife and Anne ultimately turn. Harville's list of inconstant women *(mulier mutabile)* no doubt included more recent examples than Jankyn's, for instance Hamlet's "frailty, thy name is woman," but of course it is Benwick who hastens to new sheets, though so young a mourner (p. 108). Against these Anne sets circumstances in favor of her own sex such as may be found "within our own circle," many of which "may be precisely such as cannot be brought forward without betraying a confidence, or in some respect saying what should not be said." She means, of course, her own. Generous to the last, she allows all that Captain Harville says for the sensibilities and sufferings of men—"God forbid that I should undervalue the warm and faithful feelings of any of my fellow-creatures"—but argues still, as Penelope might, that men are constant only "so long as you have an object. . . . All the privilege I claim for my own sex (it is not a very enviable one, you need not covet it) is that of loving longest, when existence or when hope is gone." "We men may say more, swear more," says the disguised Viola, but men "prove/ Much in our vows, but little in our love." Like Harriet Byron (II. 158), like Viola, Anne, like Patience on a monument, allows concealment like a worm in the bud to feed on her damask cheek; she sits smiling at grief. When at last Viola tells her love, she is like Desdemona or indeed any of Shakespeare's heroines, more than half the wooer. So too is Anne in this revised ending the active promoter of her own fate, for Wentworth hears in the debate the same admission heard by Duke Orsino, and acts with the same swift certainty as he.

Now we can see why the revised ending is so incomparably better than the first; it gives Anne a chance to act, to exert herself like her sisters in Shakespeare. Resonant and allusive, it allows her to speak in their voices; they throng about her, adding their testimony to hers, providing layers of argument about women's sphere and women's constancy that gather and convince.[13] This is her answer to Captain Harville's list, her reply to Jankyn's book. Above all, she, like the Wife, pleads for the authority not of books but of her own experience. She herself has been constant, and her example is written out for us to read. Her reward is to escape from the deadening confines of her class, her age, and her sex into a world of doing instead of being. By adding the story of Anne Elliot's to all the others, Jane Austen uses the fact of its real existence as the Wife of Bath used hers, to "prove" the worth of women. It is the same neat trick as Shakespeare's at the end of Sonnet CXVI: unless she never writ (and she obviously has), and unless no one ever loved (and they obviously have), there is no such thing as constancy (so there obviously is).

Jane Austen's juvenilia and her early works are often parodic and inverted versions of other books, for she learnt her craft through play. Even in *Pride and Prejudice* and *Mansfield Park* the same literary-critical impulse, tempered now with respectful affection, is often to be seen. In her mature novels, *Emma* and *Persuasion*, she turns rather to other authors as equals, making them new by a new and contemporary context. The parodic impulse is rarely apparent, nor does she offer her readers the special pleasure of recognizing her main allusions so frequently as she used to do. She remakes what she takes without irony, for the most part, and although she protects the Wife-like Mrs. Croft from being thought coarse and ill-humored, seems to subscribe to a view of the Wife more like Hoppner's than like Blake's. That she might permit Anne to be associated with the Wife certainly suggests so.

The evidence is all circumstantial, but these verbal echoes, these similarities in characterization and event and theme, are not mere *vraisemblances* handy to elucidate the text; they go well beyond coincidence to the likelihood of Jane Austen having read and used the earlier authors. Jane Austen's synthesizing and creative mind was filled with far more than we shall ever know, but it seems possible that in Shakespeare, Richardson, and above all Chaucer's Wife of Bath, she found energy and ideas to inspire her shaping of *Persuasion*.

*Jocelyn Harris*
*University of Otago*

# NOTES

1. Geoffrey Chaucer, *The Wife of Bath's Prologue and Tale*, ed. James Winny (London: Cambridge University Press, 1965). Sandra M. Gilbert and Susan Gubar, *The Madwoman in the Attic: The Woman Writer and the Nineteenth-Century Literary Imagination* (New Haven and London: Yale University Press, 1979), p. 11, anticipated me in identifying the allusion.
2. See D. J. Gilson, "Jane Austen's Books," *The Book Collector* 23 (1974): 27–39.
3. J. E. Austen-Leigh, *Memoir of Jane Austen* (London: Oxford University Press, 1926), p. 89.
4. *Mansfield Park*, p. 338. All references to Jane Austen's novels are to R. W.

Chapman, ed., *The Novels of Jane Austen* (London: Oxford University Press, 1931–34). Juliet McMaster, in "Jane Austen on Love," *English Literary Studies* no. 13 (Victoria, 1978), suggests links between the romantic comedies of Shakespeare and Jane Austen.

5. See my " 'As if they had been living friends': *Sir Charles Grandison* into *Mansfield Park*," *BRH* 83:iii (Autumn 1980): 360–405; unpublished paper on *Pride and Prejudice* delivered at the American Eighteenth-Century Society meeting, Washington, 1981.

6. Samuel Richardson, *The History of Sir Charles Grandison*, ed. Jocelyn Harris, 3 parts, Oxford English Novels (London: Oxford University Press, 1972), II: 289.

7. J. E. Austen-Leigh, *Memoir of Jane Austen*, p. 88. Frank W. Bradbrook, *Jane Austen and her Predecessors* (Cambridge: Cambridge University Press, 1966), p. 79, believes that she read the *Inferno*, the *Purgatorio*, and the *Paradiso* in translation.

8. See Peter Dixon, *The World of Pope's Satires: An Introduction to the Epistles and Imitations of Horace* (London: Methuen, 1968) pp. 79–82.

9. Identified by H. J. C. Grierson, *Times Literary Supplement*, 8 December 1921.

10. Garrick, who supplied Mr. Woodhouse with his riddle about Kitty, a fair but frozen maid, may here be assisting Admiral Croft. See his prologue to Goldsmith's *She Stoops to Conquer:* "I've that within—for which there are no plaisters."

11. Anne's sportings with pretty musings of high-wrought love and eternal constancy, "almost enough to spread purification and perfume all the way," are something like Richardson's rewriting of *Hudibras* for Harriet:

> Where-e'er she treads, her feet shall set
> The primrose, and the violet:
> All spices, perfumes, and sweet powders,
> Shall borrow from her breath their odours. (I. 71)

12. Byron wrote, "Man's love is of man's life a thing apart, / 'Tis woman's whole existence" (*Don Juan* I. cxciv) shortly after *Persuasion* was first published. Was he returning Benwick's compliment to his *Turkish Tales*?

13. Jane Austen's list must include Constance in Benwick's favorite, Scott's *Marmion*, a woman of "matchless constancy" in a "form so soft and fair" (II. xxi, xxvi). The dashing young gallant Lochinvar, "so faithful in love and so dauntless in war," who plucks fair Ellen from the heart of her family at Netherby Hall (Canto V) contains more than a hint of Captain Wentworth. Captain Harville, for his part, could point to

> O woman! in our hours of ease,
> Uncertain, coy and hard to please.
> And variable . . . (VI. xxx)

# Transaction Books and Journals
## 🅰 in Women's Studies 🅰

### WOMEN, THE ARTS AND THE 1920s IN PARIS AND NEW YORK
*Kenneth W. Wheeler and Virginia Lee Lussier, editors*
ISBN: 0-87855-908-6 (cloth) 1982                     250 pp.  $24.95

### WOMEN IN MUSLIM RURAL SOCIETY
*Joseph Ginat*
ISBN: 0-87855-342-8 (cloth) 1981                     259 pp.  $24.95

### WOMEN'S EXPERIENCE IN AMERICA
### AN HISTORICAL ANTHOLOGY
*Esther Katz and Anita Rapone, editors*
ISBN: 0-87855-668-01 (paper) 1980                    414 pp.  $ 7.95

### THE MADAM AS ENTREPRENEUR
### CAREER MANAGEMENT IN HOUSE PROSTITUTION
*Barbara Sherman Heyl*
ISBN: 0-87855-211-1 (cloth) 1978                     276 pp.  $16.95

### WOMEN AND SPORT
### AN HISTORICAL, BIOLOGICAL, PHYSIOLOGICAL & SPORTSMEDICAL APPROACH
*Jan Borms, Marcel Hebbelinck, and Antonio Venerando, editors*
ISBN: 3-8055-2725-X (cloth) 1981                     244 pp.  $73.95

### THE FEMALE ATHLETE
### A SOCIO-PSYCHOLOGICAL AND KINANTHROPOMETRIC APPROACH
*Jan Borms, Marcel Hebbelinck, and Antonio Venerando, editors*
ISBN: 3-8055-2739-X (cloth) 1981                     232 pp.  $73.95

### FEMINIST ISSUES: A Journal of Feminist Social and Political Theory
A Publication of the Feminist Forum, Inc., Berkeley (triannual)
*Mary Jo Lakeland and Susan Ellis Wolf, editors*
$15/1 yr., $28/2 yrs., (individuals); $25/1 yr., $47/2 yrs., (institutions).

### WOMEN'S RIGHTS LAW REPORTER
A Publication of the Rutgers School of Law (quarterly)
*Tracey Thayer, editor*
$14/yr. (individuals), $28/yr. (institutions), $12/yr. (students).

*Order from your bookstore or prepaid from:* **Transaction Books**
**Department 2505 • Rutgers University • New Brunswick, NJ 08903**

# This Kind of Woman

TEN STORIES BY JAPANESE WOMEN WRITERS
1960–1976

*Translated and Edited by Yukiko Tanaka & Elizabeth Hanson.* The short stories in this collection introduce the English-reading public to the contemporary fiction of some of Japan's leading female writers. Chosen for their high literary quality and for their sensitivity to the changes that have so dramatically altered the lives of women in postwar Japan, the stories concern single mothers, women in conventional marriages who are questioning their roles as wives and mothers, and young women who are striving to understand more completely their relationship to men, to other women their age, and to their mothers. The authors are all well known in the Japanese literary world, but most are presented to Western readers for the first time in this anthology of work originally published between 1960 and 1976. $18.75

# The Changelings

A CLASSICAL JAPANESE COURT TALE

*Translated, with an Introduction and Notes, by Rosette F. Willig.* This is the first English translation of *Torikaebaya monogatari*, a 12th-century work that tells the story of a brother and sister whose natural inclinations lead them at an early age to live as members of the opposite sex. The chronicle of their difficulties, especially the complications that arise in the course of their sexual encounters, ends with the hero and heroine taking each other's place in society, thus returning to their original sexes. It is clearly among the best of the few surviving examples of *giko monogatari*, a literary genre marked by a simple structure, a limited number of characters, an unusual problem as the basis of its plot, and many elements imitative of the classic *The Tale of Genji*. $19.50

*Order from your bookstore, please*

# Stanford University Press